T0329490

Francis Bacon's Hidden Hand

in Shakespeare's

The Merchant of Venice

FRANCIS BACON'S HIDDEN HAND IN SHAKESPEARE'S *THE MERCHANT OF VENICE*

A STUDY OF LAW, RHETORIC, AND AUTHORSHIP

Christina G. Waldman

Algora Publishing
New York

Library of Congress Cataloging-in-Publication Data —

Names: Waldman, Christina G., 1957- author.
Title: Francis Bacon's Hidden Hand in Shakespeare's *The Merchant of Venice, A Study of Law, Rhetoric, and Authorship*/ by Christina G. Waldman.
Description: New York: Algora Publishing, [2018] | Includes bibliographical
  references and index.
Identifiers: LCCN 2018017375 (print) | LCCN 2018032796 (ebook) | ISBN
  9781628943320 (pdf) | ISBN 9781628943313 (hard cover: alk. paper) | ISBN
9781628943306 (pbk.: alk. paper)
Subjects: LCSH: Shakespeare, William, 1564-1616—Authorship—Baconian theory.
  | Bacon, Francis, 1561-1626—Authorship. | Shakespeare, William,
  1564-1616. Merchant of Venice. | Shakespeare, William,
  1564-1616—Knowledge—Law. | Shakespeare, William,
  1564-1616—Characters—Bellario.
Classification: LCC PR2944 (ebook) | LCC PR2944 .W25 2018 (print) | DDC
  822.3/3—dc23
LC record available at https://lccn.loc.gov/2018017375

Printed in the United States

Certainly it partakes of a higher science to comprehend
the force of equity that has suffused and penetrated
the very nature of human society.
— Francis Bacon, *Aphorismi*

To David and the ones we love

Acknowledgments

I would like to thank Lawrence Gerald for his generous help and support on this project from its inception. It was he who first proposed that I write a review of Mark Edwin Andrews' *Law v. Equity in The Merchant of Venice* for his website, www.SirBacon.org, Sir Francis Bacon's New Advancement of Learning. Without him and the SirBacon.org website, this book would probably never have happened.

I am grateful, also, to Simon Miles, author of the foreword of this book, for his talk on *The Merchant of Venice* before the Francis Bacon Society in March 2015, which inspired me to begin writing the book. His insightful questions and comments helped tremendously. I look forward to reading any book on Bacon and Shakespeare he should happen to write. The good advice of Barry Clarke, author of the forthcoming book *The Bacon Shakespeare Connection, a Scholarly Study*, is also much appreciated. I thank Stephen Basler, too, for his encouragement and interest in the project.

I am very grateful to Prof. Daniel R. Coquillette, author of books and articles on Francis Bacon's jurisprudence, and to Prof. R. H. Helmholz and Prof. Doug Coulson, for reading of drafts and encouragement. I thank my dear "David" for living this book project with me for the past three years and all that has entailed, including careful editing of drafts.

Prof. Robert E. Beck's compilation of legal history source materials from my legal history class with him at Southern Illinois University School of Law in 1985 was a valuable resource for this project, as was British barrister N. B. Cockburn's work of scholarship, *The Bacon Shakespeare Question, The Baconian Theory Made Sane*, a copy of which Susan McIlroy, President of the Francis Bacon Society so generously provided to me. I appreciate her support.

I am very grateful to Maureen Ward-Gandy, forensic handwriting analyst, for permission to share her professional expertise and to Laurence Gerald, for sharing her July 24, 1992, report (appendix 4, infra) for publication. I am grateful to Mark Neustadt for permission to cite or quote from his translation of Bacon's *Aphorismi*. I thank "Isabel" at the Buffalo Library for her efficient and cheerful handling of interlibrary loan requests.

I thank those at Algora: Martin, my terrific editor Andrea, and all those at Algora who shared my vision for this book and have worked so hard to bring it to fruition. Working with them has been one of the best experiences of my life.

Francis Bacon said it best, "It is hard to remember all, ungrateful to pass by any."

Table of Contents

PREFACE

In 1597–1598, law students at one of the Inns of Court were being "victimized by smooth-talking scoundrels who induced them to give bond for large sums of money." In Star Chamber, Lord Burghley (William Cecil), who relished imaginative punishments, proposed ordering playwrights to write a comedy about the problem in order to shame the parents of the students into paying closer attention to their sons' financial accounts.[1]

Would it be so far-fetched to propose that Burghley's nephew, a court insider and member of an Inn of Court (Gray's Inn), may have answered the call by writing — perhaps with others — *The Merchant of Venice*?

I am speaking, of course, of Francis Bacon, the visionary genius to whom the modern world owes a greater debt than is generally recognized. His acknowledged writings alone fill fourteen volumes. His chief concern was not fame or glory but the betterment of mankind, through the use of knowledge.

Nearly four hundred years after the "first Folio" appeared in 1623, the Shakespeare plays have retained their timeless appeal, but not many people read Bacon — although that is changing.[2] One serious scholar who has studied both Bacon and Shakespeare is Brian Vickers. Historically, he notes, Bacon's work has not received the commentary, criticism, and linguistic

---

[1] Catherine Drinker Bowen, ch. 9, "1597-1598. The House in Castle Yard. Star Chamber. The Death of Brigit Coke," *The Lion and the Throne* (Boston: Little, Brown, 1957), pp. 104-116, 111-113, esp. 112 (citing John Hawarde, *Reports del. Cases in Camera Stellata* (1894 ed.), 13-250 passim, pp. 612-613). To be further cited as Bowen, *Lion*.

[2] For scholars currently involved in Bacon research, see, e.g., Rhodri Lewis, "Francis Bacon and Ingenuity," *Renaissance Quarterly* 67, no. 1 (Spring, 2014), pp. 113-163, asterisked footnote, p. 113, JSTOR, http://www.jstor.org/stable/10.1086/676154.

annotation that Shakespeare's has. He suggests several possible reasons. One is that Bacon's work overlaps disciplines and thus defies categorization. Another is that people have accepted the negative "spin" on Bacon[1] — that he was cold-hearted, conniving, and corrupt — despite ample evidence to the contrary.[2]

In consequence, many who refuse to even consider Bacon's contribution to authorship of the Shakespeare oeuvre do not really know the man. Brian Vickers, a scholar of both Bacon and Shakespeare who is heading ongoing publication of the *Oxford Francis Bacon*,[3] has stated, "No issue in Shakespeare studies is more important than determining what he wrote."[4] Francis Bacon taught that people should make their own investigations and draw their own conclusions, rather than blindly trusting in authorities. However, he also mined the past for ideas that could be given future application.[5]

One of the themes of this book is looking closely, beneath what is apparent on the surface, reading between the lines.[6] Sometimes the truth lies in the interstices, the "nooks and crannies." Of course, there is a risk of finding in Bacon or Shakespeare the qualities one seeks. Ambiguities, some caused by the passage of four hundred years, create a need for interpretation among multiple plausible possibilities.

I have been interested in the Shakespeare authorship question since my college days. However, until a few years ago, my reading was more often in authorship studies than in the actual writings of Shakespeare or Bacon. The archaic language in Shakespeare put me off, and I found Bacon's "four idols"[7] truly mystifying. These days, though, the internet gives us new ways to study these timeless works. With www.opensourceshakespeare.org, Google, HathiTrust.org, and the valuable SirBacon.org website, Bacon and

---

[1] See Brian Vickers, preface, *Francis Bacon, A Critical Edition of the Major Works*, ed. Brian Vickers (Oxford: Oxford University Press, 1996), pp. vii-viii.

[2] See Nieves Matthews, *The History of a Character Assassination* (New Haven: Yale University Press, 1996), the entire book.

[3] *Oxford Francis Bacon*, under the auspices of the British Academy, http://www. oxfordfrancisbacon.com/.

[4] Brian Vickers, *Shakespeare, Co-Author, A Historical Study of Five Collaborative Plays* (Oxford: Oxford University Press, 2004, soft cover), pp. 3, 560. He adopts Bacon's wish as his own, "that the art of discovery may advance as discoveries advance." Vickers, p. 147. On Bacon, see also pp. ii, 145, 273, 413, 526.

[5] See, e.g., *Spedding*, V, p. 110 (transl. of *De Augmentis*).

[6] This phrase is said to have originally applied to sixteenth-century cryptology, but it might also bring to mind also the interlinear and marginal notations the twelfth-century glossators made when glossing or interpreting the texts of Justinian's *Corpus iuris civilis*.

[7] See Daniel R. Coquillette, *Francis Bacon* (Stanford: Stanford University Press, 1992), pp. 228-231, 233-34, 293 (hereafter to be cited as "Coquillette, FB" or "FB." Prof. Coquillette's book is the first modern book focusing on Bacon's jurisprudence.

Shakespeare become much more accessible. I have found it fruitful to choose one term at a time and search for it in the works of "both men."

Unless otherwise stated, I used the standard (Longmans, 1857–1874) fourteen–volume *Works of Francis Bacon*, edited by James Spedding, Robert Leslie Ellis, and Douglas Denon Heath (to be cited as *Spedding*), online at HathiTrust.org. For word searches, it made sense to use the three–volume first American edition of Basil Montagu (Philadelphia: Carey & Hart, 1841–1853, to be cited as *Montagu*). There is a previous sixteen–volume Montagu edition (London: William Pickering, 1825–1837). Unless otherwise stated, references to *Shakespeare* will be to the 1864 *Globe* edition at www.opensourceshakespeare.org.

Researching this book has felt like being drawn into a game of hide-and-seek, where one clue leads to another, with an occasional wild goose chase.[1] About *The Merchant of Venice*, Marjorie Garber wrote, "From first to last, this play is about decipherment."[2] That seems fitting from the man who invented the word "hint,"[3] a word not unfamiliar to Bacon, which may be of significance.[4] Let us explore this further:

The word "hint" was used by Shakespeare eight times, always as a noun, first in *Othello* and also in *Anthony and Cleopatra*.[5] Suggested derivation is from Anglo-Saxon "hent" (the act of grabbing or seizing).[6] However, the word made me think of "hunt," which comes from the Anglo-Saxon "huntian." One meaning of "hunt" is "change ringing: to shift the order of bells in a hunt."[7] Bacon even speaks of something that is "more like a kind of hunting by scent than a science."[8] Hunt plus scent equals hint makes more sense to me than talking about grabbing.

---

[1] Coincidentally, a William Wildgoose was the binder of Shakespeare's First Folio. Adam Smyth, *Material Texts in Early Modern England* (Cambridge: Cambridge University Press, 2018), p. 164.

[2] Marjorie Garber, "The Merchant of Venice," *Shakespeare After All* (New York: Pantheon Books, 2004), pp. 282-312, 303.

[3] "Hint," Jeffrey McQuain, *Coined by Shakespeare, Words & Meanings First Penned by the Bard* (Springfield MS: Merriam-Webster, 1998), p. 95.

[4] *Significatio* means "hint" in classical Latin. *Cassell's New Compact Latin Dictionary*,compiled by D. P. Simpson (New York: Dell, 1974), pp. 293, 207 (hereinafter, *Cassell's Latin*).

[5] *Othello* first appeared in print in Quarto in 1622, though it is thought to have been written in 1604. '*Othello*,' *The Yale Shakespeare*, ed. by Tucker Brooke (New Haven: Yale University Press, 1956), appendix B, p. 175. The date for *Anthony and Cleopatra*'s composition is given as 1606-1607, but the first printed text was the First Folio, 1623. *Anthony and Cleopatra, The Yale Shakespeare* (New Haven: Yale University Press, 1955), ed. by Peter G. Phialas, appendix a, p. 159.

[6] McQuain, *Coined by Shakespeare*, p. 95.

[7] *Webster's Collegiate Dictionary*, fifth ed., s.v. "hunt" (Springfield MS: G. & C. Merriam Co., 1941), p. 485 (hereinafter, *Webster's*).

[8] Christopher Hill, ch. 3, "Francis Bacon and the Parliamentarians," *Intellectual Origins of the English Revolution Revisited* (New York: Oxford University Press, 1997), p. 78.

While McQuain and Malless report that the first "recorded" use of "hint" as a *verb* dates to 1648, without naming Bacon, they may been alluding to a 1648 text which included Bacon's writings.[1] However, a search in the three volumes of Montagu reveals that Bacon used the word "hint" even earlier than that,[2] in the *Novum Organum* (1620), for instance.[3]

Francis Bacon once described himself as the "bell-ringer who calls all the wits together."[4] In *The Merchant of Venice*, there is a mysterious old Italian jurist called Bellario who, though he never actually appears as a character, guides the plot from behind the scenes by his notes and letters to Portia. In a 1965 book, Mark Edwin Andrews first proposed that Bellario "was," or was in some way integrally connected to, Francis Bacon. To my knowledge, no one has ever challenged, or further explored, Andrews' assertion. This book does that. Does Bellario indeed point uniquely to Francis Bacon? Looking first to the play for hints, let us begin the hunt for the hidden meaning of Bellario.

Christina G. Waldman
Buffalo, July 2018

---

[1] They may be referring to *Remains of the Lord Verulam[...]* which contained some allegedly spurious, as well as genuine, works of the Lord Verulam, Francis Bacon. *Montagu*, XVI, pt. 2, in 16 vol. (London, 1824-1834)(There is no pagination of the notes. Type "1648" in the search box.), HathiTrust, https://hdl.handle.net/2027/hvd.hnug21 (Unless otherwise stated, references to *Montagu* will always be to the three-volume set). E.g., see also *Montagu*, II (of III), p. 400 (Philadelphia, 1853), pp. 4, 400-401, HathiTrust, https://hdl.handle.net/2027/ucl.b3618254. https://hdl.handle.net/2027/ucl.b3618254. Note: the 1648 *Remains* is to be distinguished from *Baconiana, or, Certain genuine remains of Sr. Francis Bacon[...]*, ed. by Thomas Tennison (London, 1679), http://name.umdl.umich.edu/A28024.0001.001.

[2] *Montagu*, I, pp. 409, 2d col. ("Thoughts on the Nature of Things"); pp. 427, 1st col.; 432, 2d col.; 434, 2d col. ("The Interpretation of Nature"); and p. 451, 2d col. ("Fable of Cupid"), HathiTrust, https://hdl.handle.net/2027/njp.32101068998481; *Montagu*, II: p. 547 ("Of the Interpretation of Nature"), HathiTrust, https://hdl.handle.net/2027/njp.32101068998499; *Montagu*, III: pp. 191 ("letter to a most dear friend"), 362 (*Novum Organum*, i, #93, first lines); 369, 1st col. (*Novum Organum*, i, #124), HathiTrust, https://hdl.handle.net/2027/njp.32101068998507.

(Note: These works I have found, some apparently prototypical fragments, with "Interpretation of Nature" in the title: "Thoughts and Observations of Francis Bacon, of Verulam, Concerning the Interpretation of Nature, or, the Invention of Things and of Works"; "*Valerius Terminus*, Of the Interpretation of Nature with the Annotations of Hermes Stella" (*Spedding*, III); "Aphorisms Concerning the Interpretation of Nature and the Kingdom of Man" in the *Novum Organon*; and proem to a planned treatise, "Of the Interpretation of Nature, *Spedding*, X).

[3] Coquillette, FB, appendix 3, p. 333.

[4] Francis Bacon letter to "Dr. Playfer" (undated), *Spedding*, X, p. 301, HathiTrust, https://hdl.handle.net/2027/ucl.b3618245.

"His greatness consists in his repeated insistence on the facts that man is the servant and interpreter of Nature, that truth is not derived from authority and that knowledge is the fruit of experience. The impetus which his inductive method gave to the future of scientific investigation is indisputable. As he himself described it, he 'rang the bell which called the other wits together.'" "Francis Bacon," *Chambers Encyclopedia: A Dictionary of Universal Knowledge*, vol. 1 (London, 1888), pp. 641-644, 643.

FOREWORD

In 1935 at the University of Colorado, Mark Edwin Andrews, a visiting student, was taking a class on Shakespeare taught by a visiting scholar, the eminent Princeton Professor of Literature J. Duncan Spaeth. A chance remark on the relationship between common law and equity in *The Merchant of Venice* led Andrews to look more closely at the extent to which the play dramatized this legal and historical problem.

He wrote up his results in a paper in which he arrived at three fascinating conclusions. First, that the famous trial scene in the play dramatizes the inherent tension between law and equity in the courts. Second, that the play actually influenced the decisive resolution of these competing claims in 1616, when King James asked a legal committee headed by Sir Francis Bacon to investigate and make recommendation as to the best course. Third, and perhaps most surprisingly, Andrews advances the suggestion that the character of Bellario in the play represents, in some sense, Francis Bacon himself.

In *The Merchant of Venice*, Bellario, an aged law professor, never appears on stage, but acts from behind the scenes to orchestrate the trial resolution, through the pleadings of Portia, in disguise as the young lawyer Balthazar. For Andrews, Bellario plays the same role within the play as Bacon does in history, even though the play, which was most likely written in 1597/1598, appeared nearly twenty years before the legal conflict was resolved by Bacon's contribution.

Andrews' manuscript languished in a box in the law library storage for three decades before being rediscovered when an exhibition on Shakespeare and the Law was planned at the University for 1964. By then he had gone on to a distinguished career in industry, rising to Assistant Secretary of the Navy. He readily agreed to publication of his original text, and it appeared under the University of Colorado publishing imprint in 1965.

It is important to note that Andrews did not consider that his textual and legal historical insights into *The Merchant of Venice* should lead to any suggestion that Francis Bacon had any role in the authorship of the play. In fact, he went out of his way to explicitly disavow any suggestion of aiding or abetting the Baconian theory of Shakespearean authorship, and made it abundantly clear he was entirely orthodox on the question and did not dispute that William Shakespeare wrote the works attributed to him.

However, he did not really attempt any more than a cursory explanation of how the Stratford actor might have acquired his detailed knowledge of the law, nor how he might have anticipated with such uncanny accuracy the role of Francis Bacon in legal history in relation to the question.

Whilst the book and some of Andrews' conclusions have received critical attention by scholars working in the discipline of Legal History, they have made little impact beyond that sphere. In particular, they have not been widely discussed, if at all, within the context of the Shakespeare authorship question. And, although there have been responses to Andrews' suggestion that the play dramatizes the conflict between common law and equity, much less, if anything, has been written on his observation that Bacon is Bellario. Christina Waldman's book changes all that and, for these reasons, is a very welcome addition to the literature.

In the current work, Waldman takes as her starting point Andrews' suggestion that Bacon is Bellario and uses this as a springboard for an extended exploration of the sources, origins, and characters of the play. She does not set out to prove or disprove anything. Instead, she offers the reader a detailed investigation into the relationship between Francis Bacon and the character of Bellario in the text of *The Merchant of Venice*, in which she is willing to entertain seriously the notion that he might have some involvement in its creation. By examining his life and legal career, and comparing this material with the themes, locations and character names which occur in the narrative, Waldman uncovers many rich threads and notable connections. The result is a thought-provoking enquiry into the legal and historical resonances between Bacon and the play, and especially the character of Bellario.

She does not need to press the point, because the conclusion is all but unavoidable: the play is Bacon's, through and through. It is permeated by his presence. There is a strong case to be made that this work does indeed present a case study of one of the crucial legal questions of its time, the relationship between the common law and equity, and it does so in a manner which closely reflects Bacon's thought and involvement. If Bacon wrote the play, these surprising connections make perfect sense. If not, then we can at least say that the playwright chose to use *The Merchant of Venice* as a vehicle to investigate Bacon's role in this critical legal debate. Either way, it is an entirely justified and long overdue strategy to interrogate the play with an open mind as to the possibility that Francis Bacon had a hand in its appearance.

The Merchant of Venice has attracted a reputation in modern times for the perception by some critics of anti-Semitism, but this view is a distraction which overlooks and downplays the incredible complexity beneath its surface. The play is infinitely nuanced and layered, and no single perspective, particularly one distorted by historical distance, can hope to encompass its depths.

It is a play about the law, certainly, and about money-lending, debt and usury. It undoubtedly has something to say about the relation between Gentiles and Jews, but it is also more broadly a play about the relationship of the foreigner to the city, of the outsider to the local. *Merchant* is a meditation on cultural and religious difference, and the markers and taboos which maintain the boundaries between groups.

In this sense, the play already had deep political sensitivities when it first appeared in the late 1590s, a time of recent riots amongst Londoners over the presence of foreigners, particularly Dutch traders and merchants, in the capital.

Yet, for all this, there is something very personal at the heart of the play. The relationship between Bassanio and Antonio, the two leading male characters, exactly mirrors that between Francis Bacon and his brother Anthony at the time. Francis was frequently in debt, and Anthony would often stand bond for his brother. Spedding, Bacon's biographer, expresses puzzlement at this relationship and notes that at no time does Anthony ever express the slightest reservation or criticism or hesitation in assisting Francis with funds in this manner. Spedding cannot understand why, but the reasons have been suggested by Baconian scholars who contend that the brothers were engaged in a joint literary enterprise, nothing less than the creation of the English Renaissance, in plays, in texts, and in printed works.

Francis suffered the indignity of being arrested for debt in 1598, at the instigation of one Giles Sympson, a moneylender and goldsmith. The name, tantalizingly similar to Shylock, has inspired some Baconians to speculate whether the incident inspired the play. In fact, the play was certainly in print prior to the arrest, so to the extent that it is echoed within the action, it was a curious case of life imitating art. As it happens, Bacon did insert some very specific references to his arrest elsewhere in the Shakespeare works, in the play of *Henry IV Part 1*, written immediately after *The Merchant of Venice*, but that story is getting too far away from the current topic. It is enough to note that we can see Francis Bacon reflected in this play in multiple guises and characters, as if showing different aspects of his life. His personal circumstances are paralleled in Bassanio, and as Andrews and Waldman argue, his legal persona is depicted in Bellario.

There are many parallels to be found between passages, words and phrases in *The Merchant of Venice* and Bacon's other writings. These are like fingerprints of thought which confirm the identity of the author, when we know where to look.

For example, Bacon kept a personal notebook in which he would jot down words, phrases and ideas. He called it the *Promus of Formularies and Elegancies*, and it is held today in the British Museum. "Promus" means "storehouse," or "larder," or a place from which one draws provisions, and the notebook supplies very many parallels to the Shakespeare works. It was compiled in the mid 1590s, in the years preceding the publication of *The Merchant of Venice*. On one page in the notebook, amongst a list of various items, appears a fascinating word written in Greek letters, which may be transliterated as *skiamachy*. It means, literally, *to fight with shadows*.

In *The Merchant of Venice*, Act 1, Scene 2, there occurs the following line, spoken by Portia:

> "He started dancing every time a bird sang, and he was so eager to show off his fencing that he'd fight with his own shadow."

This is, precisely, an instance of skiamachy.

Of course, this is not proof that Bacon wrote the play, but it demonstrates the small discoveries which await when one is willing at least to entertain the possibility. Bacon made a note about skiamachy in 1594/5; Shakespeare wrote about fighting with shadows in 1597.

There is another remarkable parallel with a line, spoken by Portia/Balthazar in the trial scene, which is of key significance to Andrews.

His book includes an intriguing re-imagining of Act IV, Scene 1, re-located from Venice to a courtroom in London, with the speeches "translated" into correct contemporary legal terminology of the day. He shows that the scene is precisely split into two distinct sections. The first takes place as if it were in a court of common law and the second as if it were in a court of equity. This conflation into a single trial occurs for dramatic purposes, but the exact language used by the playwright shows his deep nuanced understanding of the conflict between the two branches of jurisprudence. The crucial moment in the scene which Andrews identifies as the beginning of the equity court is when Portia utters the words: "Tarry a little..."

In Bacon's essay, "Of Dispatch," the following quotation appears:

> I knew a Wise Man, that had it for a byword, when he saw Men hasten to a conclusion: Stay a little, that we may make an End the sooner.

This is not the only place that the short anecdote appears amongst his writings. It was a favorite saying of Bacon's: "Stay a while, that we may make an end of it the sooner."

But notice how it is essentially the same thought as Portia expresses: "Stay a while," means nothing different from "Tarry a little." In the play, Portia employs the phrase to express the identical sentiment as in Bacon's aphorism. She urges the parties to wait, to tarry, to stay for a little while, the sooner to resolve the business at hand.

Again, it is not necessary to consider this as proof of Francis Bacon's authorship of *The Merchant of Venice*. It is sufficient simply to observe once more that if we are willing to explore the relationship between Bacon and the play, we can easily find abundant materials to work with.

But does it really matter who wrote the Shakespeare plays?

There's an old joke about the works being written by another man with the same name; there's a grain of truth in that. The point hidden behind the gentle mockery of the authorship debate in this quip is this: what does it matter whether it is this man or that man, with the same name or a different name? Surely the works stand on their own, and it is a pointless waste of time to speculate on whether his identity is known, or concealed, or substituted.

They do, and it is. If it were simply a question of this man or that man, then it would be neither here nor there. But the authorship question does matter *if the knowledge of the identity of the true author can inform and expand our understanding of the Works.*

This is the litmus test. The only point in knowing the identity of the author of the Shakespeare works is to shine light on the works themselves.

If this is true, and surely it is, then the only authorship discussion that is of value, and worthwhile engaging with, is one that by offering an appreciation of the true author, their identity, life, career, thought, and writings, allows a deeper appreciation and understanding of the works of Shakespeare themselves. By these criteria, Christina Waldman's book passes the test with flying colors.

It takes as its starting point the open-minded possibility that Francis Bacon was the author of *The Merchant of Venice*, a fruitful location from which to begin the exploration as it turns out. Armed with Mark Edwin Andrews' penetrating insights, but now freed from the constraints of the orthodox authorship position, Christina Waldman has produced a welcome and timely contribution to the literature on Shakespeare's place in legal history. At the same time, Francis Bacon's complex relationship with *The Merchant of Venice* is illuminated by a richer perspective in this engaging study.

Simon Miles
Manchester, UK
23 April 2018

TABLE OF ABBREVIATIONS/EXPLANATION OF TERMS

Baker, *Intro.*: J. H. Baker, *An Introduction to English Legal History*, third ed. (London: Butterworths, 1990).

Black's LD: Black's Law Dictionary, fifth ed. (St. Paul MN: West 1979).

Bl. Comm.: Blackstone's *Commentaries.*

Bowen, *Lion:* Catherine Drinker Bowen, *The Lion and the Throne* (Boston: Little, Brown, 1957).

BSQ: N. B. Cockburn, *The Bacon Shakespeare Question: The Baconian Theory Made Sane* (Guildford and Kings Lynn: printed for the author by Biddles Limited, 1998).

Cassell's Latin: Cassell's New Compact Latin Dictionary, compiled by D. P. Simpson (New York: Dell, 1974).

FB or Coquillette, FB: Daniel R. Coquillette, *Francis Bacon* (Stanford: Stanford University Press, 1992).

MEA: Mark Edwin Andrews, *Law v. Equity in the Merchant of Venice, a Legalization of Act IV, Scene 1* (Boulder CO: University of Colorado Press, 1965).

Merchant: The Merchant of Venice by William Shakespeare, 1864 Globe edition, www. opensourceshakespeare.org.

REB: Robert E. Beck, Professor of Law, Southern Illinois University, "Selected Materials on Anglo-American Legal History: The Development of a Legal System," Fourth Revised Edition (Not for general publication. All rights reserved). August, 1978.

Shakespeare: a name used by the true author(s) of the works attributed to William Shakespeare, whoever he/she/they may be.

Webster's: Webster's Collegiate Dictionary, fifth edition, (Springfield, MS: G & C Merriam, 1941).

SPEDDING REFERENCES HEREIN, BY VOLUME

Sources: *The Works of Francis Bacon*, collected and edited by James Spedding, Robert Ellis, and D. D. Heath, vols. I–XIV (London: Longmans, 1857–74), HathiTrust, https://catalog.hathitrust.org/Record/006685889 (useful link to all volumes). Citations will be to volumes I through XIV, never to the internally numbered "Life and Letters" (volumes VIII through XIV).

Volumes I through V are the Philosophical Works. Volumes I through III contain Bacon's original Latin writings, with prefaces and valuable editor's notes in English. Volumes IV and V contain translations.

Vol. I

"Appendix on the Art of Writing in Cipher" (p. 841).

"Rawley's Life of Francis Bacon" (p. 5).

Vol. II

Sylva Sylvarum (p. 672).

Vol. III

Of the Advancement of Learning (pp. 253–491).

Vol. IV (Books I through VI)

"Aphorisms on the Composition of the Primary History." In *Preparative Towards an Experimental and Natural History* (p. 254 ff.)

De Dignitate et Augmentis Sciantiarum (De Augmentis). 1623 (pp. 273–438). The *De Augmentis Scientiarum* (1623) is an expanded, Latin version of *The Advancement of Learning* (1605). For "Bacon on Ciphers," see p. 444.

The Novum Organum, with *Proem*, of the *Instauratio Magna* (pp. 37–248).

Vol. V (Books VII through IX)

De Dignitate et Augmentis Scientiarum (De Augmentis) (pp. 3–119).

____. *Example of a Treatise on Universal Justice or the Fountains of Equity, by Aphorisms,' De Augmentis*, book 8 (pp. 88–110).

De Principiis atque Originibus (p. 499).

History of Life and Death (Historia vitae et mortis) (p. 265).

On the Ebb and Flow of the Sea (p. 446).

Vol. VI (literary works and professional works)

Essays, or Counsels, Civil and Moral: "Of Beauty," "Of Cunning," "Of Custom and Education," "Of Custom and Education," "Of Discourse," "Of Dispatch, "Of Gardens," "Of Judicature," "Of Masques and Triumphs," "Of Simulation and Dissimulation," "Of Studies," "Of

Suspicion," "Of Travel," "Of Usury," "Of Vain Glory," "Of Youth and
Age," "On Fame." (pp. 365-518; appendices, 519-604).

In Felicem Memoriam Elizabethae, Angliae Reginae. Written by 1608 (pp.
281-304 in Latin; 305-318 in English).

De Sapienta Veterum (Of the Wisdom of the Ancients) (pp. 701-764).

The History of the Reign of King Henry VII (pp. 1-264).

The Beginning of the History of the Reign of King Henry VIII (p. 265-270).

The Beginning of the History of Great Britain (pp. 271-280).

Vol. VII (literary and professional works, including the legal works)

An Advertisement Touching an Holy War (pp. 1-36).

Apophthegms New and Old. 1625 (pp. 121-166. All *Apophthegms,* pp. 111-186).

Colors of Good and Evil. 1597 (pp. 65-93).

The Arguments in Law of Sir Francis Bacon (All arguments, pp. 517-726).

    Jurisdiction of the Marches

    The Argument on the Writ De Non Precendendo Rege Inconsulto

    The Argument of Francis Bacon in the Case of the Post-Nati of Scotland

    The Case for the Impeachment of Waste

    The Case of Revocation of Uses

The Promus of Formularies and Elegancies (excerpts, pp. 187-213).

Translation of Certain Psalms (pp. 263-272).

'*Maxims of the Law*' (pp. 307-383), published in a double tract — together
with the "spurious" '*The Use of the Law for Preservation of our Persons,
Goods, and Good Names*' (pp. 451-505) in one tract, *The Elements of the
Common Lawes of England[...].* 1631. *The Use of the Law* was first published
in 1929.

Ordinances in Chancery (pp. 755-775).

Reading on the Statute of Uses (389-451).

Volumes VIII through XIV are *The Letters and the Life*, including the "Occasional Works." They are in chronological order.

Vol. VIII (1560 to Jan.–Nov., 1594–1595)

Bacon's Speech on Motion for Supply. 1593 (pp. 212-214).

"*Mr. Bacon's Discourse in the Praise of his Sovereign*" (pp. 126-142).

"*Tower Work. 'Nature of an Examination Upon Interrogatories*'" (pp. 316-318).

Six Councillor Speeches for the Gesta Grayorum (pp. 332-343).

Letter to Lord Burghley. ca. 1592 (p. 108).

Observations on a Libel. 1592 (pp. 146-208).

Vol. IX (1595 to April, 1601)

"Advice to the Earl of Rutland on his Travels" (pp. 6-15).

"Speech in the Parliament, Elizabeth 39, upon the Motion of Subsidy."
1597–98 (pp. 85-89).

Vol. X (April, 1601 to March–July, 1506–1507)

Letter to Mr. Davys [John Davies]. March 28, 1603 (p. 65).
Letter to Mr. Foules," March 28, 1603 (p. 64).
Bacon's notes for "Speech on repealing superfluous laws" (p. 19).
Bacon's notes for "Speech on bringing in a bill concerning assurances
among merchants" (p.3 4).
Proem to planned treatise, *Of the Interpretation of Nature, Proem* (a "must
read").

Vol. XI (Oct.–April, 1607–08 to July–Dec., 1613)

Letter to George Cary. 1608 (pp. 109-110).
Letter to Tobie Matthew. 1609 (p. 132).
"Report on Project Touching the Penal Laws, to King James," ca. 1608 (pp.
96-106).

Vol. XII (1613–14 to 1616)

"A Memorial Touching the Review of Penal Laws and the Amendment of
the Common Law" (pp. 84-86).
"Sir Francis Bacon, His Accusation of Sir John Wentworth, Sir John Hollys,
and Mr. Lumsden" (pp. 213-223).

Vol. XIII (1616 to Jan., 1618–1619)

"Proceedings re Lord Coke and his law reports" (pp. 76-199).
Proposition to the king touching the compiling and amendment of the laws of England
(pp. 61-71).
"The Speech which was used by the Keeper of the Great Seal in Star Chamber before the Summer Circuits, the King then being in Scotland,
1617" (pp. 211-214).

Vol. XIV (1619 to April, 1626)

Letter to Launcelot Andrewes, ca. 1622 (p. 374).
Letter to Buckingham (p. 538).
"Note of my Lord Chancellor's Speech in Chancery, to Mr. Whitlock, June
29, 1620..." (pp. 100-104).
"An Offer to King James of a Digest" (p. 358).
"The Last Will of Francis Bacon, Viscount St. Albans" (p. 540).

CHAPTER ONE: A FRESH LOOK AT MARK EDWIN ANDREWS' INSIGHTS

> Let us all ring fancy's knell
> I'll begin it, — Ding, dong, bell.
> Ding, dong, bell.
> So may the outward shows be least themselves
> The world is still deceived with ornament.[1]

A world in which things are not what they seem can be unsettling to perceive, but so would be the end of fancy. By "ornament," Shakespeare may have simply meant "show." However, he may have also had in mind rhetorical figures of speech called "adornments." For example, there were four divisions of puns: antanaclasis, syllepsis of the sense, paranomasia, and asteismus. Punning was esteemed as "not merely an elegance of style or display of wit," but a "means of emphasis and an instrument of persuasion." It was integral to constructing an argument step-by-step, in serious applications such as the sermons of Launcelot Andrewes and the tragedies of Shakespeare. [2]

In 1964, a University of Colorado law librarian, John Moller, found, in a dusty cardboard box in storage, a paper written in 1935 by an able law

---

[1] William Shakespeare, *The Merchant of Venice*, III, 2, 1437 ff. On rhetorical style and "ornament" as considered integral to the meaning of a text in Renaissance writing, see Sister Miriam Joseph, *Shakespeare's Use of the Arts of Language* (New York: Hafner, 1966), pp. 39-40. It is good to keep in mind that there is no reason why "Shakespeare" could not have been a pen name.

[2] Sister Miriam Joseph, , *Shakespeare's Use of the Arts of Language* pp. 39-40, 164-165 n. 340; 340 (quoting Frank P. Wilson).

A study just of Bacon's use of the word "ornament" would be beneficial to those seeking to understand his method. E.g., in *Spedding*, IV, see pp. 4, 110. In *Spedding*, V, see especially p. 288 ('*Novum Organum*'). Bacon's *Ornamenta Rationalia*, or "Ornamental Speeches," are lost. Thomas Tennison, *Baconiana, or, Certain genuine remains of Sir Francis Bacon, Baron of Verulam, and Viscount of St. Albans in arguments civil and moral, natural, medical, theological, and bibliographical now for the first time faithfully published* (London, 1679), pp. 1, 22, 60, 89, Early English Books Online: Text Creation Partnership, http://tei.it.ox.ac.uk/tcp/Texts-HTML/free/A28/A28024.html; http://name.umdl.umich.edu/A28024.0001.001.

student. Realizing it had merit, law librarian Prof. Roy Mersky contacted its author, former Assistant Secretary of the Navy Mark Edwin Andrews, who agreed to its publication in 1965 by the University of Colorado Press.

Law v. Equity in 'The Merchant of Venice, a Legalization of Act IV, Scene I[1] was perhaps the first modern book to significantly point out the degree to which the play focused on the tension between two important concepts in jurisprudence, law and equity. Andrews also asserted that the play *itself* must have helped to change the law by influencing the King's decree in favor in the equity courts in the 1616 *Glanvill* case — at least for a time, as the decree was declared illegal in 1670.[2] It did this, said Andrews, by influencing two, if not three, of the major players in that case: Sir Francis Bacon and Thomas Egerton (Lord Ellesmere), although probably not Sir Edward Coke.[3]

W. Nicholas Knight agrees, citing Andrews and his sources. However, it should be noted that Knight, a Stratfordian (one who believes the orthodox teaching that William Shaxpere of Stratford wrote the plays attributed to William Shakespeare), imparts to Shakespeare legal acumen for which there is no evidence Shaxpere, an actor/theatre owner/grain merchant, ever possessed,[4] yet which Bacon surely did. For example, Knight writes, "There is substantial evidence of Shakespeare having developed a program of explicating, renovating, and defending, to meet the needs of all levels of society, the system of English law with its common law courts and competing courts of equity, offering provision for appeals to higher courts which allowed for and maximized evenhanded justice." And, "He actively, in at least the one area of equity, and vigorously pursued a program for effecting change in, and reform and the preservation of, English jurisprudence...."[5] How to explain this paradox?

Andrews' further assertion, that Francis Bacon "is" the character Bellario in the play, seems to have been largely ignored. B. J. and Mary Sokol argue

---

[1] Mark Edwin Andrews, *Law v. Equity in The Merchant of Venice, a Legalization of Act IV, Scene 1* (Boulder: University of Colorado, 1965) will be cited hereinafter as MEA.

[2] *R. v. Standish* (1670) Treby MS. Rep., LPCL 438 declared the decree illegal. J. H. Baker, *An Introduction to English Legal History*, 3d ed., (London: Butterworth's, 1990), p. 126, fn 56. The third edition will be hereafter cited as "Baker, *Intro.*"

[3] Of course, the ultimate decision in *Glanville* (associated by its issues with the *Earl of Oxford's Case*) was made by King James, by decree, although Bacon cautioned the King not to do it that way, flaunting his prerogative. See David Ibbetson, ch. 1, "The Earl of Oxford's Case (1615)," in Charles and Paul Mitchell, ed., *Landmark Cases in Equity*, (Oxford: Hart Publishing, 2012), pp. 1-32, 3, 28. https://books.google.com/books?isbn=1847319742.

[4] For the documented facts on the life of the man thought to be "Shakespeare," William Shaxpere/Shaxberd of Stratford, see Ilya Gililov, *The Shakespeare Game, The Mystery of the Great Phoenix* (New York: Algora 2003), ch. 2, pp. 89-224, 98-105.

[5] W. Nicholas Knight, *Shakespeare's Hidden Life, Shakespeare at the Law* (New York: Mason & Lipscomb, 1973), pp. 279-288, 279, 284.

that the trial scene in *Merchant of Venice* "is not concerned with the vicissitudes [changes in power and status, perhaps] of the English jurisdiction of equity."[1] The struggle for preeminence between the English courts of equity and the courts of law dates from ca. 1300. Tim Stretton seems to agree, as do I, insofar as the Sokols are saying that it was not the jurisdictional conflict between the *courts* of law and equity that Shakespeare wished to dramatize, twenty years before the matter came to a head in 1616, but the problems of ordinary sixteenth-century London debtors. Creditors were habitually holding debtors to the terms of conditional bonds which had harsh penalty clauses, disproportionate to the amount of debt.[2]

In simplest terms, the issue in the 1616 *Glanville* case was whether, after a plaintiff had obtained a judgment against a defendant in a court of law, that defendant could run to the court of equity and seek relief from the judgment on grounds of equity. Because of the importance of the issue, Lord Ellesmere had referred the matter to King James. Francis Bacon, already a special counsellor to the King, headed the special Privy Council set up to advise the King on the matter which was resolved in 1616 by a king's decree, in favor of the courts of equity and, a selling point for the king, the king's prerogative. Drawing an analogy between the fictional role of Bellario in *Shylock v Antonio* and the real-life role of Bacon in *Glanvill* twenty years later, and for other reasons, Andrews suggests that Bacon *is* Bellario. He does not say that Bacon appears "as" Bellario. For that matter, Bacon never "appears" at all. Rather, for Andrews, the identity was complete. But what would Francis Bacon be doing "in the play"?

The most obvious explanation would be that Bacon authored the play. However, Andrews assures us he is a "Stratfordian," one who believes the actor William Shaxpere wrote the plays attributed to "William Shakespeare." Having ruled out Bacon's authorship, though, Andrews seems at a loss to rationally explain Bacon's strong "presence" within the play.[3] Perhaps, he

---

[1] B. J. Sokol and Mary Sokol, "Shakespeare and the English Equity Jurisdiction, '*The Merchant of Venice*' and The Two Texts of '*King Lear*,'" *The Review of English Studies*, new series, 50, no. 200 (Oxford: Oxford University Press, 1999), pp. 417-439, 417, JSTOR, www.jstor.org/stable/517390.

[2] Tim Stretton, "Contract, Debt Litigation, and Shakespeare's The Merchant of Venice," *Adelaide Law Review* 31, no. 2 (2010). pp. 111-125, https://search.informit.com.au/documentSummary;dn=201100559;res=IELAPA.

[3] In the Revels' accounts listing provided by E. K. Chambers, *The Merchant of Venice* is one of only two plays which names an author — Shaxpere — the other play being *Measure for Measure*. The rest, which include known Shakespeare plays, are all listed anonymously. E. K. Chambers, *William Shakespeare, A Study of Facts and Problems*, vol. 2 (Oxford: Clarendon Press, 1930), appendix d, "Performances of Plays," pp. 331-332. However, the "Shaxpere" notations were discovered to be forgeries of Payne Collier. William J. Rolfe, *Shakespeare's Comedy of 'The Merchant of Venice'* (New York, 1885), p. 11.

suggests, the "mental seeds of Bacon fell upon fertile ground in the mind of the country boy from Stratford and bore fruit in the trial scene of *The Merchant of Venice.*" "One seer will influence another" in any age," he continues.[1] As a lawyer in training, he must realize how mystical these phrases sound. In the opinion of British law professor George Keeton, writing in 1967, Shakespeare had simply failed to explain Bellario "plot-wise."[2]

We are back to the most obvious explanation which is: that he wrote the play and gave himself a cameo role which did not require his appearance. Alfred Hitchcock would show up for brief cameos in his films, and nineteenth century French artist Toulouse-Lautrec would paint himself unobtrusively into the backgrounds of his paintings. The head stonemason of a Gothic cathedral would leave a small portrait of himself in the very top of the building, his signature. Cameos and miniature portraits were popular in Elizabethan England, with the cameo being part of the fascination with ancient Rome.[3]

There in his cameo, Bellario has quietly remained for four hundred years, virtually ignored.

***

It was watching Simon Miles' talk[4] on *The Merchant of Venice* in March 2015 that made me remember Mark Edwin Andrews' *Law v. Equity in the Merchant of Venice, a Legalization of Act IV, Scene 1.* I had first seen the book in my college library, thirty-five years before. The visual impact of his paraphrase of the famous trial scene into modern courtroom English, with the lines from Shakespeare's "immortal poetry" set out next to it on the right, had been powerful. I was convinced that whoever wrote that play had to have been a lawyer.

Andrews' honing in on just one act of one play has a certain appeal when the literature on Shakespeare, and on Bacon, is so extensive.[5] While many are content to enjoy the plays at face value, others become gluttons for

---

[1] MEA, p. 45.

[2] George Keeton, ch. 9, "Shylock v. Antonio," *Shakespeare's Legal and Political Background* (London: Pittman 1967), pp. 139-140 (mentioning that Karl Elze, editor of the 1878 *Shakespeare Jahrbucher* (*Yearbook*), suggested that Bellario may have been modelled on Otto Discalzio, a sixteenth-century Paduan legal scholar. Keeton, 1967, p. 140, citing [Friedrich] Karl Elze, ed., *Shakespeare Jahrbucher* (1878); appendix, *A New Variorum Edition of Shakespeare: Merchant of Venice, 7th* ed., edited by Horace Howard Furness (London, 1888), pp. 458-459). However, there may be another solution to the riddle of "who is Bellario?"

[3] Sara N. James, "Elizabethan painting: the portrait," *Art in England: The Saxons to the Tudors: 600-1600* (Oxford: Oxbow Books, 2016), p. 307. A cameo "concentrate[es] major drama into a minute space." "Cameos and Intaglios," *Extasia Jewelry*, https://www.extasia.com/retail-jewelry/cameos-and-intaglios.html; "Cameo," Online Etymology Dictionary, https://www.etymonline.com/word/cameo.

[4] "The Francis Bacon Society Lectures with Simon Miles, 'Francis Bacon and the *Merchant of Venice*,' March 2015, pub. on Aug. 27, 2015, https://www.youtube.com/watch?v=KcQCljc1Mv8.

[5] On May 23, 2018, a Google search for "Shakespeare and law" returned 42.4 million results for "all results" and 3.27 million results for "books."

punishment,[1] trying to learn more about the plays and playwright, perhaps hoping some of Shakespeare's genius will rub off on them.

Andrews sets his fictional scene in a London court of law, 1597, with Lord Chief Justice Coke presiding, Lord Ellesmere as Chancellor, and Francis Bacon as *amicus curiae*. In reality, Sir Edward Coke did not become Chief Justice of the Court of Common Pleas until 1606.[2] Lord Ellesmere did not become Chancellor until 1603, under King James.[3] However Andrews' dramatization, drawing parallels, is provided for comparative purposes.

By 1616, Francis Bacon was a legal advisor to King James, but in 1596-7, the dates proposed for the play's composition, he had had few legal briefs, and political advancement eluded him, save that the Queen had created a position just for him as "learned counsel extraordinary." In that role, he took part in Tower investigations of men accused of treason. These included the interrogations of Dr. Lopez, condemned to death in June 1594,[4] and the Jesuit priest Father John Gerard, who once evaded capture as a hunted priest by traveling incognito, pretending to be a falconer looking for his missing hawk ("Did you not hear his bell tinkle?").[5]

Perhaps more importantly, in 1596-97, he completed his "first important legal work," *A Collection of Some Principle Rules and Maximes of the Common Lawes*, a hybrid work in which he attempted to infuse the practical common law with precepts of a "higher law" he had taken from civilian legal teachings. This work he dedicated to Queen Elizabeth. It was not published until 1631, thirty-four years later. In 1597, too, his *Essays*, along with *Colours of good and evill* and *Meditationes Sacrae*, were published. He dedicated this, his first published work, to his brother Anthony.[6]

While it would make sense for the playwright to set *Merchant* in his own times, the play has a certain medieval feel to it which cannot be ignored. As Hermann Sinsheimer, author of *Shylock*, tells us, the pound of flesh as a remedy for creditors was actually part of the Roman law on the books in the

---

[1] Cormorants are adept, voracious fishing birds that Shakespeare associated with gluttony. http://acobas.net/teaching/shakespeare/masters/. Anglers do not like the cormorant, unless they have trained it to serve them. Like pork, this bird of prey was a forbidden food to the Jews (Leviticus 11: 13-14). The Hebrew for "cormorant" is "shalakh," which sounds like "Shylock." Hope Traver, "I Will Try Confusions with Him," *The Shakespeare Association Bulletin* 13, no. 2 (April, 1938), pp. 108-120, 119, JSTOR, http://www.jstor.org/stable/23675765.

[2] Gareth H. Jones, "Sir Edward Coke," *Encyclopedia Britannica*, https://www.britannica.com/biography/Edward-Coke; Bowen, *Lion*, ch. 21, pp. 278-281.

[3] "Sir Thomas Egerton, Viscount Brackley, Lord Chancellor Ellesmere (1540-1617)" Luminarium: Encyclopedia Project. http://www.luminarium.org/encyclopedia/egerton.htm.

[4] Bowen, *Lion*, p. 94.

[5] Bowen, *Lion*, pp. 98-99. Nieves Matthews in *Francis Bacon, The History of a Character Assassination*, thought Bowen treated Bacon in an unduly negative fashion in her biography of him, *The Temper of a Man* (New York: Fordham University Press, 1993). https://books.google.com/books?isbn=0823215377.

[6] FB, appendix II, p. 325; on the *Maxims*, pp. 35-48.

twelfth century — even as late as the fifteenth century.[1] The presence of the fictional Lord Falconbridge, the English suitor about whom Nerissa queries Portia, has the same name as a character in Shakespeare's play *King John* (1166–1216). This might suggest that *Merchant*, too, could be set in the twelfth century. In this, then, I disagree with Andrews who envisioned the play set in Elizabethan England. It is as if the playwright had a foot in each of two worlds, like having two computer screens open, so as to more easily draw a comparison between Elizabethan England and twelfth-century Venice.

In Part 1 of his book, Mark Edwin Andrews sets out his translation of the trial scene in *Merchant* into modern courtroom English. In Part 2, he sets out his research, sixty pages of annotations consecutively tied to the action in the play. He includes the "set-outs" of many relevant but hard-to-find cases from the Year Books, providing a valuable service.[2]

Today, lawyers look for the most current case, to prove that the law has not changed, but in Shakespeare's time, lawyers looked for the oldest case, as if to say, "It was ever thus."[3] While Bacon was not immune from the strategy,"[4] he was less likely to succumb to the temptation than Coke.[5] At one point, Coke was in trouble for misstating the law.[6] Coke would report cases as he thought they should have been decided, not as they actually were. In his defense, however, the legal historian William Holdsworth wrote that he only did this in matters where politics were involved.[7]

In Part 2 of *Law v. Equity*, Mark Edwin Andrews provides commentary to the trial scene he has paraphrased into modern courtroom English in Part 1. He notes the rising importance of the notary in the sixteenth century, due to the increase in trade and commerce.[8] He documents Francis Bacon's concerns about the obscure informer clause[9] and laws affecting aliens, both

---

[1] Hermann Sinsheimer, *Shylock* (New York: Benjamin Blom, 1963, first pub. 1947), p. 82.

[2] MEA, *part II*, pp. 17-78, appendix 1, pp. 79-81.

[3] Daniel R. Coquillette, ch. 1, "The Early Legal Works," *Francis Bacon* (Stanford: Stanford University Press, 1992), p. 59, n. 165, citing *Spedding*, XIII, p. 41, HathiTrust, https://hdl.handle.net/2027/ucl.b3618247.

[4] Bowen, *Lion*, p. 361. For example, Bacon argued in *Calvin's Case*, "Allegiance began before laws:.... The original age of kingdoms was governed by natural equity...." Francis Bacon, in Polly J. Price (1997), "Natural Law and Birthright Citizenship in Calvin's Case (1608), *Yale Journal of Law & the Humanities* 9, no. 1, art. 2, p. 109, n. 202, Digital Commons, http://digitalcommons.law.yale.edu/yjlh/vol9/iss1/2/; "Arguments of the Law, The Case of the Post-Nati of Scotland," *Spedding*, VII, 637-682, 666, HathiTrust, https://catalog.hathitrust.org/Record/006685889; Calvin v. Smith, 77 Eng. Rep. 377 (K.B. 1608).

[5] Coquillette, *Francis Bacon*, p. 246.

[6] Holdsworth, *A History of English Law*, 3d ed. (1922), pp. 553-554, HathiTrust, https://hdl.handle.net/2027/njp.32101075729283.

[7] Bowen, *Lion*, ch. 34, pp. 515; p. 635 (notes to p. 515).

[8] MEA, pp. 48-49, n. 26.

[9] MEA, p. 69. For Bacon's longstanding concern about the abuses of informers, see his "Report on Project Touching the Penal Laws" to King James, ca. 1608, *Spedding*, XI, pp. 96-106, p. 96, HathiTrust, https://hdl.handle.net/2027/ucl.31175012007939.

---

of which he finds relevant to the play.[1] He finds distinct echoes of Portia's "quality of mercy speech" in the official *Per Ipse Regum* which Bacon for King James in the 1616 *Glanville* case.[2]

Andrews expresses admiration for the playwright's correct use of over fifty precise legal terms of art, including "tender" and "cause in controversy."[3] In contrast, he provides an excerpt from the petition of "William Wayte et al." for an order of protection from "William Shaxpere" who has caused the petitioners to live in fear for their lives.[4] Suffice it to say that Shaxpere's legal experience was quite different from Francis Bacon's.

Andrews explains that his calling Bellario an *amicus curiae* or "friend of the Court" is meant "to suggest the actual fact that it was Bacon's destiny as a legal authority to solve the actual conflict [in 1616] which Portia solves in the play."[5]

According to Andrews, detailed legal procedure was Shakespeare's addition to his literary sources. Although Andrews finds Shakespeare remarkably accurate in his use of the law, he points out two aberrations.

---

[1] MEA, p. 70; Bowen, *Lion*, p. 39 (regarding a bill pending in 1593, *Against Alien Strangers retailing their goods in London*).

[2] MEA, pp. 40-41. Here is Portia: "The quality of mercy is not strain'd/It droppeth as the gentle rain from heaven/Upon the place beneath.../...It becomes the Throned monarch better than his crown.../It is enthroned in the hearts of kings.../And earthly power doth then show likest God's/When mercy seasons justice...." (*Merchant* IV, 1, 2125).
Compare, as MEA does, the decree Bacon penned for the King to sign: "Now, forasmuch as mercy and justice be the true supports of our Royal Throne, and that it properly belongeth to us, in our princely office, to take care and provide, that our subjects have equal and indifferent justice ministered to them ...." *The English Reports*, vol. 21, pp. 65, cited in MEA, p. 41.
Compare, also, Bacon's speech to Parliament on the motion of subsidy, Elizabeth 39 (1597-1598): "Sure I am that the treasure that cometh from you to her Majesty is but as a vapour which riseth from the earth and gathereth into a cloud, and stayeth not there long, but upon the same earth it falleth again...." (1597-98), Spedding, IX, pp. 85-89, 86, HathiTrust, https://hdl.handle.net/2027/ucl.b3618244.

[3] MEA, part 2, pp. 50, 53-55. *Merchant*, IV, 1. As to "cause," the canonist Gratian used the "causa" or "case" method as a teaching tool in his *Decretum*. "Since the time of Chief Justice Marshall," the U.S. Supreme Court will hear only a "cause in controversy." MEA, p. 50. (Incidentally, two United States Supreme Court justices praised Andrews' book. Letter from Justice Stone to Mark Edwin Andrews, 1937, quoted in editor's preface and letter from Mark Edwin Andrews to Roy M. Mersky, April 27, 1964, pp. ix, 85, MEA).
While Shakespeare's substantial knowledge of law is now generally accepted, scholars used to argue about how much he knew and how he could have learned it. See O. Hood Phillips, *Shakespeare and the Lawyers* (London: Methuen 1972), esp. pp. 91-140, 166 n. 2. One quibble concerned whether Antonio's bond was single or conditional. Some argued a penalty could not be a condition, but *see* Baker, *Intro.*, p. 368. William Rushton chastised Lord Campbell for using terms incorrectly, while Keeton agreed with Greenwood that Shylock was using "condition" in a general sense. *See* Sir George Greenwood, Shakespeare's Law, (London: C. Palmer, 1920), pp. 25-27; Keeton, ch. 9, "Shylock v. Antonio," *Shakespeare's Legal and Political Background*, p. 136); Baker, *English Legal History*, pp. 368-371, 368; 'The Merchant of Venice,' *A New Variorum Edition of Shakespeare*, vol. 7, ed. by Howard Horace Furness (London, 1888), pp. 50-51; William Rushton, *Shakespeare a Lawyer* (London, 1858), pp. 18-19, HathiTrust, https://hdl.handle.net/2027/hvd.32044009633488.

[4] MEA, p. 26.

[5] MEA, p. 43, n. 22.

The first is that Shakespeare has both legal and equitable issues heard in the same courtroom, although such was not the norm in late sixteenth-century England. The second is that, just once, Shakespeare used the word "decree," where Andrews thought the word should have been "judgment" *if* the case had been heard in King's Bench as Andrews assumes.[1] He suggests that Shakespeare may have been imagining the courtroom of the future where law and equity were merged. However, there may be other explanations.

The separate legal systems of law and equity did not merge in the United Kingdom until 1873.[2] The legally trained chancellor under Henry VIII, Sir Thomas More, the author of *Utopia*, had proposed such a merger.[3] Francis Bacon's writings as a mature jurist indicate he was not in favor of merger. He thought the common law would suffer![4] It bears noting that, in Shakespeare's time, the lines between the courts of law and equity were perhaps not as clear-cut as they might seem to us today. The same lawyers who made up the common law bar also made up the equity bar. Furthermore, common

---

[1] MEA, pp. 8, 54, fn. 41.

[2] Baker, *Intro.*, pp. 131-133; p. 132, n. 75. Bowen quotes Bacon in 1616, "So all that troubles us is this, that when Mr. Brownlow [notary] goes up to Westminster Hall hereafter, he shall turn a little upon his right hand, and all shall be well!" Bowen, *Lion*, pp. 356-364, 361. Chancery was on the right hand side; King's Bench was on the left.

For a brief history of equity jurisdiction (with pars. 25-33 on the 1616 jurisdictional struggle), see the speech of The Hon. T. F. Bathurst, Chief Justice of New South Wales. "The History of Equity," October 27, 2015, http://www.supremecourt.justice.nsw.gov.au/Pages/sco2_publications/SCO2_judicialspeeches/sco2_speeches_chiefjustice.aspx or http://www.supremecourt.justice.nsw.gov.au/Documents/Publications/Speeches/2015%20Speeches/Bathurst_20151027.pdf.

As of 2015, in the United States, three states had not completely merged their courts of law and equity: Tennessee, Mississippi, and Delaware. Samuel L. Bray, "The Supreme Court and the New Equity," *Vanderbilt Law Review* 68, no. 4 (May, 2015), pp. 997-1054, 1018, fn. 113 (listing other states which maintain some separation between law and equity: New Jersey, Cook County, Illinois, Georgia, and Iowa); see also Russell Fowler, "A History of Chancery and its Equity, from Medieval England to Today's Tennessee," *Tennessee Bar Journal* (January 25, 2012), reprinted by permission from Capital Area Bar Association (May 2012). http://caba.ms/articles/features/history-chancery-equity.html. For an argument for the preservation of equity within the Federal Rules of Civil Procedure, see, e.g., Thomas O. Main, "Traditional Equity and Contemporary Procedure," (2003) *Scholarly Works*, paper 740, Scholarly Commons at UNLV Law, http://scholars.law.unlv.edu/facpub/740, also Wash. L. Rev. 429-514 (2003).

Francis Bacon asserted, "For there is no law under heaven which is not supplied with equity." Francis Bacon, *"The Jurisdiction of the Marches,"* in *'Arguments of the Law,'* Spedding, VII, pp. 567-612, 602, HathiTrust, https://hdl.handle.net/2027/ucl.b3924335. Interestingly, Kenji Yoshino has observed that, within *Merchant*, there is no law that is not "inflected" by equity, and "equity" looks a lot like Portia's will. Kenji Yoshino, "The Lawyer of Belmont," *Yale Journal of Law and the Humanities* 9, no. 1 (1997), pp. 202, 209, 211, http://digitalcommons.law.yale.edu/yjlh/vol9/iss1/4/.

[3] Brendan F. Brown, "St. Thomas More, Lawyer," 4 *Fordham L Rev.* 375, p. 381, http://ir.lawnet.fordham.edu/flr/vol4/iss3/1.

[4] Daniel J. Coquillette, *Francis Bacon* (Stanford: Stanford University Press, 1992), p. 249, citing aphorism 45, *Spedding*, V, p. 96; Barbara Shapiro, "Francis Bacon and the Mid-Seventeenth Century Movement for Law Reform," *American Journal of Legal History* 24, no. 4 (Oct. 1, 1980), pp. 331-362, p. 344, JSTOR, http://www.jstor.org/stable/844906.

---

law judges would sometimes "sit" for chancery judges, as needed.[1] It would be easy to see how one court might borrow or learn from another, over time.

Common law judges called civilian, or Roman law, experts to consult them in merchant cases, at least after merchant cases began to be heard in common law courts.[2] In the play, the bringing in of a legal expert to advise the judge, as well as Portia's taking an active role in the questioning of Shylock, derived from Roman or civil law.[3] Roman law was practiced in some sixteenth-century English courts, such as admiralty.[4] The fictional Bellario is an Italian jurist, which means he is an expert in the civilian or Roman law, i.e., that based on the Sixth Century Roman Emperor Justinian's *Corpus Juris Civilis*. Canon law (ecclesiastical law), too, and its interpretation, was based to a great extent on Justinian's law as well. However, the Reformation had made it suspect in England. Somehow, it had to be "Reformed." Canon law scholars like Prof. R. H. Helmholz have studied the history of English canon law.

In contrast to Bellario, Francis Bacon was trained at Gray's Inn in the law in common use in English legal courts, with a focus on statutes. Thus, if Bacon is Bellario, there is a seeming paradox, for Roman law was distrusted by the common law bar, including the powerful Sir Edward Coke—as being Popish and foreign. And yet, Roman law (civilian law) did have its applications in some English courts, as we have just discussed.

Professor Daniel Coquillette has argued that Francis Bacon's Roman law leanings were much stronger than has usually been acknowledged. What I will argue in this book, not uniquely, is that Francis Bacon, who took all knowledge to be his province, as he told Lord Burghley, had set out to reform the law of England, continuing the efforts of his father, under the Queen's orders.

In applying his vast intelligence to this task, he strove, in at least some of his writings, to achieve a synthesis, a grafting into the common law of England of some Roman (civilian) law concepts, as he did in his *Maximes* for instance. However, he had to do so quietly, unobtrusively, so as not to arouse a forceful repression of his method, which might have resulted in confiscation of his manuscripts, as had happened to Lord Coke. For example, Bacon's treatise,

---

[1] J. P. Dawson, "Coke and Ellesmere Disinterred: The Attack on the Chancery in 1616, 36 *Ill. L. Rev.* 127 (1941), pp. 143, 146.

[2] William S. Holdsworth, *A History of English Law*, vol. 1, third ed. revised (Boston: Little, Brown, 1922) p. 554, n. 5, citing 2 Brownlow 17 (1611), Archive.org, https://archive.org/details/historyofengl3rd03holduoft or JSTOR, https://www.jstor.org/stable/2141111.

[3] *Merchant*, V, 1: 319-321. The civil law forums were inquisitional, using such fact-finding instruments as depositions, interrogatories, and subpoenae. Civilian judges cross-examined witnesses and requested the advice of experts. Daniel R. Coquillette, "Legal Ideology and Incorporation I: The English Civilian Writers, 1523-1607," *Boston University Law Rev.* 61 (1981), pp. 1-89, 29, Digital Commons @ Boston College Law School, http://lawdigitalcommons.bc.edu/lsfp/642/.

[4] The word "civilian" referred to Roman law based upon Justinian's *Corpus iuris civilis*. Canon law, church law, was also Roman, influenced by Justinian law, but written by churchmen.

sometimes known as the *Aphorismi* for short, has never been published, and his *Maximes of the Common Law* was not published until thirty-four years after his death. For more on Bacon's jurisprudence, see Coquillette's book, *Francis Bacon*.

Such contentions as these may be difficult to contemplate. However, to realize that there was animosity on the part of the common lawyers towards the civilian law, with all its centuries of accumulated wisdom, including interpretations on "higher law" bordering on theology, is important in understanding why Bacon might have hidden his civilian law knowledge which may well have been deeper than is commonly known. This may explain what Bacon was up to, in part, in his involvement in the writing of certain "Shakespeare" plays such as *Merchant*, if he did indeed play an authorship role. But let the reader read on and discern for him/herself.

Does the Play Offend?

At times, censors have banned this popular play about justice and mercy, labelling it as anti-Semitic for its portrayal of Shylock.[1] How *can* Shakespeare argue, as it seems, for justice tempered by mercy for everyone but Shylock?[2] The treatment of Shylock makes the play a challenge for directors.[3] Perhaps the play teaches mercy by antithesis, like a "devil's advocate."[4] The villain

---

[1] For "The Most Infamous Shakespeare Production in History? The Merchant of Venice at Vienna's Burgtheatre in 1943," see *Shakespeare en devenir*, no. 9, 2015, http://shakespeare.edel.univ-poitiers.fr/index.php?id=865.

On censorship, see, e.g., David C. Kupfer, "The Merchant of Venice: Schools, Libraries, and Censors," Library Philosophy and Practice (2009), http://www.webpages.uidaho.edu/~mbolin/kupfer2.htm; Melvyn Bragg, "Banned Books of Guantanamo: *The Merchant of Venice* by William Shakespeare" (Nov. 13, 2014), https://www.vice.com/en_us/article/jmb78y/the-merchant-of-venice-by-william-shakespeare-777; Dawn B. Sova, "The Merchant of Venice," Banned Plays: Censorship Histories of 125 Stage Dramas (New York: Facts on File, 2004), pp. 175-176. On anti-Semitism, see Walter Saunders, "The Merchant of Venice and Anti-Semitism" (2011), http://sirbacon.org/wsaundersMOV.htm.

[2] "Justice and Mercy" was the motto adorning the Seal of the Inquisition. Jonathan Kirsch, *The Grand Inquisitor's Manual, A History of Terror in the Name of God*, (New York: Harper Collins e-book (print, 2008), p. 3, https://www.harpercollins.com/9780061982569/the-grand-inquisitors-manual.

[3] See, e.g., Frank G. Riga, "Rethinking Shylock's Tragedy: [Director Michael] Radford's critique of anti-Semitism in 'The Merchant of Venice,'" The Free Library, 2010, Mythopoeic Society, http://www.thefreelibrary.com/Rethinking+Shylock%27s+tragedy%3a+Radford%27s+critique+of+anti-semitism+in...-a0227196961.

[4] Defining something by saying what it is not ("negation and exclusion") is important in Bacon's system of inductive reasoning. Klein, Jürgen, "Francis Bacon," *The Stanford Encyclopedia of Philosophy* (Summer 2015), ed. by Edward N. Zalta, sec. 5. http://plato.stanford.edu/archives/sum2015/entries/francis-bacon/). See Francis Bacon, *Novum Organum*, ii, aphorisms 11-12, in *Spedding, IV*, p. 127 to 137. Kenji Yoshino points out the abundant contrasting of "binaries" in *Merchant*. "The Lawyer of Belmont," pp. 185, 188. http://digitalcommons.law.yale.edu/yjlh/vol9/iss1/4/. Bacon also knew the power of the "negative pregnant." He once wrote to King James that he was saying a lot by his silence.

---

often gets to portray or proclaim the message no one wants to hear.[1] Analogy and antithesis were hallmarks of Bacon's style.

Arguably the play, with its important theme of justice,[2] is too important to relegate to obscurity.[3] Although it is classified as a comedy, there is nothing

---

Antithesis was popular among Renaissance writers, Machiavelli was among those who observed that opposites juxtaposed reveal each other more sharply in contradistinction. See his letter to R. Bechi, March 9, 1497-98. Alan H. Gilbert, ed., *The Prince and Other Works ...*(Chicago: Packard, 1941), p. 220. When the contrast is extreme, it can also be an effective device in humor. See, e.g., "William Shakespeare: Study sheds light on Bard as food hoarder." BBC News, April 1, 2013, http://www.bbc.com/news/uk-wales-mid-wales-21993857.

David Kerchner in *The Popes against the Jews* tells "an age-old story of a powerful religion or powerful people that believes in its own divinely ordained position as sole possessor of the Truth and repository of all that is good, and, pitted against it, a despised minority, the Other, the agent of the devil. It should not have taken the Holocaust to teach us how dangerous such views of the world can be, but since the destruction of the Jewish millions, we owe it to the survivors and ourselves to learn its lesson ...." David Kerchner, intro., *The Popes against the Jews* (New York: Vintage Books, 2002), p. 21.

For a history of mistreatment of Jewish persons in London, see David Hughson, *London, Being an Accurate History and Description of the British Metropolis*, vol. 2 (London, 1805), pp. 365 to 379.

[1] Michael Bryson and Arpi Movsesian, ch. 6.II, "*Post-Fin'amor French Poetry: The Roman de la Rose*," *Love and its Critics: From the Song of Solomon to Shakespeare and Milton's Eden* (Cambridge UK: Open Book Publishers, 2017)(Scroll down about two inches, under the picture of Meister des Rosenromans.), https://www.openbookpublishers.com/htmlreader/978-1-78374-348-3/ch6.xhtml#_idTextAnchor025.

[2] Prof. Daniel R. Coquillette's 1992 book, *Francis Bacon* (Stanford: Stanford University Press, 1992) is the first book to focus on Bacon's jurisprudence.

A very important Baconian text, never published, discovered and translated relatively recently, sheds much light on Bacon's "mature" views on the law. It is a text of twenty aphorisms, or in Latin, *Aphorismi* ("Aphorisms on the greater law of nations or the fountains of Justice and Law,") which, taken together with his 97 aphorisms in the '*Example of a Treatise on Universal Justice or The Fountains of Equity, by Aphorisms,*' in book 8 of the *De Augmentis*, present a good picture of Bacon's "mature" jurisprudence. Prof. Coquillette sets out highlights from this material clearly in ch. 5, "The Final Vision," Coquillette, FB, pp. 234-256.

The manuscript with the twenty new *Aphorismi*, found by Peter Beal in 1980, was translated by Mark Neustadt. For text and scholarly translation, see the appendix to his 1987 Ph.D. dissertation for Johns Hopkins University, "The Making of the Instauration: Science, Politics and Law in the Career of Francis Bacon" (microfilm). This text is also discussed in William Sessions, ch. 3, "Actual Makers of Time: the Experience of Henry VII and Bacon's Law Texts," in *Francis Bacon Revisited*, Twayne's English Author Series no. 523 (New York: Twayne Publishers, 1996), pp. 57-68, 62-68. As Sessions says, "Even in so cursory a survey as this, the reader cannot but be daunted by the legal texts that emerged from the profession that occupied the great part of Francis Bacon's every day."

[3] Theodore Roosevelt said, "Justice consists in not being neutral between right and wrong, but in finding out the right and upholding it, wherever found, against the wrong." Theodore Roosevelt Association, s.v. "Justice—Meaning of", http://www.theodoreroosevelt.org/site/c.elKSIdOWIiJ8H/b.8090921/apps/s/content.asp?ct=14739067. In 1979, *Black's Law Dictionary* defines justice as "the proper administration of the laws." *Black's Law Dictionary*, 5th ed., ed. by Henry Campbell Black (St. Paul: West, 1979), p. 776 (hereafter to be cited as *Black's LD*). The 10th edition, edited by Bryan Garner (Thomson Reuters/Westlaw, 2014), gives, inter alia, this definition: "the fair treatment of people; the quality of being fair or reasonable; the legal system by which people and their causes are judged," especially in the criminal context, and "the fair and proper administration of the laws."

funny about hatred, racism, attempted murder, or injustice. There is a form of medieval humor called the "grotesque." It involves building anxiety and dramatic tension, then invoking laughter for relief.[1] Some matters are so serious, they can only be spoken of "as if" one were joking. The fool's head or blockhead is a form of grotesque humor.[2] People may laugh at the fool when he speaks the unpleasant truth, but his frightening, traditionally grotesque appearance was thought to protect him, like a creature in nature who makes itself more formidable, a cat who hisses and arches its back, or a puffer fish (blowfish).

In the trial scene, Portia begs for Shylock to show Antonio mercy. He, of course, refuses. Mercy, the grace or pardon one does not deserve, is different from equity, a word which derives from Roman law, *aequitas*, meaning fairness. Although the word "equity" does not appear in the play, fairness is one of its major themes. Francis Bacon, who in later life was Chancellor, second only to King James, asserted that equity was a component of every law.[3] That is potentially a very powerful statement. Portia does not use the word "equity"; rather, she speaks of mercy seasoning[4] justice (IV, 1, 2125). In cooking, a seasoning becomes a part of the dish so you can no longer tell the seasoning from the main ingredients. Thus, it is an apt metaphor. While mercy differs from equity, there might be some overlap in application at times, as with the term "forbearance," for example.[5] Bacon, for one, was

---

[1] On the medieval "grotesque" as humor in a 1611 manual for lawyers, see Scott L. Taylor, "Vox populi e voce professionis: *Processus juris joco-serius: Esoteric Humor and the Incommensurability of Laughter*," ch. 17, pp. 515-530, 516-518 and Albrecht Classen, intro., both in *Laughter in the Middle Ages and Early Modern Times: epistemology of a fundamental human behavior, its meaning, and consequences*, ed. by Albrecht Classen (Berlin: Walter de Gruyter, 2010), pp. 113-114.

[2] Thomas Wright, *A History of Caricature and Grotesque in Literature and Art*, illus. by F. W. Fairholt (orig. pub. London, 1875), Project Gutenberg, released Jan. 22, 2014, https://www.gutenberg.org/files/44566/44566-h/44566-h.htm.

[3] "For there is no law under heaven which is not supplied with equity." Francis Bacon, 'The Jurisdiction of the Marches,' in *Spedding*, VII, p. 602, HathiTrust, https://hdl.handle.net/2027/ucl.b3924335.

[4] Francis Bacon uses the word "seasonable"; see *Montagu*, I, p. 80, HathiTrust, https://hdl.handle.net/2027/njp.32101068998481.

[5] For further reading, see, e.g., David Dolinko, "Some Naïve Thoughts about Justice and Mercy," *Ohio State Journal of Criminal Law* 4, pp. 349-360 (2007), http://moritzlaw.osu.edu/students/groups/osjcl/files/2012/05/Dolinko-PDF-03-11-07.pdf, and Martha C. Nussbaum, "Equity and Mercy," *Phil. & Pub. Aff.* 22, no. 2, pp. 83-125, 92-97 (Spring, 1993). https://www.law.upenn.edu/live/files/3901-martha-nussbaum-equity-and-mercy — excerptpdf, JSTOR. http://www.jstor.org/stable/2265442).

On mercy as a theme in medieval and Renaissance romantic love poetry, see Michael Bryson and Arpi Movsesian, ch. 7.II, "Post-Fin'amour Italian Poetry: The Sicilian School to Dante and Petrarch," *Love and its Critics* ...(Cambridge: Open Book Publishers, 2017, online), pp. 300-330, p. 306, https://www.openbookpublishers.com/htmlreader/978-1-78374-348-3/ch7.xhtml#_id-TextAnchor031.

precise in his use of language, and the same precision has been attributed to Shakespeare.[1]

> "Season" as a noun has to do with "time generally," a "fit and convenient time," the four seasons, and "that which keeps fresh and tasteful." The verb means: (1) "to spice, relish, make fresh and tasteful" (2) to "render more agreeable, recommend and set off by some admixture" (3) "to qualify, to temper" (4) "to mature, to ripen, to prepare"; and (5) "to gratify the taste of."[2]

> In "Of Dispatch," Bacon writes, "To choose time is to save time; and an unseasonable motion is but beating the air..." He goes on to speak of "that negative that is more pregnant of direction than an indefinite."[3]

> Colossians 4:6 (KJV) says, "Let your speech be always with grace, seasoned with salt, that ye may know how ye ought to answer every man." Due to its elegance in language, it is plausible that Bacon was the final editor of the King James Bible.[4]

Did the Play Influence the Results in 1616?

Reportedly, King James saw the play twice in short succession (1604–1605).[5] The comments of Sir Thomas Egerton, later Lord Ellesmere, suggest that he, too, had seen it.[6] Lord John Campbell reported that Ellesmere had argued that the king needed his prerogative, "for otherwise the King would be no more than the Duke of Venice." Egerton arranged for *Othello* to be performed by Shakespeare's company at his estate, Harefield, for Queen Elizabeth, in August 1602.[7] Bacon and Ellesmere were acquainted. Bacon had written a letter to Lord Ellesmere in 1597, in which he introduced the word

---

[1] Andrew Zurcher, ch. 1, "Preamble: How Shall I Understand You?" *Shakespeare and Law*, (London: Arden Shakespeare, 2010), pp. 1-24, 13.

[2] "Season," Alexander Schmidt, *Shakespeare Lexicon and Quotation Dictionary*, vol. 2, N-Z (New York: Dover 1971, rev. and enlarged from the Berlin: George Reimer 1902 ed.), pp. 1016-1017.

[3] "Of Dispatch," *The Works of Francis Bacon* (Roslyn NY: Walter J. Black, 1932), pp. 92-93.

[4] See A.E. Loosley, "Francis Bacon and the James [the] First Bible"; William Smedley, ch. 17, "The Authorized Version of the Bible 1611," *The Mystery of Francis Bacon*, and Tony Bushby, ch. 1, "What Was the Church Trying to Hide?" from the book, *The Bible Fraud*, all excerpted at Sir Francis Bacon's New Advancement of Learning, SirBacon.org, http://www.sirbacon.org/links/bible.html.

[5] E. K. Chambers, *William Shakespeare: A Study of Facts and Problems*, vol. 2. (Clarendon Press: Oxford, 1930), appendix d, p. 332.

[6] MEA, citing [John] Lord Campbell, *Lives of the Lord Chancellors*, vol. 2 (Boston, 1874), p. 385. HathiTrust, https://catalog.hathitrust.org/Record/100266555. As to errors in Campbell, see Nieves Matthews, ch. 28, "The Two-Souled Monster," *Francis Bacon, The History of a Character Assassination*, pp. 339-341.

[7] William Reynolds, intro, 'The Merchant of Venice,' in *The Bankside Shakespeare*, vol. 3, ed. by Appleton Morgan (New York, 1888), p. 36, HathiTrust, https://hdl.handle.net/2027/mdp.39015082503056.

"competition" into the English language,[1] and he sent Ellesmere a copy of his work, *The Advancement of Learning* after its publication, in 1605.[2]

Mark Edwin Andrews wrote, "If I were asked to name the three men in all England who were most profoundly affected by Shakespeare's *The Merchant of Venice*, I should unhesitatingly name the following: Sir Edward Coke, Sir Thomas Egerton, later to become Lord Ellesmere, and Sir Francis Bacon. This statement is made after due consideration, for these three men were to English jurisprudence of the late sixteenth and early seventeenth centuries what Shakespeare, Marlowe, and Johnson were to Elizabethan drama; and *The Merchant of Venice* was the one instance in which jurisprudence and drama came together *vis-à-vis*."[3] In contrast, Lord Campbell believed it was not in Sir Edward Coke's "nature" to attend plays.[4] Paul Raffield considered Coke to be no friend to stage actors.[5]

While Bacon did not ever mention the name of Shakespeare, according to Spedding, or, apparently, *The Merchant of Venice*, E. A. Abbott, who was not a Baconian, wrote in his preface to Mrs. Henry Pott's work on Bacon's *Promus* that he believed Bacon must have seen *Romeo and Juliet*, based on similarities between the *Promus* and the play.[6] Bacon wrote and co-wrote masques,[7] speeches for the Gray's Inn revels in 1594, and other dramatic works.[8] Mark

---

[1] See *Spedding*, II, p. 63; George Stronach, letter to editor, "Shakespeare, Bacon, and Dr. Murray," *The Academy and Literature*, vol. 64 (25 April 1903), pp. 421-423. *https://books.google.com/books?id=xvXQ3PTqthYC*,

[2] Letter, *The Works of Francis Bacon*, in ten vols., vol. 5 (London, 1803), no. 80, p. 290 (from Rawley's *Rescuscitatio*), HathiTrust, https://hdl.handle.net/2027/inu.30000108528492. Note: E. Kantorowicz wrote in *The King's Two Bodies* that Egerton was a patron of the playwright/poet Samuel Daniel. This is now disputed. However, Egerton did hire John Donne to be his private secretary. On Daniel, see David Ibbetson, *Law and Equity, Approaches in Roman Law and Common Law*, ed. by E. Koops and W. J. Zwalve (Leiden: Martinus Nijhoff, 2014), p. 72. On Donne, see British Library, "Letters from John Donne about his secret marriage to Ann More," https://www.bl.uk/collection-items/letters-from-john-donne-about-his-secret-marriage-to-ann-more.

[3] MEA, p. 21.

[4] MEA, foreword, p. xii; 40-41, 41 n. 16; see also George W. Keeton, ch. 4, "Sir Edward Coke and Shakespeare," pp. 43-67, p. 43, in *Shakespeare's Legal and Political Background*, (London: Pittman, 1967), Lord John Campbell, *"Lives of the Chief Justices*, vol. 1 (London, 1849), p. 243, HathiTrust, https://catalog.hathitrust.org/Record/000272904.

Allen D. Boyer found no evidence that Coke had ever attended a play. *Sir Edward Coke and the Elizabethan Age* (Stanford: Stanford University Press, 2003), p. 34.

[5] Paul Raffield, intro., *The Art of Law in Shakespeare* (Oxford: Hart Publishing, 2017), p. 3.

[6] E. A. Abbott, preface, Mrs. Henry Pott, *The Promus of Formularies and Elegancies*[...] (London, 1883), p. vii. See also Potts, pp. 25, 65-67, appendix L), HathiTrust, https://hdl.handle.net/2027/umn.31951002288344z.

[7] Brian Vickers, intro., *Francis Bacon, a Critical Edition of the Major Works*, pp. xxiv to xxix.

[8] Brian Vickers, "Bacon's use of theatrical imagery," in *Francis Bacon's Legacy of Texts*, edited by W. A. Sessions (New York: AMS Press, 1990), pp. 171-213; R. J. W. Gentry, "Francis Bacon and the Stage," *Baconiana*, reprinted at http://www.sirbacon.org/links/bacon&_the_stage.htm; Amy Alicia Leith, "Bacon on the Stage," *Baconiana* (July 1909), pp. 150-162, HathiTrust, https://

Edwin Andrews, a Stratfordian, believed it was likely that Bacon would have seen the play. As he wrote, "The author can advance no irrefutable proof as to the influence of the play on Elizabethan thought, or on the final decision regarding the case of *Glanville v. Courtney*. Nevertheless, is it not significant that Coke, Ellesmere, and Bacon saw each other frequently and must have had many opportunities to see the play, to discuss it with others who had seen it, and to discuss it amongst themselves? It is even possible that one or more of them may have known Shakespeare personally...."[1] Yes...

> According to O. Hood Phillips, Bacon set forth the law on bribery to King James "a little later" than when the play was written (1596-98).[2] It was actually in April 1621, when Bacon was facing charges of corruption, that Bacon wrote a memorandum setting forth the law on bribery, in preparation for his audience with King James. He wrote, "There be three causes of bribery charged or supposed in a judge: the first, of bargain or contract for reward to pervert justice; the second, where the judge conceives the cause to be at an end by the information of the party or otherwise, and useth not such diligence as he ought to inquire of it; and the third, when the cause is really ended, and it is sine fraude, without relation to any precedent promise." Lord Normand reasoned that Portia's case fell into the third category.[3]

> Corruption was rampant in the Elizabethan justice system, where presents could be seen not as bribery but as allowed fees which moved a case through a backlog. A failure to provide a consistent rubric as to what constitutes actionable bribery can provide ammunition for one's political enemies, as we have seen in recent times; e.g., in the case of Don Siegelman, former governor of Alabama.[4]

> In twelfth-century Italy, honored doctors of jurisprudence who were called to serve as podesta (judges in criminal matters in small republics) "did not render [their] opinions gratuitously" but expected to be paid. Portia had turned Shylock v. Antonio into a criminal matter. Thus, if we set the play in the twelfth century, Bassanio's gracious compensation of Portia was completely respectable and expected of him.[5]

---

hdl.handle.net/2027/iau.31858001735426; http://www.sirbacon.org/leithbaconstage.htm; L. Biddulph, "Lord Bacon and the Theatre," *Baconiana*, no. 108 (July 1943), http://www.sirbacon.org/links/lord_bacon_&_the_theatre.htm; Edwin Bormann, *Francis Bacon's Cryptic Rhymes and the Truth They Reveal*, appendix to ch. 2, (London: Siegle, Hill, 1906), pp. 227-234, HathiTrust, http://hdl.handle.net/2027/ucl.$b681854.

[1] MEA, foreword, *Law v. Equity*, p. xii.

[2] O. Hood Phillips, ch. 8, "The Trial in 'The Merchant of Venice,'" *Shakespeare and the Lawyers* (London: Methuen, 1972), p. 110, n. 41.

[3] Lord Normand, p. 43. I am indebted to Simon Miles for inquiring into Phillips' "a little later."

[4] On corruption in the Elizabethan justice system, see *Spedding*, XIV, pp. 237-238, HathiTrust, https://hdl.handle.net/2027/ucl.31175012007947; Baker, *Intro.*, p. 129.

[5] See Henry Hallam, *Intro. to the Literature of Europe in the Fifteenth, Sixteenth, and Seventeenth Centuries*, vol. 1 (London, 1872), p. 83, HathiTrust, https://catalog.hathitrust.org/Record/011559899.

James Spedding presumed that Bacon had most likely never heard of the plays of Shakespeare, since he never mentioned Shakespeare in his writings.[1] Spedding wrote to Baconian judge Nathaniel Holmes that he "no longer" believed that Bacon had written Hamlet.[2] However, he did compare Bacon to Shakespeare[3] and praised Bacon's poetic faculty.[4] Spedding excluded from publication some works which arguably bear on the question of authorship.[5]

---

[1] *Spedding*, I, p. 519, as cited in Edwin Bormann, appendix to ch. I, "Did Mr. James Spedding Really Know 'Everything' About Bacon?" *The Cryptic Rhymes of Shakespeare and the Truth They Reveal*, pp. 217-226, p. 220, HathiTrust, https://hdl.handle.net/2027/ucl.$b681854. Spedding notes two similarities between Bacon and Shakespeare in *Spedding*, VI, p. 139 (*Bacon's History of the Reign of King Henry VII*), and p. 486 ("Of Gardens"). HathiTrust, https://hdl.handle.net/2027/ucl.b3618247.

Edwin Reed points out the need to read Bacon in English, Latin, and French to gain the full benefit of his cryptic meanings, since he wrote in foreign languages both to conceal and to reveal. Edwin Reed, "An Idiosyncracy," *Coincidences, Bacon and Shakespeare* (Boston: Coburn, 1906), coincidence no. 36, pp. 70-71, HathiTrust, https://hdl.handle.net/2027/hvd.32044019185958.

[2] James Spedding's Feb. 15, 1867 response to St. Louis, Missouri judge Nathaniel Holmes, author of *The Authorship of Shakespeare* (Boston, 1894), after reading Holmes' book is reprinted in "Lochithea," *Baconian Reference Book, Commentarius Solutus*, (New York: iUniverse, Inc., 2009), p. 596, https://archive.org/stream/BaconianReferenceBook/baconian_reference_book_archive#page/n333/mode/2up. The experts closing ranks against Holmes is reported in Alan Stewart, "The Case for Bacon," in *Shakespeare Beyond Doubt: Evidence, Argument, Controversy*, ed. by Paul Edmondson and Stanley Wells (New York: Cambridge University Press, 2013), pp. 16-29, 21-22.

[3] Spedding wrote, "What Milton said of Shakespeare may as truly be said of Bacon." *Spedding*, XIV, p. 574, HathiTrust, https://hdl.handle.net/2027/ucl.31175012007947 ("That each heart/ hath from the leaves of thy unvalued book/Those Delphic lines with deep impression took."). Spedding also said that if Bacon were called upon to pronounce judgment upon himself, he would do so in the words of Isaac Comnenus in the play, *Isaac Comnenus*, written by Spedding's friend, Sir Henry Taylor. *Spedding*, XIV, pp. 576-577; Sir Henry Taylor, Isaac Comnenus, end of Act III (London, 1827), https://books.google.ca/books?id=mlgJAAAAQAAJ. For more on Taylor, see "Taylor, Sir Henry," *Dictionary of National Biography*, vol. 55, ed. by Leslie Stephen and Sidney Lee (London, 1898), pp. 410-412, 411. The Online Books Page may be useful. http://onlinebooks.library.upenn.edu/webbin/metabook?id=dnb.

For the Taylor-Spedding correspondence related to whether Bacon was Shakespeare, see *Henry Taylor's Correspondence*, (London, 1888), ed. by Edward Dowden, pp. 306-307. Also of interest may be pp. 313, 339, 355-357.

I think Bacon said what he wanted to say on the subject when he wrote to a friend, *Dat veniam corvis; vexat censuram Columbas*, a quotation from Juvenal *Saturae* I, 63: "The censor's office is indulgent towards the crows but harasses the doves." See "Latin Proverbs, Mottoes, Phrases, and Words: Group D," English — Word Information, *Robertson's Words for a Modern Age*, copyright 2003 to 2014, http://wordinfo.info/unit/3466/s:adages; Montagu's preface to vol. I, *Montagu*, I, p. vi, HathiTrust, https://hdl.handle.net/2027/uc2.ark:/13960/t6zw1952d.

[4] Spedding's preface to Bacon's *Translation of Certain Psalms* (1625), *Spedding*, VII (Longmans), pp. 267-268, as discussed in Mrs. Henry [Constance] Pott, *Did Bacon Write Shakespeare?* (in 2 parts) (London, [1884-189-?], p. 6, HathiTrust, https://hdl.handle.net/2027/mdp.39015082256259.

[5] J. E. Roe, *Sir Francis Bacon's Own Story*, p. 152, HathiTrust, http://hdl.handle.net/2027/njp.32101068587755. Helen Hackett used just twenty lines of the late Roe's book to say that "most" anti-Stratfordian scholarship was of poor quality. The category would presumably include doubters, Oxfordians, Marlovians, Baconians, and those of other persuasions. For Baconians alone, the published scholarship would include at least all of *Baconiana*, the journal

Spedding discussed how Bacon guarded and preserved his ideas from the scorn and derision of those who would likely not understand them. He may have felt it was his duty as editor of his works to keep Bacon's secrets.[1]

Law in Shakespeare as Probative Evidence of Authorship

It is now accepted that there is an abundance of law in the works of Shakespeare.[2] However, there seems to be a tendency to simply sidestep the implications of that fact as to the authorship question.[3] For example, it has been argued that Shakespeare could have picked up all the law he needed to infuse his plays with legal knowledge from living in a litigious society or possibly clerking in a law office, *and* that he was an *authority* on legal topics such as "libel, inheritance, sovereign immunity, conveyance, and delegation."[4] Normally, becoming an authority on such topics would require years of study and practical experience.

Arguably, no legitimate reading should disregard highly probative evidence. Any bald statement, such as that it was a "virtual"[5] or "almost virtual"[6] certainty that Bacon did not write Shakespeare, does not become true merely by being repeated often. Bacon taught that one should look first to the facts and then derive rules from them, rather than to force-fit

---

of the Francis Bacon Society, and all of the writings listed/linked to at www.SirBacon.org. See Helen Hackett, *Shakespeare and Elizabeth, The Meeting of Two Myths* (Princeton: Princeton University Press, 2009), pp. 159-160.

[1] See Robert Ellis, ed., preface, *Novum Organum*, iii, in *Spedding*, I, pp. 85-86; 110, 112-113, HathiTrust, https://hdl.handle.net/2027/hvd.32044011598257.

[2] Andrew Zurcher, ed. "Preamble: How Shall I Understand You?" *Shakespeare and Law*, pp. 8, 282, n. 3. Zurcher opens ch. 1 with a quotation from Francis Bacon and ch. 2 with a quotation from Edward Coke.

[3] Zurcher, pp. 2, 282.
For a sample of the arguments against Shaxpere as Shakespeare, see William F. and Elizebeth S. Friedman, ch. 1, "The Great Controversy," *The Shakespearean Ciphers Examined* (Cambridge: Cambridge University Press, 1958 and repr. in 2011), pp. 1-14, 10-11; N. B. Cockburn, ch. 30, "Was Shake-Speare a Lawyer?" *The Bacon Shakespeare Question: The Baconian Theory Made Sane* (Guildford and Kings Lynn: printed for the author by Biddles, Ltd, 1998), pp. 338-367, to be further cited as "BSQ"; Andrea E. Mays, ch. 2, "Adieu...Remember Me," *The Millionaire and the Bard: Henry Folger's Obsessive Hunt for Shakespeare's First Folio* (New York: Simon and Schuster, 2015), pp. 26-28; The Shakespeare Authorship Page, www.shakespeareauthorship.com (site managed by David Kathman and Terry Ross); Penn Leary, "A Reply to 'The Code That Failed' by Terry Ross," *The Shakespeare Authorship Page* (July 20, 1996). http://shakespeareauthorship.com/bacpl2.html.

[4] Daniel J. Kornstein, prologue, *Kill All the Lawyers, Shakespeare's Legal Appeal* (Princeton: Princeton University Press, 1994), pp. xiii.

[5] David Simpson, "Francis Bacon 1561-1626," *Internet Encyclopedia of Philosophy*. http://www.iep.utm.edu/bacon/.

[6] Robert P. Ellis, "Preface," *Francis Bacon: The Double-Edged Life of the Philosopher and Statesman* (Jefferson NC: McFarland, 2015), p. 2.

---

facts to rules.[1] In discussing legal fictions, legal scholar J. H. Baker wrote, "The implication of a material fact is tantamount to a conclusion of law."[2] Shakespeare's knowledge of law is such a fact.

In sum, then, research since Andrews has proven correct his argument that the author of *The Merchant of Venice* demonstrated vast knowledge of the English legal system and legal language. His second assertion, that the play actually influenced legal history-in-the-making twenty years after the play was produced, is difficult to prove with certainty, but seems plausible, as far as it goes.

Andrews' last, novel assertion, that Bacon "was" in some way the character Bellario, yet remains to be explored to its fullest — as Simon Miles says in his Foreword — without a restriction on consideration of Bacon's authorship, and using modern tools of online research not available to Andrews, whose time on the project was, at any rate, limited.

Thus, this book attempts to take up where Andrews left off, looking for clues within the play, in Bacon's writings, and other sources to try to understand the meaning, function and purpose of Bellario within the play and what, if anything, he can teach us about Francis Bacon and, in a bigger picture, the law.

[1] For Jean de La Fontaine (1621-1695), reteller of *Cinderella*, as an authority on both fables and the *Gesta Romanorum*, see T. F. Crane, "Medieval Sermon-Books and Stories," *Proceedings of the American Philosophical Society* 21, no. 114 (Mar., 1883), pp. 49-78, 53-54, JSTOR, http://www.jstor.org/stable/pdf/982361.pdf.

[2] J. H. Baker, ch. 12, "Law Making," *An Introduction to English Legal History*, 4th ed. (London: Butterworths, 1990), p. 202.

CHAPTER TWO: BELLARIO AS A CAMEO: CLUES

What do we know about Bellario? Very little; therefore, we might assume each fact is potentially significant. The Duke calls him both "learned" and "old." (IV, 1, 2103–5). He is a learned Italian jurist,[1] a legal expert whom the Duke summons to court to advise him in the matter of *Shylock v. Antonio*. While he never appears on the stage, his hand, through his notes for Portia ("what notes and garments he doth give thee"), guides the plot. In Bellario's letter introducing "Balthasar" who will appear in his stead, he apologizes that he is "very sick."[2] Bellario praises "Balthasar," saying he never knew "so young a body with so old a head."[3]

---

[1] *Black's Law Dictionary*, 5th ed., defines "jurist" as one versed or skilled in the law," a *jurisperitus* in Latin; "a legal scholar, one who has distinguished himself by his writing on legal subjects or to judges." (p. 767). The 10th edition provides: "someone who has a thorough knowledge of the law, especially a judge or eminent legal scholar; a jurisprudent" (person learned in the law). *Black's Law Dictionary*, 10th ed., ed. by Bryan Garner (Thomson Reuters Westlaw 2014), https://legalsolutions.thomsonreuters.com/law-products/westlaw-legal-research/?login=true.

[2] Francis Bacon struggled with poor health all his life. Bowen, *Lion*, p. 80; see, e.g., Francis Bacon, 'Proem' to planned treatise, "Of the Interpretation of Nature," *Spedding*, X, p. 84 ("...a man not old, of weak health, my hands full of civil business..."), HathiTrust, https://hdl.handle.net/2027/ucl.b3618245. For the Latin original, see Spedding, III, p. 518); see also *Spedding*, XIII, p. 200, HathiTrust, https://hdl.handle.net/2027/ucl.b3618247.

[3] *Merchant*, IV, 1, 2098 (Bellario's first letter); IV, 1, 2194, "How much more elder art thou than thy looks!" (Shylock); II, 7, 1058-1060 (Morocco reading: "Had you been as wise as bold/Young in limbs, in judgment old/Your answer had not been enscroll'd."), www.OpenSourceShakespeare.org (Cambridge, 1864 "Globe" edition). In *Timon of Athens*, the soldier speaks: "Our captain hath in every figure skill/ An aged interpreter, though young in days (V, 3, 2551), www.opensourceshakespeare.org. See Andrew Zurcher, *Shakespeare and Law*, ch. 1, p. 9. On p. 8, Zurcher had written that, in Bacon's essay, "Of Judicature,"" ...Bacon's merestone suggests that Shakespeare's obsessive interest in law is of fundamental importance not only to many particular places in his works, but to our critical approach to his works in general."

Desiderius Erasmus in *The Praise of Folly*, wrote, "Everybody hates a prodigy, detests an old head on young shoulders."[1] Another translation is: "For who would not look upon that child as a Prodigy that should have as much Wisdome as a Man? — according to the common Proverb, 'I do not like a Child that is a Man too soon.'"[2] Bacon quotes Erasmus in his *Promus* (infra, ch. 4). Erasmus' influence on Shakespeare has been acknowledged.[3]

What was "Jan Rasmus" trying to accomplish? Biographer Van Loon says Erasmus promoted the kind of world in which "decent human beings" could live "simple, decent lives." He wanted to set mankind free from fear and disaster by being set free from its own ignorance; he hoped for a world in which intelligence, common sense, good manners, tolerance, and forbearance should dominate the scene instead of violence, ignorance, prejudice, and greed."[4] Fellow humanist Bacon had similar goals. Van Loon was writing two years after the Germans had bombed Rotterdam, destroying a statue of Erasmus— but not his vision.

In the last scene, Portia presents another letter "from Bellario" disclosing the secret that Portia was the juris doctor and Nerissa her clerk all along. Again, Bellario guides the plot.

Portia calls Bellario her cousin. However, the word "cousin" then had a number of meanings besides being the child of one's aunt or uncle. It could simply mean "akin," as two jurists might be "akin." *Cousin* was also a way one sovereign might refer to another sovereign or nobleman.[5] Portia could be seen to represent Queen Elizabeth, head of the English justice system.[6] To "cozen" was "to dupe, deceive," or "a deception." Was Portia telling us,

Bacon's "old head on young shoulders" is discussed in Mrs. Henry Pott [Constance], *Did Francis Bacon Write Shakespeare?* (London: Robert Banks & Son, 1900), pp. 14-15, HathiTrust, https://hdl.handle.net/2027/mdp.39015082256259. See also Shakespeare's sonnet 73 and Bacon's letters to Burghley 1592, 1599 and Sir Edwin Reed, "Premature Old Age," *Coincidences, Bacon and Shakespeare*, (Boston: Coburn, 1906), coincidence no. 7, p. 16), HathiTrust, https://hdl.handle.net/2027/hvd.hnpyfp.

[1] *The Columbia Dictionary of Quotations*, ed. by Robert Andrews (New York: Columbia University Press, 1993), s.v. "genius," p. 366.

[2] *Desiderius Erasmus of Rotterdam, The Praise of Folly,'* with a life of the author and illus. by Hendrik Willem van Loon, transl. by John Wilson (1627-1696)(New York: Walter J. Black, 1942, first pub. in Paris, 1511), p. 110.

[3] See, e.g., T. N. Greenfield, "A Midsummer Night's Dream and the Praise of Folly," *Comparative Literature* 20, no. 3 (Summer, 1968), pp. 236-244, JSTOR, https://www.jstor.org/stable/1769442.

[4] Van Loon, dedication to Elmer Davis, pp. viii–ix.

[5] *Webster's*, p. 234. In more detail is Tamsin Hekala, ORB Encyclopedia: Online Essays, "Who's a Relative? Kinship Terminology in the Middle Ages," The ORB: On-line Reference Book for Medieval Studies, copyright 1996, pp. 1-8. https://www.arlima.net/the-orb/essays/text03.html. Kinship terms indicated a relationship that was "safe" and "reciprocal," like a family, and could emphasize a "similarity of outlook" among those engaged in the same activity. Hekala, under "Kinship as a Job Title" and "Conclusion."

[6] Clare Asquith, *Shadowplay, The Hidden Beliefs and Coded Politics of William Shakespeare* (New York: Public Affairs, 2006), pp. 114-121; Marjorie Garber, *'The Merchant of Venice,'* in *Shakespeare After All* (New York: Pantheon Books, 2004), pp. 282-312, 288; see also Roy Strong, *The Cult of*

then, that Bellario was her deception?[1] Did he exist at all? Or was he the legal fiction that allowed a woman to appear in a medieval Venetian court, albeit in disguise?

Bellario was "old." Bacon was in the class of distinction called "Ancients" at Gray's Inn. The meaning of "Ancients" seems clear cut: old, perhaps older than others. However, for some, it might have had a hidden meaning. Scholar/legal historian John Selden wrote that the twelfth-century jurist Odofredus (c. 1200–1265)[2] had divided the jurists from the twelfth-century revival into "antients" [sic] (up through Azo and Bassianus) and "moderns" (Accursius and forward).[3] Selden was one of the "Society of Antiquarians," a "historical society" interested in mining the past for arguments that could be used to improve the state of the law in England and, more specifically, fight King James' claim to a prerogative over Parliament. Selden did write about Odofredus' "antients."

The Roman law of Justinian as it was revived in the twelfth century would not have been popular among common law lawyers such as Coke. It was associated with Catholicism.

While allusions to classical Greek and Roman would pass the censors, King James was perhaps justifiably suspicious of the "Society of Antiquarians" whose ranks included William Camden, Robert Cotton, William Lambarde,[4] and Ortelius.[5] The Earl of Leicester, Robert Dudley (1532–1588), had protected the Antiquarians, just as he had protected those involved in the theatre by having his own theatre company. Bacon wrote a piece called "Wisdom of the Ancients," a collection of fables, ostensibly, but with much written between

---

Elizabethan Portraiture and Pageantry (London: Thames & Hudson, 1977), pp. 15-17, 46, 52, 54, http://www.ucpress.edu/op.php?isbn=9780520058415.

[1] "Cozen,"Alexander Schmidt, *Shakespeare Lexicon and Quotation Dictionary*, p. 257; "cozen" (ca. 1573, 1583) *The Oxford Universal Dictionary on Historical Principles*, prepared by William Little, 3d ed., rev., with addenda, by C. T. Onions (Oxford: Clarendon Press, 1955), p. 414.

[2] "Odofredus, c. 1200-1265), report c034, "Bio-Bibliographical Guide to Medieval and Early Modern Jurists, Ames Foundation, last updated 5/5/2018, http://amesfoundation.law.harvard.edu/BioBibCanonists/author_main_entry_list.php?author_id=489&author_abb=G.%20Nicolosi%20Grassi&surname=Nicolosi%20Grassi.

[3] *The Dissertation of John Selden Annexed to Fleta*, translated with notes by [Robert Kelham, the] editor of Britton 1771, p. 160, HathiTrust, https://hdl.handle.net/2027/nyp.33433008667663. *Fleta*, an anonymous treatise on Bracton and Glanvill, is thought to have been written by a judge while he was incarcerated in the Fleet Prison; hence, *Fleta*. See Jonathan A. Bush and Alain Wijffels, eds., *Learning the Law: Teaching and the Transmission of English Law, 1150-1900* (London: Continuum, 2006), p. 153.

[4] Raymond J. S. Grant, "The Transcribers and Editors," *Lawrence Nowell, William Lambarde, and the Laws of the Anglo-Saxons*, Costerus new series 108 (Amsterdam: Rodopi, 1996), pp. 9-11, https://books.google.es/books?isbn=9042000767.

[5] Tine Luk Meganck, *Erudite Eyes: Friendship, Art and Erudition in the Network of Abraham Ortelius (1527-1598)*(Boston: Brill, 2017), p. 19. https://books.google.es/books?isbn=9004342486.

---

the lines. Traditionally, the fable has been used by the powerless to convey deeper truths. Aesop was, after all, only a humble slave.

Bacon as a "Lucretian" Poet, Conveying Scientia (Knowledge)

The reason most commonly given for discrediting Bacon's authorship is that he was too busy to write *Shakespeare*[1] or that he lacked the temperament and imagination, the assumption being it was simply impossible for the same person to be both a philosopher of science and a narrative poet/dramatist. Today, it would be unusual for one who had devoted himself to the study of science to be also an accomplished poet. However, the lines between disciplines were not as clear-cut then. Modern science did not yet exist, although Bacon's ideas would help it to emerge. There was one "ancient" in the classical Roman sense, the poet Lucretius, who was both a philosopher of science and a poet. When his poem, *De rerum natura*, was rediscovered, it contributed to the humanistic, secularizing spirit of the Italian Renaissance. I believe Bacon sought to emulate Lucretius.

There is a passage in Bacon's *De Augmentis* in which he very beautifully, seemingly effortlessly, "changes keys," to use a musical metaphor, in one paragraph from "poesy is as a dream of learning" to the "clear air of philosophy and the sciences" through which he would now "wing his way," rising "above the earth," "awake."[2]

When he was about thirty-one, Bacon had famously told Burghley he had taken all knowledge to be his province.[3] He also had told Burghley that if he

---

[1] BSQ, ch. 5, "Bacon's Spare Time," pp. 55-62.

[2] *De Augmentis*, at the beginning of iii, *Spedding*, IV, p. 336, transl., HathiTrust, https://hdl.handle. net/2027/ucl.31175002901968.

Shakespeare uses the metaphor of "wing" or "winged" extensively, often in the sense of protection under a wing or winged thoughts. For example, in *Henry V*, 3, opening lines: 1053, the Chorus says, "Thus with imagined wing our swift scene flies/Its motion of no less celerity than that of thought." Also, in Line 2846: "Heave him away upon your winged thoughts athwart the sea." In Part II of *Henry VI*, IV, 7: 2694, Lord Say (*Se* is Latin reflexive, meaning "himself." Is the playwright referring to himself?), who claims his judgment was never swayed by gifts, says: "And seeing ignorance is the curse of God, knowledge the wing wherewith we fly to heaven." Bacon warned Essex of Icarus in the Greek myth who flew too close to the sun, melting his waxen wings. *Montagu*, II, p. 335, HathiTrust, https://hdl.handle.net/2027/hvd.hn34hu.

In the 1623 *De Augmentis*, dedicated to King James (*O King, if you are still reading in Latin by Book 3!*), Bacon coyly writes, "[That p]utrefaction is more contagious before than after Maturity" is a rule in Physics; the same is true in Morals, for the men who are the most wicked and profligate produce less corruption in the public manners than those who appear to have some soundness and virtue in them, and are only partly evil." *Spedding*, IV, p. 338, HathiTrust, https://hdl.handle.net/2027/ucl.31175002901968.

[3] *Spedding*, VIII, pp. 108-109, 109, Bacon to Burghley, HathiTrust, https://hdl.handle.net/2027/ucl.b3618243 , cited in BSQ, ch. 7, "The Learning of Shakespeare," p. 73.

---

did not obtain the kind of "position" or "advancement" he sought, he was considering becoming a "sorry book-maker." It seems he did just that. He hired scriveners, his "good pens,"[1] to help him in his many literary endeavors. Although he did not finish all the writing he had begun, due largely to the pressures of public life, what he did finish was enough to set the modern world on a new course.

Bacon's works include his writer's prayer, a group prayer ("By our hands").[2] Collaboration on the writing of *Shakespeare* has been acknowledged, even by Stratfordians.[3] Bacon was acknowledged to be a poet during his lifetime.[4] In fact, in a letter to John Davies, he referred to himself as a "concealed poet."[5]

Ovid is said to have been Shakespeare's favorite poet.[6] Since Ovid borrowed extensively from Virgil,[7] we might expect to find much of Virgil's

---

[1] Commander Martin Pares, "Francis Bacon and the Knights of the Helmet," *American Bar Association Journal* (April, 1960), pp. 402-409, 405. In the same issue is Arthur E. Briggs, "Did Shaxper Write Shakespeare?" at pp. 410-412. Pares, a retired Royal Navy commander, was President of the Francis Bacon Society from 1956 to 1962. See also, Martin Pares, "Parallelisms and the Promus," http://www.sirbacon.org/mp.html; J. E. Roe, *Sir Francis Bacon's Own Story* (Rochester NY: DuBois, 1918), pp. 44, 151, 112, 236, HathiTrust, http://hdl.handle.net/2027/njp.32101068587755; "Shakespeare," *Francis Bacon Research Trust.* https://www.fbrt.org.uk/pages/shakespeare.html.

[2] *Montagu*, II, p. 406, HathiTrust, https://hdl.handle.net/2027/hvd.32044098248545.

[3] See, e.g., the fifteen-minute debate, "Who Wrote Shakespeare? Sir Jonathan Bate and Alexander Waugh," How to: Academy, published on September 26, 2017, YouTube. https://www.youtube.com/watch?v=HgImgdJ5L6o.

[4] BSQ, ch. 2, "Bacon was a Poet," *The Bacon Shakespeare Question*, pp. 13-21; see "Francis Bacon, Baron Verulam, Viscount St. Albans (1561-1626), Verse Legitimately or Doubtfully Attributed to Bacon," *Catalog of English Literary Manuscripts* 1450-1700, http://celm-ms.org.uk/authors/baconfrancis.html; Barry R. Clarke, *The Shakespeare Puzzle, a Non-Esoteric Baconian Theory*, appendix D, "Bacon's Verse," pp. 221-227, Feb. 2007, http://barryispuzzled.com/shakpuzz.pdf or http://citeseerx.ist.psu.edu/viewdoc/download?doi=10.1.1.116.944&rep=rep1&type=pdf (pp. 207-213); *Manes Verulamiani* [Shades of Verulam], *32 Elegies Written on the Death of Francis Bacon[...]*, William Rawley, ed. (1626); translated from Latin into English Verse by Willard Parker, President, Francis Bacon Society, *American Baconiana*, no. 5 (November, 1927), http://sirbacon.org/Parker/Parker_ManesVerulamiani.pdf.
A "shade" is "a shadow, unreal image, unsubstantial semblance; phantom, spirit; the underworld; a covered place, sheltered spot." A "shadow" is, also, a "fictitious name, invented man." "To shadow" or "to shade" meant to "hide, conceal, or cover up." "Shade" and "shadow," *Shakespeare's Words, a Glossary & Language Companion*, ed. by David Crystal and Ben Crystal, preface by Stanley Wells (London: Penguin Books, 2004), pp. 394-395.

[5] In his March 28, 1603 letter asking Sir John Davies to use his "good offices" on Bacon's behalf with the King, he concludes, "So desiring you to be good to concealed poets, I continue, your very assured, Fr. Bacon." Letter to John Davys [Davies], *Spedding*, X, p. 65, https://hdl.handle.net/2027/ucl.b3618245.

[6] See., e.g., A. D. Nuttall, "A Kind of Scandal," a review of Jonathan Bate, *Shakespeare and Ovid*, *London Review of Books* 15, no. 16, (August 19, 1993), pp. 15-16, https://www.lrb.co.uk/v15/n16/ad-nuttall/a-kind-of-scandal.

[7] See, e.g., Jas Elsner, ch. 5, "Late Narcissus: Classicism and Culture in a Late Roman Cento," in Jas Elsner and Jesus Hernandez Labato, eds., *The Poetics of Late Latin Literature* (New York: Oxford University Press, 2017), pp. 176-207, 177, 179, 184, 186, 192-194, 199-200. Elsner stresses that it is important to our understanding of modern poetry to know what was happening

thoughts in Shakespeare as well. Bacon read Virgil; for that matter, what did Bacon not read? He read Lucretius, as Virgil had done before him, as well as other pre-Socratic philosophers who wrote in a style of poetry which preserved, like a treasury, all of the knowledge and wisdom known at the time.[1]

Consider this passage from Bacon:

> Being at some pause, looking back into that I have passed through, this writing seemeth to me, '*si nunquam fallit imago*,' as far as a man can judge of his own work, not much better than the noise or sound which musicians make while they are tuning their instruments, which is nothing pleasant to hear, but yet is a cause why the music is sweeter afterwards: so have I been content to tune the instruments of the muses, that they may play that hath better hands."[2]

It is surprising how much has been written about the simple Latin phrase, *si numquam fallit imago*, found in Virgil's eclogue 2.27.[3] It has been translated, "if the image never deceives" or "if a reflected image never deceives the viewer...."[4] It had become accepted by Virgil's time that the reflection of one' self which one saw in a still pond or a mirror provided a true, reliable image.

In that eclogue, Virgil, or rather his comic *persona*, the shepherd Corydon,[5] is a would-be suitor in courtship. He has engaged in a song duel. He says he has observed his own reflection, which he ought to be able to trust, and he does not look too bad, or so he thinks. Virgil is thought to have taken this "scientific" idea about the accuracy of a reflection from the Epicureans (School of Siron), who stressed that sensory perceptions were valid and trustworthy.[6] The problem comes, however, when we err in the judgments we make *based* on these sense perceptions. Virgil's taking on the *persona*

---

with poetry in the "thirteen centuries between Vergil and Dante." Elsner, intro., pp. 1-2. On Shakespeare and Ovid, see Charles and Michelle Martindale, ch. 2, "Shakespeare and Ovid," *Shakespeare and the Uses of Antiquity: An Introductory Essay* (London: Routledge, 1994), p. 198, nn. 16, 17, 18; A. D. Nuttall, "Virgil and Shakespeare," Charles Martindale, ed., *Virgil and His Influence: Bimillennial Studies* (n.p.: Bristol Classical Press, 1984), pp. 71-93.

[1] Robert Schuler, ch. 4,'Bacon and Lucretius' in "Francis Bacon and Scientific Poetry," *Transactions of the American Philosophical Society* 82, no. 2 (1992): pp. 1-65, 34-42, JSTOR, http://www.jstor.org/stable/3231921.

[2] Preface, *Montagu*, I, p. viii, HathiTrust, https://hdl.handle.net/2027/hvd.32044098248545.

[3] Philip Hardie, part 2, "The Eclogues," *Virgil*, Greece & Rome 28 (Oxford: Oxford University Press, 1998) pp. 5-9.

[4] Gregson Davis, ch. 6, "Coping with Erotic Adversity: *Carmen et Amor* (*Ecl.* 2 & 8)," *Parthenope: The Interplay of Ideas in Vergilian Bucolic* (Leiden: Brill, 2012), pp. 99-120, 107. https://books.google.ca/books?isbn=9004233083.

[5] Corydon appears in "Passionate Pilgrim,"line 246. See www.opensourceshakespeare.org.

[6] A. Traina, ch. 7, "*Si Numquam Fallit Imago*: Reflections on the Eclogues and Epicureanism," in *General Articles and the Eclogues* , Virgil, edited by Philip Hardie (London: Routledge, 1999), 84-91, 84. https://books.google.ca/books?isbn=0415152461.

---

of a common shepherd lends an element of self-deprecating humor, in his framing of a "standard Epicurean precept as mediated by Lucretian verse."[1]

What is notable is that Corydon is not only a shepherd; he is an artist. As Judith Haber writes, Corydon "continues to reflect upon his self-definition and proceeds to define himself primarily as an artist." He is "a self-conscious creator of reflections."[2] Bacon may be telling us he, like Virgil, identifies with Corydon. This passage is associated with the myth of Narcissus who fell in love with his own reflection in a pool ("autoeroticism").

While I did not find the specific phrase *si numquam [or nunquam] fallit imago* in Shakespeare (www.opensourceshakespeare), Shakespeare clearly is exploring the reliability of perception in *Merchant*. For example, Lorenzo says of Jessica, "For she is wise, if I can judge of her" (II, 6, 966). Salanio says, "That's certain, if the devil may be her judge" (III, 1, 1269), while Shylock predicts, "Thy eyes shall be thy judge, the difference of old Shylock and Bassanio" (IV, 1, 847). Antonio directs, "And when the tale is told, bid her be judge whether Bassanio had not once a love (IV, 1, 2221).[3]

The word "judge" appears twenty times in the play. The uses in the preceding paragraph refer to judgment more generally. Then there is Portia's observation: "To offend, and judge, are distinct offices and of opposed natures" (II, 9, 119; IV, 1, 2221). Nerissa repeats Gratiano's lines when she says: "Gave it a judge's clerk! No, God's my judge."[4]

Shylock and Gratiano flatter Portia as judge, calling her "upright," "learned," "rightful," and "noble."[5] Gratiano says, "In christening shalt thou have two god-fathers: Had I been judge, thou shouldst have had ten more, to bring thee to the gallows, not the font." (IV, 1, 2349). Debate about the number of witnesses required for wager of law or the number of jurors on a jury is a common topic among the legally-trained, which could be a hint about Gratiano and who the intended audience of the play might have been.

Lucretius's long scientific poem, *De Rerum Natura*, is the vehicle by which the philosophy of Democritus was preserved. He was an atomist. Long before microscopes existed, he taught that everything in the world was made up of tiny particles, as Bacon discussed in his *Novum Organum*.[6]

[1] Davis, "Coping with Erotic Adversity," p. 108; *Lucretius*, IV; Traina, "Si Numquam[...]," pp. 84-87.

[2] Judith Haber, ch. 2, "*Si numquam fallit imago*: Virgil's revision of Theocritus," *Pastoral and the Poetics of Self-Contradiction: Theocritus to Marvel* (Cambridge: Cambridge University Press, 1994), pp. 36-53, 44. https://books.google.ca/books?isbn=0521034612.

[3] http://opensourceshakespeare.org/search/search-results.php.

[4] *Merchant*, V, 1: 2608, 2628, 2645 (Gratiano), 2622 (Nerissa).

[5] Shylock, *Merchant* IV, 1, 2247, 2250, 2164, 2177, 2189, 2193. Gratiano in IV, 1, 2259, 2264, 2271. https://www.opensourceshakespeare.org/search/.

[6] *Spedding*, IV, p. 193, HathiTrust, https://hdl.handle.net/2027/ucl.31175002901968.

Bacon said the rule that the nature of everything is best seen in its smallest portions is "a rule of physics of such force that it produced the atoms of Democritus...."[1] In his *Novum Organum*, Bacon translates the first lines of Lucretius's famous poem: "As well said the poet, 'To man's frail race great Athens long ago, first gave the seed whence waving harvests grow, and *recreated* all our life below'" (italics Bacon's).[2] Bacon's translation is more elegant than the Mallock translation which does not use the word "recreated," though the sense is, perhaps, there with "speaks though dumb and lives being dead." I believe Bacon is saying he sees himself as an heir to Epicurus, the Greek philosopher celebrated by Lucretius in his *De rerum natura*. Epicurus was a teacher of the arts, framer of laws, and speaker of the truth "whose glory through the world is spread."[3] Perhaps Bacon identifies with "the world" in a personal symbolism.

He also may be saying he is like the poet Lucretius, who gave the world two things: his treatise on natural science and the poem in which he set it forth, *De rerum natura*."[4] After its discovery during the early Italian Renaissance, this poem was influential on many thinkers seeking to wrest science free from theology. The poem can seem surprisingly modern.[5]

Drama as a Tool for Influence

It could reasonably be argued that subtly persuading the sovereign to exert her/his power to bring about needed change might have been a goal of the author of *The Merchant of Venice*. As well, the ruling powers knew the power of the theatre to influence public opinion and used it to their advantage.[6] From ancient times, drama has served important civic and cultural functions.

A court trial is a form of drama. Queen Elizabeth, as head of the justice system, intervened at times in court cases. For example, the Queen intervened in the case of Simon Taylor (1587), who had obtained a judgment

---

[1] *De Augmentis, Spedding*, IV, p. 338, HathiTrust, https://hdl.handle.net/2027/ucl.31175002901968.

[2] *Spedding IV*, p. 114.

[3] W. H. Mallock, ch. 4, "The Poem of Lucretius in six books," VI, lines 1-7, series ed. by W. Lucas Collins (Philadelphia, 1881), pp. 83-143, 138. HathiTrust, http://hdl.handle.net/2027/coo.31924026921837. On Bacon's reliance on Lucretius as a source for the ideas of the pre-Socratics, see Robert Schuler, 'Bacon and Lucretius' in "Francis Bacon and Scientific Poetry," *Transactions of the American Philosophical Society* 82, no. 2 (1992): 1-65, 34-42, JSTOR, http://www.jstor.org/stable/3231921.

[4] Mallock, ch. 5, "Lucretius as a Poet," pp. 144-151, 144.

[5] Mallock, ch. 1, pp. 1-11; Stephen Greenblatt, *The Swerve* (New York: W. W. Norton, 2011). For its influence on: Giordano Bruno, see pp. 233-241; Bacon, pp. 8, 243, 261; Shakespeare, pp. 3, 9, 75-77, 206, 233, 242-43; Montaine (friend of Bacon's brother, Anthony Bacon), pp. 243-49; on Sir Thomas More, pp. 227-33.

[6] E.g., Bowen, *Lion*, ch. IX, p. 112.

at law, violating Chancery's injunction against further litigation.[1] She loved the theatre.[2] So did Robert Dudley, the Earl of Leicester, her intimate friend and advisor.[3] So did Francis Bacon.[4]

The Earl of Leicester was the first to sponsor an acting company, The Lord Leicester's Men, by royal patent of 1574 (founded by James Burbage). This was the beginning of professional theatre in London. As Peter Dawkins relates, the July 1575 "Woodstock Entertainment" was the "first truly great Elizabethan pageant of poetry, drama and chivalry." The Earl of Leicester also put on the "sumptuous Kenilworth Entertainment" for the Queen,[5] about which much has been written.

And yet, the ruling powers felt compelled to control the public conversation through censorship. While a courtier might be able to exert positive influence on a sovereign by mingling his advice with flattery, a playwright who intended to subtly offer advice or suggest change to a sovereign was treading a more dangerous path.

As a statesman on the floor of Parliament in 1593, thirty-two-year-old Francis Bacon had not pleased the sovereign when he spoke out against a subsidy increase she sought in order to finance a potential war with Spain. This earned him the Queen's royal ire and, it would seem, her continuing refusal of political advancement to him for several years, or so the story goes.[6] It should be remembered, however, that, at the time, others were simply better qualified for the posts he aspired to. Coke had sixteen years of practical experience before he was made Attorney General in 1593.[7]

---

[1] J. P. Dawson, "Coke and Ellesmere Disinterred: The Attack on the Chancery in 1616," 36 *Ill. L. Rev.* 127 (1941), pp. 127-146, 132.
  The Queen prayed for God's wisdom in her role of providing justice to her people. William P. Haugaard, "Elizabeth Tudor's Book of Devotions: A Neglected Clue to the Queen's Life and Character," *The Sixteenth Century Journal* 12, no. 2 (Summer, 1981), pp. 79-106, 99 (in her French, English, Latin and Greek prayers). The Queen attempted to conceal her most personal matters in her diary by writing in foreign languages. Haugaard, p. 99.

[2] Clare Asquith, ch. 2, "Secret Voices," *Shadowplay*, p. 26.

[3] S. L. Lee, "Dudley, Robert, Earl of Leicester (1532? To 1588)," *Dictionary of National Biography* 16, ed. by Leslie Stephen and Sidney Lee (London, 1885-1900), pp. 112-114. To locate volumes, see the Online Books Page for the *Dictionary*, http://onlinebooks.library.upenn.edu/webbin/metabook?id=dnb.

[4] See BSQ, ch. 3, "Bacon's Interest in the Theatre," pp. 21-40.

[5] Peter Dawkins, *The Wisdom of Shakespeare in The Merchant of Venice* (Warwickshire U.K.: I.C. Media Productions, 1998), p. 184.

[6] MEA, p. 45; Bowen, *Lion*, pp. 14, 33-43, 77; "Bacon's Speech on Motion for Supply," *Spedding*, VIII, pp. 212-226, pp. 232-235.

[7] Bowen, *Lion*, pp. 81-83.

While Bacon may have been sometimes lavish in his personal expenses, to some extent, this was expected of him as a courtier. In fiscal matters of state, I believe the record would show that he was prudent.

It is possible that somewhat more has been made than the facts warrant regarding Bacon's "all but ruining himself" (as Coke's biographer Bowen wrote) by what he said in the famous subsidy debate. In his 1987 Ph.D. dissertation, Mark Neustadt relates that, in opening the debate, Lord Puckering, the Lord Keeper, had requested that people stick to the subject of the subsidy. Bacon, however, speaking for his first time publicly, began to talk about the need for law reform. The report breaks off, incomplete, at that point, leaving room for some conjecture.[1]

The famous story is told that the Holy Roman Emperor Frederick II (d. 1250) asked two of the famous "Four Doctors," twelfth-century jurists, Bulgarus and Martinus, to tell him whether he was "lord of the world" (Dominus mundi). Bulgarus answered honestly that, under the law, he was not. Martinus, however, said that he was. This pleased the emperor so much that he gave Martinus his horse. Bulgarus quipped that, on account of equity, he had lost an equine.[2]

Frederick II was a great patron of the arts, in whose reign the poetry of Dante, Petrarch, and Boccaccio flourished, "heavily influenced," as they were, by the troubadours.[3]

Francis Bacon, a Brief Resume

According to law professor Daniel Coquillette, Francis Bacon is *the* "most overlooked example of a common law lawyer influenced by the civil (Roman) law."[4] The precocious Bacon, having attended Trinity College, Cambridge

---

[1] Mark Neustadt, "The Making of the Instauration: Science, Politics and Law in the Career of Francis Bacon" (Johns Hopkins University, Ph.D. diss., 1987 (microfilm), pp. 71-75, 71, fn. 7 (citing Simon D'Ewes, *The Journals of All the Parliaments during the Reign of Queen Elizabeth* (London, 1682), p. 473; Bacon's speech, "Motion for Committee of Supply," Spedding, VIII, pp. 212-228, 213-214; see also 360. Bowen also relied on D'Ewes' *Journals* (22 Feb. to 3 Mar.), pp. 478-515 (Bowen, *Lion*, ch. 4, pp. 33-35, 43; 610).

[2] Kenneth Pennington, ch. 1, "The Emperor is Lord of the World," *The Prince and the Law, 1200-1600, Sovereignty and Rights in the Western Legal Tradition* (Berkeley: University of California Press, 1993), pp. 15-16-17. https://books.google.ca/books?isbn-0520913035. Reviewed by Charles J. Reid, Jr., "Am I, by Law, the Lord of the World? How the Juristic Response to Frederick Barbarosa's Curiosity Helped Shape Western Constitutionalism," *Michigan Law Rev.* 92 (1994), pp. 1646-1674. On Frederick II, see Richard Cavendish, "Death of Emperor Frederick II," *History Today* 50, no. 12, (Dec. 2000), http://www.historytoday.com/richard-cavendish/death-emperor-frederick-ii.

[3] Michael Bryson and Arpi Movsesian, ch. 7.II, "Post Fin'amor Italian Poetry: The Sicilian School to Dante and Petrarch," *Love and Its Critics: From the Song of Songs to Shakespeare and Milton's Eden* (Open Book Publishers, 2017), pp. 295-352, pp. 300-301, JSTOR, http://www.jstor.org/stable/pdf/j.ctt1sq5vd6.11.pdf.

[4] Coquillette, "Legal Ideology ...I ," pp. 9-10, n. 16. For Bacon's jurisprudence, see Daniel R. Coquillette, *Francis Bacon* (Stanford: Stanford University Press, 1992), to be further cited as "Coquillette, FB" or "FB." For an explanation of legal terminology, see Daniel Williman, "Legal

from age twelve to fifteen (without graduating[1]), was sent by the hand of the Queen herself to France when he was yet in his teens as a secretary to England's ambassador to France, Sir Amyas Paulet, from 1576–1579.[2] While there, it is likely he received instruction in civil law from Jean Hotman (1552–1636), the eldest son of civilian jurist and Protestant reformer François Hotman (in Latin "Hotomanus," 1524–1590),[3] with whom he resided for a time in France. Certainly, it seems logical he would have been exposed to the writings of François Hotman. In fact, I find myself wondering whether Reformation proponents Nicholas and Anne Bacon did not name Francis Bacon *after* François Hotman. Bacon also studied with Lambert Daneau, a Reformed theologian, during his time in France as a youth.[4]

After the death of his father, Sir Nicholas, Francis returned to England, in March 1579. He had been admitted to Gray's Inn before he left for France, and would begin his study there in October, 1579, bypassing the customary first year of preliminary legal training at an Inn of Chancery. Coke, for example, had spent his first year at Clifford's Inn, 1571–72.[5] Gray's Inn was one of the four regular Inns of Court for the study of the common law: Gray's Inn, Inner Temple, Middle Temple, and Lincoln's Inn.

Terminology, an Historical Introduction to the Technical Language of Law," sect. 2, http://www.corsanoandwilliman.org/latin/work/legalterminology.htm.

[1] Edward Coke, too, beginning at age 15, attended Trinity College, Cambridge for three-and-a-half years without graduating. This was not uncommon. Less than forty percent graduated. Bowen, *Lion*, p. 58. How much civil law a particular student learned at a particular university at a particular time may have varied. Sir Thomas Egerton's notes show that he studied civil law at Brasenose College, Oxford (also without graduating), as well as classics, logic, and history, before matriculating into Furnivals Inn, an Inn of Chancery, in 1560, to begin his common law studies. Louise A. Knafla, *Law and Politics in Jacobean England: The Tracts of Lord Chancellor Ellesmere* (Cambridge: Cambridge University Press, 1977), intro., p. 6; ch. 1, "The Making of a Legal Mind," pp. 39-64, 39.

[2] Mark Neustadt, "The Making of the Instauration," p. 14.

[3] Coquillette, "Legal Ideology ...I," p. 9, n. 16; Peter Dawkins, *Bacon-Shakespeare Timeline*, Francis Bacon Research Trust, http://fbrt.org.uk/pages/essays/Bacon-Shakespeare_Timeline.pdf.

François Hotman's history of "ancient French laws and liberties" from its early origins, *Franco-Gallia*, may have influenced John Selden in entitling his analogous work, *Anglo-Britainnicon*. Graham Parry, ch. 4, "John Selden," *The Trophies of Time* (New York: Oxford University Press, 1995) p. 98, fn 4.

Jean (John) Hotman, a friend of Philip Sidney who was nephew to the Earl of Leicester, served as the Earl of Leicester's secretary, after Edmund Campion, the martyred Jesuit priest. H. R. Woudhuysen, *Sir Philip Sidney and the Circulation of Manuscripts, 1558-1640* (Oxford: Clarendon Press, 1996), p. 79, https://books.google.com/books?isbn=0191591025. On Campion, see also Bowen, *Lion*, p. 84.

John (Jean) Hotman is the author of a burlesque, *Antichopinus*, and *Anticolason*, "an apology for his treatise of *Ambassador*." M. Claude de Ferriere, *The History of the Roman or Civil Law[..]*, transl. by "J. B.," Esq. (London, 1724), p. 151.

[4] Brian Vickers, intro., *Francis Bacon, A Critical Edition of the Major Works*, p. xi.

[5] Baker, *Intro.*, pp. 182-184, 184.

Edward Coke, whose father had died when he was nine, was in court arguing cases as soon as he had been admitted to the bar, in 1578, at age twenty-six.[1] In contrast, Bacon pled no cases in court until 1594,[2] when he was thirty-three. He argued only two cases in court before the age of forty. Yet, Bacon's cases include important ones still taught in law schools, such as *Slade's Case*,[3] *Chudleigh's Case*,[4] and *Calvin's Case*, also known as the *Case of the Post-Nati*.[5]

According to Bacon's biographer and executor, William Rawley, in 1594, when he was just thirty-two years old, the Queen did create a special office just for him, making him her "learned counsel extraordinary." It was, however, a non-paying position.[6] Spedding thinks William Rawley must have been mistaken because it would have been unprecedented. There were no "contemporary allusions" to it.

---

[1] Bowen, *Lion*, p. 69.

[2] Bowen, *Lion*: on Coke, pp. 68-75, 68; On Bacon, p. 79; MEA, p. 23; Peter Dawkins, *Bacon-Shakespeare Timeline*, http://www.fbrt.org.uk/pages/essays/Bacon-Shakespeare_Timeline.pdf.

[3] *Slade v. Morley*, 4 Co. Rep. 94b, 76E, 1602, argued 1597–1602; see FB, ch. 3, "The Theorist as Advocate," pp. 127-189, 136-143.

A case in which Coke opposed Bacon was the *Surgeon's Case* (1370). A. W. B. Simpson, "The Place of Slade's Case in the History of Contract," *Law Quarterly Review* 74 (1958), pp. 381-396, 393. As Shylock prepares to take "execution" on his judgment, Portia tells him, "Have by some surgeon, Shylock, on your charge." *Merchant*, IV, I, 2202. www.opensourceShakespeare.org.

[4] *Dillon v. Freine*, 1594, (B. & M. 150–157); FB, ch. 3, pp. 128-136.

[5] *Calvin v. Smith*, 77 Eng. Rep. 377 (K. B. 1608). For *"The Argument of Francis Bacon in the Case of the Post-Nati of Scotland,"* see *Spedding*, VII, page 641. This case is "one of the most important common law decisions adopted by courts in the early history of the United States." Polly J. Price, "Natural Law and Birthright Citizenship in Calvin's Case (1608)," *Yale Journal of Law and the Humanities*, pp. 73–145, 73, Digital Commons, http://digitalcommons.law.yale.edu/yjlh/vol9/iss1/2/.

Harvey Wheeler called this case "the Baconian genome out of which both [the] English and American constitutions evolved." Harvey Wheeler, "Francis Bacon, the Case of the Post-Nati...," a paper delivered at the University of London Symposium, September, 1999, http://www.sirbacon.org/wheelerpostnati.html.

Although on opposing sides in this important case, Bacon and Coke worked well together on it, without animosity. Price, "Natural Law," p. 76, n. 12; see Coquillette, FB, ch. 3, pp. 155-166; "Three speeches of the Right Honorable, Sir Francis Bacon Knight, then his Majesties Sollicitor Generall [sic], after Lord Verulam, Viscount Saint Alban. Concerning the post-nati [after birth] naturalization of the Scotch in England union of the lawes of the kingdomes of England and Scotland. Published by the author's copy, and licensed by authority." (London, 1641), Early English Books Online: Text Creation Partnership, http://quod.lib.umich.edu/e/eebo/A71317.0001.001?view=toc.

[6] *Spedding*, I, 'Rawley's Life of Francis Bacon,' p.5, HathiTrust, https://babel.HathiTrust.org/cgi/pt?id=nyp.33433081627303;view=1up;seq=39; Bowen, *Lion*, pp. 98, 111; *Spedding*, VIII, pp. 107-108.; "Lochithea," *Baconian Reference Book, Commentarius Solutus* (New York: iUniverse, 2009), pp. 1-12, Internet Archive, https://archive.org/details/BaconianReferenceBook ; https://www.fbrt.org.uk/pages/essays/baconian_reference_book_archive.pdf.

James kept Bacon on as King's Counsel,[1] for pay, after which he appointed Bacon as Solicitor General, Attorney General, Lord Keeper, and Lord Chancellor. This last post included running the country as Vice Regent when James was in Scotland in 1617.[2] Bacon served in Parliament for forty years, beginning in 1581 when he was only twenty years of age, a year before he had been "called to the bar." His claim to have been even younger might call into question the information on his baptismal certificate.[3]

Evidence shows the Queen and Francis Bacon had a special closeness. In fact, he may have even been her son, perhaps through a secret marriage to Robert Dudley, Earl of Leicester after the death of his wife Amy Robsart in 1560. A scandalous publication about the event was *Leicester's Commonwealth*.[4]

When Sir Nicholas Bacon (Dec. 28, 1510–Feb. 20, 1579) died, he left an inheritance to each of his seven children, save Francis, the youngest. Rawley in his *Life of Bacon* writes that Nicholas had intended to leave an inheritance to Francis but died before he had arranged it. Eighteen-year-old Francis became a ward of William Cecil, Lord Burghley, until he turned twenty-one.[5]

---

[1] Nieves Matthews, *Francis Bacon, The History of a Character Assassination* (New Haven: Yale University Press, 1996), p. 79; Baker, *Intro.*, pp. 188-189.

[2] Brian Vickers, ed., "Principal Events in Bacon's Life" in *Francis Bacon, The History of the Reign of King Henry VII and Selected Works* (Cambridge: Cambridge University Press, 1998), pp. xxvi-xxviii.

[3] "Bacon, Francis (1561-1626) of Gray's Inn and Gorhambury, Herts.," http://www.historyofparliamentonline.org/volume/1558-1603/member/bacon-francis-1561-1626. As to questions about Bacon's birth, see Alfred Dodd, "The Sublime Prince of the Royal Secret," *The Marriage of Elizabeth Tudor* (London: Rider, 1940), pp. 38-42, excerpted at http://www.sirbacon.org/doddsublimeprince.htm.

A copy of Bacon's baptismal certificate lists *custodis* next to Nicholas Bacon's name and calls the baby "Mr." http://www.sirbacon.org/baptismalregistration.htm. Note: In Helen Hackett's opinion, Dodd reads "too much" of an autobiographical nature into Shakespeare's sonnets. Helen Hackett, *Shakespeare and Elizabeth, The Meeting of Two Myths* (Princeton: Princeton University Press, 2009) pp. 162-165.

Peter Beal explains that a birthdate, when given as 1560/1561 ("old style"/"new style"), accounts for the Julian/Gregorian calendar change which affects dates between January 1 and March 24. Peter Beal, *A Dictionary of English Manuscript Terminology: 1450-2000* (New York: Oxford University Press 2008), p. 107. Thus, Bacon's birthdate is January 22, 1561, new style. The Gregorian calendar, proclaimed by the Pope on February 24, 1582, was not adopted in England until 1752. John J. Bond, *Handy-book of Rules and Tables for Verifying Dates within the Christian Era* (London, 1869, reprinted Charlestown, MS: Acme Bookbinding, 2003), preface, p. xxvii; pp. 7, 10.

[4] See Frank J. Burgoyne, ed., *Intro. to History of Queen Elizabeth, Amy Robsart and The Earl of Leicester, Being a Reprint of Leycester's Commonwealth*, 1641 [orig. printed on the Continent in 1584] (New York: Longmans, 1904), p. vii; Parker Woodward, ch. 1, "The Master Mystic," *Sir Francis Bacon, Poet — Philosopher — Statesman — Lawyer — Wit* (London: Grafton, 1920), pp. 1-5, HathiTrust, https://hdl.handle.net/2027/ucl.$b691466.

[5] See Amelie Deventer von Kunow, *Francis Bacon, Last of the Tudors*, transl. by Willard Parker (New York: Francis Bacon Society of America, 1924), p. 87. Reprinted at http://www.sirbacon.org/vonkunow.html; see also http://www.sirbacon.org/parentage. Von Kunow's lecture at Weimar on her book was labeled a "German atrocity," akin to calling the royal family of

Lady Anne had been head lady-in-waiting to both Queen Mary and Queen Elizabeth. Anne Bacon's father, Anthony Cooke, had been an unofficial tutor to Edward VI.[1] Leicester is "one of the most hotly debated figures of Elizabeth I's reign."[2]

James kept Bacon on as King's Counsel,[3] for pay, and appointed him Solicitor General, Attorney General, Lord Keeper, and Lord Chancellor. As Vice Regent, he ran the country when James was in Scotland in 1617.[4] Bacon served in Parliament for forty years, beginning in 1581 at age twenty, although he claimed to have been even younger.[5]

England "Hohenzollerns." *The Literary Digest*, 68, ed. by Edward Jewitt Wheeler (New York: Funk & Wagnalls, February 19, 1921), p. 30.

[1] Lady Anne Bacon, "An Apology or Answer in Defense of the Church of England: Lady Anne Bacon's Translation of bishop John Jewel's 'Apologia Ecclesiae Anglicanae,'" MHRA *Tudor and Stuart Translations* 22, ed. by Patricia Demers (Cambridge: Modern Humanities Research Association, 2016), ch. 1, "Introduction," pp. 1-34, 6, 16, 18, https://books.google.com/books/about/An_Apology_or_Answer_in_Defence_of_The_C.html?id=xeZcCwAAQBAJ.

[2] Simon Adams, "A Godly Peer? Leicester and the Puritans," *History Today* 40, no. 1 (Jan. 1990). http://www.historytoday.com/simon-adams/godly-peer-leicester-and-puritans, later pub. as Simon Adams, "A Godly Peer? Leicester and the Puritans," ch, 11, *Leicester and the Court: Essays on Elizabethan Politics* (Manchester: Manchester University Press, 2002), pp. 225-235. See also "Dudley, Robert, Earl of Leicester," by S. S. Lee., *Dictionary of National Biography* 16 (London, 1888), pp. 112-113.

[3] Nieves Matthews, *Francis Bacon, The History of a Character Assassination* (New Haven: Yale University Press, 1996), p. 79; Baker, Intro., pp. 188-189.

[4] Brian Vickers, ed., "Principal Events in Bacon's Life" in *Francis Bacon, 'The History of the Reign of King Henry VII and Selected Works* (Cambridge: Cambridge University Press, 1998), pp. xxvi-xxviii.

[5] "Bacon, Francis (1561-1626) of Gray's Inn and Gorhambury, Herts.," http://www.historyofparliamentonline.org/volume/1558-1603/member/bacon-francis-1561-1626. As to questions about Bacon's birth, see Alfred Dodd, "The Sublime Prince of the Royal Secret," *The Marriage of Elizabeth Tudor* (London: Rider, 1940), pp. 38-42, excerpted at http://www.sirbacon.org/doddsublimeprince.htm.

A copy of Bacon's baptismal certificate lists *custodis* next to Nicholas Bacon's name and calls the baby "Mr." http://www.sirbacon.org/baptismalregistration.htm. Note: In Helen Hackett's opinion, Dodd reads "too much" of an autobiographical nature into Shakespeare's sonnets. Helen Hackett, *Shakespeare and Elizabeth, The Meeting of Two Myths* (Princeton: Princeton University Press, 2009) pp. 162-165.

Peter Beal explains that a birthdate, when given as 1560/1561 ("old style"/"new style"), accounts for the Julian/Gregorian calendar change which affects dates between January 1 and March 24. Peter Beal, *A Dictionary of English Manuscript Terminology: 1450-2000* (New York: Oxford University Press 2008), p. 107. Thus, Bacon's birthdate is January 22, 1561, new style. The Gregorian calendar, proclaimed by the Pope on February 24, 1582, was not adopted in England until 1752. John J. Bond, *Handy-book of Rules and Tables for Verifying Dates within the Christian Era* (London, 1869, reprinted Charlestown, MS: Acme Bookbinding, 2003), preface, p. xxvii; pp. 7, 10.

Francis Bacon, Reformer

The Queen charged Francis with reforming the laws of England, a task his father, Sir Nicholas, had begun[1] and one which Francis pursued for nearly thirty years.[2] Lord Ellesmere, too, had issued a call to the bar to weed out archaic texts and modernize the law.[3] Bacon's interest in reform is obvious from the speeches he wrote for the Christmas festivities at Gray's Inn, preserved in the *Gesta Grayorum*, involving the setting up of a mock government.[4] Bacon sought to prune, shape and organize the law so lawyers could find it, thus aiding legal certainty. To this end, Bacon composed his twenty-five *Maxims of the Law*, dated January 8, 1596/1597,[5] and his *Ordinances in Chancery*.[6] Bacon's maxims are not short, pithy statements, but lengthy expositions of civilian, not common, law. He is setting forth new rules, which he calls aphorisms, though he purports to be providing a mere restatement of existing law.[7] Cheeky devil, was he not? Although he wrote the *Maxims* for the use of lawyers, he dedicated it to Queen Elizabeth.[8]

Improving the practice of law in England necessitated improving the quality of legal education. Law, of course, exists in the broader context of culture. According to Prof. Coquillette, English common law books when Bacon began legal study in 1579 were "genuinely medieval in both structure

---

[1] Paul H. Kocher, "Francis Bacon on the Science of Jurisprudence," *Journal of the History of Ideas* 18, no. 1 (Jan. 1957), pp. 3-24, 4, first pub. in *Essential Articles for the Study of Francis Bacon*, ed. by Brian Vickers (Hamden CT: Archon Books, 1968); David Chan Smith, *Sir Edward Coke and The Reform of the Laws: Religion, Politics, and Jurisprudence, 1578-1616*, Cambridge Studies in English Legal History (Cambridge University Press: Cambridge, 2014), p. 54. Bacon took up his theme of law reform in 1594 at the Gray's Inn Christmas revels, as well as in his *Maxims*. Smith, p. 54. For Bacon's later "Proposition to the King Touching the Compiling and Amendment of the Laws of England," see *Spedding*, XIII, pp. 57-71, HathiTrust, https://hdl.handle.net/2027/ucl.31175012007921.

[2] Baker, *Intro.*, pp. 249-250. For Bacon's reforms under King James, see Coquillette, FB, ch. 2, "The Initial Jacobean Works," pp. 70-126, 70-76. For examples, see *Spedding*, X: pp. 19 (notes for, "speech on repealing superfluous laws") and 389 ("Attempt to improve the constitution of petty juries"), HathiTrust, https://hdl.handle.net/2027/ucl.b3618245.

[3] The quotation is provided by MEA; see pp. 33-34, n. 15, from Lord [John] Campbell, *Lives of the Lord Chancellors*, vol. 2 (Boston, 1874), p. 341, HathiTrust, https://catalog.hathitrust.org/Record/100266555.

[4] See *Spedding*, VIII, pp. 334-343, 343, HathiTrust, https://hdl.handle.net/2027/uc. In Coquillette, FB, see pp. 33-34, 259, 313, 324.

[5] Preface to *Maxims of the Law*, *Spedding*, VII, pp. 310, 311.

[6] For more on Bacon's *Maxims*, see Coquillette, FB, ch. 1, "The Early Legal Works," pp. 35-48. For his *Ordinances in Chancery*, see Spedding, VII, pp. 755-775, HathiTrust, https://hdl.handle.net/2027/ucl.b3924335; FB, ch. 4, "The Theorist as Judge," pp. 201-206. For his *Ordinances for the Reporters*, see FB, pp. 210, 214 n. 54, 329. For his '*Example of a Treatise on Universal Justice or the Fountains of Equity, by Aphorisms*,' viii of the *De Augmentis*, *Spedding*, V., HathiTrust, https://hdl.handle.net/2027/ucl.b3618241), see FB, pp. 236-9, 243-256, 283-4, 289, 295.

[7] FB, p. 36.

[8] Mark Neustadt, "The Making of the Instauration," p. 52.

and substance, with only a few arguable exceptions."[1] The main texts were Littleton's *Tenures* (a book on feudal property law), the yearbooks, and the writ system. Some Roman law was taught in the Universities.[2] Prof. Allen Boyer writes that Coke's first law books were probably the same books his parents had owned.[3] More "radical" books such as those by Christopher St. Germain, Sir Thomas Smith, or Sir John Fortescue[4] were small studies, "isolated...in a professional world dominated by Law French Yearbooks, abridgements, registers of writs, and professional treatises on feudal land law and procedure. They had little to do with the actual world of the practitioner, law student, and judge."[5]

Prof. Coquillette identifies three "points of tension" within the legal profession of Bacon's time, in the order of his priority: "(1) fundamental changes in legal literature and corresponding disputes about legal education; (2) struggles between the common law courts and the Chancery and conciliar courts of civil law and equity; and (3) major controversies about legal doctrines and ideologies, including both the public and the private law."[6]

One of Bacon's practical reforms was the "confession of judgment," an efficiency measure which Lord Coke, finding it "too novel," would not allow.[7] Where did Bacon get the idea? Around 1600, one remedy the English ecclesiastical courts used to enforce their decrees with respect to the behavior of married parties was the penal bond with conditional defeasance, borrowed from the common law. Prof. Helmholz observes that it worked like a confession of judgment. If the party did not do what he or she was supposed to do, he or she would be required to pay money into court by a

---

[1] Coquillette, FB, "intro.," pp. 6-7. For the legal literature influencing Bacon, see FB, pp. 6-14.

[2] Coquillette, FB, p. 9.

[3] Allen D. Boyer, ch. 3, "Learning the Law," *Sir Edward Coke and the Elizabethan Age* (Stanford: Stanford University Press, 2003), pp. 32, 33, n 19. Coke owned copies of *Glanville* and the *Statutes at Large*, a *Book of Entries*, a *Yearbook* of Edward III, St. German's (St. Germain's) *Doctor and Student*, and Plowden's *Commentaries* of 1571, the first case reports printed in Coke's lifetime. Boyer, p. 32. According to Prof. Coquillette, it is largely due to *Doctor and Student* that a doctrine of equity in English common law survived the English Reformation, and with it, Henry VIII's "secularization of the Chancery." FB, p. 8.

[4] John Selden's annotated, anonymously-published translation of Sir John Fortescue's *De Laudibus Legum Angliae (In Praise of the Laws of England*, written ca. 1470) was dated "1616, Inner Temple." Fortescue was Chief Justice during the reign of Henry IV. His book is a dialogue between the Chancellor and the King's son, whom the Chancellor is instructing in the law. Graham Parry in *The Trophies of Time*, pp. 106-108. Fortescue's *De Laudibus* had been translated from the Latin by 1567. Id.

[5] Intro. to Coquillette, FB, p. 8-9.

[6] Coquillette, FB, p. 6.

[7] This was in a 1613 case. See MEA, p. 41, n. 17 (citing Lord [John] Campbell, *Lives of the Lord Chancellors* , vol. 2, p. 385, HathiTrust, https://catalog.hathitrust.org/Record/100266555, and *The English Reports*, vol. 21, p. 295), also p 4. Antonio comments, "Let me have judgment and the Jew his will." *Merchant*, IV, 1, 84.

---

date certain.[1] Shylock's deed after confession was analogous: if he did not comply, his life would be forfeit.

There is evidence that it was during Bacon's Chancellorship that legal title began to pass to a mortgagor.[2] Bacon instigated official court reporting, although it took two more centuries for it to become common.[3] As Chancellor, he efficiently resolved a massive backlog of cases.[4] When Bacon was Chancellor, in 1617, he hired a court reporter to sit at his feet and record the court proceedings.[5] Oh, the novelty! Bacon did not think judges should write the reports for their own decisions, as Coke did when he was a judge.[6] Regrettably, only a few of Bacon's reported decisions have survived. His description of what a law report should entail is still considered valuable today.[7]

Francis Bacon, "Closet" Civilian

Prof. Coquillette has shown that Bacon's interest in civil law has been underestimated. "His use of Roman models throughout Book 8 of the *De Augmentis*," in his *Treatise on Universal Justice*, where he sets out his jurisprudence on equity, is "striking and substantive."[8] It would have been political suicide, says Coquillette, for Bacon to have publicly identified with the university-trained "civilian" lawyers who dined together at Doctors' Commons.[9] One

---

[1] Richard H. Helmholz, "Canonical Remedies in Medieval Marriage Law: The Contributions of Legal Practice Founding," *University of St. Thomas Law Journal* 1 (2003), pp. 647- 655, 650, University of Chicago Law School, Chicago Unbound, http://chicagounbound.uchicago.edu/cgi/viewcontent.cgi?article=2479&context=journal_articles.

[2] Baker, *intro.*, pp. 355-356, 356, fn. 88, 359R, *Emmanuel College, Cambridge v. Evans* (1625), 1 Ch. Rep. 18. The doctrine of equity of redemption grew out of the "same root" as the "doctrine of penalties" on a conditioned bond. Baker, p. 355, 370. It evolved in the reign of Queen Elizabeth. MEA, p. 67 n. 70, see also pp. 53 n. 38, 68 n. 71. Portia asked, "Is he not able to discharge the money?"

[3] *Spedding*, XIII, p. 262, 264, HathiTrust, https://hdl.handle.net/2027/ucl.31175012007921; Coquillette, FB, pp. 191-2, 210, 253.

[4] *Spedding*, XIII, p. 208.

[5] Baker, *Intro.*, p. 127, n. 61. For Bacon's proposed reforms, see Barbara Shapiro, "Francis Bacon and the Mid-Seventeenth Century Movement for Law Reform," *The American Journal of Legal History* 24, no. 4 (Oct., 1980), pp. 331-362, p. 353.

[6] For Coke's downfall, see *Spedding*, XIII, pp. 76-199, HathiTrust, https://hdl.handle.net/2027/hv.

[7] Coquillette, FB, p. 253.

[8] Coquillette, FB, ch. 5, "The Final Vision," p. 270, n. 149; see also notes to ch. 5, pp. 269-271, nns. 122, 139, 167.

[9] On Doctors' Commons, see Coquillette, Daniel R., *The Civilian Writers of Doctors' Commons, London: Three Centuries of Juristic Innovation in Comparative, Commercial, and International Law*, (Berlin: Duncker & Humblot, 1988), I.II.A, pp. 19-28, 20; 45, 94, 147, 198, 268; G. D. Squibb, *Doctors' Commons: a History of the College of Advocates and Doctors of Law* (Oxford: Clarendon Press, 1977); reviewed in Peter Stein, "'Doctor's Commons[...]' by G. D. Squibb," Review, *Cambridge Law Journal* 37, no. 2 (Nov., 1978, online Jan. 1, 2009), pp. 355-356; JSTOR, https://www.jstor.org/stable/i406653, and Brian P. Levack, "A Review of G. D. Squibb, 'Doctors Commons,'" *Am. J. Leg. History* 23, no. 3 (1979), pp. 274-276, JSTOR, www.jstor.org/stable/i235116.

might imagine him, rather, studying quietly and conversing privately with like-minded friends such as his nephew by marriage, Sir Julius Caesar, the son of an Italian physician, in whose arms Bacon reportedly died.[1] Caesar suffered professionally for "want of law," presumably of the common kind.[2] Bacon, however, sought to "enrich the existing English national law with civilian methodology and principles, most particularly the techniques of comparative legal study and the doctrines of the *ius gentium*."[3] The reforms he proposed to King James — the drafting of Institutes, Code, and Digest, as well as a law dictionary for England, all based on Justinian's *Corpus iuris civilis* — were civilian.[4] As Bacon told his students, he wrote out his "Arguments of Law" in order to provide models of speeches for the law students, similar to what had been done in ancient Rome and was being done at the time on the Continent.[5]

It seems plausible that Bacon may have been influenced in his views on civil law by Alberico Gentili (1552–1608), a refugee civilian jurist[6] who was

---

[1] Catherine Drinker Bowen, *The Temper of a Man* (New York: Fordham University Press, 1993), p. 226. https://books.google.com/books?isbn=0823215377; Basil Montagu, "A Letter to the Right Honorable Thomas Babington Macaulay," *The Monthly Review* 3, ed. by Ralph and George Griffiths (London, 1842), pp. 206-228, 221. *https://books.google.com/books?id=r0xQAQAAMAAJ.*

[2] "Caesar, Sir Julius," The History of Parliament, at n 152, http://www.historyofparliamentonline.org/volume/1604-1629/member/caesar-sir-julius-1558-1636.

[3] Coquillette, "Legal Ideology and Incorporation I[...]," p. 10; see also pp. 22-27, 42-45, 57-72, 83-84, Digital Commons at Boston Law School, http://lawdigitalcommons.bc.edu/cgi/viewcontent.cgi?article=1645&context=lsfp. The *ius gentium* or "law of nations" is a fascinating concept which originated in ancient Rome. It was the law applicable to non-Roman-citizens. *Black's Law Dictionary* gives this definition: "that law which natural reason has established among all men, is equally observed among all nations, and is called the "law of nations," as being the law which all nations use." It encompasses, but is broader than, international law (*Blacks LD*, p. 772).

[4] See, e.g., Francis Bacon, "An Offer to King James of a Digest," *Spedding*, XIV, p. 358, HathiTrust, https://hdl.handle.net/2027/ucl.31175012007947; "A Memorial Touching the Review of Penal Laws," *Spedding*, XII, pp. 84-86, HathiTrust, https://hdl.handle.net/2027/ucl.b3618248, and Proposition to the King Touching the Compiling and Amendment of the Lawes of England," *Spedding*, XIII, pp. 61-71, HathiTrust, https://hdl.handle.net/2027/ucl.b3618243 ; see Daniel R. Coquillette, ch. 1, "Introduction," *The Civilian Writers of Doctors' Commons[...]*, pp. 20-21, n. 16.

However, as Bacon wrote to Bishop Launcelot Andrewes ca. 1622, without the King's financial support, he lacked funds to pay writing assistants and so was unable to bring the project to fruition. *Great matters ...have (many times) small beginnings. Spedding*, XIV, p. 374, HathiTrust, https://hdl.handle.net/2027/ucl.31175012007947; See Coquillette, "Legal Ideology and Incorporation I ...." pp. 1-89, 9-10, nn. 16, 18; p. 17, n. 48, available at http://works.bepress.com/daniel_coquillette/; Coquillette, "Legal Ideology and Incorporation IV: The Nature of Civilian Influence on Modern Anglo-American Commercial Law," *Boston University Law Rev.* 67 (1987), pp. 877-970, 922-924, Digital Commons at Boston College Law School, http://lawdigitalcommons.bc.edu/lsfp/644/.

[5] Francis Bacon, *The Arguments in Law of Sir Francis Bacon, Spedding*, VII, p. 523, HathiTrust, https://hdl.handle.net/2027/hvd.32044069750248.

[6] On Gentili, see Coquillette, "Legal Ideology ...I," pp. 54-63; Douglas M. Johnston, *The Historical Foundations of World Order: the Tower and the Arena*, (The Hague: Martinus Nijhoff, 2008), pp. 385-387, https://books.google.ca/books?isbn=9004161678.

Regius Professor of Civil Law at Oxford University for twenty-one years. Gentili joined Gray's Inn in 1600. Gentili never joined Doctor's Commons, the community of university-trained civilian lawyers. Gentili argued that the English common law was not as well suited to resolving disputes involving foreigners as was the *ius gentium*.[1] Some have criticized Shakespeare for not setting his merchant case in a specialty court such as admiralty. The civil jurisdiction of Admiralty, liberal under Henry VIII (extending to contracts made abroad between two Englishmen),[2] became increasingly curtailed under Queen Elizabeth, with Coke bringing writs of prohibition to enforce a 1574 jurisdictional agreement which Admiralty had been largely ignoring for years. The agreement was completely repudiated when Coke came to the bench in 1606, despite the fact that, as Gentili argued, Admiralty was the best court for hearing trade disputes involving foreigners.[3] Even Coke, in 1611, told the common law judges that, when hearing merchant cases, it was all right for them to consult a civilian doctor of laws.[4] That is, of course, precisely what the Duke does in *The Merchant of Venice*, much earlier than 1611.

As I understand it, the opinion of a civilian even held sway in the afterlife....

Francis Bacon tells how Nicholas Bacon died and reached the pearly gates of heaven, but the gatekeeper (Bacon does not call him St. Peter; this is the Reformation, after all!) would not let him in. "Remember that bad court ruling you made," the gatekeeper reminded him. Nicholas could only vaguely recall the case, but he thought it had been a Star Chamber case. "I know," said Nicholas. "Let's ask Cordal, the Master of the Rolls." Cordal had recently died, and he was soon located.

Cordal checked and found out that Nicholas' ruling in that case was, in fact, sound, because he had based his decision on the certificate of one "Dr. Gibson," a doctor of civilian law. That was enough for the gatekeeper, and Nicholas was ushered into paradise.[5]

---

[1] Johnston, *Historical Foundations*, p. 387.

[2] William Searle Holdsworth, ch. 7, "Courts of Special Jurisdiction," *A History of English Law*, 3rd ed. rewritten, vol. 1 (Boston: Little Brown, 1922), p. 552-555, https://archive.org/details/ahistoryenglish01holdgoog.

[3] That the medieval law merchant has long been misunderstood is argued in Emily Kadens, "The Medieval Law Merchant: The Tyranny of a Construct" (June 26, 2015), *Journal of Legal Analysis* 7 (2015), pp. 251-89, online at Northwestern Law & Econ Research Paper No. 16-06, SSRN: http://ssrn.com/abstract=2773689.

Holdsworth, ch. 7, "Courts of Special Jurisdiction," pp. 554-555.

[4] Holdsworth, ch. 7, p. 554, fn. 5, citing *2 Brownlow 17* (1611).

[5] Francis Bacon, *Apothegms*, in *Spedding*, VII, p. 171; Thomas and Henry Roscoe, *Westminster Hall: Or Professional Relics and Anecdotes of the Bar, Bench and Woolsack*, vol. I (London, 1825), p. 218.

Sir Thomas Gresham, Royal Merchant

In his book *Law and Literature*, Judge Posner of the Seventh Circuit has observed that *Merchant*, the "most celebrated" of Shakespeare's legal plays, is the one "most concerned with commerce."[1] It may be that, in writing *Merchant*, the dramatist intentionally meant to pay homage Sir Thomas Gresham (1519–1579) who had been financier and fiscal officer to three royal sovereigns, Edward, Mary, and Elizabeth. His will called for the founding of Gresham College, the first college in London, after the death of his widow. Thus, the college was founded in 1597, about the time the play was written.[2] The College gave free public lectures (45 minutes in Latin with a 15-minute summation in English) in seven subjects: theology, jurisprudence (notably, civil law, which Gresham had studied at Cambridge), medicine, astronomy, geometry, rhetoric, and music.[3] Today, the College still gives free public lectures.[4]

Sir Thomas Gresham was Francis Bacon's uncle by marriage, since Gresham's wife was Nicholas Bacon's first wife's sister, prior to Nicholas's marriage to Anne Cook, Bacon's mother.[5] In addition, Francis's older half-brother Nathaniel Bacon had married Thomas Gresham's illegitimate daughter.[6] Gresham College in 1660 became the first home of the Royal Society, established for the improvement of natural knowledge. The Royal Society's motto is *Nullius in verba*, or, "Take nobody's word for it."[7]

There is an old story associated with the Gresham name which involved one called "Antonio the rich." Antony is, of course, the name of Francis

---

[1] Richard A. Posner, ch. 3, "Antinomies of Legal Theory," in *Law and Literature*, 3d ed. (Cambridge: Harvard University Press, 2009). pp. 124-169, 139.

[2] Gresham College, https://www.gresham.ac.uk/about/history/.

[3] John Ward, *The Lives of the Professors of Gresham College, to which is prefixed The Life of Sir Thomas Gresham* (London, 1740), pp. vi, x, 36, 70, appendix 12.

[4] See, e.g., Gresham College, https://www.gresham.ac.uk/attend/.

[5] Christopher Hill, ch. 3, "Francis Bacon and the Parliamentarians," *Intellectual Origins of the English Revolution Revisited* (New York: Oxford University Press, 2002), p. 77. https://books.google.es/books?isbn-0191588679.

[6] "Nathaniel Bacon" (1604-1629), http://www.historyofparliamentonline.org/volume/ 1604-1629/member/bacon-nathaniel-1546-1622. He is not to be confused with Bacon's nephew Nathaniel Bacon (1593-1660), son of his half-brother Edward Bacon, who co-authored a book with John Selden, *An Historical and Political Discourse of the Laws and Government of England* (London, 1689), HathiTrust, https://hdl.handle.net/2027/mdp.35112204858940; http://www.historyofparliamentonline.org/volume/1660-1690/member/bacon-nathaniel-1593-1660, or Nathaniel Bacon (1647-1676) who led Bacon's Rebellion in 1676. See "Jamestown. Bacon's Rebellion, Historic Jamestowne," National Park Service, last updated Feb. 26, 2015, https://www.nps.gov/jame/learn/historyculture/bacons-rebellion.htm. There was also Nathaniel Bacon the Jesuit, who assumed the name "Southwell" (1598-1576). "Nathaniel Bacon," *Catholic Encyclopedia*, vol. 2 (1913), New Advent.org, http://www.newadvent.org/cathen/02191c.htm. They are all related to Francis Bacon. See also https://en.wikipedia.org/wiki/Nathaniel_Bacon.

[7] The Royal Society, History, https://royalsociety.org/about-us/history/.

Bacon's older brother who generously loaned him money on numerous occasions.[1]

> George Sandys (*Travels*, B.IV.194) relates how in 1558 or so the merchant Thomas Gresham (1519–1759) set sail from Palermo: "where there then dwelt one Antonio called the rich, who at one time had two kingdoms mortgaged unto him by the king of Spain, who, being crossed by contrary winds, was constrained to anchor under the lee of this island. Now about midday when for certain hours it accustomedly forbeareth to flame, he ascended to the mountain with eight of the sailors; and approaching as near the vent as they durst, amongst other noises they heard a voice cry aloud, 'Dispatch, dispatch, the rich Antonio is a coming.' Terrified, herewith they descended, and anon the mountain again evaporated fire." The Catholics called these islands the "very jaws of hell."

> "But from so dismal a place they made all the haste that they could." When they got back to Palermo, they asked about 'rich Antonio.' As it turned out, he had just died, just at the time they heard the voice cry out. Gresham and his eight sailors swore to these facts before the king. The event so affected him that he gave away all his wealth and retired from secular doings.[2]

> The Jesuit and alchemist Athanasius Kircher (1602–1680) tells this story in his preface to his book, *Mundus Subterraneus*.[3] Kircher may have been a secret disciple of Giordano Bruno.[4]

---

[1] Thomas Birch, *Memoirs of the Reign of Queen Elizabeth: From the Year 1581 Till Her Death, in which the Secret Intrigues of her Court, and the Conduct of her Favorite, Robert Earl of Essex, both Home and Abroad, are Particularly Illustrated, from the Original Papers of his Intimate Friend, Anthony Bacon, Esq., and other Manuscripts never before published*, vol. 2 (London, 1754), pp. 355-357. https://books.google.com/books?id=rL4_AAAAcAAJ; Edwin Bormann, transl. by Harry Brett, *The Shakespeare-secret*, 2 (London, 1895), pp. 355-357. https://books.google.com/books?id=eceEAAAAIAAJ (and HathiTrust); Hon. Ignatius Donnelly, "Francis Bacon," in *Great Men and Famous Women, a Series of Pen and Pencil Sketches of the lives of more than 200 of the most prominent persons in history*, 3, ed. by Charles Francis Horne (New York, 1894), pp. 154-172, 157; *Spedding*, VIII, ch. 7, pp. 243, 322, HathiTrust, https://hdl.handle.net/2027/ucl.b3618243; *Spedding*, III, pp. 11-14 (discussing the credibility of Wotton's recount in *Birch*), HathiTrust, https://hdl.handle.net/2027/ucl.b3618240; Peter Dawkins, "Baconian History," Francis Bacon Research Trust (under "Courtship — Merchant of Venice — Essex's Insurgency"). https://www.fbrt.org.uk/pages/bacon_history.html.
[2] John Ward, "The Life of Sir Thomas Gresham," *The Lives of the Professors of Gresham College, to which is prefixed The Life of the Founder, Sir Thomas Gresham* (London, 1740), pp. 1-2.
[3] (London, 1665), reprinted at Sedimentary Basin Analysis and Modeling Lab (SBAML), Wichita State University (See last four paragraphs), last updated Feb. 8, 2010, http://webs.wichita.edu/?u=wparcell&p=/kircher/volcanoes/chapter6; for more information, see W. C. Parcell, "Signs and symbols in Kircher's Mundus Subterraneus," *The Revolution in Geology from the Renaissance to the Enlightenment*, Geological Society of America Memoir 203, ed. by Gary D. Rosenberg, p 51-62 (Boulder CO: The Geological Society of America, 2009), pp. 51-62, http://georegister.org/publications/2011_Kircherfull.pdf, doi: 10.1130/2009.1203(04).
[4] Daniel Stolzenberg, *Egyptian Oedipus: Athanasius Kircher and the Secrets of Antiquity* (Chicago: University of Chicago Press, 2013), p. 131, n. 4, citing four works by Ingrid Rowland.

Thomas Gresham, in his efforts to get King Edward VI (Queen Elizabeth's brother) out of debt had proposed that he buy up all the lead he could, make a staple of it, and then proclaim that none should convey it for five years, in order to drive up the price.[1] Lead would be used in printing type, too, and Gresham's new stock exchange would rely on printing for the rapid dissemination of information. Gresham also established a paper mill.[2] "Lead" also hints at "being led," as in "leading the witness"[3] or Portia's "leading" Bassanio to choose the right casket, the leaden one.[4]

Sir Thomas Gresham used his own money to build the Royal Exchange, a stock exchange based on the Antwerp Exchange. It was a place for London merchants to trade and do business indoors. After Antwerp fell to the Spanish in 1576, many Dutch persons fled to England.

Architecturally, Gresham modelled his Bourse on the Flemish and Venetian exchanges.[5] He imported workers and materials were imported from Flanders. Gresham reportedly used wood from his own estate Rinxhall (Ringshall) to build the Bourse.[6] The bell of the large bell tower which stood at the main entrance rang every day at noon and six p.m.[7] When Elizabeth first visited the Bourse in 1570, bells rang in every part of the city.[8] She promptly named the Bourse the "Royal Exchange."[9] References to the "royal merchant" in *Merchant*[10] would have been readily understood by Elizabethans to refer to Sir Thomas Gresham.[11]

---

[1] Ward, "The Life of Sir Thomas Gresham," pp. 6-8.

[2] [M. Hackett, according to Google], "A brief memoir of Sir Thomas Gresham[...]" (London, 1833), p. 8. https://books.google.com/books?id=Zkx4ffEXHgcC.

[3] An article using Bacon's "Idols of the Cave" theory to help explain witness bias is Deborah Davis and William C. Follette, "Foibles of Witness Memory for Traumatic/High Profile Events," *Journal of Air Law and Commerce* 66, no. 4 (2001), pp. 1421-1549, 1481-1482, Law Journals at SMU Scholar, https://scholar.smu.edu/jalc/vol66/iss4/6.

[4] For an image of a Venetian casket, see "Golden Casket from Venice," British Library, Collection Items https://www.bl.uk/collection-items/golden-casket-from-venice.

[5] Walter Thornbury, *Old and New London* 1 (London, 1878), *British History Online* http://www.british-history.ac.uk/old-new-london/vol1.

[6] Saunders, "The Old Royal Exchange," p. 291.

[7] Saunders, "The Old Royal Exchange," p. 291.

[8] Saunders, "The Old Royal Exchange," p. 291.

[9] Walter Thornbury, *Old and New London*, vol. 1 (London, 1878), *British History Online*, http://www.british-history.ac.uk/old-new-london/vol1.

[10] *Merchant*, III, 2, 1614; IV, 1, 1961. http://opensourceshakespeare.org/search/search-results.php.

[11] William J. Rolfe, *Shakespeare's Comedy of 'The Merchant of Venice'* (New York, 1885), notes, p. 156, n. 29; *The Merchant of Venice*, rev., ed. by Ebenezer Charlton Black (Boston: Ginn, 1906), p. 102, fn. 29; *Shakespeare Select Plays, Merchant of Venice*, ed. by W. G. Clark and W. A. Wright (Oxford: Clarendon Press, 1902), p. 110, fn. 235.

CHAPTER THREE: TRIFLES AND DEVILS: LITERARY PRECEDENTS

Roots of Play in Law and Culture

It is interesting that the origins of the word "play" includes the concept of a champion who fights for another, a notion still incorporated in our conception of an attorney. In former times, trial was by battle. The German *plega, plegan* meant "to vouch or stand guarantee for, to take a risk, expose oneself to danger, or to bind or engage oneself to attend." Both playing (games or roles) and pledging involve risk and ceremony. According to Johann Huizinga, "play" was elemental in the formation of our various cultural institutions, including religion, ethics, and law.[1] In Chaucer's time, "pley" could refer to "funeral games."[2] Children today still favor forms of play which involve heightened risk or uncertainty.[3]

There is a traditional children's hide-and-seek/tag game called "Ring-lairio/Ring-o-lairio/Ring-o-leavio" (spelled variously).[4] In this game, players on one team hide, and the other team tries to capture them and keep their

---

[1] Huizinga, p. 39.

[2] Skeat, "Pley," glossarial index, *The Student's Chaucer*, p. 83.

[3] Chris Richards and Andrew Burn, eds., *Children's Games in the New Media Age, Childlore, Media, and the Playground* (London: Routledge, 2016), p. 103; 101, https://books.google.ca/books?isbn=1317167562.

[4] See Amy Packham, "13 Traditional Games Parents Played in Their Childhood" ("Forty-Forty-In"), last updated August 1, 2016, http://www.huffingtonpost.co.uk/2016/08/01/fun-traditional-games-parents-played-when-children_n_7553124.html; "The Games of Spain," *A Playful World*, Streetplay.com, copyright 2018 (chart showing English names for Spanish games: ringoleavio and manhunt), http://www.streetplay.com/playfulworld/spain.shtml; http://www.streetplay.com/rulesheets/pdf/ringoleaviosheet.pdf.)

teammates from setting them free."[1] A same or similar game, "Relievo,"[2] came to the United States from the British Isles. The game of "Bedlams," a type of "Prisoner's Base," is similar.[3]

Shakespeare referred to the game "Country Base" in *Cymbeline* (V, 3).[4] Two more Shakespearean references to the "Hide and Seek" type of game are Biron's line, "All hid, all hid, an old infant play," in *Love's Labour Lost* (IV, 2, 1402) and Hamlet's line, "Hide fox, and all after," (IV, 2, 2705).[5] Another

---

[1] "Ring-a-levio," https://www.merriam-webster.com/dictionary/ring-a-levio.

[2] "Street Games," 'So-Th,' *Encyclopedia of Children and Childhood in History and Society.* copyright 2008 Advameg, http://www.faqs.org/childhood/So-Th/Street-Games.html.

[3] See Stuart Cullin, "Street Games of Boys in Brooklyn, N.Y.," *Journal of American Folklore* 4 (Sept.-Oct., 1891): 221-237; "Street Games," Encyclopedia.com (under "Variations in Games), from *Encyclopedia of Children and Childhood in History and Society*, ed. by Paula S. Fass (New York: Macmillan Reference, 2004, Gale Virtual Reference Library), Encyclopedia.com, copyright 2016, http://www.encyclopedia.com/children/encyclopedias-almanacs-transcripts-and-maps/street-games; "Street Games," *Traditional Games of England, Scotland, and Wales*, vol. 2, ed. and collated by Alice Berthe Gomme (London, 1894), pp. 40, 79, 107, 213, 465-466; "Bedlams or Relievo," *The Traditional Children's Games of England, Scotland and Ireland in Dictionary Form*, vol. I, p. 25. www.traditionalmusic.co.uk/traditional-games-1/traditional-games-1-0125.htm.

For rules, see Carmel Corr, *Play Better Games: Enabling Children with Autism to Join in with Everyday Games* (London: Routledge, 2017), p. 125.

Playing ringolevio is fondly remembered by Doug Adams, "Ringoleavio," *Hitchhiker's Guide to the Galaxy*, http://hitchhikersgui.de/Ringoleavio; David Banks, *Soar: How Boys Learn, Succeed, and Develop Character* (New York: 37 Ink/Atria, 2014), p. 28; Richard Quarantello, *Surviving the Warzone: Growing Up: East New York: Brooklyn* (n.p.: Xlibris Corporation, 2013), p. 10; and Emmett Grogan, *Ringolevio: A Life Played for Keeps* (New York: Rebel Incorporated, 1999).

[4] Gromme, *Traditional Games*, vol. 2, pp. 79-82, 79.

[5] https://www.opensourceshakespeare.org/, https://www.reddit.com/r/AskHistorians/comments/3nhltp/how_old_is_the_childrens_game_hide_and_seek/ (comment by "Yottle in the Bottle"). While we are on the subject of *Hamlet*, in an excellent article, T. Baluk-Ulewiczowa explores possible connections between the renaming of "Corambis" to "Polonius" in *Hamlet*, a diplomatic incident involving a Polish diplomat insulted by Queen Elizabeth, and the subsequent English (redacted) publication of Polish nobleman, bishop, and doctor of law Wawrzyniec (Laurence) Goslicki's book, *De optimo senator*, HathiTrust, https://catalog.hathitrust.org/Record/001139977. See T. Baluk-Ulewiczowa, *Goslicius' Ideal Senator and His Cultural Impact over the Centuries: Shakespearean Reflections*, ed. by Lucyna Nowak (Krakow: Polska Akademia Umiejetnosci and Jagiellonian University, 2009), ch. 8, pp. 140-149, 152-156 and ch. 10.2, pp. 183-187). If Baluk-Ulewiczowa's theory is correct, did "Shakespeare" change the name to preserve the memory of the book and its writer?

The name Polonius sounds a little like Polynices, Antigone's brother in Sophocles' *Antigone*, the "traitor" whom she buried — despite King Creon's orders — following a "higher law."

For "a" Robert Chester, Cambridge student, as the probable first English translator of *De optimo senator*, see T. Baluk-Ulewiczowa, ch. 7, pp. 132-138, 132-133. For Robert Chester as the putative author of "Rosalind's Complaint" and the "Love's Martyr" poetry collection which includes "The Phoenix and the Turtle," see Ilya Gililov, *The Shakespeare Game: The Mystery of the Great Phoenix* (New York: Algora, 2003), pp. 11-14.

---

related variation is "King by Your Leave" or "Old Shewe."[1] Thomas Dekker alluded to a game called "All-Hid" in his *Satiromatrix*.[2]

There was apparently a time when childhood extended into the teens and beyond, insofar as people of all ages played outdoor games. "In 1600, a sharp distinction between the world of the adult and the world of the child did not exist."[3] It is hard not to be nostalgic for such times.

Devils

It had surprised me to learn first from reading Prof. Keeton of an unlikely source for *The Merchant of Venice*. During the Middle Ages, certain books such as the *Processus Sathanae* and *Processus Belial*[4] taught trial procedure in the guise of a mock trial in which Satan sued in God's court for the souls of humankind. These books were popular, entertaining and irreverent. They went through many printings.[5] One of these books was the *Processus Sathanae*, (sometimes spelled *Sathane*; in Italian, e.g., *Processo di Satana*),[6] the authorship of which is ascribed to Bartolus of Saxoferratus (1313/14–1357). An even earlier book of this type was written by Cardinal Lotario (Lothar) de Conti di Segni (1160–1216) who became Pope Innocent III. His book was called *Litigacio Sathanae Contra Genus Humanum*. It is the last tract in a volume of his

---

[1] Elizabeth Tucker, "Hide and Seek," *Encyclopedia of Play in Today's Society*, vol. 1, ed. by Rodney P. Carlisle (Los Angeles.: Sage, 2009), pp. 286-287 and, briefly, p. 756. See also "Europe, 1200 to 1600," pp. 197-200, and Christine Walker, "Europe, 1600 to 1800," pp. 200-203, *Encyclopedia of Play[...]*, vol. 1.

[2] *Encyclopedia of Play*, vol. 1, p. 1.

[3] Walker, p. 203, *Encyclopedia of Play*, vol. 1, https://books.google.com/books?isbn=1452266107.

[4] The *Processus* is separate but related to the mystery plays. Both of them dramatize the Last Judgment "in which Justice and Mercy debate for the possession of mankind's soul," with the Virgin Mary as advocate for mercy before God. *Processus* refers to legal procedure, as in "due process of law."

[5] Keeton, ch. 9, "Shylock v. Antonio," *Shakespeare's Legal and Political Background* (London: Pittman, 1967), pp. 132-150, 140-142 (referring to both Nevill Coghill, author of *The Basis of Shakespeare's Comedy: A Study in Medieval Affinities* (London: Wyman and Sons, 1950) and John D. Rea's Note, "Shylock and the Processus Belial," *Philological Quarterly* 8 (Jan. 1, 1929), pp. 311-313, http://search.proquest.com/openview/ab2a34efac8128f15105dd5f789515af/1?pq-origsite=gscholar; Hope Traver, "The Four Daughters of God, A Mirror of Changing Doctrine," *Publication of the Modern Language Association [PMLA]* 40, no. 1 (March, 1925), pp. 44-92, JSTOR, http://www.jstor.org/stable/457268; Doug Coulson, "The Devil's Advocate and Legal Oratory in the Processus Sathanae," pp. 409-30, 413, http://ssrn.com/abstract=2745281.

[6] Pages from a 1505 Cologne *Processus Sathane* and Gratian's *Decretum* may be viewed at: Winroth, Anders and Widener, Michael, "The Pope's Other Jobs: Judge and Law-giver" (2015), *Italian Statutes*, book 6, pp. 12, 18. 23 fig. exhibit, http://digitalcommons.law.yale.edu/itsta/6; see also *Processus Satanae contra genus humanum* (Memmingen: Albert Kunne, 1500), Europeana Collections, https://www.europeana.eu/portal/en/record/09428/show_inc_ii_163.html; images at *Modello Processo di Satana*, The MOSAICO Project, last updated June, 2012, http://mosaico.cirsfid.unibo.it/templates/index.php?table=SATANA&action=show mokup.

works.[1] It, however, contained no law, so that would have been Bartolus's addition, if the great Roman law jurist and founder of the law school at Perugia did write the *Processus Sathanae*.[2]

The literary themes in the *Processus* plays go back a thousand years to Hebrew, Egyptian, and Babylonian sources.[3] Related literature includes the Apocalypses and mystery plays.[4] The *Processus Sathanae*, which taught lawyers rhetoric and trial procedure,[5] contained more law than the *Processus Belial*, a later book which contained more theology, but "still much law."[6]

One of Bartolus's teachers, for a brief but — he says — influential time, was poet and jurist Cino Da Pistoia (also Guittoncino, Cino dei Sighibuldi, Cinus, less often Cina)[7] who wrote the *Lectura super codice*, a commentary on Justinian's *Corpus iuris civilis*.[8] Cina had studied with, and served as a secretary to, canonist Johannes Andreae (c. 1275–1348).[9] Cina taught Dante Alighieri,

---

[1] David Murray, *Lawyer's Merriments*, p. 153 n.2. For a recent biography of Pope Innocent III, see John C. Moore, *Pope Innocent III, To Root Up and to Plant* (Notre Dame IN: Notre Dame University, 2009).

[2] For Bartolus's legal accomplishments, see Manlio Bellomo, *The Common Legal Past of Europe 1000-1800*, 2d ed., trans. from the Italian by Lydia G. Cochrane (Washington D.C.: Catholic University of America Press, 1995), pp. 191-193.

[3] Traver, Hope. "The Four Daughters of God, a Study of the Versions of this Allegory, with Special Reference to those in Latin, French, and English." *Monograph Series* 6. (Bryn Mawr: n.p., 1907), pp. 1-195, 164. https://ia902704.us.archive.org/13/items/fourdaughtersgo02travgoog/fourdaughtersgo02travgoog.pdf; HathiTrust, https://hdl.handle.net/2027/hvd.32044021642061.

[4] Traver, "Four Daughters of God, A Mirror[...]," pp. 48-76; Coulson, "The Devil's Advocate[...]," pp. 420, 425.

[5] As late as 1877, Charles Barton, in *History of a Suit in Equity, from its Commencement to its Final Termination*, includes Bacon's *Ordinances in Chancery* to "increase the practical value of this volume" (p. 5). Barton, *History of a Suit in Equity*, ed. by James P. Holcombe (Cincinnati, 1877), HathiTrust, https://hdl.handle.net/2027/cool.ark:/13960/t4qj800lf. For the *Ordinances*, see *Spedding*, V, pp. 755-775.

Bartolus was a practical lawyer and teacher who concerned himself with solving practical problems like traffic signals and preventing the plagiarism of watermarks. "Paper," *Encyclopedia of Library and Information Science*, vol. 3, 2d ed., ed. by Miriam Drake (New York: Marcel Dekker, 2003), pp. 1591-2378, 2289. https://books.google.ca/books?isbn=0824720792. As to modern concerns about the plagiarism of watermarks, *see*, e.g., Chris Reed, "Remove Watermarks Online? Be Prepared to Answer to the DMCA," *Art Law Journal*, September 27, 2017, https://alj.orangenius.com/watermarks/.

[6] Coulson, "The Devil's Advocate[...]," p. 411.

[7] Augosto P. Miceli, "Forum Juridicum: Bartolus of Sassoferrato," *Law La. Rev.* 37, no. 5 (1976-1977), pp. 1027-1036, p. 1027, n. 1, LWU Law Digital Commons, http://digitalcommons.law.lsu.edu/lalrev/vol37/iss5/3.

[8] "Cino Da Pistoia, Italian author," https://www.britannica.com/biography/Cino-da-Pistoia#ref260093. For Cino's contribution to jurisprudence, see Manlio Bellomo, *The Common Legal Past of Europe 1000-1800*, pp. 186-190; 147, 184, 211.

[9] "Johannes Andreae Contents," The Ames Foundation, copyright 2014, http://amesfoundation.law.harvard.edu/digital/JohannesAndreae/JohannesAndreaeMetadata.html.

On Cino, see, "The Sixth Age of the World," folio CCXXVII, recto, the *First English edition of the Nuremberg Chronicle, being the Liber chronicarum of Dr. Hartmann Schedel (1440-1514)* (Madison:

---

the author of the *Divine Comedy*,[1] as well as Boccaccio[2] and Petrarch (Francesco Petrarca, 1304–1374).[3] He probably taught them a mixture of law and poetry. Cino had been a student of Franciscus d'Accorso (1225–1293), son of Accursius, the jurist who compiled the "Great Gloss." After Accursius, jurists who wrote about the *Corpus iuris civilis* of Justinian were no longer called Glossators, but Commentators. Franciscus d'Accorso had a reputation for avarice, for lending money to students at interest and taking bribes from them.[4]

David Murray relates the narratives of the *Processus Sathanae* and *Processus Belial* in his book, *Lawyer's Merriments*.[5] Parallels to *The Merchant of Venice* will be fairly obvious. In the *Sathanae*, the Devil, who lacks standing, cannot appear in court. He is represented by "the procurator of the wickedness of hell," the devil's advocate who states his case before the judge, Jesus Christ. Since the fall of Adam in the Garden of Eden, man is a sinner, and God demands righteousness. The Lord Jesus asks if there is anyone willing to act as advocate to defend the hapless human race. At first, there is no one, and the human race is in contempt of court. At last, the Virgin Mary appears as *Advocata*, a female advocate.

In *Merchant*, Portia's route to court is more convoluted.[6] Her role, too, is complicated — conflicted, we would say. For that matter, the Virgin's role is also complicated, for, as the devil's advocate complains, his opponent is the mother of the judge!

The devil says he stands for justice; Shylock, too, says he stands for justice. The Virgin Mary pleads for mercy; Portia, too, pleads for mercy. The scales of justice are presented, for, once the devil realizes he is losing, he proposes a

---

University of Wisconsin Digital Collections Center, 2010), http://digital.library.wisc.edu/1711. dl/nur.001.0004.

[1] On legal structure in Dante's *Commedia*, see Justin Steinberg, *Dante and the Limits of the Law* (Chicago: University of Chicago Press, 2013). This is on my personal list for further reading.

[2] Janet Levarie Smarr, "Giovanni Boccaccio (1313-1375)," *Key Figures in Medieval Europe, an Encyclopedia*, ed. by Richard K. Emmerson (New York: Routledge, 2006), pp. 79-84.

[3] Christopher Kleinhenz, "Petrarcha, Francesco," *Key Figures in Medieval Europe, an Encyclopedia*, pp. 517-524; "Francesco Petrarca," Yale University exhibition, 2004, http://brbl-archive. library.yale.edu/exhibitions/petrarch/about.html; "poet Petrarch," poets.org, https://www. poets.org/poetsorg/poet/petrarch.

[4] Christopher Kleinhenz, "Cino da Pistoia (c. 1270-c. 1336-37)," *Key Figures in Medieval Europe, an Encyclopedia*, pp. 141-142.

[5] David Murray, '*Processus Satanae*' in *Lawyer's Merriments*, (Glasgow: James Maclehose, 1912), pp. 134-152, 134 n. 1; '*Processus Luciferi*,' pp. 154-157, HathiTrust, https://hdl.handle.net/2027/ hvd.32044010322881.

[6] In early fourteenth-century Venice, at least, a woman was not permitted to appear in court unless she was appearing on behalf of someone else who was unable to appear, due to sickness or another good reason. Linda Guzzetti, ch. 3, "Women in Court in Early Fourteenth-Century Venice," in *Across the Religious Divides, Women, Property and Law in the Wider Mediterranean (ca. 1300-1800)*, edited by Jutta Gisela Sperling and Shona Kelly Wray (New York: Routledge, 2010; Taylor & Francis e-library 2009), p. 52

compromise. If God will not agree to turn over the whole human race to him, he will settle for a portion.[1] Shylock, too, was willing to compromise, but he had lost his chance. In reality, he never had a chance. He always loses. He must lose, for Christ had already paid the ransom. In some versions, Mary presses her hand down onto the scale, "cheating,"[2] but God allows it. After all, she is only an untrained mother, and the fate of the entire human race "hangs in the balances." She even breaks down and cries, eliciting the Judge's sympathy.[3] Similarly, in *Merchant*, it has been observed that "Portia cheats." Bassanio urges Portia: to do a great right, do a little wrong (*Merchant* IV, 1). That she refuses, but she certainly gave him some strong hints in selecting the leaden casket.

Some scholars do not believe Bartolus wrote the *Processus Sathanae* to Bartolus of Saxoferrata (a.k.a. "Severus," the name of the Roman emperor in the *Processus Sathanae*).[4] However, the fact that the drama includes a scene where documents are signed in "1311," whereas Bartolus was born in 1313-14, cannot be taken as serious proof of his non-authorship — unless you really believe that John the Evangelist notarized the signatures of John the Baptist, St. Peter, St. Paul, and the Archangel Michael![5] Rather, it could be taken as a lesson to lawyers and others to read documents carefully and take their authenticity "with a grain of salt." Underlying themes in the *Processus* are compassion, seen with the Virgin Mary, and God's mercy for imperfect sinners, seen through the sacrifice of Christ.

---

[1] Murray omits mention of the scales; but see Hope Traver, *The Four Daughters of God, A Study of the Versions of this Allegory*, pp. 55, 57-61, 73, 136; pp. 53, 56, 65-66 are on compromise. HathiTrust, https://hdl.handle.net/2027/hvd.32044021642061.

[2] "Portia cheats." Kenji Yoshino, ch. 2, "The Lawyer: The Merchant of Venice," *A Thousand Times More Fair* (New York: Ecco 2011), p. 31; Kenji Yoshino, "The Lawyer of Belmont," *Yale Journal of Law & the Humanities* 9, no. 1 (1997), pp. 206, 212. http://digitalcommons.law.yale.edu/yjlh/vol9/iss1/4/.

[3] Hope Traver, "The Four Daughters of God, A Mirror[...]" (1925), p. 75, JSTOR, http://www.jstor.org/stable/457268.

[4] "Bartolus de Saxoferrato (Bartolis Severus de Alphanis)," *CERL Thesaurus*, https://thesaurus.cerl.org/record/cnp00397421.

[5] Scott L. Taylor, ch. 17, "Vox populi e voce professionis: Processus juris joco-serius: Esoteric Humor and the Incommensurability of Laughter," in Albrecht Classen, ed., *Laughter in the Middle Ages and Early Modern Times: Epistemology of a Fundamental Human Behavior, its Meaning and Consequences* (Berlin: Walter de Gruyter, 2010), pp. 515-530, 516-518; Augusto P. Miceli, "Forum Juridicum: Bartolus of Sassoferrato," pp. 1027-1036, p. 1027 n. 1; Hope Traver, "The Four Daughters of God, A Mirror[...]," (1925), pp. 44-92, JSTOR, http://www.jstor.org/stable/457268.

Scott Taylor mentions an expanded version of the *Processus Sathanae*, published in 1597 in Frankfurt, by lawyer/dramatist Jakob Ayer (Ayerer) called the *Historischer Processus Juris*. There is also a 1617 Ayer edition. Scott Taylor, "Vox populi e voce professionis[...]," p. 516, n. 7, https://books.google.ca/books?isbn=3110245485. *David Murray gives a synopsis in* D. Murray, *Lawyer's Merriments*, p. 158.

Francis Bacon writes: "Queen Elizabeth, being to resolve upon a great officer, and being by some, that canvassed for others, put in some doubt of that person whom she meant to advance, called for Mr. Bacon, and told him; She was like one with a lantern seeking a man; and seemed unsatisfied in the choice she had of men for that place. Mr. Bacon answered her; That he had heard that in old time there was usually painted on the church walls the Day of Doom, and God sitting in judgment, and St. Michael by him with a pair of balance; and the soul and the good deeds in the one balance, and the faults and the evil deeds in the other; and the soul's balance went up far too light: Then was our Lady painted with a great pair of beads, casting them into the light balance, to make up the weight: so (he said) place and authority, which were in her hands to give, were like our lady's beads, which though men, through diverse imperfections, were too light before, yet when they were cast in, made weight competent."[1]

The *Processus Belial* or *Processus Luciferi*, short names for the *Consolatio peccatorum, seu Processus Luciferi contra Jesum Christum*, was written by Jacopo Theramo (1349–1417), also known as Palladini and Ancharano. He was, consecutively, Bishop of Monopoli, Florence and Spoleto, and Archbishop of Taranto.[2] This book differed from the *Processus Sathanae* in that it contained several trials. Not only Biblical persons (Moses, Solomon, Jeremiah, and Isaiah), but also King Octavius and Aristotle played parts. God the Father was the judge; Christ was the respondent; and King Solomon was the "judge delegate." Moses was the procurator, advocate for mankind.[3]

About one-third of the citations in the *Belial* were to canon and Roman law,[4] including citations to Gratian's *Decretum*.[5] Law books, including the *Processus* books, were printed with wide margins (borders) on all sides, to leave room for the lawyer to write his own notes. These marginal notes served as the hyperlinks of yesterday.

Although the popular *Processus* books were banned by the first Council of Trent (1545–1547), numerous editions were printed during the late

---

[1] Apophthegms, no. 65, *Spedding*, VII, p. 134, HathiTrust, https://hdl.handle.net/2027/ucl.b3924335.

[2] Keeton, *Shakespeare's Legal and Political Background*, pp. 140-142.

[3] Doug Coulson, "The Devil's Advocate," p. 411. SSRN: http://ssrn.com/abstract=2745281; David Murray, *Lawyer's Merriments*, pp. 153-159. Murray mentions a lengthy article, in French, on Palladini in Prosper Marchand, Dictionnaire historique, vol. 2 (n.p., "A la Hate, chez Pierre de Honde," 1759), p. 117-125, https://books.google.ca/books?id=liBJCxRt7KIC). Murray, Lawyer's Merriments, p. 154, fn. 1, HathiTrust, https://hdl.handle.net/2027/hvd.32044010322881.

[4] (1) Francesco Mastroberti, "The *Liber Belial*," http://www.historiaetius.eu/uploads/5/9/4/8/5948821/mastroberti.pdf, p. 2.

[5] Kenneth Pennington, "The Biography of Gratian, The Father of Canon Law," *Vill. L. Rev.* 59 (2014), pp. 679-706, 689, n. 30. https://scholarship.law.edu/cgi/viewcontent.cgi?referer=&httpsredir=1&article=1839&context=scholar.

fifteenth and early sixteenth centuries.[1] In England, publishers printed copies "even after the change in religion."[2] In 1606, Parliament passed an *Act to Restrain Abuses of Playes*, restricting references to the Christian God, jests, and profanity on stage.[3] There are twenty-two instances of the name of "God" alone in *Merchant*.[4] The Revels accounts show no performances of the play after the two recorded in 1605, occurring either on the same day or on Shrove Sunday and Shrove Tuesday, before King James at Whitehall.[5] Although it is often said that James must have liked the play, for he asked to see it again, perhaps he was displeased by its use of the name of God "in vain."

Traver reports that both the *Processus Belial* as well as the *Gesta Romanorum*, a source of *Merchant*,[6] are offshoots of the same allegory: the "Four Daughters of God" — Mercy, Truth, Justice, and Peace.[7] There was, at least at one time, a tapestry depicting this allegory at Hampton Court Palace.[8]

The allegory may help explain some lines in *Merchant*. For example, in the allegory, one man typically asks another man who is burdened with sins, "What is the cause of your sadness?"[9] In the very first line of *Merchant*,

[1] Karl Shoemaker, "The Devil at Law in the Middle Ages," *Revue de l' histoire des religions* 4 (2011), in English and French. http://rhr.revues.org/7826#text.

[2] Traver, *The Four Daughters of God, A Study[..]*, p. 163, HathiTrust, https://hdl.handle.net/2027/hvd.32044021642061.

[3] Cyndia Susan Clegg, "Censorship," in *The Oxford Encyclopedia of British Literature*, vol. 1, ed. by David Scott Kastan (Oxford: Oxford University Press, 2006), p. 418. For a summary of Tudor laws affecting liturgical drama, up to the Elizabethan *Injunctions* of 1559 which forbade "monuments of idolatry and superstition" and were followed by Bishop Bentham's *Articles* in 1565, see E. K. Chambers, *The Medieval Stage*, vol. 2, pp. 24-25.

[4] Search, s.v. "God," www.opensourceshakespeare.org.

[5] E. K. Chambers, *William Shakespeare: A Study of Facts and Problems*, vol. 2 (Oxford: Clarendon Press, 1930), appendix D, p. 332. The two marginal additions of the name "William Shaxberd" as "the poet who made the play" next to the entries for *The Merchant of Venice* performances are considered spurious. William J. Rolfe, *Shakespeare's Comedy of 'The Merchant of Venice'* (New York, 1885), p. 11. For current stage history, see Royal Shakespeare Company, "The Stage History of the "The Stage History of The Merchant of Venice." https://www.rsc.org.uk/the-merchant-of-venice/about-the-play/stage-history. "The history, as presented in Chambers' standard work, *The Elizabethan Theatre*, has been revised." W. R. Streitberger, intro., *The Masters of the Revels and Elizabeth I's Court Theatre* (Oxford: Oxford University Press, 2016), pp. 1-31, 15.

[6] See "G. B.," *Evenings with the Old Story Tellers, Select Tales from the 'Gesta Romanorum'* (New York, 1845), pp. 46-51. https://books.google.es/books?id=D5APAAAAIAAJ.

On the Gesta, see C. D. Warner, comp. The Library of the World's Best Literature. An Anthology in Thirty Volumes (1917), Bartleby.com, http://www.bartleby.com/library/prose/2181.html.

[7] Hope Traver, *The Four Daughters of God, a Study [...]* (1907), p. 164, HathiTrust, https://hdl. handle.net/2027/hvd.32044021642061."The *Gesta Romanorum* is a collection of fictitious narratives in Latin, compiled from Oriental apologues, monkish legends, classical stories, tales of chroniclers, popular traditions, and other sources, which it would now be difficult and perhaps impossible to discover." Intro., *The Merchant of Venice, The Yale Shakespeare*, ed. by Wilbur L. Cross and Tucker Brooke (New York: Barnes & Noble, 2005), p. 155.

[8] Hope Traver, *The Four Daughters of God, a Study[..]* (1907), p. 163, n. 15.

[9] Hope Traver, "The Four Daughters of God, a Mirror[...]" (1925), p. 59, JSTOR, http://www.jstor.org/stable/457268.

we find Antonio *answering* that very question, asked, presumably, before the play begins by an unseen and unknown questioner. E. Kantorowicz observes, "The melancholy of Justice is traditional."[1] In his article on marine insurance, Luke Wilson provides David Hume's analysis that Antonio does not fit the pattern: he should be afraid, not sad, because he has no way to accurately assess the risk of his ships at sea. For Antonio, risk is like *a fait accompli*.[2] Antonio's relationship with Bassanio is about to change drastically. A troubadour poet revered by Dante wrote about a lover's melancholy.[3]

We are shocked by Shylock's cruel intent towards Antonio. It is interesting, however, that in the allegory, it was because of his cruelty that Satan forfeited any putative claim to man. According to Hope Traver, the allegory evolved as theology evolved. St. Anselm was the first theologian to deny Satan any rights to the souls of humankind. Satan was tricked even in the crucifixion, for the death of Christ was in the fulfillment of God's plan.[4]

Doug Coulson points out that these "devilish" fictional trials of humanity had a role to play in teaching students the art of oratory, as opposed to just memorizing rules and laws.[5] The theological underpinnings were integral to the pedagogy, acting as memory triggers. The *Processus* served to teach students how to resolve antitheses and to "approach legal rules as a topic for thought and argument."[6]

Since the days of ancient Rome, equity had been so closely associated with rhetoric that the two were almost synonymous,[7] as they had been for

---

[1] "Ernst Kantorowicz, *The King's Two Bodies, A Study in Medieval Political Theology* (Princeton: Princeton University Press, 2016, first pub. 1957) p. 108, n. 60; Peter Goodrich, ch. 1, "Introduction: *Melancholia Juridica*," *Oedipus Lex: Psychoanalysis, History, Law* (Berkeley: University of California Press, 1995), pp. 1–15.

Robert E. Lerner has published a new biography, *Ernst Kantorowicz, A Life* (Princeton: Princeton University Press, 2017). See Robert E. Norton, "Ernst Kantorowicz, Man of Two Bodies," *Times Literary Supplement* (2/22/2017), https://www.tls-co.uk/articles/public/ernst-kantorowicz-life/.

[2] Luke Wilson, "Drama and Marine Insurance in Shakespeare's London," in Constance Jordan and Karen Cunningham, *The Law in Shakespeare* (Houndsmills UK: Palgrave Macmillan, 2007), pp. 127-143, 127-130.

[3] See the discussion of Guiraut de Bornelh, praised by Dante, in H. J. Chaytor, *The Troubadours* (Cambridge, 1912), p. 54, The Project Gutenberg Ebook of the Troubadours, Ebook 12456, https://www.gutenberg.org/files/12456/12456-h/12456-h.htm.

A lovely, illustrated article on the Troubadours is Sylvia Huot, "Visualization and Memory: The Illustration of Troubadour Lyric in a Thirteenth-Century Manuscript," *Gesta* 31, no. 1 (Chicago: University of Chicago Press, 1992), pp. 3-14, http://www.jstor.org/stable/767046.

[4] Travers, "The Four Daughters of God, a Mirror...," (1925), pp. 6466, JSTOR, http://www.jstor.org/stable/457268.

[5] Coulson, Doug, "The Devil's Advocate and Legal Oratory in the *Processus Sathanae*," pp. 409-30, p. 413, SSRN: http://ssrn.com/abstract=2745281.

[6] Coulson, "The Devil's Advocate[...]," pp. 427-428.

[7] Coulson, "The Devil's Advocate[...]," p. 429.

the Roman statesman and orator Cicero (first century B.C.E.). Bacon cites or mentions Cicero thirty-eight times, second only to the number of times he cites Aristotle, in his 1605 *Advancement of Learning*, according to Matthew Sharpe,[1] although he also cites Virgil to a significant degree.[2] Sharpe explores how Bacon relied on Cicero's *De invention, De oratore,* and *Proemia* and the writings of other ancient writers in his *Advancement of Learning.* According to Sharpe, Bacon "proposes an apology, a defense for the life of the mind," explaining how "philosophy and wider learning inculcate both intellectual and civic virtues."[3] In his "Letter to Bishop Launcelot Andrewes," probably ca. 1622, Bacon wrote that he looked to Demosthenes, Cicero, and Seneca as models for how to bear up under adversity.[4]

One of the main purposes of the *Processus Sathanae* type of book was to "illustrate the tension between law and equity in legal practice,"[5] with a view towards their reconciliation. Might not this have been a goal of the playwright who wrote *Merchant*? Rhetoric may help explain why Shylock elicits sympathy, despite his intent to kill Antonio. The use of rhetorical devices, including puns, for achieving enhanced effect from words is discussed in Sister Miriam Joseph's *Shakespeare's Use of the Arts of Language.*[6]

The common theological framework of the *Processus Belial* was integral to the learning process. The framework also aided memorization, just as

---

[1] Matthew Sharpe, "'Not for personal gratification, or for contention, or to look down on others, or for convenience, reputation, or power': Cultura Animi in Bacon's 1605 Apology for the "Proficiency and Advancement of Learning," in *Journal of Early Modern Studies (JEMS)* 4 (2015), ed. by Sorana Corneanu, 2:37-68, at p. 44. Available from http://deakin.academia.edu/MatthewSharpe.

[2] Robert Schuler, "Francis Bacon and Scientific Poetry," *Transactions of the American Philosophical Society* 82, no. 2 (1992), pp. 1-65, 42-43, JSTOR, http://www.jstor.org/stable/3231921.

[3] Sharpe, "Not for personal gratification[...]," pp. 43-44.

[4] *Spedding, XIV*, p. 372, HathiTrust, https://hdl.handle.net/2027/ucl.31175012007947.

[5] Coulson, "The Devil's Advocate[...]," pp. 414-415.

[6] Sister Miriam Joseph, *Shakespeare's Use of the Arts of Language* (Philadelphia: Paul Dry Books 2005, first pub. 1947), pp. 43-89.

As to *Merchant*, Joseph notes Shakespeare's familiarity with *The Orator*, "translated from the French of Alexandre van den Busche (Le Silvayn) by Lazarus Pyott, almost as soon as it was published in 1596." She believes Shakespeare drew on *The Orator's* ninety-fifth oration for the "order and motives of Shylock's argument in court" in *Merchant*. Joseph, pp. 139-52, 46.

For rhetorical devices which Joseph found in *Merchant*, see Joseph, pp. 75 (malapropism (II, 5, 19); 99-100 (proverbs, maxims), 113-114 ("division," parietem); see also her Index.

At least 180 different rhetorical devices existed during Shakespeare's time. Joseph, p. 4; see Index, pp. 413-415. Just to name a few: paradox (p.136), antithesis (pp. 133, 137), homoeosis ("general figure of similitude," includes parabola, paradigm, fable, and icon)(p. 143), and etymology (argument from a name, pp. 162, 339).

A newer book is Victoria Kahn and Lorna Hutson, eds. *Rhetoric and Law in Early Modern Europe* (New Haven: Yale University Press, 2001, currently out of print). https://yalebooks.yale.edu/book/9780300084856/rhetoric-and-law-early-modern-europe.

"fantastical elements" had aided memory in classical orations in the days of Cicero.[1] This raises an important question: how *did* England "purge "the "Catholic" from its ecclesiastical law after the nation became Protestant? How does a country sever its law from its roots? After the English universities stopped teaching courses in canon law under Henry VIII,[2] how was ecclesiastical law taught? Henry VIII established Regius professorships in civil law at the universities, but there must have still been a tremendous gap. The civilians of Doctors' Commons did not teach.[3] This strikes me as an enormous problem that would impact all aspects of society, one which Bacon would have tried to address.[4]

Today, when courts are increasingly secular, how do we preserve the concepts of equity that have their roots in Christian theology but which one might argue are universal to humankind?

One fifteenth-century rendition of the "Four Daughters of God" allegory is *The Booke of the Pylgremage of the Sowle*, by Guilliame de DeGuileville. In the introduction to an 1859 edition of this work, Katherine Cust traces the "scales of justice" motif back to Homer, Virgil, and Aeschylus.[5] The plot involves the now-familiar theme of Satan demanding his right to the soul of one poor sinner. Michael the Archangel intercedes on behalf of the man, with

---

[1] Coulson, "The Devil's Advocate[...]," pp. 414-415.

[2] Coquillette, "'The Purer Fountains," p. 4, notes 22, 23.

[3] Baker, *Intro.*, pp. 193-194.

[4] See, *Spedding*, VIII, preface, p. iv.

[5] *The Book of the Pylgremage of the Sowle* by "Guilliame or Guillaume de DeGuileville" or de Digulleville, edited by Katherine Cust (London, 1859, transl. 1413; first pub. William Caxton, 1483), appendix B, pp. xxi, xxvi, 14-16, at 18, Plate II (with exquisite illustrations from Egerton MS 615), Hathitrust, https://hdl.handle.net/2027/mdp.39015053684802; Traver, "The Four Daughters of God..., a Mirror," (1925), p. 60 n. 35.

"De DeGuileville" was a monk of the Cistercian Abbey of Chaalis. Jessica Brantley, ch. 6, "Envisioning Dialogue in Performance," in *Reading in the Wilderness: Private Devotion and Public Performance in Late Medieval England* (Chicago and London: University of Chicago Press, 2007), p. 240. The *Book of the Pylgremage of the Sowle* (English) is the second poem in a trilogy consisting of 1) *Le Pelerinage de Vie humaine* (a play); 2) *Le Pelerinage de l'ame*; and 3) *Le Pelerinage Jhesucrist*." Cust, p. 383, n. 95.

The larger part of these works by de DeGuileville (or just DeGuilleville) is present in "Cotton Manuscript Vitellius C. xiii (leaves 2-308). See introductory material, p. 4, headed "Texts Preparing, DeGuilleville, Anglo-Saxon Psalters." Richard Morris, *Cursor mundi (the Cursor of the world), Northumbrian poem of the XIVth Century in four versions* (n.p.: Trubner for the Early English Text Society) E.E.T.S. vol. 99, 1874, 1893, p. 30. https://books.google.com/books?id=AAEVAAAAQAAJ. *Francis Bacon borrowed manuscripts from Robert Cotton's library.* Brian Vickers, ed., *History of the Reign of King Henry VII*, pp. xiii, xxviii, 128 n., 221 n.

Misericorde,[1] Justice, Reason, Truth and Equity[2] (five virtues) personified, interceding in the trial.[3]

Of note, the authorship of Guilliame de DeGuileville is established only by acrostic.[4] Although Guilliame (Guillaume, "William") is a perfectly respectable name, it sounds like "guile," which is defined as wile, cunning, deceit, whereas a "gull" is a "dupe," who would swallow anything (down the gullet), perhaps even that John the Baptist and Michael the Archangel signed as witnesses![5]

Influence of Aristophanes and Saturnalian Release

The scales motif is also found in connection with the character "Aeschylus" in Aristophanes' comedy *The Frogs*.[6]

Wondering whether Ben Jonson's reference to Shakespeare's "small Latin and less Greek" might have been alluding to classical comedies, I searched for the word "trifle," first recorded in use during Elizabethan times. Then, the layered dessert called "trifle" was a novel delicacy.[7] Literature, of course,

---

[1] The definition for "misericorde" includes mercy, compassion, and a thin-bladed dagger for giving the "death" or "mercy" stroke. "Misericorde," *Webster's*, p. 638.

[2] Interestingly, the concept of *aequitas*, or equity, was first mentioned--in Rome, at least--by Plautus (254-184 B.C.), the Roman writer of comedies, even before Cicero had written of it. A. Arthur Schiller, sec. 183, *Roman Law, Mechanisms of Development* (The Hague: Mouton Publishers, 1978), p. 555. For interesting connections between the goddesses Aequitas and Moneta, see, e.g., Barbara F. McManus, "Trutina: Roman Balance scales, Aequitas, and Moneta" (with images of coins), http://www.vroma.org/-bmcmanus/aequitas.html.

The concept of *aequitas*, or fairness, has also been traced from Christopher St. Germain (St. German) back to *epiekeia* in Aristotle's *Nichomachean Ethics* (David Ibbetson, *Law and Equity*, pp. 71-74), as well as to French theologian Jean Gerson (1363-1429). Thomas C. Bilello, "Accomplished with What She Lacks: Law, Equity, and Portia's Con," condensed version reprinted from *Law and Literature*, 16:1 (Spring 2004) 11-32, in *The Law in Shakespeare*, ed. Constance Jordan and Karen Cunningham (Houndsmills UK: Palgrave MacMillan, 2007), pp. 109-127, 110-112. Aristotle lived from 384 B.C. to 322 B.C. One would think, however, that most, if not every, culture must have some conception of *aequitas*.

[3] Cust, *Pylgremage*, preface, pp. xi-xiv.

[4] William Stone Booth and Penn Leary are two who have found acrostics revealing Bacon's name, in the works of *Shakespeare*. See William Stone Booth, *Subtle Shining Secrecies Writ in the Margents of Books Generally Ascribed to William Shakespeare, The Actor, and Here Ascribed to William Shakespeare, the Poet* (Boston: Walter H. Baker, 1925), pp. 32-33.

[5] Walter W. Skeat, "Guile" and "Gull," *An Etymological Dictionary of the English Language* (Oxford, 1898), p. 248.

[6] *The Frogs* by Aristophanes, Project Gutenberg, http://www.gutenberg.org/ebooks/7998; "Ancient Greece — Aristophanes," *Classical Literature* http://www.ancient-literature.com/greece_aristophanes.html (with links to his major works).

[7] In 1598, John Florio, Italian translator of Montaigne's *Essays* and Italian language tutor to King James's family, described the "trifle" or "foole" as a popular dessert. Rita D. Jacobs, "Fare of the Country; English Trifle; Serious Dessert," travel section, *The New York Times*, March 27, 1988, http://www.nytimes.com/1988/03/27/travel/fare-of-the-country-english-trifle-serious-dessert.html?pagewanted=all, citing the *Oxford English Dictionary*, 2d ed., 1989. In a

is made up of layers of meaning, like a trifle. In *The Frogs*, the word translated "trifle" (*nuga*) occurs eight times. In Aristophanes' play, *The Clouds*,[1] *nuga* appears twice. In a collection of five plays by the Roman writer of comedies, Titus Maccius Plautus,[2] the word "trifle" appears five times, and twice more in an additional play, Plautus' *Mostellaria*.[3]

In *The Frogs*, one of the occurrences of "trifle" is near the place in the text where Charon, who ferries the dead across the River Styx to Hades in Greek mythology, says, "If you listen, you will hear sweet music"; i.e., the music of the frogs. Whether a bullfrog chorus qualifies as music is debatable, unless you are a female frog. In *Merchant*, Jessica says she is never merry when she hears sweet music (V, 1, 2525) — for good reason, if Charon, ferryman on the River Styx, is near! Perhaps she is starting to feel the pangs of conscience.

The plots of both *The Frogs* and *The Clouds* concern usury, and both plays contain imagery of debtors being eaten up by debts and creditors. C. L. Barber in *The Saturnalian Pattern* writes:

> Once Shakespeare finds his own distinctive style, he is more Aristophanic than any other great English comic dramatist, despite the fact that the accepted educated models and theories when he started to write were Terentian and Plautine. The Old Comedy case of his work results from his participation in native saturnalian traditions of the popular theater and the popular holidays. Not that he "wanted art" — including Terentian art. But he used the resources of a sophisticated theatre to express, in his idyllic comedies and in his clowns' ironic misrule, the experience of moving to humorous understanding through saturnalian release.[4]

Shakespeare's comedy is Aristophanic, Barber explains, because it is "shaped by the form of feeling" of the special day. Aristophanic comedy involves two "gestures": "invocation," such as May Day "garlanding," and "abuse," the flouting of things otherwise deserving of respect, just for the

---

1585 cookbook, Thomas Dawson gave a recipe he called "trifle" which sounds like a pudding. Wikipedia. https://en.wikipedia.org/wiki/The_Good_Huswifes_Jewell.

[1] The Project Gutenberg e-book of 'The Clouds' by Aristophanes," http://www.gutenberg.org/files/2562.

[2] "The Project Gutenberg e-book of 'Amphitryo,' 'Asinaria,' 'Aulularia,' 'Bacchides,' 'Captivi' by Plautus, Titus Maccius, http://www.gutenberg.org/files/16564.

[3] "The *Captivi* and the *Mostellaria* by Titus Maccius Plautus," http://www.gutenberg.org/ebooks/7282..

[4] C. L. Barber, "The Saturnalian Pattern," *Approaches to Shakespeare*, ed. by Norman Rabkin (New York: McGraw-Hill, 1964), pp. 230-245, esp. 231, 239.

day.[1] The pattern "involves inversion, statement and counterstatement, and a basic movement from release to clarification."[2]

Typically, a Saturnalian plot will involve one who is a "kill-joy," such as Malvolio or Shylock.[3] In the Saturnalian pattern, the holiday spirit reigns, and behaviors not normally permitted are tolerated.[4] As England's universal culture of Catholic holy-day holidays and revelries, consisting of "morris dances, sword-dances, wassailings, mock ceremonies of summer kings and queens and of lords of misrule, mummings, disguisings, masques, and a bewildering variety of sorts, games, shows, and pageants," celebrated by the rich and poor alike" was fading, giving way to Protestant culture, "Shakespeare's theatre" began "taking over on a professional and everyday basis functions which until his time had largely been performed by amateurs on holiday."[5]

The holidays were seasonal, with roots in nature worship, "built around the enjoyment of the vital pleasure of moments when nature and society are hospitable to life. The holiday and the comedy are parallel manifestations of the same pattern in culture, a way men can cope with their life."[6] When the Lord of Misrule was on his throne, mockery of all things, both natural and unnatural, was the "order" of the day.

In Portia's famous speech on mercy, she tells us that mercy seasons justice. Since these holidays were, or had been until recently, so much a part of the English culture, I find myself wondering whether the word "seasoning" would have had for people then a mental association with merry old England's holidays. There was a spirit of "overlooking" for behavior that happened on a holiday that would have been inexcusable on a regular day. This suggests to me that Shakespeare saw a parallel between this holiday spirit and a relaxation of the strict spirit of the law, akin to equity or mercy's "forbearance, compassionate treatment of an offender."

Perhaps Shakespeare was suggesting that mercy is to law as necessary as holidays, play time, are to a healthy society. Just as "the season to be jolly" makes the rest of the year more "palatable," so a little salt makes the meat taste better, and a little flexibility makes the law more accommodating to human nature, which, like nature as a whole, has its seasons. A "seasoned" practitioner will not be so likely to "cook by the book." Jessica's theft from her father might have been a mere holiday prank, but one does not get that

---

[1] Barber, pp. 234-235.
[2] Barber, pp. 234-238.
[3] Barber, p. 236.
[4] Barber, pp. 237-238.
[5] Barber, pp. 233, 243.
[6] Barber, pp. 234-235.

sense. In the play, we see revelers but no revelries, and Charon, or at least, the music of the frogs, is invoked.

Or, perhaps Ben Jonson's cryptic reference to Shakespeare's "small Latin and less Greek" was an example of Aristophanean irony. It cannot be denied that Shakespeare had abundant classical knowledge and language facility. We are told that an Elizabethan schoolboy could have learned all the Latin that Shakespeare knew. That, however, is debatable. True, Ben Jonson, a proficient classicist, never went to a university, yet he had studied Latin and Greek at Westminster School, headed by "Antiquarian" William Camden, and was an accomplished classicist. However, (1) that school was probably superior to a Stratford grammar school; and (2) there is no proof William Shaxpere ever attended a Stratford grammar school. He seems to have had difficulty signing his name the same way twice. Also, it is difficult to stay fluent in a language unless one continues to use it. Bacon wrote in Latin during all of his adult life. At any rate, there is room for discussion about what Jonson meant.[1]

Trifles

The word "trifle" is found in the writings of both Bacon and Shakespeare to a significant degree. Others did use the word, of course, including Queen Elizabeth[2] and Lord Coke. We find the word in Bacon's *Promus*, his private literary notebook which contains words and expressions found in both Shakespeare and Bacon.[3] The *Promus* includes two quotations from Horace and one from Ovid which use the Latin word *nuga* ("trifle").[4] Horace called his fine lyric poems mere "trifles" (*lusimi*, like Catullus's use of *nugae*).[5] Horace also asked, "What prevents one from speaking truth with a laughing

---

[1] See Colin Burrow, intro., *Shakespeare and Classical Antiquity* (Oxford: Oxford University Press, 2013), pp. 1-2. An earlier book with the same title is Paul Stapfer, *Shakespeare and Classical Antiquity, Antiquity as Presented in Shakespeare's Plays* (C. Kegan Paul, 1880).

[2] Elizabeth Jenkins, *Elizabeth the Great* (New York: Coward-McCann, 1959), p. 19 ("There is only one Christ Jesus and one faith; the rest is a dispute about trifles"); p. 28 (Elizabeth to Thomas Seymour, "I am a friend not won with trifles, nor lost with the like").

[3] Dutch humanist Desiderius Erasmus reportedly advocated the keeping of a "personal treasury of words and expressions for use in future speeches and letters" in his *De Copia* (1512), according to Henry Hitchings, ch. 6, "Genius," *The Secret Life of Words: How English Became English* (New York: Picador, 2008), pp. 110-139, 119. Keeping such a notebook became a common habit among Renaissance humanists. Brian Vickers, intro., *Francis Bacon, a Critical Edition of the Major Works* (Oxford: Oxford University Press, 1996), p. xli-xliv. For more on the *Promus*, see infra, ch. 4.

[4] Mrs. Henry [Constance] Pott, ed., *The Promus of Formularies and Elegancies, (being Private Notes, circ. 1594, hitherto unpublished) by Francis Bacon illustrated and elucidated by passages from Shakespeare*, preface by E. A. Abbott (London, 1883), pp. 191, 339, and 345, item nos. 295, 1039, 1060, HathiTrust, https://hdl.handle.net/2027/hvd.32044086726981.

[5] Ross S. Kilpatrick, "Two Horatian Proems, *Carmen* 1.26 and *Carmen* 1.32, pp. 213-241, 231, in *Studies in Latin Poetry*, vol. 21, YALE CLASSICAL STUDIES, ed. by Christopher M. Dawson

face?"[1] As Simon Miles points out in his talk on *Merchant*, the opening to the play juxtaposes the laughing philosopher, Democritus, with the weeping philosopher, Heraclitus.[2]

We know that Francis Bacon wrote works of imaginative literature which he referred to as "toys" or "trifles," words associated with play. See, e.g., the opening lines of Bacon's essay, "Of Masques and Triumphs:" "These things are but toys to come amongst such serious observations."[3] The censors, too, might refer to a play as a "toy" from which they would pick out the hidden meanings.[4]

The word "trifle" seems to recur frequently in Shakespeare commentary, as well. In relating the Queen's fondness for young Bacon (calling him her

and Thomas Cole (Cambridge: Cambridge University Press, 1969), https://books.google.ca/books?id=qLU8AAAAIAAJ.

Bacon uses "trifle" or "triflers" in the following examples. In *Spedding*, IV, 'Novum Organum,' i, no. 88, p. 87 ("It is no wonder if noble inventions and worthy of mankind have not been brought to light, when men have been delighted with such trifling and puerile tasks..."); 'Novum Organum', ii, p. 178; 'Novum Organum,' ii, no. 48, p. 224; 'De Augmentis, v, ch. 3," p. 424.; 'De Augmentis, vi, no. 34, p. 486, HathiTrust, https://hdl.handle.net/2027/uc1.31175002901968.

In *Spedding*, V: p. 133, "out of scanty and trifling experience"; "On the Ebb and Flow of the Sea," p. 446; "History of Life and Death," pp. 265; "De Principiis atque Originibus," p. 499; p. 513, "a trifling and ridiculous mistake." HathiTrust, https://hdl.handle.net/2027/uc1.b3618241.

In his essay "Of Seeming Wise, "Bacon speaks, in Latin, of his disdain of "those that do nothing, or little very solemnly (*magno conatu nugas*, "trifles with great effort"). He finds the "shifting" of these formalists ridiculous and "fit for a satire to persons of judgment." He speaks of foolish men who hide their ignorance with subtlety (A. Gellius in Latin, *Hominem delirum, qui verborum minutiis rerum frangit pondera*: "A foolish man, who fritters away the weight of matters by finespun trifling on words." "Vide. *Quint. X. 1.*" *The Works of Francis Bacon, The Wisdom of the Ancients and Other Essays* (Roslyn, NY: Walter J. Black, 1932), pp. 93, n.2; 94, n. 4. *Spedding*, VI, p. 436, HathiTrust, https://hdl.handle.net/2027/uc1.31175002285222.

In his essay "Of Beauty," he writes, "A man cannot tell whether Apelles or Durer were the more trifler." *Spedding*, VI, p. 570, HathiTrust, https://hdl.handle.net/2027/uc1.b3618242.

A search of Shakespeare at www.OpenSourceShakespeare.org reveals forty-one uses of "trifle," including seventeen of "trifles," one use of "trifler," five of "trifling," and seven of "trivial." In *The Merchant of Venice*, the word trifle appears three times, in II, 2, 718 (Launcelot); IV, 1, 2240 (Shylock: "We trifle time"), and IV, 1, 2385 (Bassanio).

[1] Horace, *Sat.* I. i. 24., as quoted by Bacon in his *Promus*; see Mrs. Henry Pott, ed., *The Promus...*, p. 339; infra, ch. 4.

[2] Simon Miles, lecture on *The Merchant of Venice*, https://www.youtube.com/watch?v=KcQCljc1Mv8.

[3] *Spedding*, VI, p. 467, HathiTrust, https://hdl.handle.net/2027/uc1.b3618242. Walter W. Skeat finds uses of the word "toy," defined as "trifle, trifling ornament," in eight Shakespeare plays (*Hamlet, Winter's Tale, Twelfth Night, Othello, King John, Richard III, Two Noble Kinsmen,* and *Henry VI*, and one use in Bacon's essay, "Of Empire" (princes setting their hearts upon toys). *A Glossary of Tudor and Stuart Words, especially from the Dramatists*, collected by Walter W. Skeat, ed. with additions by A. L. Mayhew (Oxford: Clarendon Press, 1914), pp. 214, 293, 415, HathiTrust, https://catalog.hathitrust.org/Record/001441055. Note: Skeat did not have an entry for "trifle." The essay, "Of Masques and Triumphs," begins, "These things are but toys to come amongst such serious observations...."

[4] John Huntington, "intro.," to *Ambition, Rank, and Poetry in 1590s England*, crediting Cyndia Susan Clegg (Urbana: University of Illinois Press, 2001), p. 16.

"little Lord Keeper"), Catherine Drinker Bowen writes, "Of such trifles might a man's career be built."[1] John Heminges and Henry Condell refer to the First Folio submissions not as "plays" but as "trifles" three times in their second and third sentences of their dedicatory epistle in the First Folio.[2]

Marjorie Garber relates how Freud considered the theme of the three caskets a "trifle," a "little problem" that had to do with death.[3]

> Freud proposes that the Gesta Romanorum tale of the three caskets is an inversion of the tales where there are three sisters and one is chosen, such as Cinderella. He relates this to the three fates, the Greek Moirae: Clotho who spins the thread of life, Lachesis who allots it, and Atropos who cuts it.[4] In these tales, it is always the third, chosen one who represents both death and love.[5]

> Thus, it is worth considering whether Bassanio is in any way associated with death. In Merchant, II, 2, 738, Leonardo says of Bassanio, "Yonder, sir, he walks." Of twenty-eight uses of the word "walks" in Shakespeare, "walks" is clearly used of a ghost in two plays: Julius Caesar, V, 3, 2610; and King Lear, III, 4, 1911. He also uses "walks" in the personification of a spirit in others, such as Hamlet I, 1, 190 (But look, the morn in russet mantle clad,/ walks o'er the dew of yon high eastward hill").

> According to Freud, these fates (Moirae in Greek) are associated with the "ineluctable severity of law and its relation to death and dissolution." The Moirae are "very closely related" to the Horae (the Seasons, associated with Time, the guardians of natural law and of the divine order), and the three Graces,[6] Joy, Charm, and Beauty. Freud says the dramatist intentionally "reduced the theme to the original myth," thereby achieving a more profound effect. Shakespeare's "mercy seasons justice" may well embody the concepts for which these goddesses stand.

The court official and lawyer Walter Map (*Gualteri Mapes*) (1140–1210), one of the Goliardi, a brotherhood of student and cleric poets, wrote a book of jests, *De Nugis Curialiam* or *Courtier's Trifles* during his spare time while serving in the busy court of Henry II. Map or Mapes also had countless Latin poems of the Goliardi ascribed to him; in fact, "To say that a poem

---

[1] Bowen, *Lion*, p. 77.

[2] E. K. Chambers, *William Shakespeare, A Study of Facts and Problems*, vol. 2, appendix B, "Contemporary Allusions" (Oxford: Clarendon Press, 1930), p. 228.

[3] See, Marjorie Garber, ch. 3, "Freud's Choice: The Theme of the Three Caskets," in *Shakespeare's Ghost Writers: Literature as Uncanny Causality* (New York: Routledge, 1997), pp. 74-86, 75.

If the casket were to be interpreted as symbolic of female genitalia (Yoshino, *The Lawyer of Belmont*," p. 194, and sources cited therein), so, too, might "Belmont," (L. *bellus* = pretty, handsome and *mons, montis*, as in *mons veneris*).

[4] Sigmund Freud, "The Theme of the Three Caskets," Leonard and Eleanor Manheim, eds., *Hidden Patterns, Studies in Psychoanalytic Literary Criticism* (New York: MacMillan, 1966), pp. 79-92, pp. 80-81.

[5] Manheim, pp. 87-88.

[6] Freud, pp. 86-89.

was written by Walter Mapes was almost equivalent to saying that the real author was unknown, or wished to remain unknown."[1]

Bacon had been exposed to the idea of a literary "bund" when he was in France, with the group called the *Pleiade*, a royal academy.[2] The Areopagus, too, was an informal literary society which met at Leicester House, formed for the discussion of law and poetry.[3] The lawyer/poet dramatists writing at/for the Inns of Court were not so unlike the Goliardi in some ways. Both groups were composed of young men, students. Both probably wrote home for money. However, most Goliardic poetry is not of high quality.

As for trifles, although small or insignificant, their appearance may be deceiving. Coke once insulted Bacon, calling him "less than little, less than the least."[4] Bacon said, "For common and trivial things are (many times) the best."[5] He also said, "But I, who am well aware that no judgment can be passed on common or remarkable things, much less anything new brought to light, unless the causes of common things, and the causes of those causes, be first duly examined and found out, am of necessity compelled to admit the commonest things into my history...."[6] The word "trivial" comes from the Latin *trivium:* a place where three roads — *tri via* — meet; hence, it came to mean "common."[7] The *trivium*, pl. *trivia*, were the three liberal arts: grammar, rhetoric, and logic or dialectic.[8] *Trivia* is, of course, seemingly unimportant but interesting knowledge. The Renaissance poet Petrarch referred to his own poems in vernacular Italian as *nugae vulgares*, Latin for "trifles." And yet, ironically, it is for these poems rather than his serious writings in Latin that he is remembered.[9]

[1] Sebastian Evans, *Quest of the Holy Grail...* (London, 1898), p. 186.

[2] Peter Dawkins, *The Shakespeare Enigma* (London: Polair, 2004), pp. 160, 233, 310.

[3] Margaret J. Howell, *The Spirit of Understanding, English Literature in an Age of Confusion* (n.p.: Xlibris 2013), p. 102.

[4] Catherine Drinker Bowen, *Francis Bacon: the Temper of a Man* (Boston: Little, Brown, 1963), Archive.org, https://archive.org/details/francisbaconthet002428mbp, p. 91, cited in Coquillette, FB, p. 212, n. 2. Alfred Dodd recounts the insult in Dodd, *Francis Bacon's Personal Life Story,* excerpted at "Francis Bacon and his Nemesis Edward Coke," http://www.sirbacon.org/cokeandbacon.htm.

[5] Francis Bacon to King James, "Offer of a Digest of the Laws," March 20, 1620, *Spedding,* XIV, pp. 358-364, 360, HathiTrust, https://hdl.handle.net/2027/uc1.31175012007947; see also preface, note "b," *Novum Organum, Spedding,* I, p. 99, HathiTrust, https://hdl.handle.net/2027/hvd.32044011598257.

[6] Francis Bacon, *New Organon, Spedding,* IV, p. 106, HathiTrust, https://hdl.handle.net/2027/mdp.35112104256922.

[7] *Webster's,* p. 1071.

[8] Mario Ascheri, ch. 1, "Irnerius," *The Laws of Late Medieval Italy (1000–1500): Foundations for a European Legal System* (Leiden: Brill, 2013), pp. 22-23. Irnerius taught the trivium before he famously became the first law professor at the University of Bologna in the twelfth century.

[9] Frances Edward Harrison, "Some Notes on Language," in *Millennium, a Latin Reader A.D. 374-1374* (Bristol UK: Bristol Classical Press, 1991), pp. xix to xxvii, xxiii, https://books.google.ca/

Sir Philip Sidney protested that his 180,000-word romance, *The Countess of Pembroke's Arcadia*, was a mere "trifle, and that triflingly handled."[1] Rhetorical understatement, a diminishing or making smaller, often in the form of belittling, is called "meiosis."[2] Francis Bacon plainly tells us, perhaps with modest understatement, that he wrote "trifles."

The Goliardi

The Goliardi were wandering students and clerics (*scholars vagantes* and *clerici vagantes*) whose poetry was full of youthful exuberance, lust, and irreverence. Some wrote plays as well.[3] Many of their writings parodied and satirized the Church,[4] notwithstanding the fact that two of their best poets, known as the "Archpoet" and the "Primate," were clerics.[5] In fact, the moniker "Goliardi" was probably first hurled at these satirical versifiers as an insult, just as "Cathars" and "Hebari" were first hurled as insults at the Albigensians and Hebrews by the Catholics and Canaanites, respectively.

In his introduction to the *Commentaries on the Laws of England* (Oxford, 1765-1769), William Blackstone wrote that in 1152, King Stephen (1135–1154) had forbidden the study of Roman law. Walter Mapes wrote a poem, *De judicio extremo*, about how this ban might keep Roman civil law out of the courts, but it would not stop the clergy from reading and teaching it.[6]

The school of canon law at Oxford was said to have begun with the Italian jurist/canonist Vacarius who, in 1140, imported Gratian's *Decretum* into England. Vacarius was the author of the abridgment of the civil law, *Liber pauperum*, which he made for the English students who could not afford the full set of required books (The school at Oxford was *utrumque ius*, a school of "both laws," civil and canon.[7] However, after Pope Gregory issued his Decretals, the faculty split into two schools. [8]

---

books?isbn=0862922453.

[1] William Andrew Ringler, "Sir Philip Sidney, English Author and Statesman," *Encyclopedia Britannica*, copyright 2018, https://www.britannica.com/biography/Philip-Sidney.

[2] "Meosis," Literary Devices, copyright 2018, https://literarydevices.net/meiosis (explaining three examples from Shakespeare!).

[3] E. K. Chambers: *The Medieval Stage*, vol. 1, pp. 60, 280, 327; vol. 2, pp. 8, 23, 37, 52, 72, 107.

[4] Charles Homer Haskins, ch. 6, "Latin Poetry," *The Renaissance of the Twelfth Century* (Cambridge: Harvard University Press, 1982, first pub. 1927), p. 178-179; see also pp. 148, 175-192. J. A. Symonds, *Wine, Women and Song* (London, 1884), pp. 23-33, 44, 49-50, appendix, pp. 198-205.

[5] Haskins, ch. 6, "Latin Poetry," *The Renaissance of the Twelfth Century*, pp. 179-182: "...[T]he whole conception of the order of Golias is a burlesque on the regular orders of monks." pp. 183-192, 184.

[6] Ferdinand Mackeldey, intro., "History of the Roman Law," in *Compendium of Modern Civil Law*, ed. by Philip Ignatius Kaufmann (New York, 1845), div. 3, p. 72, https://books.google.com/books?id=xLEBAAAAYAAJ.

[7] L. E. Boyle, "Canon Law before 1380," ch. 14, in *The History of the University of Oxford: The Early Oxford Schools*, vol. 1, ed. by T. H. Aston (Oxford: Clarendon Press, 1984), pp. 531-565, 538.

[8] Boyle, p. 536.

While the ban did affect Vacarius, the greater the opposition, the more the law flourished (Tacitus had said something similar about banned books). Before long, Vacarius was teaching again.[1]

Another ban, Henry III's ban on the teaching of civil law in London, took effect in 1234 after news of Pope Honorarius's ban (*"Super specula"*) of 1219 reached England, fifteen years after it was proclaimed! Would-be clerics wishing to teach or study the civil law in London had to do so before they were ordained or risk recommunication! [2]

One discouraging effect of Henry's ban was that students could no longer study, at the same time in London, both civil law and common law pleading. This added years to the training time.[3]

John Matthews Manly thinks the term "Goliardi" originated in the Biblical story of "David and Goliath," based on his study of church breviaries. A popular sermon, one of several erroneously attributed to Augustine, based on 1 Samuel 17, likened David to Christ and Goliath to the Devil.[4] A passage which would have been read later the same day (the fourth Sunday after Pentecost) began: "Alligatus est enim." The word *alligatus* struck me, because it looks like the word "alligator," which Shakespeare is said to have been the first to use, in Romeo and Juliet.

In law and theology, too, John of Salisbury reasoned that the prince as *persona publica* was both bound by the law (*legibus alligatus*) and freed by the law (*legibus solutus*) — both "lord and serf of the law."[5] This was an important concept in political theory. Bacon might well have read John of Salisbury. In addition, as St. Germain in "Doctor and Student" had written, "For the law is derived of *ligare*, that is to say, to bind."[6] A legator in Latin was a testator, a witness. One can imagine a man with Bacon's background and his fertile

---

[1] Sir Arthur Duck, "The Use and Authority of the Civil Law in England," transl. by "J. B.," appended to Claude Joseph de Ferriere, *The History of the Roman or Civil Law* (London, 1724), pp. xix-xx. Note: Duck's dates do not coincide with Blackstone's.

[2] Boyle, pp. 536, 551

[3] J. L. Barton, ch. 13, "The Study of Civil Law before 1380," in *The History of the University of Oxford*, vol. 1, ed. by J. I. Catto (Oxford: Clarendon Press, 1984), pp. 519-531, 521, https://books.google.com/books?isbn=0199510113.

[4] John Matthews Manly, "Familia Goliae," *Modern Philology* 5 (Oct. 1907), 200-209, 203, JSTOR, http://www.jstor.org/stable/pdf/432490.pdf.

[5] E. Kantorowicz, *The King's Two Bodies*, pp. 96, 105-107; see also "John of Salisbury," *Stanford Encyclopedia of Philosophy*, first pub. Aug., 2016, https://plato.stanford.edu/entries/john-salisbury/.

[6] Christopher St. Germain, *The Doctor and Student, or, Dialogues between a Doctor of Divinity and a Student of the Laws of England [...]*, revised and corrected by William Muchall, (Cincinnati, 1886; first published in Latin, London, 1518), HathiTrust. http://hdl.handle.net/2027/uc2.ark:/13960/t1jh3nw58?urlappend=%3Bseq=28; http://lonang.com/library/reference/stgermain-doctor-and-student/.

---

imagination likening some malicious court witnesses to large Spanish lizards, *el legarto*, the usual explanation attributed to Shakespeare.[1]

Public opinion is moulded by allegations of one kind or another. Does an allegation "bite" like an alligator? "Never smile at a crocodile," as a children's song warns. Bacon warned repeatedly about the dangers of rumor and false report. One way that "Shakespeare" coined new words was by combining two different words. For example, he coined "eyeball," "birthplace," "undervalue," "cold-blooded," "soft-hearted," and "downstairs."[2] It might be interesting to see whether Bacon had actually used those any of those words first.

"Golias" may also be related to the Latin word for gluttony, *gula* (gulls and cormorants).[3] The vagrant (wandering) students were often poor and hungry, so when there was food, they ate their fill. Jessie Weston pondered whether the characters "Golishan" in the St. George mumming play and "Golagros" and "Golerotheram" in Arthurian romances might be etymologically linked to "Goliath."[4]

Simon de Montfort, the Fifth Earl of Leicester

At some time between 1220 and 1231, before the expulsion of the Jews in 1290, the French count Simon de Montfort (a.k.a. Mountfort; Duke of Narbonne, 5th Earl of Leicester) began a twenty-year crusade against the Albigensians.[5] His son, also named Simon, had put his seal to a charter prohibiting Jews from living in Leicester. The younger Simon's aunt, Countess Margaret de Quincy, née de Beaumont,[6] widow of crusader Saher

---

[1] See Francis Douce, "Romeo and Juliet," in *Illustrations of Shakespeare, and of Ancient Manners, with Dissertations on the Clowns and Fools of Shakespeare, on the Collection of Popular Tales entitled Gesta Romanorum, and on the English Morris Dance* 1 (London, 1839), p. 436; Walter W. Skeat, "Alligator," *An Etymological Dictionary...*," p. 17. *Alligatus* is not in Cassell's classical Latin dictionary, but the verb *ligo -are,- avi,- atus*, "to bind, unite," is. *Cassell's Latin*, s.v. *legator*, p. 130.

[2] McQuain, *Coined by Shakespeare*, p. ix. The word was spelled "allegater" in the First Folio of 1623. It was not spelled "alligator" until 1699. McQuain, s.v. "alligator," pp. 6-7.

[3] Manly, "*Familia Goliae*," p. 201.

[4] Jessie Weston, *From Ritual to Romance* (Mineola NY: Dover 1997, first pub. 1914), pp. 91, n. 2; 183.

[5] Bryson and Movsesian, ch. 6.I, "The Death of Fin'amor: The Albigensian Crusade and its Aftermath," *Love and its Critics*, pp. 223, 227-230. When the Albigensians attacked while he was at Mass, Simon de Montfort finished his prayers before going to battle "in the name of the Trinity," killing 20,000 Albigensians. Gregory Johnson, "Simon de Montfort's Good Habit," http://www.traditioninaction.org/religious/h063rp.Montfort.html. For a brief history of Simon de Montfort, see "Who was Simon de Montfort?" Intriguing History, http://www.intriguing-history.com/simon-de-montfort/; "Simon de Montfort," The Simon de Montfort Society, http://www.simondemontfort.org/montforts-life.

[6] The name "Beaumont" is said to derive from old French "beau, bel" meaning fair, lovely and "mont," meaning hill. Last name: Beaumont," SurnameDB.com, copyright 1980-2017, http://www.surnamedb.com/Surname/Beaumont.

(Saer, Saier) de Quincy, the Earl of Winchester, had written to Robert Grosseteste (Grossetete), then Archdeacon of Leicester, offering to give the displaced Jews a place of refuge on her land. Grosseteste's letter to her, in Latin, "throws light on the charter" of Simon de Montfort, as to its dating (1220–1231), according to one author who saw the parallel with *Merchant* (IV, 1, 1970).[1] In his reply to her, Grosseteste supported with Scripture his conviction that these displaced Jews should not be killed.[2]

The name "Belmont" is in Shakespeare's assumed source, a story from the collection, *Il Pecorone.*[3] It was written ca. 1378 but not published until 1558.[4] The vowel sounds in "Shylock" mimic those in "Simon" de Mountfort, who, like Shylock, was an overtly religious man. If Shylock is Simon de Montfort, enemy of the Jews, then he is his own worst enemy.[5] The story in *Il Pecorone* thought to be closest to *The Merchant of Venice* is from the *Gesta Romanorum*, but these sorts of stories are well represented both in *Il Pecorone* and in the *Gesta*.

For example, in the *Gesta Romanorum*, there is a story about a man who pawned his body to a merchant and used the money to woo an emperor's daughter. He cannot make good on the bond, but is saved, nevertheless, by the princess, disguised as a knight, who informs the merchant in no uncertain

---

The Norman Beaumonts (Belmonts) came in 1066 from Normandy to live in Dorset and Gloucestershire. Margaret de Quincy was the daughter of Robert, Third Earl of Leicester (d. 1190). Justin Glenn, *The Washingtons: A Family History, 3: Royal Descents of the Presidential Branch* (El Dorado Hills, CA: Savas Publishing, 2015), p. 139-140. https://books.google.com/books?isbn=1940669286. *Janet and Robert Wolfe Genealogy.* http://www-personal.umich.edu/-bobwolfe/gen/person/gl6593.htm.

[1] James Thompson, "The Jews and the Jewry Wall," *Leicestershire Architectural Society* 4 (1878), pp. 48-51, 51, https://www.le.ac.uk/lahs/downloads/JewsJewryWPagesfromIVpartl-3.pdf (Also pub. in *Spencer's Illustrated Leicester Almanac* 9 (Leicester, 1898), pp. 60-64. https://books.google.com/books?id=FvVSAAAAYAAJ); *The Letters of Robert Grosseteste, Bishop of Lincoln,* transl. by F. A. C. Mantello and Joseph Goering (Toronto: University of Toronto Press, 2010), no. 5, pp. 65 et seq.

Oliver D. Harris points out that the "Jewry Wall" in Leicester may have once been the site of a Roman temple to the god Janus. Harris, "Jews, Jurat and the Jewry Wall: a Name in Context," Trans. *Leicestershire Archaeol. and Hist. Soc.* 82 (2008), pp. 113-133 (the name "Jewry Wall" may have come from "Jury Wall"), https://www.le.ac.uk/lahs/downloads/2008/2008%20(82)%20113-133%20Harris.pdf.

Shakespeare *may* have used the term "Duke" rather than "Doge" because he wanted to suggest the story of Simon de Montfort and the merciful Margaret Belmont. The Queen might have appreciated a story related to the Leicester family. The play calls Portia's late father a "cruel Duke." Kenji Yoshino, "The Lawyer of Belmont." (pp. 202, 206), Digital Commons, http://digitalcommons.law.yale.edu/yjlh/vol9/iss1/4/.

[2] Thompson, "The Jews and the Jewry Wall," p. 51.

[3] Robert Ornstein, "The Merchant of Venice" in *William Shakespeare's The Merchant of Venice*, new ed., ed. with intro. by Harold Bloom (New York: Bloom's Literary Criticisms, 2010), pp. 65-97, 67.

[4] *Barron's Book Notes, A Simplified Approach to Shakespeare: The Merchant of Venice*, ed. by Edward F. Nolan (Woodbury NY: Barron's Educational Services, 1971), pp. 4-11, p. 4.

[5] Cf. "Colors of Good and Evil" (fragment, 1597, about the time *Merchant* was written), *Spedding,* VII, no. 8, p. 86, HathiTrust, https://hdl.handle.net/2027/ucl.b3924335.

terms that the forfeiture does not give him the right to shed her lover's blood. The first English telling of this story is found in a long fourteenth-century poem, the *Cursor Mundi*, a history of the world in verse. In this version, a goldsmith who serves Queen Helena, the mother of the Roman Emperor Constantine, borrows money from a Jew and pledges to either repay it or give up a piece of his flesh in equal weight. The Jew may not enforce the promise, for the bond gave the merchant no right to shed blood.[1]

Another story which was a "direct source for a similar story in the *Gesta*" is a religious allegorical poem by the highly influential Bishop of Lincoln, Robert Grosseteste (1175–1253).[2] The story, *Chasteau d'Amour*, written in French, was incorporated into the *Cursor mundi*. Grosseteste transformed a heavenly court scene, in an allegory from a sermon by St. Bernard involving the Four Daughters of God, into a feudal romance, an important evolutionary step.[3] From the *Gesta Romanorum*, the allegory made its way into French morality plays.[4]

The best source of the *Cursor mundi* is said to be the Cotton Manuscript. Francis Bacon borrowed manuscripts from the library of Robert Cotton.[5] The "original owner" of this manuscript is thought to be William Cosyn.[6] It may mean absolutely nothing, but Portia referred to Bellario as her "cousin." A "cousin" in literary terms could refer to a version of a play which descended independently from an ur-text.[7] Perhaps Portia was hinting at a "Cosyn" connection.

A William Cosyn, mentioned in 1276, had a brother, Peter, who was a rich wool merchant. He had a son, William, who married a rich heiress by

[1] *Barron's Book Notes*, p. 4; H. Hupe, "On the Filiation and the Text of the MSS. of the Middle English Poem, 'Cursor Mundi,'" pp. 57-103, 62, in *Cursor Mundi (The cursur o the world). A Northumbrian poem of the XIVth century in four versions*, ed. by the Rev. Richard Morris[...], Early English Text Society, orig. series, 99, vol. 6, (London, 1874-93), http://scans.library.utoronto.ca/pdf/2/1/cursormundicupt600morruoft/cursormundicupt600morruoft_bw.pdf.

[2] Grosseteste was a friend of Simon de Montfort (1208-1265). "Simon of Montfort, Earl of Leicester," https://www.britannica.com/biography/Simon-de-Montfort-earl-of-Leicester.

[3] Hope Traver, *The Four Daughters of God, a Study of the Versions of this Allegory, with Special Reference to those in Latin, French, and English*, Bryn Mawr College Monographs, vol. VI (Bryn Mawr: n.p., 1907), pp. 1-195, p. 29. For a summary of the *Chasteau*, see pp. 30-31, HathiTrust, https://hdl.handle.net/2027/hvd.32044021642061; https://ia902704.us.archive.org/13/items/fourdaughtersgo02travgoog/fourdaughtersgo02travgoog.pdf; "Dr. Haenisch," "Inquiry into the Sources of the 'Cursor Mundi,'" in *Cursor mundi*, ed. by Robert Morris, p. 24. For Grosseteste, see "Robert Grosseteste," *Stanford Encyclopedia of Philosophy*, first published July 10, 2007; subst. rev. 3/8/2013. https://plato.stanford.edu/entries/grosseteste/.

[4] Traver, *The Four Daughters of God, a Study[...]*," pp. 39-40.

[5] Dr. Haenisch," "Inquiry into the Sources[...]," in *Cursor mundi*, p. 3; "On the Filiation and the Text[...]," in *Cursor mundi*, p. 63; Brian Vickers, ed., *The History of the Reign of King Henry VII and Selected Works*, (Cambridge: Cambridge University Press, 1998), pp. xiii-xiv, xxviii, 128 n, 221.

[6] H. Hupe, "Cursor Studies and Criticism on the Dialects of its MSS," in *Cursor mundi*, ed. by Robert Morris, pp. 122-123.

[7] Arthur Freeman gives as examples of "cousin" used this way several works "related to" Shakespeare's *Henry IV*. Arthur Freeman, "The Tapster Manuscript: an Analogue of Shakespeare's *Henry the Fourth Part One*," *English Manuscript Studies 1100-1700*, 6, ed. by Peter Beal and Jeremy Griffiths (1997): 93-105, p. 102.

whom he had two sons, Peter and Thomas. Peter had a son, William, who is thought to be "the" William Cosyn who was the owner of the Cotton MSS. There are certain parallels with the play *Merchant*. The merchant in *Merchant* was named Antonio. Bacon and William Cosyn each had a brother named Anthony. William's brother was a rich merchant. William Cosyn married a rich heiress; Portia was a rich heiress who called Bellario her cousin.[1]

There are other stories which may have served as background material for *Merchant*, such as the story of Abraham and Theodore, "The Merchant's Surety," and the legend of Theophilus. This last story has the traditional elements of the Virgin Mary as *Advocata* tricking the Devil. In one version, legal procedure is followed so closely that it is said to bear comparison to Bracton. "Shakespeare's story of a Jewish contract ultimately renegotiated by a chast (Christian) female lawyer deserves genuine consideration as a descendant of the legend of Theophilus."[2]

Another possible source of the play is the untranslated Italian "Story of Giannetto" ("Little John"). In that story, the female lead has just finished her studies at Bologna and is a doctor of laws.[3] Hmm....

In sum, the writer of *Merchant* appears to have been very well read and a student of history. The stories mentioned here existed in the popular culture, but the *Processus* versions would hold special interest for lawyers. I do not think Shakespeare relied on just one or two sources. He had many stories percolating in his brain, and some were not yet translated into English or readily accessible.[4]

---

[1] Hupe, p. 124.

[2] Adrienne Williams Boyarin, *Miracles of the Virgin in Medieval England: Law and Jewishness in Marian Legends* (Cambridge: D. S. Brewer 2010), pp. 29-31, 96-102, 100 n. 107. Bracton is translated at The Ames Foundation, Online Edition of Bracton's *De legibus et consuetudinibus Angliae*, copyright 1999-2009, http://www.law.harvard.edu/programs/ames_foundation/bracton.html; http://hlsl.law.harvard.edu/bracton/index.htm.

[3] William Reynolds, "intro.," *The Merchant of Venice*, pp. 2-8, 29. Reynolds also relates "The Famous History of Fryer Bacon," in which the devil secures a bond for the forfeit of a man's soul, but is cheated by a clergyman (Reynolds, p. 32). A source for the Jessica elopement plot may have been a 1470 story by Massucio di Salerno, also not translated from the Italian. (Reynolds, p. 12). Note: While Reynolds argues Shakespeare did not have great knowledge of the law, this is not the modern view.

[4] "Sources for Merchant" are listed at British Library, *Shakespeare Quartos, the Merchant of Venice* (2016), http://www.bl.uk/treasures/shakespeare/merchant.html.

Chapter Four: Two *Mentes* in One

Language Doubling (i.e., Saying Things Twice)

Up to the fifteenth century, the law was written in Law French, or, as Mark Edwin Andrews put it, a mixture of "the Latin of Julius Caesar, the French of William the Conqueror, and the English of Geoffrey Chaucer."[1] After the "1362 Statute, Pleading" required English to be spoken in the courts, the lawyers, loathe to abandon tradition, did not drop the Latinate usage of words that came from Latin, but merely tagged on the English. There are many examples of "legal doubling" still in use today, such as "he deposes and says." The Anglo-Saxons were themselves prone to doubling. For example, "to have and to hold" is pure Anglo-Saxon. Doubling is redundant and frowned upon today, but long ago, repeating things in Anglo-Saxon would have helped those who did not understand the Norman French know what was going on in court.[2]

In "Shakespeare and the Norman Conquest," George Watson discussed Shakespeare's habit of saying things twice, first in the Norman/Latin-derived English words of the upper class, and then again in common Anglo-Saxon. Said Watson, "English is the only great European language firmly and extensively based on a system of double derivation" (Germanic and

---

[1] MEA, p. 17.

[2] "Doublet," Bryan Garner, ed., *Garner's Dictionary of Legal Usage*, 3d ed. (New York: Oxford University Press, 2011). https://books.google.com. For examples of doubling (word pairings), see Garner, secs. 2.42 to 2.53. For further explanation of Anglo-American's tri-language roots, see Peter Butt, *Modern Legal Drafting*, 3d ed. (Cambridge: Cambridge University Press, 2013), secs. 2.34 to 2.42, *https://books.google.ca/books?isbn=1107607671.*

Romance).[1] Shakespeare was the only Elizabethan dramatist to write an entire scene in a foreign language, in *Henry V*. He even invented a language in *All's Well that Ends Well* (Act IV).[2] By the end of a scene, everyone in the audience understood the action. Shakespeare was a teacher. Watson called him a "conscious theorist of language," a "conscious linguist."[3] Nineteenth-century German Shakespeare scholar Karl Elze called "him" a "perfect master" of both Italian and Latin.[4]

When speaking of the making of laws and proclamations in his '*Example of a Treatise on Universal Justice or the Fountains of Equity, by Aphorisms,*' Francis Bacon said, "Everything should be more fully explained, and pointed out, as it were with the finger, to the capacity of the people."[5] And yet, Bacon could be intentionally obscure, observed Spedding. Pseudonyms and ambiguity are two different ways of adding a layer of protection from censorship or derision at exposure to new ideas to one's work.[6] Nicholas Copernicus (1473–1543) watered down his revolutionary new theory about the earth revolving around the sun in his book, *de revolutionibus orbium coelestrium*. Even then, he did not publish it until he was dying.[7] Galileo hid his discovery of the moons of Venus in an acrostic. In his Will, Bacon directed his executor,

---

[1] George Watson, "Shakespeare and the Norman Conquest: English in the Elizabethan Theatre." *VQR, Virginia Quarterly Review* 66, no. 4, (Autumn, 1990; online, Dec. 12, 2003), http://www.vqronline.org/essay/shakespeare-and-norman-conquest-english-elizabethan-theatre, pp. I-V, "II."

[2] Watson, p. 1.

[3] Watson, p. 4. For Bacon on language, see, e.g., the (transl.) *De Augmentis*, vi, *Spedding*, IV, pp. 438-444, HathiTrust, https://hdl.handle.net/2027/ucl.31175002901968.

More "pleonasms" (language doublings) include: "so, and in such manner," "many a time and oft" (*Merchant* I, 3), "the inaudible and noiseless foot of time," "that old and antique song we heard last night," and "I see report is fabulous and false." Charles Cowden Clarke and Mary Cowden Clarke, *The Shakespeare Key, Unlocking the Treasures of his Style...*, (London, 1879), pp. 610-612 https://books.google.ca/books?id=2wx66C5PejwC. To these could be added, "melt, thaw, and resolve itself into a dew" (*Hamlet*).

John Crowe Ransom notes that a powerful linguistic tension is created when Latinate words share the same space with Anglo-Saxon words. John Crowe Ransom, "On Shakespeare's Language," *Sewanee Review* 55 (1947), pp. 181-198, JSTOR, http://www.jstor.org/stable/27537724?seq=1#page_scan_tab_contents, as noted in Robert Bechtold Heilman, *This Great Stage Image and Structure in King Lear*, (n.p.: University of Washington Press, 1963), p. 5. https://archive.org/stream/thisgreatstageim001480mbp/thisgreatstageim001480mbp_djvu.txt.

[4] Karl Elze, *Essays on Shakespeare*, trans. L. Dora Schmitz (London, 1874), ch. 7, "The Supposed Travels of Shakespeare," pp. 254-316, 289.

[5] Aphorism 68, '*Example of a Treatise on Universal Justice,*' *De Augmentis*, viii, trans., in *Spedding*, V, pp. 88-110, 102-103, HathiTrust, https://hdl.handle.net/2027/ucl.b3618241, as discussed by Coquillette, FB, p. 252.

[6] See Robert Leslie Ellis, *Spedding*, I (1872 ed.), preface, *Novum Organum*, iii, pp. 85-86, 110, 112-113, HathiTrust, https://hdl.handle.net/2027/hvd.32044011598257.

[7] Michael White, *The Pope and the Heretic* (New York: William Morrow, 2002), pp. 58-62.

William Rawley, not to publish his yet-unpublished writings until some years after his death, and only in foreign countries.

Coined Words

Bacon was an inventor of words, as was "Shakespeare."[1] Coriolanus, says, "So shall my lungs coin words till their decay" (*Coriolanus*, III, 1, 1826). According to Jeffrey McQuain and Stanley Malless, the writings attributed to Shakespeare introduced approximately 1,500 to 1,700 invented words to the English language.[2] This count includes words already used as one part of speech which he changed into another, such as nouns he changed into verbs. One word first used in *Merchant* is "shudd'ring," as in "shudd'ring fear and green-eyed jealousy" (III, 2, 110), from an old German word, *skutten*, "to shake."[3] It has a certain "ring" to it (Forgive me, but the theme is Bellario). Legal words Shakespeare is credited with inventing include "petition," "premeditated," "negotiate," "compromise," "consanguineous," "circumstantial," "premeditated," "baseless," "questioning," "unmitigated," and "the accused" (from *causa*).[4]

One timely word coined by Shakespeare is "climature," from climate and temperature.[5] He is thought to have been the first to use the word "torture," which dates from 1540, as a verb. He used "torture" more than thirty times, both as a noun and as a verb.[6] Bacon also wrote about torture; specifically, about men remaining strong under torture.[7]

---

[1] Mrs. Henry [Constance] Pott, ed., *Francis Bacon and Shakespeare, The Promus …* ; the *Promus* webpage, with links, http://www.sirbacon.org/links/notebook.html; Sir Edward Durning Lawrence, "[Francis] Bacon and the English Language" in *The Shakespeare Myth* (London: Gay & Hancock, 1912), pp. 27-30. http://www.sirbacon.org/links/BaconEnglishLanguage.htm; HathiTrust, http://hdl.handle.net/2027/mdp.39015030034436?urlappend=%3Bseq=29, pp. 27-30; George Stronach, editor, "Shakespeare, Bacon, and Dr. Murray," *The Academy and Literature*, 64, 25 April 1903, pp. 421-422, https://books.google.com/books?id=xvXQ3PTqthYC. Stronach gives many examples of words first used by Bacon that Dr. Murray omitted. While Murray consulted the *Shakespeare Concordance*, Stronach doubts that he consulted Spedding, especially as to Bacon's correspondence.

[2] "Words Shakespeare Invented," Shakespeare Online. 20 Aug. 2000. Copyright 1999-2014 by Amanda Mabillard, http://www.shakespeare-online.com/biography/wordsinvented.html; Jeffrey McQuain and Stanley Malless, intro., *Coined by Shakespeare, Words and Meanings First Penned by the Bard*, p. viii.

[3] McQuain, p. 210.

[4] McQuain, p. 177; 107; 153; 33; 31-32; 177-178; 16; 185-186; 234-235; 4.

[5] Sister Miriam Joseph, *Shakespeare's Use of the Arts of Language*, p. 51.

[6] McQuain, pp. 222-223.

[7] See ch. 1, '*De Augmentis*,' trans., *Spedding*, IV, pp. 374-375. On Bacon's "coining" words, see *Spedding*, IV, pp. 344, 440, HathiTrust, https://hdl.handle.net/2027/ucl.b000353568.

On Bacon and torture in the case of Peacock, see *Spedding*, XIV, p. 78ff, HathiTrust, https://hdl.handle.net/2027/ucl.31175012007947.

It is difficult to be certain, of course, about the first recorded instance of any word's use. For example, the word "assassination" was thought to have been used first in *Macbeth* in 1605. However, my editor found that Thomas Smith, then an English ambassador to France, used the word in a letter to "Dr. Wilson" in 1571. This was five years before Bacon was in France as a young secretary to the English ambassador Amyas Paulet (from 1576 to 1579[1]). In addition, Matthew Suttcliffe, an English clergyman, used "to assassinate" in 1600, five years before *Macbeth*, in *A Briefe Replie to a Certaine Odious and Slanderous Libel, Lately Published by a Seditious Jesuite*.[2]

The author of the works of Shakespeare frequently "coined" new words from Latin words.[3] Bacon exhibits this trait in his literary notebook, the *Promus*, to be discussed shortly.

In an undated letter, purportedly from Gray's Inn member Henry Gosnold to Francis Bacon's brother Anthony Bacon, sent February 12, 1594, "Gosnold" reports that in Francis Bacon's first court speech against Lord Coke, he "spangled his speech" with unusual words and "presumed somewhat" on the judges' "capacities." The letter continued, "All is as well as words can make it, and if it please her Majesty to add deeds, *the Bacon* may be too hard for *the Cook*." Bowen clearly attributed these last sentiments to Bacon.[4]

The *Promus*; Spanish Proverbs

Edwin J. Des Moineaux described Bacon's *Promus* as his notebook of "1560 phrases, poetical expressions, quotations, and proverbs from various languages for use in literary composition" which he used in his writings, many of which have parallels in the works of Shakespeare."[5] Mrs. Henry Pott

---

[1] Brian Vickers, "Principle Events in Bacon's Life," *The History of the Reign of King Henry VII*, p. xxxvi.

[2] McQuain, p. xi (disclaimer); *assassination*, pp. 8-9, *but see* "Letter from Sir Thomas Smith to Dr. Wilson," April 11, 1572, British History Online, http://www.british-history-ac.uk/cal-state-papers-foreign/vol17/pp438-490, no. 460; "Assassination," Wikipedia, nn. 6, 7.

[3] See, e.g., McQuain, beginning with the first entry, "abstemious," p. 3.

[4] *Spedding*, VIII, pp. 267-268, HathiTrust, https://hdl.handle.net/2027/ucl.31175012007830; Bowen, *Lion*, ch. 7, p. 79. Henry Gosnold in 1596 became Chief Justice of Munster. *John Nichols's The Progresses and Public Processions of Queen Elizabeth I, a New Ed. of the Early Modern Sources*, vol. I (1579-1595), ed. by Elizabeth Goldring (Oxford: Oxford University Press, 2014), p. 599. https://books.google.com/books?isbn=0199551405.

[5] Edwin G. Des Moineaux, *Manuscript Said to be Handwriting of William Shakespeare Identified as Penmanship of Another Person. Mystery of "Sir Thomas More Document Unravelled, an Entirely New Phase of the Baconian-Shakespeare Controversy* (Los Angeles: printed for the author by Phillips Printing, 1924), pp. 1-31, 28.

(Constance), founder of the Francis Bacon Society, has studied the *Promus* and published her findings.[1]

Is there anything in *Merchant* that we find in Bacon's *Promus*? To begin with, Portia says to Shylock, "To offend and judge, are distinct offenses/And of opposed natures" (II, 9, 1191-92). In the *Promus*, we find Bacon's: *Chi offende maj perdona* ("Spanish and English Proverbs," no. 602, "He who offends never pardons"; p. 239). A famous Italian jurist, Baldus de Ubaldis (1327–1400),[2] once said, "Judges may err; justice never errs."[3]

Turning to Mrs. Pott's work, her item no. 625 is a Spanish proverb, "Por mejoria mi casa dexaria ("I will leave my house for a better").[4] This is what Launcelot Gobbo dramatizes, and, figuratively, what we might say Launcelot Andrewes has done in giving up his Catholic faith to become a Protestant theologian. In Mrs. Pott's work, we find another Spanish proverb, *El mozo por no saber y el viego por no poder dexan las cosas pierder* ("The boy from want of knowledge, and the old man from want of power, let things go to ruin"). With Launcelot and Old Gobbo, we do have a boy and a powerless old man. The proverb meant something to Bacon, or else he would not have written it down in his *Promus*.

The Earl of Essex, Robert Devereux, was the driving force behind Dr. Roderigo Lopez's prosecution for treason. Bacon may have felt he was powerless to persuade the hot-headed younger Essex to let Lopez be. Since Sidney Lee's 1888 essay, many have believed the prosecution and execution of Lopez inspired the character of Shylock.[5]

If Bacon were perusing his collection of Spanish proverbs while, let us say, writing *Merchant*, he would also have found *El lobo et la vulpeja a son todos d'una conseja* ("The wolf and the vulture are both of one mind").[6] He would also have found *Quien al ciel escupe a la cara se le vuelve* ("He who spits at heaven, it returns in his own face").[7] Compare to the Prince of Morocco's

---

[1] "The *promus* of formularies and elegancies (being private notes, circ. 1594, hitherto unpublished) by Francis Bacon, illustrated and elucidated by passages from Shakespeare," by Mrs. Henry [Constance] Pott, with preface by E. A. Abbott (London, 1883), HathiTrust, https://hdl.handle.net/2027/hvd.32044086726981. For a video presentation on Constance Pott's work, see "Mrs. Constance Pott," videos, The Francis Bacon Society, http://francisbaconsociety.co.uk/the-society/videos/; https://www.youtube.com/watch?v=mlIMJ8psP_Q. See her essay reprinted at http://www.sirbacon.org/links/pott.html.

[2] "Kenneth Pennington, "Baldus de Ubaldis," http://legalhistorysources.com/Canon%20Law/BALDBIO.html.

[3] E. Kantorowicz, *The King's Two Bodies*, p. 142.

[4] Mrs. Henry [Constance] Pott, *The Promus*, p. 242.

[5] "Who was the Real Shylock?" The National Library of Israel, n.d., http://web.nli.org.il/sites/NLI/English/library/reading_corner/Pages/Shylock.aspx.

[6] Pott, *The Promus*, p. 239.

[7] Pott, p. 241.

"The watery kingdom whose ambitious head/Spits in the face of heaven, is no bar." *Merchant*, II, 7, 1030-31. A Spanish proverb Mrs. Pott found in *Merchant*, which is not in the *Promus*, is *De hambre poco vir morer, di mucho comer cien mil.* "Of hunger I have seen few die; of surfeits, a hundred thousand." This sentiment is expressed in "They are as sick that surfeit with too much, as they that starve with nothing." *Merchant* I, 2, 199–200 (Nerissa).[1] A *HathiTrust* search of Mrs. Pott's work on the *Promus* brought up sixty-three references to *The Merchant of Venice*. Barry R. Clarke discusses a number of them, as well as other *Promus* findings.[2]

Saying he did not consider it important, Spedding did not give us the full fifty-page text of Bacon's *Promus*, only extracts.[3] Was he trying to protect Bacon's secrets?

Counter-Argument

In *Shakespeare Beyond Doubt, Evidence, Argument, Controversy*, Paul Edmonson and Stanley Wells cursorily dismiss Mrs. Pott's 628-page work. "One example will suffice," they say. They simply ignore the Spanish proverbs.[4] They do note instances where Bacon used material in the *Promus* in "his own" writings, including the Ascension Day Device which Bacon wrote for Essex to present before the Queen, November 1595, thus conceding it was Bacon who ghost-wrote that dramatic work.[5] It is true that Bacon included some proverbs or epigrams in common usage, but he tended to see them as raw material which he improved.[6]

"Promus" rhymes with "Momus," the Roman god of satire.[7] While *promus* could stand for "storehouse" or "larder," its first meaning was "a butler, cellarman who brought up provisions from the cellar (also *cellarius*).[8] The *promus* assisted the "condus," or steward, butler. However, since these were often the same person, the Romans came to call such a person the *promus*

---

[1] Pott, appendix C, pp. 526-527. As to Bacon's prevalent use of Spanish proverbs, see Pott, intro., pp. 6, 16, 17, 26, 28, 29, and 84, HathiTrust, https://hdl.handle.net/2027/hvd.32044086726981.

[2] Barry R. Clarke, *The Shakespeare Puzzle, a Non-Esoteric Baconian Theory,*" (2010) ch. 8, "Verbal Parallels," pp. 183-193, 184 ("All that glisters is not gold."), 186 (Charon), 191 ("plain set gem"). http://barryispuzzled.com/shakpuzz.pdf. On Aristophanes, see infra, ch. 3.

[3] Preface, *Spedding*, VII, pp. 187, pp. 197-211.

[4] Paul Edmonson and Stanley Wells, *Shakespeare Beyond Doubt, Evidence, Argument, Controversy* (Cambridge: Cambridge University Press 2013), pp. 25-27.

[5] Edmonson, p. 27.

[6] Mrs. Henry Pott, *The Promus*, p. 21.

[7] In *Spedding*, V, see pp. 17-18, 122, 645 (satire) and pp. 59, 621, 645 (Momus).

[8] *Promus, Cassell's Latin*, p. 181; "butler," p. 255.

condus.[1] Spedding suggested the term "storehouse," but for Bacon to call his notebook the *Promus* could also be seen as a personification.

Similarly, *Palladis Tamia* by Francis Meres is sometimes translated *Wit's Treasury*, but *tamia* is Greek for housekeeper. In Elizabethan times, the meaning of "housekeeper" was expanded to include the landlord or owner of a theatrical house.[2]

Hermann Sinsheimer has called *The Merchant of Venice* "the most ingenious satire on justice and courts of law in the literature of the world."[3] In Bacon's *De Augmentis,* book 7, he makes four references to "serious satires" in the same context in which he is discussing the word "promus."[4]

Writing to King James in Latin, Bacon explains *promus majus quam condus* ("The promus is greater than the condus). There are two appetites in people, one to "preserve or continue," and one to "multiply or propagate," he says. The word *promus* in the context of *active* (with a pun on acting, perhaps) pursuits done for the benefit of the self, not for the common good, fulfilling a human desire for novelty, variety, and for leaving works to posterity.[5]

Bacon deliberately distinguished *promus* from *condus.* The Latin verb *promo* means "to bring out, disclose, express," while the meanings of *condo* include "to compose or write a literary work."[6] Right under King James's nose, under the guise of "There goes Bacon being obscure again" — in Latin, no less — could he have made his meaning plainer? He was writing literary works for his own purposes, not necessarily for the benefit of the public good. As was his fashion, Bacon used the Latin words *promus* and *condus* in a sense close to their original meanings.[7]

In the cast list for *Merchant,* the character "Salerio" is identified as a "friend or messenger." *Sal* is Latin for "salt,"[8] in French, *sel.* "Bellario" rhymes

---

[1] Anthony Rich, *The Illustrated Companion to the Latin Dictionary and Greek Lexicon* ...(London 1849), pp. 196, 529, citing Plautus's *Pseud.* ii.2.14. https://books.google.com/books/.../The_Illustrated_Companion_to_the_Latin_D.html?id...

[2] McQuain, intro., p. ix.

[3] H. Sinsheimer, *Shylock,* p. 139.

[4] *De Augmentis,* vii, transl. by Francis Headlam, *Spedding,* V, p. 17-18, 122, and 645.

[5] *De Augmentis,* vii, *Spedding,* V, ch. 2, pp. 10-11. On the *Promus,* see also "Promus new.txt" webpage, http://www.sirbacon.org/links/notebook.html and Martin Pares, "Parallelisms and the Promus," from the Francis Bacon Society journal, Baconiana 1963, http://www.sirbacon.org/mp.html. On Bacon and the Ciceronian choice between the *vita activa* and *vita contemplativa,* see Vickers, intro., *Francis Bacon,* pp. xxvii to xxviii.

[6] *Cassell's Latin,* pp. 46 (*condo*), 181 (*promo*).

[7] *An Anthology of English Literature,* ed. by Roger Philip McCutcheon and William Harvey Vann (New York: Henry Holt, 1936), p. 196. Prof. Coquillette has observed the same. Part of this could be due to the translation, but a translator does have to come up with a meaning that makes sense.

[8] Salt was once used as money. The word "salary" comes from "sal." See "A Brief History of Salt," *TIME,* May 15, 1982. http://content.time.com/time/magazine/article/0,9171,925341,00.html.

with *cellario* and Salario. In *Henry IV, Part I* (II, 4, 1024), the "puny drawer" who would be bringing up the beer from the inn's cellar is named — imagine that! Francis![1] *Cel* means "seal," the insignia of the chancellor.[2] The sound of "cellar" might also suggest "chancellor." Bacon, the son of a chancellor, would one day become one himself.

Bacon notes in his *Promus*, "*vita salillum*," "life is a little salt cellar." Erasmus in his *Adagia* quoted Plautus's expression "*salillum animae*," or "little salt cellar of life."[3] Bassanio says he has a wife he loves more than life itself (IV, 1, 2228–29). On "salt," note Bacon's preface his *Apophthegms New and Old* (1625).[4] Bacon, for recreation during his periods of illness, collected short, pithy sayings called apophthegms (or apothegms), useful for enlivening one's speech, as had been advocated by the Roman orator Cicero, who called them *salinas*, salt pits, good for sprinkling about.[5] Plautus actually wrote about *aequitas*, or equity, before Cicero did.[6]

It is interesting, also, that the word "prompt," with its theatrical connotations, seems to come from the same root as *promus*. *Promo, promere* meant "to bring out, produce, bring forward, disclose," with the participle *promptus, -a -um*: "ready, at hand, easy, visible, apparent; of persons, prepared, resolute, prompt."[7]

In *The Merchant of Venice*, in true Aristophanean fashion, "Salerio" (*cellario*) gives himself away as a person of inferior rank to the other two "gentleman attendants," Salarino and Salanio, by his manner of speech.[8]

Perhaps I am easily fascinated, but it has long bemused me that the word "act" could refer both to a theatrical act and a legislative act, a law. Both law

---

[1] See *Edwin Bormann, sec.8.9.* "*Mutual Hints at Each Other, B, Shakespeare Hints at Bacon,*" *The Shakespeare Secret*, transl. by Harry Brett (London, 1895), pp. 234-236, p. 236, HathiTrust, http://hdl.handle.net/2027/ucl.b4500360.

[2] Adrienne Williams Boyarin, *Miracles of the Virgin in Medieval England: Law and Jewishness in Marian Legends* (Cambridge: D. S. Brewer 2010), ch. 3, pp. 96-100 (recounting how in the medieval story of Theophilus, the seal ("cel") on the charter (the devil's contract with Theophilus for his soul), is one of the elements with which the devil is "comically over-concerned." Yes, the contract is "legal," the devil is assured, but then the Virgin Mary, attorney-at-law, finds an exception. Sound familiar?).

[3] See Pott, *The Promus*, pp. 194-195.

[4] *Spedding*, VII, p. 123, HathiTrust, https://hdl.handle.net/2027/ucl.b3924335.

[5] Thomas Tennison, *Baconiana* p. 91, Early English Books Online: Text Creation Partnership, University of Oxford, copyright 2018, http://tei.it.ox.ac.uk/tcp/Texts-HTML/free/A28/A28024.html.

[6] Israel B. Greene and Sara Mann Greene, "Fundamentals for Equity Studies...Papers presented at the Second International Conference on Aequitas and Equity, the Faculty of Law, The Hebrew University of Jerusalem, May, 1993," (Jerusalem: Hebrew University of Jerusalem 1997), pp. 26, 31; A. Arthur Schiller, *Roman Law, Mechanisms of Development* (The Hague: Mouton Publishers, 1978), p. 555.

[7] *Cassell's Latin*, pp. 78, 181.

[8] W. Rolfe, *Shakespeare's Comedy of The Merchant of Venice*, p. 167; *Merchant*, III, 3, 214).

---

and theatre are representational. In classical Latin (200 B.C. to A.D. 100), the verb *actio* meant "to be busy, in law court or theatre." Similarly, the English words "statue" (L. *statua*) and "statute" (L *statutum*) both come from Latin verb *statuo*, "to cause to stand." *Actio* in classical Latin was: "an action, doing; with *gratianum*, the giving of thanks; the action of a magistrate, a proposal; in the theatre, a plot; at law, an action or the bringing of it or right to bring it; or a legal formula or speech on an indictment."[1] In the ninth century, *Actio* was used to refer to the "canon" or unchangeable portion of the Mass. At least once, it was used to refer to a play.[2] Another literary word with a legal past is "narrator." A "narrator" was the name for a pleader in the civil law in the latter part of the reign of King Henry III.[3]

---

[1] *Cassell's Latin* (1963), p. 4, 212; "statue, statute," *Webster's*, p. 973.

[2] E. K. Chambers, *The Medieval Stage*, vol. 2, p. 105, 105 n. 6(discussing "nomenclature," including the origins of the words "mystery" — which Chambers says probably derived from *ministerium* (similar to the way in which *métier* in English became "mystery," denoting the "function of the craft guilds" — and "miracle," as names for religious plays, pp. 104-105).

[3] Fabian Philips, [Latin title omitted]...*A Vindication of the Government of the Kingdom of England under our Kings and Monarchs[...]* (London, 1686), Early English Books Online: Text Creation Partnership (waiving copyright), http://name.umdl.umich.edu/A54686.0001.001. This work early on mentions "hintsham" and "Cuffs of the Dark" on p. 288. It may warrant a closer reading "between the lines."

CHAPTER FIVE: A GOOD PSEUDONYM IS HARD TO PROVE

We know that Bacon had a close relationship with Queen Elizabeth, as did the Earl of Essex. In fact, she may have been their mother, perhaps secretly married to Robert Dudley, Earl of Leicester, whose wife Amy Robsart died in 1560.[1]

Dudley, the Queen, and Francis Bacon had all loved the theatre.

In ancient Rome, Herodes Atticus (to be distinguished from Cicero's friend Pomponius Atticus[2]) had built a theatre called the "Herodeum" to commemorate the death of his wife. It is still standing. In Italy, the famous Renaissance architect Andrea di Pietro della Gondola, who took the humanist name "Palladio," had built the Teatro Olimpico, the first permanent theatre in Renaissance Italy.[3] England had had no permanent theatre until Richard Burbage built his *Theatre* in London, beginning construction in 1576.[4] Dudley

---

[1] As to evidence of Bacon's royal birth, see Amelie Deventer von Kunow, *Francis Bacon, Last of the Tudors*, trans. Willard Parker, President, Francis Bacon Society of America (New York: Francis Bacon Society of America, 1924), 124 pp. http://www.sirbacon.org/vonkunow.html; "Francis Bacon and his Nemesis Edward Coke," from ch. 11, "The Last of the Tudors," in Alfred Dodd, *Francis Bacon's Personal Life Story*, vol. I (London: Rider, 1949), http://www.sirbacon.org/cokeandbacon.htm; "Bacon's Royal Parentage." References prepared by Frances Carr and Lawrence Gerald. See also http://www.sirbacon.org/links/parentage.htm.

[2] Bacon mentioned Cicero's letters to Titus Pomponius Atticus, the finding of which by Petrarch is said to have begun the Italian Renaissance, on four occasions in Book 8 of his *De Augmentis, Spedding*, V, pp. 31-33, 56, 69-70, HathiTrust, https://hdl.handle.net/2027/hvd.32044069750222.

[3] Teatro Olimpico Vicenza, Vicenza and the Palladian Villas, http://www.teatrolimpicovicenza.it/en/; Mary Richardson, "Andrea Palladio," *Encyclopedia Britannica*, copyright 2018, https://www.britannica.com/biography/Andrea-Palladio.

[4] Leslie MacIntyre, "The Theatre," via *London Remembers, Atlas Obscura*, 2018, http://www.atlasobscura.com/places/the-theatre.

(1531–1588) was a supporter of the arts, "midwife" of Oxford University Press,"[1] and patron (i.e., protector) of his own theatre company, the Earl of Leicester's Servants.[2]

> With the architect's name "Gondola," as association of ships with architecture and theatre is established. This would lend support to Richard Roe's theory that a villa built by Palladio corresponds geographically to Portia's villa, Belmont.[3] The date of the capture of the Spanish ship *San Andreas* in Cadiz, of which Londoners were aware by July 30, 1596, has been used for dating the play no earlier than 1596.[4] One might suspect, though, that the playwright, who could have chosen the name of any ship, might have had a special reason for choosing one called the *Andreas*.

> The other boundary for determining the play's composition date is Francis Meres' *Palladis Tamia*, entered in the Stationer's Registry in 1598, in which he names *Merchant* as one of Shakespeare's.[5] By continuing to associate ships with architecture, one might also see an allusion to the Cathedral of St. Andrew which was falling into ruin from 1559 on, with the central tower collapsing by the late 1500s,[6] as a symbol for the decline of Catholicism. If so, the "sandy hour-glass" in *Merchant*, I, 1, 27 may be an allusion to the sermons of Reformation preachers like Launcelot Andrews. To control the length of the sermons, they might be timed by a sand-glass. A "merry-Andrew" was also a name for a clown.

Chez sphere or *eschec esperer*

I am going to propose a possible explanation for the pseudonym "Shakespeare" for Francis Bacon that I have not seen before, but it makes sense to me: *Eschec esperer*, or possibly, *chez sphere*, in French. It might be loosely translated "putting one's hope in the sovereign" or, possibly, "king of the world." It is at least worth exploring.

---

[1] Dr. Martin Maw, "Sir Robert Dudley, Midwife of Oxford University Press," Oxford University Press Blog, June 24, 2012. https://blog.oup.com/2012/06/sir-robert-dudley-midwife-of-oxford-university-press/.

[2] Ralph Wewirtzer, *A Brief Dramatic Chronology of Actors, etc., on the London Stage...*, new ed., with appendix (London, 1817), p. 2; Michael Shapiro, "Patronage and the companies of boy actors," in *Shakespeare and Theatrical Patronage in Early Modern England*, edited by Paul Whitfield White and Suzanne R. Westfall (Cambridge: Cambridge University Press, 2006), pp. 272-295, 281; Richard Dutton, ch. 2, "Beginnings," *William Shakespeare: A Literary Life* (London: Palgrave, 1989), pp. 17-36, 23.

[3] Richard Roe, *The Shakespeare Guide to Italy, Retracing the Bard's Unknown Travels* (Harper Collins: New York, 2011), p. 5, n. 25.

[4] Stanley Wells, "The Canon and Chronology of Shakespeare's Plays," in *William Shakespeare: A Textual Companion*, pp. 69-145, 119.

[5] G. Gregory Smith, ed., *Elizabethan Critical Essays*, 1904 (copyright 1993-2015), http://www.bartleby.com/359/31.html; Francis Meres, *Palladis tamia, Wits treasury being the second part of Wits commonwealth. By Francis Meres Maister of Artes of both universities* (London, 1598): Early English Books Online: Text Creation Partnership, http://name.umdl.umich.edu/A68463.0001.001.

[6] See Campbell Brown and Steven Wiggins, ch. 2, *St. Andrews and Fife Walks* (Edinburgh: Black and White Publishing, 1992).

In Middle French *eschec* (Old French *esches*), meaning "king," is the root of "exchequer."[1] In Medieval Latin, the word for a chessboard was *scaccorum*.[2] The table upon which the English court of Exchequer kept accounts was called the *scaccorum*. In modern French, *eschecs* means "chess" and *eschec* means to "check, defeat (in chess, *faire eschec*)."[3] Additionally, "Shake" comes from the Old English *scacan, scoc, scacen*, which once had a poetical usage of "to go, pass, move, journey; to flee, depart, shake, quiver, vibrate."[4]

Chess is an example of a "divided game", *joc partit*, in which two are opposed, from which the legal words "jeopardy" and "party" derive.[5] *Jocus partitus* (jeopardy) was a chess term meaning a "set problem."[6] *Joc partit* also referred to a question-and-answer game, played since ancient times, which served to store up a vast quantity of useful knowledge in verse form.[7] The troubadours sang question-and-answer songs.[8] Shakespeare portrays a game of chess in his last play, *The Tempest* (V, 1, 2216).[9]

A globe, or orb, was one of the Queen's symbolic images.[10] "Speare" sounds a lot like "sphere," from Old French *espere*, Latin *sphaera*, and Greek *sphaira* (sphere, ball).

---

[1] "The name for the Court of Exchequer was said to have derived from the "chequered cloth, resembling a chess-board, which anciently covered the table there," on which the king's accounts were tallied and the sums "scored and marked with counters." 3 *Bl. Comm.* 44; *Black's LD*, p. 506; see also "Check, Chequer," *The Oxford Universal Dictionary* (1955), pp. 297-298.

[2] Bill Wall, "The Etymology of Chess" (March 24, 2015), http://www.chessmaniac.com/the-etymology-of-chess/.

[3] *Cassell's French and English Dictionary*, edited by J. H. Douglas (New York: Collier Books, p.b., 1986), s.v. *Echecs, echec*, and *check*, pp. 125, 375.

[4] *The Oxford Universal Dictionary*, 3d. ed., (1955), s.v. "shake," pp. 1861-1862.

[5] *Black's LD*, p. 749. *Iocus partita* became *juparte* or *jupartye*. "Anglo-Norman Words," Oct. 23, 2014. http://anglonormandictionary.blogspot.com/2014/10/word-of-month-anglo-norman-chess.html#uds-search-results; Walter Wm. Skeat, ed., *The Student's Chaucer: Being a Complete Edition of His Works* (New York, 1891), glossarial index, s.v. "jupartye" p. 59. *Iocus* meant "joke" or "jest" in Latin. The "i" later became a "j." Latin had no "j."

[6] In old English law practice, *jocus partitus* was an "allowed gamble upon the results of a suit." Bracton analogized the agreement, in pleading, of both parties to stake the outcome of a suit upon the determination of just one issue to a "set problem" in chess. Baker, *Intro.*, p. 91.

[7] J. Huizinga, *Homo Ludens*, pp. 125-126, 126.

[8] Samuel N. Rosenberg, "Joc-partit," *Medieval France: An Encyclopedia*, ed. by William W. Kibler (New York: Routledge, 2011), p. 495.

[9] Bryan Loughrey, Neil Taylor, "Ferdinand and Miranda at Chess, *Shakespeare Survey* 35 (Cambridge: Cambridge University Press, 1982; online, March 2007), pp. 113-118, https://doi.org/10.1017/CCOL0521247527.011; William Poole, "False Play: Shakespeare and Chess," *Shakespeare Quarterly* 55, no. 1 (Spring, 2004), pp. 50-70, doi.10.1353.shq.2004.0055, Project Muse, https://muse.jhu.edu/article/171292; Bill Wall, "Chess and Shakespeare," ChessManiac.com, March/30/2013, http://www.chessmaniac.com/chess-and-shakespeare/; Edward Winter, "Chess and Shakespeare," Jan./1/2018, http://www.chesshistory.com/winter/extra/shakespeare.html.

[10] In the Spanish Chapel of the Church of Santa Maria Novella, Florence, Italy, there are a series of frescos by Andrea di Bonaiuto dating from 1365-1368 called "Triumph of St. Thomas: Allegory of the Sciences, Allegory of the Sacred Sciences, and Allegory of the Secular Sciences.

The French word *chez* can mean "at the place of," "in the name of" or "in the care of."[1] Perhaps Bacon as Shakespeare was counting on the protection of the Queen.[2] And/or, he may have been entrusting his literary offspring to the care of the world, as one might send a letter "in care of" another. His *Last Will and Testament* reads, "For my name and memory, I leave it to men's charitable speeches, and to foreign nations, and the next ages." As Spedding has acknowledged, Bacon wrote in foreign languages to conceal/selectively reveal his meanings.[3]

Chez as associated with "place" could be a play on the word "plays." Actors take their "places," and "take the place of" or stand for, some entity or person. In the legal Latin, the word for "pleas" was *placita*.[4] The Queen did not give Bacon a "place" or position (other than making him her "learned counsel extraordinary"), but the *plea* rolls for the court of King's Bench, Coram Rege, depict the "Queen's image" within a large letter "P," the first letter of *Placita juris*.[5] Like lawyers making pleas, actors need to *please*. In his *A Collection of Some Principal Rules and Maximes of the Common Lawes*, or *Maximes*, he distinguished between maxims and rules of reason, "rational grounds of law," and *placita iuris* which he explained were "not maxims and conclusions of reason, but yet are learnings received, which the law hath set down and will not have called into question."[6]

For images, see Art in Tuscany, http://www.travelingintuscany.com/art/andreadibuonaiuto/ spanishchapel.htm (Scroll down about three-quarters). In the Allegory of the Sacred Sciences; the civil and canonic law are depicted as women. The woman representing civil law dresses in red. She wears a golden circlet around her head. In her hand, she holds an orb, a symbol of world dominion. Isabella M. Pettus, "The Legal Education of Women," *Albany Law Journal* 61 (Jan.-July 1900), pp. 325-331, 325-326, HathiTrust, https://hdl.handle.net/2027/ osu.32437010639850. In portraits, Queen Elizabeth holds such an orb.

[1] *Cassell's French & English Dictionary* (Collier Books, p.b., 1986), s.v. *chez*, p. 68.

[2] "Her opening prospects Fortune hath chequer'd with uncertainty."[William Shakespeare et al?], speech of Henry VIII upon the birth of Elizabeth, *The Tragedy of Anne Boleyn, a Drama in Cipher..., as deciphered by Elizabeth Wells Gallup from the 'Novum Organum' of Sir Francis Bacon by means of the Biliteral Cipher, described in his Advancement of Learning"* (Geneva Illinois: Riverside Laboratories, 1916), HathiTrust, https://hdl.handle.net/2027/hvd.hnlczc, pp. 90-91. For explanation, please see appendix 2, infra.

[3] On how Bacon and his mother Anne Bacon would write to one another in one language with the alphabet of another, see Edwin Reed, "An Idiosyncracy," *Coincidences, Bacon and Shakespeare* (Boston: Coburn, 1906), coin. no. 52, pp. 70-71; see also *Spedding*, XI, p. 278, cited in BSQ, ch. 7, "The Learning of Shakespeare," p. 74.

[4] *Placita* comes from *placeo*, "to please, be agreeable to"; plural, "opinions, teaching." *Cassell's Latin*, p. 170.

[5] See "Coram Rege Rolls initial detail Elizabeth I," National Archives, UK, http://www. nationalarchives.gov.uk/education/resources/the-english-reformation-c1527-1590/coram- rege-rolls-initial-detail-elizabeth-i/.

[6] Mark Neustadt, "The Making of the Instauration," p. 54. For a discussion of the *Maxims*, see Coquillette, FB, pp. 35-48.

Placit or *placitum* may mean an "agreement between the parties, that which is their pleasure to arrange, or an imperial ordinance (literally, the prince's pleasure), or the judgment, decree, or sentence of a court."[1] Bacon spoke of the *placita* (opinions, teaching) of Plutarch.[2] He also used the term *ad placitum* to mean things made by "real characters...adopted and agreed upon at pleasure," as distinguished from *ex congruo*, "notes of things which carry significance without the help and intervention of words" (hieroglyphics, gestures). By "real characters," Bacon explained that he meant non-nominal "picture writing," such as Chinese character writing.

One cannot know for certain whether Bacon's thought progressed from *chez* to place, to plays, to pleas, to *placita*, but such a progression could be made.

The great Roman jurist Ulpian (d. A.D. 228) had written about the expression *Quod principi placuit* (as the prince pleases). He likened jurists to priests. Bracton had "qualified" Ulpian's expression, saying that while what pleased the king was the law, what pleased the king had to first please the council.[3] *Placuit*, what pleased the sovereign, was an important legal concept.

As for William — Wilhelmus in Latin — "helm" could refer to a helmet, or to taking the helm. One of the meanings of "bell," as in, say, Bellario, is "the body of a helmet."[4] When young Elizabeth Tudor was first released from her imprisonment in the Bell Tower, the parishioners of Shoreditch would ring bells to welcome her along the Hatfield road. "She would pause and listen attentively and commend the bells" which she took as a mark of her people's affection for her.[5]

The connection between "Shakespeare" and Pallas Athena "shaking a spear at ignorance" has been well argued.[6] I do think there could be multiple meanings, for it seems to have been Bacon's way to leave things ambiguous,[7] to bury truth beneath layers of protection. Multiple meanings of a pseudonym

---

[1] *"Placit"* through *"placitum nominatum," Black's LD*, pp. 1034-1035.

[2] *Cassell's Latin*, p. 170.

[3] E. Kantorowicz, *The King's Two Bodies*, pp. 151-152.

[4] "Bell," *Webster's*, p. 96.

[5] Elizabeth Jenkins, *Elizabeth the Great*, p. 58, based on Nichols, *Progresses*.

[6] Peter Dawkins, *The Shakespeare Enigma* (London: Polair Publishing 2004), p. 103; Peter Dawkins, "The Name William Shakespeare," http://fbrt.org.uk/pages/essays/The_Name_William_Shakespeare.pdf, pp. 1-6. There is also a Bible story: in the early days of King David, one of his men, Benaiah, slew an Egyptian "of great stature," plucking the man's spear "like a weaver's beam" out of his hand with a staff and slaying the Egyptian with his own spear. 1 Chronicles 11:23; see also 1 Samuel 17:7 and *The Merry Wives of Windsor*, V, 1, 3001 (Falstaff). Mark Twain said all writers are weavers, but Shakespeare wove on a Gobelin loom. Mark Twain, ch. 1, "What is Man? And Other Essays," Project Gutenberg, https://www.gutenberg.org/files/70/70-h/70-h.htm.

[7] The word "ambiguous," a word familiar to lawyers, comes from the French *ambigu*, a meal in which all the courses, including dessert, were put out on one banquet table at once. Lynn

are possible, and a more obvious meaning might provide cover for a hidden, more personal meaning.

York House or York Place?

Rawley, Bacon's biographer, wrote that Bacon was born "at York House, or York *Place*" (italics mine). They are very different. York House was the home of Nicholas and Anne Bacon, where Anthony and Francis Bacon spent their childhoods,[1] while King Henry VIII had turned nearby York Place into a palace, a love nest for his new bride, Anne Boleyn, and himself.[2]

York House, which had been at the corner of Villiers Street,[3] not far from Whitehall Palace, is gone now. As Shakespeare explained in *Henry VIII*, "You must no more call it York Place — that is past: For since the Cardinal fell that title's lost; 'Tis now the King's, and called Whitehall" (*Henry VIII*, IV, 1, 2524). It seems plausible that Bacon himself might have drafted what Rawley later caused to be published as a "Life of Bacon." Creating ambiguity about Bacon's place of birth does not seem to be the sort of thing Rawley would do unless he was authorized to do so by Bacon. In using "chez sphere" as a pseudonym, Bacon may have been subtly stating he identified with York *Place*. Perhaps it is significant that Shakespeare coined the word "birth-place."[4]

A search for "York Place" in www.opensourceShakespeare.org reveals thirteen uses of the two words — York and place — within some proximity to one another, while a search for "York House" revealed 27 uses. Some of these passages are worth noting. For instance, in *Richard III* — twenty or so lines above the place where Queen Margaret's line, "Thou didst usurp my place," appears five longs above "Farewell, York's wife and queen of sad mischance/England's woes will make me smile in France (IV, 4, 2904 to

---

Olver, "Dessert," Food Timeline Library last updated 2/2015, http://www.foodtimeline.org/foodfaq7.html.

[1] Aubrey tells how, while Bacon was living at York House, he watched some fishermen casting out their nets. He offered them a certain sum for their catch, but they refused, wanting more money. They only hauled in a few small fish. "You should have taken my offer," he told them. They replied that they had hoped to catch more. "Out," Bacon said, "Hope is a good breakfast but an ill supper." "A Fine Day in the Strand," *Fraser's Magazine* 29, no. 172 (London, 1844), p. 387. https://books.google.com/books?id=BGYyAQAAMAAJ. See John Aubrey, *Aubrey's Brief Lives, Chiefly of Contemporaries Set Down Between the Years 1669 and 1696* (Oxford, 1898).

[2] Annis Castellina, "Whitehall and Anne Boleyn," On the Tudor Trail, http://onthetudortrail.com/Blog/anne-boleyn/guest-articles/whitehall-and-anne-boleyn/. For "Francis Bacon's Foster Parents," see Alfred Dodd, *The Marriage of Queen Elizabeth* (London: Rider, 1940) and *Francis Bacon's Personal Life Story* (London: Rider, 1986), excerpted at http://www.sirbacon.org/links/anne_&_sir_nicholas_bacon.htm.

[3] Basil Montagu, note A to his *Life of Bacon*, XVI, pt. 2 (London: William Pickering, 1825-34). It is unpaginated but follows p. ccccxcviii (last page of index). HathiTrust, https://hdl.handle.net/2027/hvd.hnug2l. I t may be in the Philadelphia three-volume edition as well.

[4] McQuain, p. 20 (*Cor*.IV, 4, 2744, "birth-place," hyphenated).

2909-10)" — Queen Margaret says, "A dream of what thou wert, a breath, a bubble" (IV, 4, 2883. "Bubble" appears eleven times in Shakespeare). Here are the first lines in Francis Bacon's poem, "The Life of Man":

> The world's a bubble, and the life of man less than a span/In his conception wretched; from the womb so to the tomb:/Curst from the cradle, and brought up to years, with cares and fears.[1]

Portia's question-and-answer song tells us fancy dies in the cradle where it lies (III, 2, 1034). How sad the circumstances that would cause a mother's fancy to turn from her infant![2] In a prayer, Bacon wrote, "May God never permit us to give out the dream of our fancy as a model of the world, but rather in his kindness vouchsafe to us the means of writing a revelation and true vision of the traces and stamps of the Creator on his creatures."[3] One interpretation might be: May God help us see and write about things as they are, in the natural world, without distortion. Marcus Aurelius had expressed a similar thought: "The first rule is to keep an untroubled spirit. The second is to look things in the face and know them for what they are."[4]

The first Parliament under Queen Mary had revoked the divorce of Henry VIII and Catherine of Aragon, rendering Queen Elizabeth illegitimate and disinherited.[5] For personal reasons, she did not wish to marry. That choice, however, entailed sacrifice. Edwin Reed said that, besides the Queen herself, it was Francis Bacon, Shakespeare, and Ben Jonson (who "knew both men") who promoted the public image of Elizabeth as a virgin queen.[6] Spenser, too,

---

[1] Francis Bacon, *The Life of Man* and four other poems by Bacon, https://www.poemhunter.com/poem/the-life-of-man/#content.

[2] The form of the Greek deity associated with divine law and order is female. The Greek Titan goddess Themis conveys the "moral influence attributed to mothers." See J. Resnik, *Representing Justice*, p. 21, n. 58. See also Peter Goodrich, ch. 5, "Haec Imago, This Mask, This Man, This Law," sub-chapter "Of Fate, Fortune, Justice, and Other Illustrious Women," *Oedipus Lex*, Psychoanalysis, History, Law, especially pp. 121-126; "Themis," Theoi Greek Mythology, http://www.theoi.com/Titan/TitanisThemis.html.

[3] Montagu, "Life of Bacon," in *Montagu*, XVI (of 16), pt. 2, p. ccccxxxv, HathiTrust, https://hdl.handle.net/2027/hvd.hnug21.

[4] Marcus Aurelius, Quotable Quote, https://www.goodreads.com/quotes/20870-the-first-rule-is-to-keep-an-untroubled-spirit-the.

[5] Elizabeth Jenkins, *Elizabeth the Great*, p. 43.

[6] Sir Edwin Reed, *Coincidences, Bacon and Shakespeare* (Boston: Coburn Publishing Co. 1906), coin. no. 52, pp. 96-97, 97, HathiTrust, https://hdl.handle.net/2027/hvd.hnpyfp. A verse referring to "this mayden Queene" appears beneath a print entitled "Henry VIII and his Successors," after Lucas de Heere, ca. 1573-4. The British Collection Online, http://www.britishmuseum.org/research/collection_online/collection_object_details.aspx?objectId=1502473&partId=1. It is reported that the Queen had made certain admissions when she was thought to be dying from smallpox in 1562, including that she had a sexual relationship with Robert Dudley that stopped short of the sexual act. Jenkins, *Elizabeth the Great*, pp. 99-100.

---

praised the virgin queen. Bacon wrote in her defense regarding the "libel" that she must have borne illegitimate children.[1]

Valerius Terminus

A fragmentary manuscript exists known as "Valerius Terminus," a fictional author Bacon created. He even proposed, but did not get around to, annotating Terminus's writings under the name of another fictional author, "Hermes Stella."[2] Regrettably, this intriguing topic will be beyond the scope of this book, other than to provide a few suggestions for further reading.[3]

Henry Cuffe; "the Earl of Essex his Bee"

Stanley Wells gives Bacon's writing under the name of "Henry Cuffe" as an example of "internal evidence decisively contradicting and refuting the external evidence" on a title page. Speeches in a dramatic "interlude" or "device" performed before Queen Elizabeth on Nov. 17, 1595, at Essex House were attributed by title page to "Mr. Henry Cuffe, servant to the Earle of Essex." However, the speeches survive in both rough draft and fair manuscript form in a handwriting "identifiable" as Francis Bacon's.[4]

The real Henry Cuffe was tried in conjunction with the Essex rebellion. Testimony was given that no man was closer to the Earl than Henry Cuffe.[5]

---

[1] *Spedding*, VIII, pp. 146-208, 208 ("primo"), HathiTrust, https://hdl.handle.net/2027/ucl. b3618243; *Montagu*, II, "Observations on a Libel," pp. 242-265, 265, HathiTrust, https://hdl. handle.net/2027/ucl.b3618254.

[2] As to *Valerius Terminus*, see Spedding, III, p. 201, HathiTrust, https://hdl.handle.net/2027/ucl. b3618240; IV, p. 374, discussed in BSQ, ch. 4, "Bacon's Reasons for Anonymity," p. 53, fn. 7; Montagu, XVI part 2, pp. 81-95, HathiTrust, https://hdl.handle.net/2027/hvd.hnug2l.

Valerius Terminus, a precursor to the *De Augmentis*, was circulated privately but not printed until 1734. R. Serjeantson, "The Philosophy of Francis Bacon in Early Jacobean Oxford, with an Edition of an Unknown Manuscript of the Valerius Terminus," *The Historical Journal* 56, no. 4 (December, 2013), pp. 1087-1106. Available from Dr. Richard Serjeantson faculty page, University of Cambridge, 2017, https://www.hist.cam.ac.uk/directory/rws1001@cam.ac.uk.

[3] For further reading, see R. Serjeantson: "Francis Bacon's Valerius Terminus and the Voyage to the "Great Instauration," *J. Hist. Ideas* 78, no. 3 (July 2017), pp. 341-368; "Francis Bacon and the 'Interpretation of Nature' in the Late Renaissance," *Isis* 105, no. 4 (2014), pp. 681-705. Available from Dr. Richard Serjeantson faculty page, University of Cambridge, 2017, https:// www.hist.cam.ac.uk/directory/rws1001@cam.ac.uk. Serjeantson is Assistant Director of the *Oxford Francis Bacon* project.

[4] Stanley Wells and Gary Taylor, *William Shakespeare: A Textual Companion* (New York: W. W. Norton, 1997, corrected. and reprinted from 1987 ed.), p. 76. On handwriting as evidence of Baconian authorship, see appendix 4, infra.

[5] Holger Schott Syme, ch. 2, "Judicial Digest: Edward Coke reads the Essex papers," *Theatre and Testimony in Shakespeare's England: A Culture of Mediation* (Cambridge: Cambridge University Press, 2012), pp. 72-111, 80, n. 22. On Cuffe's examination, see *Spedding* IX, ch. 10, pp. 326, 342, 351, 352.

Another manuscript attributed to Cuffe is "The Earle of Essex his Bee, A Poem made on the Earle of Essex (being in disgrace with Queen Elizabeth): by mr. henry Cuffe his Secretary" [*sic*]. It was first published in *The Third and Last Booke of Songs or Aires* (London, 1603) in a musical setting.[1]

According to James Phinney Baxter, the author of *The Arte of English Poetry*, 1598, wrote, "Henry Cuffe, a scholar of distinction, not wishing to use his own name on a manuscript, sent it to a correspondent to ask Greville to permit him to publish it with his initials R. B. which, he said, "some no doubt would interpret to be Beale."[2]

Bees pollinate flowers. "Posy" could mean both a motto, such as one engraved on a ring, and poesy or the poetic arts.[3] Chief Justice Popham called the Bacon family motto, *Mediocria firma*, "the posy of the wisest and greatest counsellor of his time in England," referring to Sir Nicholas Bacon.[4] Reformation historian A. G. Dickens links this motto to Cromwell's policy of *via media*, "a middle road in affairs of Church and state" adopted by Sir Nicholas Bacon, John Jewell, Queen Elizabeth, and William Cecil.[5] *Mediocria firma* comes from Seneca: *In medio spatio mediocria firma locantur*, "the firm ground is in the middle."[6]

Shakespeare actually coined the word "immediacy," meaning "closeness or nearness, urgency or directness, a state of being not-being-in-the-middle. He only used "immediacy" once, but he used "immediate" over twelve times.[7]

Francis Bacon praised *both* Luther and the "divines" of the Protestant Church, as well as the Jesuits, "for enterprising to reform, the one the doctrine, the other the discipline and manners of the church of Rome...," [seeing] "well how both of them have awakened to their great honour and succor, all human learning."[8] Launcelot Andrewes, too, sought a middle way, a *via media*, in matters of religion.[9]

---

[1] Catalog of English Literary Manuscripts, EsR86, pp. 368-9 [Feilde MS, c. 1642]. http://www.celm-ms.org.uk/repositories/pirie-robert-s-new-york.html. For more on Bacon as "Essex's literary ghost," see BSQ, ch. 3, "Bacon's Interest in the Theatre," pp. 21-40, 38, fn. 3; 229.

[2] James Phinney Baxter, *The Greatest of all Literary Problems* (Boston: The Riverside Press Cambridge, 1915), p. xxiii.

[3] Perhaps relatedly, *pensée* in French means both "thought, opinion, idea, conception, meaning," as well as the flower "pansy." "A pensive Pansy?" Linda Sonntag, *Naming Your Baby* (New York: Random House, 1993), p. 66, https://books.google.com/books?isbn=1856985121; *Cassell's French and English Dictionary* (Collier Books, p.b., 1986), s.v. *pensee*, p. 240.

[4] BSQ, p. 208, n. 6 (The reference is, I believe, to p. 198.).

[5] A. G. Dickens, *The English Reformation*, 2d ed. (University Park, PA: Penn. State University, 1991), ch. 7, p. 135.

[6] See BSQ, pp. 198, 202

[7] E.g., *Hamlet* I, 2, 109; McQuain, *Coined by Shakespeare*, pp. 102, 104.

[8] Francis Bacon, *Scala Intellectus Filum Labyrinthi*, *Montagu*, I, p. 98, HathiTrust, https://hdl.handle.net/2027/uc2.ark:/13960/t6zw1952d. Bacon's good friend, Tobie Matthews, had become a Jesuit priest. For Bacon's praise of the Jesuits for education, see Coquillette, FB, pp. 80, 273 n. 200.

[9] Jonathan Warren, "Launcelot Andrewes, The Star of Preachers," *Anglican Pastor*, June 30, 2014, http://anglicanpastor.com/lancelot-andrewes-the-star-of-preachers/.

Francis Bacon characterized the practice of the bee as being "midway," combining both approaches, for it "draws materials from the flowers of both garden and field, but transmutes or digests them by a faculty of its own."[1] "Such should be the practice of genuine philosophy," says Bacon in the *Redargutio Philosophiarum (The Refutation of Philosophies)*. In contrast, he continues, there are the ants who, like Empiricists, gather and consume, and the spiders who, like Rationalists, "spin webs out of themselves."[2]

A search at www.opensourceshakespeare.org for "ants" and "bees" brought up too many words containing the letters of those words. However, a search for "spider" brought up a reasonable fourteen references. Spiders are often found in the same text as toads and adders in Shakespeare.[3] Spiders ensnare or entrap.[4] In *Henry VIII*, reference is made to a "self-drawing web" (I, 1, 105). In *Measure for Measure*, Vincentio says, "To draw with idle spiders' strings/ Most ponderous and substantial things! (III, 2, 1783). In *King John*, Philip the Bastard says, "And if thou want'st a cord, the smallest thread/That ever spider twisted from her womb/Will serve to strangle thee." (IV, 3, 2157).

"Little less than little wit" will not deliver a fly from a spider in *Troilus and Cressida* (II, 3, 1229). In *Winter's Tale*, Leontes says that if you drink a spider steeped in a cup, unknowing, you "partake of no venom" (II, 1, 649ff.). Queen Mab, the fairies' midwife, had wagon spokes made of spider legs and "traces" of spider's web (*Romeo and Juliet* I, 4, 559).

---

[1] *Montagu*, I, pp. 125, Apophthegm no. 21; p. 433 ("Interpretation of Nature"). Other references to the bee: *Montagu*, I, p. 208 (Who taught the bee?); *Montagu*, II, pp. 82 (honeycomb is "like a cellar"), p. 25 (bee-moll, the key of b-flat-minor in music), 69, 116, 123, 573; *Montagu*, III, p. 362 (*Novum Organum*, i, Apoph. no. 95: the method of the bee, a "mean" between that of the ant who merely gathers and uses (Empiricists) and the spider who spins from itself (Rationalist), resembles that of the natural philosopher who "changes and works" raw data into something new. In HathiTrust: *Montagu*, I https://hdl.handle.net/2027/umn.31951002094295e; *Montagu*, II. https://hdl.handle.net/2027/umn.31951002094294g; *Montagu*, III. https://hdl.handle.net/2027/umn.31951002094297a.

[2] Coquillette, FB, pp. 94-96, 96, 123 n. 123, citing *The Philosophy of Francis Bacon: an Essay on its Development from 1603 to 1609*, transl. by Benjamin Farrington (Liverpool, 1964), p. 131. Virgil wrote of bees in the *Georgics*, IV. Aristotle, who taught that women were inferior to men, thought king bees ran the hive. That began to change in the seventeenth century with a book by the curiously-named author, "Char: Butler Magd," *Feminine Monarchie[...]* (Oxford, 1609). See Sarah Kaplan, "What Bees Aristotle, and Aliens Can Teach Scientists about Bias," *The Washington Post* (Jan. 24, 2018), https://www.washingtonpost.com/news/speaking-of-science/wp/2018/01/24/what-bees-queen-elizabeth-and-aliens-can-teach-scientists-about-bias/?noredirect=on&utm_term=.569cb1ee0f8b.

[3] *Cym.*, IV, 2, 2439; *Mid. Night's Dream*, II, 2, 669; *Richard II*, III, 2, 1422; *Richard III*, I, 2, 192; IV, 4, 2876.

[4] *Henry VI*, Part 2, III, 1, 1626 (a brain more busy than a laboring spider, seeking to entrap his enemies; ensnaring bottled spider called "bunch-back'd toad"); *Richard III*: I, 3, 709; IV, 4, 2876. In *Merchant*, III, 2, 1489, Bassanio comments on Portia's portrait, "The painter plays the spider and has woven a golden mesh to entrap the hearts of men."

Thus, in both works attributed to Shakespeare and Bacon we see spiders associated with "self-drawing webs," the making of which requires mental activity.

"Draw" is a word with multiple meanings. Lawyers "draw up" or draft documents. Shakespeare "puny drawer" of ale in *The First Part of Henry IV* was named Francis. In French, *droit*, pronounced "draw," is a word for "right, equity, law."[1]

Labeo

There is a "be" in the middle of Labeo. Walter Saunders, N. B. Cockburn, and Walter Begley are among those who have argued that Joseph Hall and John Marston in their satires and Thomas Freeman in his epigram had Francis Bacon in mind when they wrote of "Labeo."[2]

There have been several Labeos in history, but Marcus Antistius Labeo ("M. A. L.") seems a good place to start. He was an early Roman jurist at about 30 B.C., under Caesar Augustus. His father Quintus (aka Pacuvius) Antistius Labeo (d. 42 B.C.) sided with Brutus against Caesar. Both Francis Bacon and M.A.L. were sons of famous jurists. Like Bacon, M. A. L. was interested in literature, history, and philosophy. Like Bacon, M.A.L. was passed over for political advancement, a circumstance which gave him time to write; in M.A.L.'s case, over four hundred books. Bacon, too, was a prolific writer. That circumstance also gave M. A. L. time to judge cases and instruct new lawyers.[3] Bacon, too, instructed new lawyers at Gray's Inn, as he did with his *Arguments of the Law*, and he, too, was a judge. Both men had political enemies. Bacon's was Coke; Labeo's, Capito.[4]

Tacitus, whom Bacon quoted frequently, wrote of Labeo.[5]

---

[1] *Cassell's French-English Dictionary*, s.v. "droit," (first Collier Books ed., 1986, p.b.), p. 123.

[2] See BSQ, ch. 14, "The Hall and Marston Satires and a Freeman Epigram," pp. 184-209; Peter Dawkins, "Labeo is Shakespeare," Francis Bacon Research Trust (2016), pp. 1-12. https://hdl.handle.net/2027/hvd.hnpyfp; Walter Begley, ch. 3, "New Evidence — Hall's Satires," *Nova Resuscitatio*, vol. 2 (London: Bird & Gay 1905), pp. 22-31, HathiTrust, https://hdl.handle.net/2027/ucl.b3310681; Barry R. Clarke, appendix E, "The Hall-Marston Satires," *The Shakespeare Puzzle: A Non-Esoteric Baconian Theory*, pp. 228-234, http://barryispuzzled.com/shakpuzz.pdf; Walter Saunders, "The Identification of 'Labeo' and 'Mutius' as Francis Bacon in Hall and Marston's Satires" (2011), http://sirbacon.org/wsaundersHallandMarston.htm.

[3] Matthew Bunson, *Encyclopedia of the Roman Empire*, rev. ed., illus., with maps (New York: Facts on File, 2002), p. 298.

[4] See Henry John Roby, ch. 9, *An Intro. to the Study of Justinian's Digest* (New York: Cambridge University Press, 2010, digital), pp. cxxvi, cxxviii, https://books.google.ca/books?id=t_U_AAAAYAAJ.

[5] "Labeo," *Dictionary of Greek and Roman Biography and Mythology by Various Writers*, vol. 2, ed. by William Smith (London, 1872), Ann. iii.75, pp. 692-693, https://books.google.ca/books?id=WA1QAAAAcAAJ.

Twelfth-century Italian jurist Azo cited Q. Antistitius Labeo in a discussion about when a seller is liable for latent defects, such as a seller who has unknowingly purchased from a thief. Labeo is also the name of a character in "Shakespeare's" *Julius Caesar* (V, 3, 108).[1]

Name of the World; Fool's Cap Map

What if Bacon took the pseudonym "Shakespeare" (*chez sphere*), and, by doing so, assumed "the name of the world"?[2] In at least one letter to King James, Bacon referred to the King's son as his "image." As "World," he would, in a sense, become the Queen's "image" with which she is often depicted, the globe. Other references, too, suggest the use of *world* to refer to the concealed poet Bacon.[3]

---

[1] Alexander Schmidt, *Shakespeare Lexicon* , vol. I, 3d ed., rev. and enlarged by Gregor Sarrazin (New York: Dover 1971, first pub. 1902), p. 622.

[2] Bacon said: "But men have got a fashion now-a-days, that two or three busy-bodies will take upon them the *name of the world* (italics added) and broach their own concepts, as if it were a general opinion..." "Sir Francis Bacon, His Accusation of Sir John Wentworth, Sir John Hollys, and Mr. Lumsden," *Spedding,* XII, pp. 2130223, 222, HathiTrust, https://hdl.handle.net/2027/ucl.b3618248. See also Bacon's "Declaration of the Treason of Robert, Earl of Essex" (*Montagu,* II), p. 348 (last par.: "For first of all, the world can now expound why he [Essex] did aspire... [to greatness]"), HathiTrust, https://hdl.handle.net/2027/ucl.b3618254.

In "Mr. Bacon's Discourse in the Praise of his Sovereign," Bacon said, "The queen has made the *world* [italics mine] the limits of her name." *Spedding,* VIII, p. 128. Ostensibly, he is flattering the Queen. However, if he is calling himself *the world*, there may be a sly double entendre. He could be seen to represent the "limits" of the Queen's name" because she acknowledged no heirs. Actually, the Welsh patronymic for "Owen Tudor," grandfather of Henry VII, should have been "Meredith," not "Tudor," according to the Welsh system. "Tudor" was not really a last name. "Sir Owen Meredith Tudor," North Isles Family History, https://www.bayanne. info/Shetland/getperson.php?personID=I357779&tree=ID1; Dr. John Rickard, "Owen Tudor, c. 1400-1461, http://www.historyofwar.org/articles/people_tudor_owen.html.

"Bal" meant "not" in Hebrew. Arie Uittenbogaard, "Belial meaning," http://www.abarim-publications.com/Meaning/Belial.html#.V5cAk-Bf3IU, last updated November 21, 2017 . Thus, *Bellario* could mean "not an heir" (Bal-heir-io).

"In things that a man would not be seen in himself, it is a point of cunning to borrow the *name of the world*, as to say, "The world says," or "There is a speech abroad." Francis Bacon, "Of Cunning," *Spedding,* VI, pp. 428-429, 429, HathiTrust, https://hdl.handle.net/2027/ucl.31175002285222.

[3] John Taylor ("the Water Poet"), a ferryman who had brought the "watermen's case" which Bacon decided (in favor of the watermen), changed the dedication of his collected works (1630 folio) to include a dedication to "the World." It might mean nothing, but it did seem as if he might have been in on the private joke about the Droeshout Portrait. See Basil Brown (1860-1928) and John Taylor (1580-1683), *Supposed Caricature of the Droeshout Portrait* (New York: privately printed, 1911), p. 8, HathiTrust, https://catalog.hathitrust.org/Record/001018476.

In a discussion of how poets evaded the censors through "crypticism," John Huntington quotes the poet/playwright George Chapman (1559?-1634): "He that shuns trifles shuns *the world*" [italics added]. John Huntington, intro., to *Ambition, Rank and Poetry in 1590s England* (Urbana: University of Illinois Press, 2001), pp. 14-17, p. 17, https://books.google.ca/books?isbn=0252026284. Chapman's victimization by a money-lender, John Wolfall, in 1585 when he was an inn-of-court student may have inspired *The Merchant of Venice.* Huntington, p.

A "map of the world" is an image of the world, *imago mundi*. An interesting "take" on this image is the "Fool's Cap map" which depicts a fool's *belled* cap with the map of the world where the fool's face should be. In 1575, Jean de Gourmont had published a fool's cap map with French philosophical mottos about the folly of mankind written all over the cap, shortly after Ortelius's map, "Typhus Orbis Terrarum," was published in *Theatrum Orbis Terrarum*.[1] Ortelius was apparently associated with the "Family of Love," a group related to the Rosicrucians and possibly to Queen Elizabeth.[2]

Another version, anonymous, ca. 1580–1590, bore a great many mottos in Latin, including a reference to Heraclitus and Democritus. The motto over the brow, *O caput elleboro dignum*, has been translated "O head, worthy of a dose of hellebore."[3] I have seen this interpreted to mean "a poison that would make you mad if it didn't kill you first." However, hellebore was used

---

3. For more on Chapman, see Gerald Snare, "George Chapman (1559-1634)," Poetry Foundation, https://www.poetryfoundation.org/poets/george-chapman.

William Rawley wrote, in his "Life of Bacon" (*Vita Baconi*, first pub. in England, 1657), "No doubt his memory and works will live, and will in all probability last as long as *the world* lasteth" (italics added). William Rawley, 'The Life of the Honorable Author," (Rawley's *Rescuscitatio, 2d. ed.*), *Spedding*, I, pp. 3-18, 18,

According to Edwin Bormann, Spedding seemed unaware of the line which follows—only in the Latin editions published on the Continent: "They will not yield to fate, until the theatrical machinery of the globe is dissolved." William Rawley, "Life of Bacon" in Francis Bacon, *Opuscula Philosophica* (Holland, 1658). Spedding found that line in a French book published near the end of the 18th century, "quoted as if from Rawley," but Spedding did not believe it was Rawley's line. Bormann says Spedding must not have consulted the foreign language editions of Bacon's works. Edwin Bormann, *Francis Bacon's Cryptic Rhymes and the Truth They Reveal* (London: Siegle, Hill, 1906), pp. 221-223. According to Bormann, that line and the continuation of that passage for two more paragraphs is found in the first *complete* editions of Bacon's works, in Latin, printed in Frankfurt in 1665 and Leipzig in 1694. Bormann reproduces the passage. Bormann, pp. 223-224, HathiTrust, https://hdl.handle.net/2027/ucl.$b681854.

The headings of certain manuscripts also associate Bacon with "the world." "Francis Bacon, Baron Verulam, Viscount St. Albans (1561-1626), Verse Legitimately or Doubtfully Attributed to Bacon," Catalog of English Literary Manuscripts, 1450-1700, http://celm-ms.org.uk/authors/baconfrancis.html, BcF9, BcF41.2, BcF43, BcF51.

[1] Richard Helgerson, "Epilogue: The Folly of Maps and Modernity" in Andrew Gordon and Bernhard Klein, *Literature, Mapping and the Politics of Space in Early Modern Britain* (Cambridge: Cambridge University Press, 2001), p. 243.

[2] Francis Yates, 'Rosicrucian Enlightenment,' *Selected Works of Francis Yates*, vol. 4 (London: Routledge 1999), pp. 216, 72, 268, 263; see Robert Thuerck, "The Fool's Cap Map — Solving a 450 Year Old Mystery," *Sustainable Diversity* (July 16, 2013), www.sustainablediversity.com/?p=208; Frank Jacobs, "The Fool's Cap Map of the World," no. 480, Big Think, copyright 2007-2018, http://bigthink.com/strange-maps/480-the-fools-cap-map-of-the-world.

[3] "Fool's Cap World Map," Royal Museums Greenwich Collection, http://collections.rmg.co.uk/collections/objects/206385.html; Frank Jacobs, "The Fool's Cap Map of the World," http://bigthink.com/strange-maps/480-the-fools-cap-map-of-the-world. High resolution image, http://cartanciennes.free.fr//maps/monde_fou.jpg. The *Norton Shakespeare*, 2d ed. (2008), uses this image for its dust cover.

medicinally, in small doses, to cure such ailments as worms.[1] The court fool was unique in being given *carte blanche* to speak freely and make fun of the court. There was frequently something about his appearance, perhaps a deformity or disfigurement, that contributed to his not being taken seriously.[2] To the careful observer, the Droeshout portrait is, arguably, not intended to be taken seriously.[3]

E. K. Chambers, in providing a collection of references to Shakespeare by his contemporaries, provides the last stanza of William Barksted's 1607 poem *Myrrha, the Mother of Adonis*, which he calls a "prequel" to Shakespeare's *Venus and Adonis*. Chambers gives the last line as "Cypres, thy brow shall fit."[4] That might refer to a cap, or a wreath of cypress, although a wreath of laurel is more what one might expect. The ending lines of the last stanza of Barksted's poem are given in Chambers and an 1813 edition of Shakespeare edited by Samuel Johnson and George Steevens as:

> His song was worthy merit; Shakespeare, hee [*sic*]/Sung the fair blossom, thou the withered tree, /Laurel is due to him, his art and wit/ Hath purchased it; Cypres, thy brow will fit.[5]

Now, "cy-pres" ("sigh-prey") is a rule of construction in equity which literally means "as nearly as possible." For example, when it would be impossible or illegal to carry out the intent of a testator in a particular bequest in a will, such as when a charitable gift would violate a rule against perpetuities, the doctrine of *cy pres* allows the court, in its discretion, to make changes so as to fulfill the intent of the testator as much as possible.[6] As a judge, Francis Bacon actually applied something close to the modern doctrine of *cy-pres* to "rectify" wills in at least two cases, *Emmanuel College, Cambridge v.*

---

[1] Robert Bevan-Jones, "hellebore, helleborus," *Poisonous Plants, a Cultural and Social History* (Oxford: OxBow Books, 2009).

[2] Frank Jacobs, The Fool's Cap Map of the World," http://bigthink.com/strange-maps/480-the-fools-cap-map-of-the-world.

[3] Basil Brown (pseud.), "Supposed caricature of the Droushout portrait of William Shakespeare, with facsimile of a rare print taken from a very scarce tract of an Elizabethan poet. Printed for private circulation (New York: n.p. 1911), HathiTrust, https://catalog.hathitrust.org/Record/001018476. "Basil Brown" is the pen name for Isobelle Kittson Brown who also wrote *Law Sports at Gray's Inn, 1594* (1921). BSQ, p. 127.

[4] E. K. Chambers, *William Shakespeare, a Study of Facts and Problems*, vol. 2, p. 216.

[5] William Barksted, "Mirrha the Mother of Adonis; or Lustes Prodegies," as printed in "Extracts of Entries on the Books of the Stationers' Company," in *The Plays of William Shakespeare, containing Prolegomena, etc., in twenty-one volumes, with the corrections and illustrations of various commentators, to which are added notes*, vol. 2, sixth ed. edited by Samuel Johnson and George Steevens, revised and augmented by Isaac Reed with a glossorial index (London, 1813), p. 120, n. 206, HathiTrust, http://hdl.handle.net/2027/njp.32101068143328.

[6] *Black's LD*, p. 349.

English and others (1617) and *Grant and others v. Huish and others* (1621).[1] *Cypres* is also French for the evergreen cypress tree, a symbol of death/mourning and immortality. Hades, god of the underworld, wore a wreath of cypress.[2]

The spelling in at least one modern printed version of Barkstead's poem was changed from "cypres" (one "s") to "cypress,"[3] perhaps by someone trying to standardize spelling; however, it demonstrates the risk in modernizing spelling. Indeed, my word processing program's "autocorrect" feature keeps changing it for me. Thus, the Court of Autocorrect demonstrates the application of the doctrine of *cy pres*. The doctrine of cy-pres is about making things "fit," as is equity, tailoring the remedy to the situation. The original spelling of "cypres" with one "s" should be maintained, since the author may have been cleverly alluding to one who utilized the doctrine of cy pres in court practice; i.e., Francis Bacon.[4]

"Felix and the Spider"

Claire Asquith found it puzzling that there is no record of King James ever having had a conversation with Shakespeare.[5] Of course, the King would have spoken regularly with Bacon, his learned counsellor. There is no record of any contact between Queen Elizabeth and Shakespeare,[6] although there is abundant evidence that the Queen and her counsellor Francis Bacon were in close communication.

"Shakespeare" was also the only major poet not to have written anything specifically to commemorate the Queen's death.[7] It has been asserted that "Shakespeare" eulogized the Queen in the plays themselves, unlike other poets of the day who wrote elegies at the time of her death. Bacon was close to the Queen. He wrote a memorial piece for her in Latin, *In Felicem*

---

[1] Coquillette, FB, ch. 4, "The Theorist as Judge," p. 207.

[2] Steven Olderr, "wreath," *Symbolism: A Comprehensive Dictionary*, 2d ed. (Jefferson NC: McFarland, 2012), p. 224.

[3] E.g., see Sarah Anne Brown and Andrew Taylor, eds., *Ovid in English 1480-1625. Part One: Metamorphoses*, (London: The Modern Humanities Association, 2013), pp. 95-123, 123, 233. Another difference is that Brown and Taylor, utilizing a 1967 source, print "Shaxpere, he" instead of "Shaxpeare hee." "Hee," a sound of laughter, could indicate a lack of seriousness about "Shakespeare he."

[4] Johnson and Steevens, "Extracts of Entries on the Books of the Stationers' Company," *The Plays of Shakespeare*, p. 120.

[5] Clare Asquith, *Shadowplay*, p. 189.

[6] Helen Hackett, intro., *Shakespeare and Elizabeth, the Meeting of Two Myths* (Princeton: Princeton University Press, 2009), pp. 3, 5.

[7] George James, *Frances Bacon: The Author of Shakespeare* (London, 1893), pp. 102-103, https://books.google.ca/books?id=tgU5AQAAMAAJ; Raymond MacDonald Alden, ed., *The Sonnets of Shakespeare: From the Quarto of 1609, with Variorum Readings* (Boston: Houghton Mifflin and Cambridge: The Riverside Press, 1916), p. 246.

Memoriam Elizabethae.[1] Five years after her death, in 1608, he showed it to two people, his intimate friend Tobie Matthew and Sir George Carey, whom he asked whether the piece sounded sufficiently "disinterested."[2] Bacon begins his tribute to the Queen by saying she was a "wonderful person among women." It sounds much more like the expression of a grieving son than of a mere statesman paying his respects. In an earlier Will, Bacon had made a specific request that this memoriam be published.[3] Spedding felt that a "disproportionate" part of the piece was devoted to a defense of Anne Boleyn.[4]

Bacon's elegy, *In Felicem Memoriam Elizabethae*, is unfortunately, awkwardly translated in Spedding as *On the Fortunate Memory of Elizabeth, Queen of England*.[5] However, the first meaning listed in *Cassell's Latin* for *felix, felicis* is "fruitful, fertile," followed by the altered sense meanings "of good omen, favorable, bringing good luck, fortunate, lucky, and successful." Bacon stayed close to the original meanings of words when he wrote in Latin.[6] For "felicitous," a modern dictionary gives "happily applied or expressed; apt; happily expressed; appropriate."[7]

When the work was finally published in England in 1651, its title was *The Felicity of Queen Elizabeth: and her times, with other things*.[8] Graham Rees observed that some problems with translation in Spedding were caused by hiring out

---

[1] *Spedding*, VI, pp. 283-291 (Spedding's preface); 291-304 (in Latin, *In Felicem Memoriam Elizabethae*); 305-318 (transl. in Spedding, *On the Fortunate Memory of Elizabeth, Queen of England*), HathiTrust, https://hdl.handle.net/2027/ucl.31175002285222; Catalogue of English Literary Manuscripts 1450-1700, [CELM], BcF 299; http://www.celm-ms.org.uk/repositories/bibliotheque-nationale-paris.html#bibliotheque-nationale-paris_id429553.

[2] *Spedding*, XI, pp. 107-108 (letter to George Cary, sometimes spelled Carey, not to be confused with George Carew which is also sometimes spelled Carey); p. 132 (Letter to Tobie Matthew, as Bacon spells the name), HathiTrust, https://hdl.handle.net/2027/ucl.31175012007939. Spedding refers the reader to his vol. VIII, p. 283, but it should be vol. VI, pp. 305-318, HathiTrust, https://hdl.handle.net/2027/ucl.31175002285222.

[3] "The Last Will of Francis Bacon, Viscount St. Alban," *Spedding*, XIV, pp. 539-540, 540, HathiTrust, https://hdl.handle.net/2027/ucl.31175012007947.

[4] *Spedding*, XIV, pp. 539-540, HathiTrust, https://hdl.handle.net/2027/ucl.31175012007947.

[5] *Spedding*, VI, pp. 305-318, HathiTrust, https://hdl.handle.net/2027/ucl.31175002285222.

[6] Roger Philip McCutcheon and William Harvey Vann, *An Anthology of English Literature* (New York: Henry Holt, 1936), p. 196.

[7] "Felicitous" and "happily," *Webster's*, pp. 452, 368. "Felicitous" is more formal and elevated than "happily," but both can include the sense of "fortunately" or "done gracefully, with dexterity." See also William Whitaker's Words Online, s.v. "felix, felicis," https://Latin.ucant.org (2017).

[8] Francis Bacon, *The Felicity of Queen Elizabeth and her Times, and Other Things* (London, 1651), Early English Books Online: Text Creation Partnership, http://name.umdl.umich.edu/A76741.0001.001. The Latin version had been privately circulated in France in 1620 in the esteemed French historian Jacques August de Thou's *Histoire Universelle*, published in "1734, French edn 1739." Nieves Matthews, *The History of a Character Assassination*, pp. 296, 439, 559 n. 74.

the translation.[1] While Bacon seems to have particularly associated the word with Queen Elizabeth, it is not out of place with regard to the "happy reign" of any monarch. For example, in just the dedication of his book of sermons to Edward VI, the Queen's brother, Henry Bullinger had used the word "felicity" in relation to kings as many as ten times, citing St. Augustine. For example: "Again, St. Augustine, Lib. v, *de Civit. Dei*, affirmeth that incredible victories, very great glory, and most absolute felicity hath been given by God unto those kings, which have in faith sincerely embraced Christ their Lord...."[2] In one passage, Bacon associated "felicity" with "beatitude" and the "highest good."[3]

According to tradition, St. Felix of Nola, a priest in the service of the Bishop Maximus, in the third century under the Emperor Decius, escaped capture by Roman soldiers because a spider's web appeared over the door to his hiding place, making the soldiers think the place was deserted.[4] One wonders whether this story might have inspired E. B. White's children's story, *Charlotte's Web*.[5] St. Felix may have nothing to do with Bacon's association of "felicity" with Queen Elizabeth, but she would have had reason to feel fortunate, and spared.

The need for honor "of a stouter web, and not so fine as that everything should catch in it, and rend it" comes up on the same page where Bacon discusses saints and "promus" in relation to "active" pursuits for private benefit.[6] As previously discussed, proverbs, words and phrases in his *Promus* are found in the Shakespeare plays. *Felix and Philomena* is a lost play, thought to have influenced Shakespeare.[7] *Philomela* is a novel, said to be by Robert Greene. "Active" pursuits could suggest the theatre. Bacon may have associated "hidden writing" with the imagery of St. Felix's web and the protection of others.[8] Bacon used Latin words close to their Latin meanings,[9] and he wrote in foreign languages to conceal and selectively reveal.[10]

---

[1] Graham Rees, introduction, *Collected Works of Francis Bacon: Philosophical Works*, vol. 1 (Routledge, Thommes, 1996), p. vii; *Spedding*, V, preface, p. vi.

[2] Henry Bullinger, "Dedication to King Edward VI," The Third Decade, *The Decades of Henry Bullinger*, transl. by H. I., ed. by Thomas Harding (New York: Johnson Reprint, 1968, first pub. Cambridge, 1850), pp. 3-16, 13-14.

[3] *Spedding*, V, p. 5 (found by searching "ornament").

[4] Grace Hall, "Felix and the Spider," *The Baldwin Project, Stories of the Saints*, Yesterday's Classics LLC (2000-2018), http://www.mainlesson.com/display.php?author=hallg&book=saints&story=felix.

[5] New York: Harper & Row, 1952.

[6] On Bacon's *Promus*, see ch. 4, infra.

[7] Lost Plays Database, University of Melbourne (2009-2017), https://www.lostplays.org/index.php?title=Felix_and_Philomena.

[8] *De Augmentis*, vii, *Spedding*, V, p. 10.

[9] Roger Philip McCutcheon, *An Anthology of English Literature* (New York: Henry Holt, 1936), p. 196.

[10] Edwin Reed, "An Idiosyncracy," *Coincidences, Bacon and Shakespeare*, coincidence no. 36, pp. 70-71, HathiTrust, https://hdl.handle.net/2027/hvd.32044019185958.

The famous anecdote is given that, when Bacon was a boy, the Queen, when visiting York House, asked him how old he was, and he answered, "Two years' younger than her majesty's happy reign." The Queen was delighted by his answer. Her pet name for him had been "my young Lord Keeper."[1] I do find myself wondering whether she had asked, and he had answered, in Latin. He was a precocious youth and was taught Latin at an early age.

In his will, Bacon had directed his executor, Rawley, to seek the advice of an unnamed, trusted "singular person" before publishing any of his private papers. Spedding thinks Launcelot Andrewes was intended. However, Andrewes died just a few months after Bacon's demise.[2]

In Andrewes' sermon delivered at Whitehall when James was king, Andrewes talked about worms and spiders "even in the king's palace." Then, after a reference to Job 31:22, he said, "It is said in the Acts, after two years Felix went his way, and another governor came in his place. And then the places were changed — some were diseased; and so is the case of all felicity here." "Felicity" may be "code" for the "happy reign of Elizabeth," which Andrewes and Bacon, who might have been in the congregation, would have shared.[3] For more on Job, see ch. 8, infra.

---

[1] Ellen Ross called the young Bacon's response "felicitous." Ellen Ross (Nelsie Brook), "A Lesson from English History," *The Day of Rest* 4, no. 24 (1875), p. 370. https://books.google.ca/books?id=lnIOAAAAQAAJ.

[2] *Spedding*, VI, pp. 283–290, p. 285, HathiTrust, https://hdl.handle.net/2027/ucl.31175002285222.

[3] *Ninety-Six Sermons by the Right Reverend and Father in God Launcelot Andrewes...*, p. 320, https://books.google.com/books/about/The_Library_of_Anglo_Catholic_Theology_N.html?id=BzDxoQEACAAJ.

Chapter Six: A Law Professor by Any Other Name...

Background

The first university was established with the founding of a law school at Bologna in 1088.[1] Tradition has it that a group of liberal arts graduates (masters) engaged a man named Irnerius (Guarnerius, Wernerius) to teach them Roman law from the books of Justinian.[2] One chronicler, Burchard of Biberach, wrote that Matilda, Countess of Tuscany, may also have engaged Irnerius to teach the books of Justinian.[3] Prior to this time, there had been centers for legal study at Rome, Ravenna, and Pavia, and teachers in private studia, such as that run by Irnerius' teacher, Pepo. However, the discovery, around A.D. 1070, of a complete manuscript of Justinian's *Digest* sparked a twelfth-century renaissance in all legal learning and practice. This rebirth began in Bologna, but soon spread across Europe.[4]

"The great compilation of Roman law, upon which virtually all our knowledge of the classical law depends, was undertaken by the Emperor

---

[1] University di Bologna, "The University from the 12th to the 20th Century," http://www.unibo. it/en/university/who-we-are/our-history/university-from-12th-to-20th-century.

[2] Peter Stein, *Roman Law in European History* (Cambridge: Cambridge University Press, 2003, first. pub. 1999), pp. 53-54; Kenneth Pennington, "The Beginning of Roman Law Jurisprudence and Teaching in the Twelfth Century: The Authenticae," *Rivista Internazionale di Diritto Commune* 22 (2011), pp. 35-53, 35.

[3] Kenneth Pennington, ch. 4.1, "Politics in Western Jurisprudence," in *A Treatise of Legal Philosophy and General Jurisprudence*, ed. by A. Padovani and P. G. Stein (Dordrecht: Springer International, 2007), pp. 157-211, 158.

[4] Haskins, ch. 7, "The Revival of Jurisprudence," *The Renaissance of the Twelfth Century*, pp. 193-223, 198-199.

Justinian and his minister Tribonian in the first half of the sixth century. What came to be called the *Corpus iuris civilis*, the fruit of their plans and labor, consisted of four books....": the Digest, "an extensive and rich collection of extracts from the classical jurists"; the Codex, comprising twelve books of the Imperial Constitutions of Rome; the Institutes, a "basic manual of instruction for students beginning the study of law," and later, the Novels, "imperial constitutions issued after the year 530." Of these, the entries in the Digest, sometimes called the "Pandects," were the most important. They comprised the "specific and best" examples of legal reasoning."[1]

In a story that marks the beginnings of the legal profession in England, we find another story (like *Merchant*) of legal tables turned. In 1139, King Stephen had seized the castles of three powerful bishops because he feared they were going to wage war against him. They probably were.

The bishops sought help from the king's powerful brother, Henry of Blois, Bishop of Winchester, grandson of William the Conqueror. However, King Stephen refused to give back the castles.

In Henry's view, the king ought not to decide the matter himself, since he had a stake in the outcome. Rather, it should be heard in an ecclesiastical court. As papal legate, Henry called a council meeting of the bishops for August 26, 1139. Though this Bolognese-based legal procedure was new to them, no bishop disregarded the notice. Each bishop either appeared at the council or made an appropriate excuse.

Henry opened with a Latin speech, bringing the charges against his brother. The king did not appear, but was represented by counsel, Aubrey (Alberic) de Vere, who did what any wise lawyer in his situation would have done: he sought an adjournment. De Vere requested that the case be put to the Archbishop of Rouen.

The Archbishop agreed to hear the case. At first, it looked like he was going to rule in favor of the bishops. They were prematurely elated ("A Daniel come to judgment!" observes the storyteller). However, there was one final point to be decided, which would determine the case. Did the canons allow prelates of the church to possess castles? Unfortunately, no. In the interests of national security, the king was allowed to keep the castles, though he had to do penance for taking them.[2]

[1] R. H. Helmholz, ch. 2, "From the Norman Conquest to the Establishment of Consistory Courts," *Oxford History of the Laws of England*, vol. 1, "The Canon Law and Ecclesiastical Jurisdiction from 1597 to the 1640s" (Oxford: Oxford University Press, 2004, published at Oxford Scholarship Online, March, 2012, p. 82, DOI:10.1093/acprof:oso/9780198258971.003.0002; see also Antonio García y García ch. 12, "The Faculties of Law," in *A History of the University in Europe*, I, "Universities in the Middle Ages," ed. by H. [Hilde] de Ridder-Symoens, (Cambridge: Cambridge University Press, 1992), pp. 388-409, 388-389; Joseph Kelly, "Pandects" [*Digesta*], *The Catholic Encyclopedia*, vol. 11 (New York: Robert Appleton, 1911), http://www.newadvent.org/cathen/11439a.htm.

[2] Walter F. Hook, "Theobald," *Lives of the Archbishops of Canterbury 2, Anglo-Norman* Period (London, 1862) pp. 50-51, sec. 6, pp. 334-337 (relying on Malmesbury, *Hist. Nov.* ann. 1139; *Gesta Stephani*, pp. 50-51). https://books.google.ca/books?id=q68AAAAcAAJ. See also J. A. Giles,

While Roman law was taught in England, from the time of Edward I, it never surpassed the English common law in importance there. "England was, indeed, unique in having schools of purely national law, schools where Justinian held no sway."[1] When Francis Bacon and Edward Coke studied law at their Inns of Court, they studied the English common law. While students who had attended a university prior to coming to an Inn of Court would have been exposed to some civilian law and rhetoric, many Inn of Court students had never previously attended a university.

Fast Forward to ca. 1597

One might not ordinarily think of Francis Bacon as a law professor, but in a sense he was; for, in the Inns of Court system, all the lawyers taught and learned from each other. As an older, more established member of Gray's Inn, Bacon would have served as a mentor and teacher of the younger, less experienced students.[2] The Inns of Court were called the "Third University." Students who could not afford or chose not to attend a university could still obtain advanced learning and gentlemanly finishing, after which they might go on to careers in public office.[3]

In 1586, four years after having been admitted to the bar, Francis Bacon had become a bencher at Gray's Inn, "one of the first men to do so without having first been elected as a reader."[4] Benchers comprised the highest, governing class of the hierarchy of students at the Inn.[5] As a member already of the "Ancients," a distinction only Gray's Inn had, he gave his first "Reading," or lecture, in 1588 and his second in 1600.[6]

William of Malmesbury's Chronicle of the Kings of England (London, 1847), pp. 498-505. https://books.google.ca/books?id=dMk_AAAAcAAJ.

[1] J. H. Baker, "Law and Legal Institutions," in John F. Andrews, *William Shakespeare: His World, His Work, His Influence*, I (New York: Charles Scribner's Sons, 1985) p. 49.

[2] Richard J. Ross, "The Memorial Culture of Early Modern English Lawyers: Memory as Keyword, Shelter, and Identity, 1560-1640," *Yale Journal of Law & the Humanities* 10, no. 2, (May 8, 2013), pp. 229-326, 271, 305-306.

[3] *The Third University: The Inns of Court and the Common-law Tradition*, Selden Society Lecture for 1990 (London: Selden Society, 1990); Baker, *Intro.*, pp. 182-185, 184; Margaret McGlynn, *The Royal Prerogative and the Learning of the Inns of Court*, Cambridge Studies in English Legal History Series, ed. by J. H. Baker (Cambridge: Cambridge University Press, 2004), p. 17, 25.

[4] "Francis Bacon," Grays Inn, https://www.graysinn.org.uk/history/members/biographies/francis-bacon; "History timeline, Francis Bacon," Grays Inn, https://www.graysinn.org.uk/history/timeline/sir-francis-bacon; Coquillette, FB, pp. 49, 312.

[5] Coquillette, FB, pp. 49, 312; "Past Members, Benchers," Grays Inn, https://www.graysinn.org.uk/history/past-members/benchers.

[6] Brian Vickers, ed., "Principle Events in Bacon's Life," *The History of the Reign of King Henry VII*, (Cambridge: Cambridge University Press, 1998), p. xxxvi-xxxviii, xxxvi.

Bacon was devoted to his Inn. He served as its treasurer for eight years.[1] He designed beautiful gardens where the students could walk. He dedicated his "Arguments of the Law" to the students of his Inn.[2]

The Education of an Elizabethan Law Student

It was the common law, not civilian law, that was taught in the Inns of Court, just as it had been taught since Edward I.

While little is known of the Inns' early history, it was the Templars who built the Temple where the Inner Temple and Middle Temple Inns of Court came to be located.[3]

A law student would typically spend the first year at an Inn of Chancery, learning the "fundamentals," preparing for further study at an Inn of Court. While it has been assumed that equity would be studied in an "Inn of Chancery," that was apparently not so. The first year involved "drill work." One would imagine, a great deal of memorization. Rhetoric would have been taught either in grammar school or at the university.[4] Coke attended Clifford's Inn, an Inn of Chancery, in 1571, before attending the Inner Temple the following year.[5] Bacon never attended an Inn of Chancery.[6]

Law students would typically spend seven years or so at an Inn of Court as "inner" barristers. They would attend court, participate in moots, attend readings (lectures), and "keep commons;" i.e., live and eat with their fellow students. After this training, a student could anticipate being called to the bar as an "utter barrister."[7] At Gray's Inn, two "Readers" would be chosen per year from the "Ancients," a designation above utter barrister but not a class per se. Readers would give a reading (lecture) during a "vacation," expounding on a statute of their choice. Usually, a reader was a "barrister of at least ten years' standing."[8] After two or three readings, the barrister could

[1] Gray's Inn, Treasurers, https://www.graysinn.org.uk/sites/default/files/documents/history/ Treasurers%20websitre%202016%20upd1.pdf.

[2] *Spedding*, VII, p. 523.

[3] "Inns of Court," *Encyclopedia Britannica*, vol. 13. 88/2 (Chicago, 1881, 1896); "Magna Carta and the Rule of Law from the Knights Templar," Order of the Temple of Solomon, http:// www.knightstemplarorder.org/templar-magna-carta; "Address by Mr. William Latey, Q.C., Master of the Bench of the Middle Temple, of the Medico-Legal Society on Monday, May 25, 1959, in the Middle Temple Hall," *Medico-Legal Journal* 27, no. 2, 1959, Hein Online, https:// heinonline.org/hol-cgi-bin/get_pdf.cgi?handle=hein.journals/medlgjr27...31; .http://journals. sagepub.com/doi/pdf/10.1177/002581725902700205.

[4] Allen D. Boyer, *Sir Edward Coke and the Elizabethan Age* (Stanford: Stanford University Press, 2003), p. 31.

[5] Bowen, *Lion*, pp. 61-62.

[6] Coquillette, FB, appendix 1, "Chronology of Bacon's Career (1561-1626)," pp. 311-322, 311.

[7] Baker, *Intro.*, ch. 10, "The Legal Profession," p. 184.

[8] Baker, ch. 10, "The Legal Profession," p. 184.

become a Sergeant and leave the Inn.[1] However, Sergeantry was falling into decline. Coke was never a Sergeant,[2] and neither was Bacon.

Being chosen as a Reader could be an expensive proposition, for a Reader was required to provide an ongoing feast, a "constant and splendid table" for three weeks and three days. One was expected to invite guests, which could include nobility, state officers, bishops, judges, and royalty.[3] A "Reading" would be an exposition on a particular statute, not an argument for change in the status quo.[4]

Francis Bacon as a Law Instructor

In his writings, we find Bacon teaching law students how to construe a statute. Seek out the main verbs first, he advised. "In every statute certain words are veins where the life and blood of the statute is and runneth...."[5] Law school graduates will recognize the familiar "White Acre, Green Acre, and Black Acre," in his teaching hypotheticals, as well as the use of rhyming names for parties like "Vale, Sale, and Dale."[6]

Bacon gave his famous six-day *Reading on the Statute of Uses* in 1600.[7] D. D. Heath, who edited his legal writings, found him to be progressive in his

---

[1] Boyer, *Sir Edward Coke and the Elizabethan Age*, p. 31.

[2] Baker, pp. 180-181.

[3] "Inns of Court," 1881 and 1896 *Encycl. Brit.* 13.88/2, in *Mapping English Metaphor Through Time*, ed. by Wendy Anderson (New York: Oxford University Press, 2016), p. 249.

For a fuller account of Francis Bacon's higher education, see Daniel R. Coquillette, "The Purer Fountains: Bacon and Legal Education," Boston College Law School, Legal Studies Research Paper Series, no. 52 (Jan. 27, 2005), SSRN: http://ssrn.com/abstract=655261; http://works.bepress.coquillette. Also published in *Essays to Commemorate the Advancement of Learning* (1605-2005), ed. by Julie Solomon and Catherine Gilmetti Martin (New York: Routledge, 2016; first pub. Aldershot: Ashgate Press, 2005).

[4] M. McGlynn, *The Royal Prerogative*, pp. 22-23.

[5] Francis Bacon, *The Reading on the Statute of Uses*, Spedding, VII, pp. 389-451, 423-424, HathiTrust, https://hdl.handle.net/2027/ucl.b3924335.

[6] *Spedding*, VII, 'Maxims of the Law,' regula 3, pp. 334-342; p. 335, HathiTrust, https://hdl.handle.net/2027/ucl.b3924335; "The Case of Revocation of Uses," pp. 557-567, esp. pp. 562-563.

[7] Spedding in his preface to the "Reading on the Statute of Uses" says a "double reading" would be a second reading by the same "Ancient." *Spedding*, VII, p. 391, HathiTrust, https://hdl.handle.net/2027/ucl.b3924335. Spedding says Bacon's first reading had been on Advowsons, in 1587 (Gray's Inn's website says 1588). *Spedding*, VII, p. 305. On Advowsons, see "Advowsons," *Legal Dictionary of the Encyclopedia of Law Project*, copyright 2014, http://legaldictionary.lawin.org/advowson/.

Bacon's *Reading on the Statute of Uses* reads much like Coke's *Reading on the Statute of Uses*. Sometimes, the law is just the law. According to David Chan Smith, they both relied upon the same, now extremely rare, source. David Chan Smith, *Sir Edward Coke and the Reformation of the Laws: Religion, Politics and Jurisprudence, 1578-1616*, Cambridge Studies in English Legal History (Cambridge: Cambridge University Press, 2014), p. 115, fn. 1.

views on uses,[1] just as he was progressive in his views on usury, seeing both as tools for the common good.

Former law students no doubt remember wrestling with the Statutes of Uses, perhaps in conjunction with the Statute of Wills, Rule in Shelley's Case, and Rule Against Perpetuities. One might imagine those late adolescent Gray's Inn students squirming in their seats through even one entire day devoted to the Statute of Uses! Their eyes were probably glazing over, their thoughts drifting to lunch, girlfriends, or perhaps "that new play just out." There was a recognized culture of play-writing and performing among the Inns of Court.[2] About twenty percent of the known playwrights of the time belonged to the Inns of Court.[3] It has been generally accepted that "Troilus and Cressida" was specifically written for an Inns of Court audience.[4] Jessica Winston's book, *Lawyers at Play: Literature, Law, and Politics at the Early Modern Inns of Court, 1558–1581*, is a valuable recent study.

Drama can be an important teaching tool. Bacon heartily endorsed the discipline of stage-playing in his writings on education for the development of skills, including stage presence, useful for public speaking. In this regard, he praised the pedagogy of the Jesuits, "for nothing better hath been put into practice."

> It will not be amiss to observe also, that even mean faculties, when they fall into great men of great matters sometimes work great and important effects. Of this I will adduce a memorable example; the rather, because the Jesuits appear not to despite this kind of discipline; therein judging (I think) well. It is a thing indeed, if practiced professionally, of low repute; but if it be made part of a discipline, it is of excellent use. I mean stage-playing: an art which strengthens the memory, regulates the tone and effect of the voice and pronunciation, teaches a decent carriage of the countenance and gesture, gives not a little assurance, and accustoms young men to bear being looked at. The example which I shall give, taken from Tacitus, is that of one Vibulenus, formerly an actor, then a soldier in the Pannonian legions.... He played the whole thing as if it had been a piece on the stage....[5]

---

[1] D. D. Heath, editor's preface, *Reading on the Statute of Uses*, Spedding, VII, pp. 389-450, 391, HathiTrust, https://hdl.handle.net/2027/ucl.b3924335.

[2] Jessica Winston, *Lawyers at Play: Literature, Law, and Politics in the Early Modern Inns of Court, 1558-1581* (Oxford: Oxford University Press, 2016), p. 3.

[3] O. Hood Phillips, ch. 2, "Shakespeare and the Inns of Court," *Shakespeare and the Lawyers*, p. 23; Arthur Underhill, "Law," in Sir Walter Raleigh, *Shakespeare's England, An Account of the Life and Manners of his Age*, I, (Oxford: Clarendon Press, 1916, repr. 1962), pp. 381-412, 410.

[4] Peter Ure, "Troilus and Cressida," in *Four Centuries of Shakespearian Criticism*, ed. by Frank Kermode (New York: Avon Books, 1965, p. b.), pp. 258-268, 258.

[5] *De Augmentis*, vi, transl., *Spedding*, IV (London: Longmans, 1883), p. 496, HathiTrust, http://hdl.handle.net/2027/hvd.hn6e7y.

Bacon had written much of the script for the Gray's Inn Revels of Christmas 1594–95, a Saturnalian celebration.[1] *The Comedy of Errors* was also performed at Gray's Inn in 1594, while *Twelfth Night* was performed at the Middle Temple in 1602.[2]

Portia tells "Morocco," "First forward to the temple; after dinner your hazard shall be made."[3]

What temple? Could Shakespeare have meant the Middle Temple?[4] The students ate at their Inns which also had a tradition of hospitality. Tradition says Queen Elizabeth gave the Middle Temple a twenty-nine foot dining table, still in its possession.[5] The Temple was the site of entertainments on a grand scale, such as a Christmas extravaganza sponsored by Robert Dudley, as "Palaphilos" and other Christmas festivities, presided over by the Lord of Misrule.[6]

Might Shakespeare have been alluding to Justinian's "Temple of Justice," that Roman emperor's poetic name for the *Corpus Iuris Civilis* which he commissioned ca. A.D. 529–565?[7]

In a poetical prologue of a work called the *Quaestiones de iuris subtilitatibus*, the author, whom Hermann Kantorowicz believes was Placentinus,[8] "one of the greatest jurists of his age,"[9] describes his vision of "Jurisprudence at work within the shrine of Justice." Three goddesses of law preside, Reason, Justice,

---

[1] BSQ, ch. 8, "'The Comedy of Errors' and the Gray's Inn Revels of Christmas 1594-95," pp. 105-129 and ch. 16, "Shake-Speare's Links with the Inns of Court," pp. 217-223.

[2] J. H. Baker, "Law and Legal Institutions," in *William Shakespeare, His World, His Work, His Influence*, vol. I, ed. by John F. Andrews (New York: Charles Scribner's Sons, 1985), pp. 41-54, 49; http://middletemplehall.org.uk/video/guided-tour.html.

[3] *The Merchant of Venice*, II, 1: 560-561.

[4] See Otto Vervaart's Rechtsgeschiedenis Blog, "In search of the true history of the Templars" (Feb. 13, 2014). https://rechtsgeschiedenis.wordpress.com/tag/templars/.

[5] But see Frederick Litchfield, *Illustrated History of Furniture*...2d American ed. (Boston: The Medici Society of America, 1922), pp. 118-119, https://books.google.com/books?id=7csLAQAAMAAJ (doubting the table came from the Queen). I had also read that the Queen had given the Middle Temple an oak screen. For an overview, see Linda Alchin, "Middle Temple Inn Theatre Playhouse (2012)," www.elizabethan-era.org.uk/middle-temple-inn-theatre-playhouse.htm.

[6] John Thomas Smith, *An Antiquarian Ramble in the Streets of London, with Anecdotes of their more celebrated residents*, 2d ed., 2, ed. by Charles Mackay (London, 1846), pp. 12-19 ("Palaphilos"); 19-20 (Lord of Misrule and Christmas festivities). From Dugdale's *Originales Judiciales*.

[7] Ernst Kantorowicz, *The King's Two Bodies*, p. 107-111, 109, esp. pp. 108-110 nn. 58-64. "The *templum Iustitiae* is often quoted and interpreted by the medieval jurists..." François Hotman (1524-1590), an important French Reformation writer of jurisprudence, "connected the *sacerdotes iustitiae* (that is, the *iurisconsulti*) with the *templum*." E. Kantorowicz, p. 109, n. 63. Bacon may have received instruction in the civil law from François's eldest son, Jean Hotman, when he was in France, 1576-79.

[8] Hermann Kantorowicz, ed., *Studies in the Glossators of the Roman Law: Newly Discovered Writings of the Twelfth Century* (Cambridge: Cambridge University Press, 1938), p. 3.

[9] "Placentinus," Ames Foundation, Bio-Bibliographical Guide to Medieval and Early Modern Jurists, Report No. c013, http://amesfoundation.law.harvard.edu/BioBibCanonists/Report_Biobib2.php?record_id=c013, last updated 4/18/2018.

and Equity, the "last-born daughter," of which Justice is central. They dwell together "in a pleasant grove at the top of a hill." Six "other" daughters, the civic virtues: *Religio, Pietas, Gratia, Vindicatio, Observantia, and Veritas*, surround them as guardians.[1]

Portia may suggest the goddess Iustitia (Justice)[2] or perhaps Jurisprudentia. There is a Neoplatonic literary pretense of putting a woman on a pedestal but denying her real power, but Portia has power. Bassanio's praise of her has been called hyperbole.[3] There may be an allusion with Portia to Astraea, in flattery of Queen Elizabeth.[4] Kenji Yoshino has remarked on the world's perpetual fascination with "The Lawyer of Belmont."[5]

In the poetical prologue ascribed to Placentinus, its author, in beautiful language, describes a "celestial banquet" where Reason (*Ratio*) had "star-like eyes" and "flashing keenness of mind." Iustitia, with dignity, "observed with many sighs the things of both God and men." Aequitas was there, too, "mirror[ing] nothing but kindness and good-will as she tried to balance the scales held by her mother." Note that it is the job of "law-weighing equity" to balance the scales of justice.[6]

Another temple worthy of mention is Francis Bacon's "holy temple." Bacon, in his *Novum Organum*, spoke of the need for mankind to question causes in nature, even if they seem self-evident and obvious, without ignoring things which might seem useless and abhorrent, like musk and civet — even they are used to make perfumes. By so doing, humanity would

---

[1] E. Kantorowicz, *The King's Two Bodies*, p. 108. https://books.google.ca/books?isbn=1400880785. Cicero was the glossators' source for the Virtues (*De. Invent.*, II,159ff). E. Kantorowicz, p. 108, nn. 59, 61.

Edmund Spenser had used *Iustitia* of the *Templum Iustitiae* to represent the Virgin Queen Elizabeth, with the Church of Isis standing for the ancient church of England. Frank Kermode, *Shakespeare, Spenser, Donne: Renaissance Essays* (Oxford: Routledge 2005, first pub. 1971), pp. 49-57, 54.

[2] The city of Venice had chosen to be personified *as* Justice (Resnik, *Representing Justice*, 79-82, images at 82). Those who knew, and who knew of Bruno's treatment, might have seen scope for satire and scorn in that.

[3] See, e.g., Kenji Yoshino, ch. 2, "The Lawyer, The Merchant of Venice," *A Thousand Times More Fair* (New York: Ecco 2011, Harper Collins e-book), pp. 29-54, *https://books.google.ca/books?isbn=006208772X*; Daniel Kornstein, ch. 4, "Fie Upon Your Law!," in *Kill All the Lawyers?* pp. 65-89, 76-77.

[4] Francis Yates, "Queen Elizabeth as Astraea," *Warburg Journal* 10 (1947), 27-82, as cited in E. Kantorowicz, *The King's Two Bodies*, p. 147, fn. 176; Judith Resnik, *Representing Justice*, pp. 21, 397 n. 63.

[5] Kenji Yoshino (1997), "The Lawyer of Belmont," *Yale Journal of Law and the Humanities* 9 (1997): no. 1, http://digitalcommons.law.yale.edu/yjlh/vol9/iss1/4/.

[6] E. Kantorowicz, IV.2, "'Iustitia Mediatrix,'" *The King's Two Bodies*, pp. 107-142, 109.

lay the foundation in human understanding for a "holy temple" based on "the model of the world."[1]

Bacon told Lord Burghley he intended to take all knowledge as his province. However, his temple of knowledge was not to be an edifice to pride.[2]

Perhaps, though, the last temple I found is the correct one. In the Villa Foscari (which is also known as *La Malcontenta*), which Richard Roe found matched geographically with Belmont in *Merchant*, there is actually a Roman temple within the house, complete with frescoes of Astraea. There are "grotesqueries," horribly ugly stone statues, within the garden, for those tracking the literary theme of the grotesque.[3] These facts lend further support to Roe's argument that the Villa Foscari was the "Belmont" Shakespeare had in mind.

The Author of *Merchant* and Law of a Higher Order

Shakespeare's legal accuracy is now acknowledged, but it used to be contested. Mark Edwin Andrews may have been right in dividing the case into four parts and finding that the first two parts concern law and the latter two concern mostly equity.[4]

In Act IV, Scene I, when Bassanio urges Portia: "To do a great right, do a little wrong," she refuses. "It must not be," she says, lest error be "recorded for as a precedent." "There is no power in Venice can alter a decree established."[5] The final decision of a court of common law would be a "judgment," while that of a court of equity, or of a sovereign, would be a "decree." Andrews, imagining the scene set in the court of King's Bench, thought "decree" was either a misnomer for "judgment," or else Shakespeare was imagining a courtroom of the future (or past?) in which law and equity were merged. Sir Thomas More had advocated for such a merger.[6] The decision of a sovereign would have been

---

[1] Preface to *Novum Organum*, *Spedding*, IV, pp. 99, 107; *Novum Organum*, i, aphorism 120; Peter Dawkins, *The Shakespeare Enigma* (London: Polair Publishing, 2004), p. 348; on the Temple of Solomon, see Dawkins, p. 218; Solomon 6:22-38, KJV.

[2] Peter Dawkins, "Baconian Philosophy," Francis Bacon Research Trust, fn. 10, citing the *Novum Organum*, i, aphorism 120 (*Spedding*, IV, pp. 106-107); http://www.fbrt.org.uk/pages/hermes_philosophy.html, , HathiTrust, http://hdl.handle.net/2027/hvd.hn6e7y.

[3] "Architecture," Villa Foscari, La Malcontenta, http://www.lamalcontenta.com/index.php/en/architecture and "Frescoes," http://www.lamalcontenta.com/index.php/en/frescoes.

[4] MEA, author's foreword, xiii-xiv.

[5] MEA, p. 8 (*Merchant*, IV, 1, 2157-61). Portia uses the equitable word "injunction" ((IV, 1, 1146). Of the three places where "decree" is found, one is Shylock's (IV, 1, 2021) and two are Portia's (I, 2, 17 and IV, 1, 2159).

For an example of interrogatories Bacon prepared for his "Tower work" in 1594, see "Nature of an examination upon interrogatories," *Spedding*, VIII, *ch.* 9, beginning at p. 316.

[6] MEA, pp. 54-55, n. 41.

---

by decree, but Shakespeare had been using the term "judgment" previously. What was on Shakespeare's mind when he wrote this passage?

A provision in the *Ordo Bambergensis*, a twelfth-century legal procedural treatise of Roman law, has been translated by Bruce Brasington thus: "When called to court, the one standing surety shall make good concerning that to be given the one for whom he has interceded. The debt is made good neither by fixed date nor condition, nor shall it be compensated for another as suits your convenience, even when the other party desires it, as in D. 14. c. 1, where it is said when compensation is not admitted *so that we do something evil lest another do something worse*" (italics added).[1] Bruce Brasington, the translator, says the *Ordo Bambergensis* was the only one of those he studied which connected the canon concerning the question of "greater or lesser evil" to debt ("Do a little wrong to do a little right").

This *Ordo* did not have a wide audience; it was soon overshadowed by those of Tancred and Richardus Anglicus.[2] The fact that the author of *Merchant* applied the concept of a lesser evil in the context of debt, as the *Ordo Bambergensis* did (and others considered by Brasington did not) is of course not definite proof that Bacon read this *Ordo* — but it does seem good evidence of it. He would have had the opportunity and incentive to consult it while composing his *Maxims*. What business would Shaxpere have had with it, as the bare facts depict him? The contrast between the legal mind and experience of Bacon, as he attempted to graft civilian law into English common law, and Shaxpere, as plaintiff or defendant in common law suits, is stark.

Until about the 1590s, judgments of law, but not equity decrees, were recorded. That changed under the chancellorship of Lord Ellesmere. A "case precedent" did not yet have binding authority, though. The word was just starting to refer to "prior, privately published judicial decisions, as well as to statutes and charters" used as evidence of a legal principle or rule.[3]

Perhaps Portia was being satirical. How to keep error out of human perception and judgment was, of course, one of Bacon's primary concerns.[4] It seems also to have been a primary concern of this play.

---

[1] Brasington, ch. 5, "The Ordo Bambergensis," in *Order in the Court* (Brill: Leiden, 2016), pp. 197-275, 238, n. 309.

[2] Brasington, preface, p. xiv and ch. 5, pp. 203, 217, 277.

[3] Polly J. Price, "Natural Law and Birthright Citizenship in Calvin's Case 1608," pp. 89-90, 107. http://digitalcommons.law.yale.edu/yjlh/vol9/iss1/2/.

[4] See Coquillette, FB, ch. 5, "The Final Vision," pp. 227-234. Bacon's use of the word "idol" came from the Greek *eidola*. The pre-Socratic atomist Democritus imagined that errors in our perception were due to distortion caused by tiny, interfering particles. It is *imaginative*. See FB, p. 228-231, 233-34, 293, citing *The Dictionary of Philosophy*, 4th ed., edited by Dagobert D. Runes, (New York 1942), p. 140, https://hdl.handle.net/2027/mdp.39015029913673.

I found myself wondering whether Ben Jonson's cryptic comment that "Shakespeare," whom he claimed to love "this side *idolatry*," had "small Latin and less Greek" might be alluding to Bacon's theory of the *eidola*, "sense perception by the means of emission of particles." See FB,

Bacon was averse to the rote citation of authority; in fact, he rarely cited authority and did not consider it binding.[1] Bacon advised: "First then, away with antiquities, and citations or testimonies of authors, and also with disputes and controversies and differing opinions — everything, in short, which is philological. Never cite an author except in a matter of doubtful credit."[2] When he was Chancellor, he did not cite case precedents as authority for his decisions, as Coke did.[3] Rather, Bacon decided cases based on the facts in individual cases. In time, he predicted that general rules or guidelines (maxims, or "laws of the laws"[4]) would evolve for dealing with

---

pp. 228-31, 233-34, 293. Jonson was a classicist. He would have known that Shakespeare had deep classical learning. His comment simply cannot be taken at face value.

The precocious Bacon had been tutored in Latin at home by his mother, Anne Cooke, a classical scholar and translator, as well as by a private tutor, Walsall. He entered Trinity College in 1573, at age twelve, with his older brother Anthony. Both he and Anthony were placed under the care of John Whitgift, later Archbishop. Brian Vickers, intro., *Francis Bacon, a Critical Edition of the Major Works*, pp. xxxviii to xl; Brian Vickers, ch. 8, "Bacon and Rhetoric," *The Cambridge Companion to Bacon*, (Cambridge: Cambridge University Press 1996), pp. 200-231, 206.

[1] Coquillette, "Legal Ideology and Incorporation I: The English Civilian Writers, 1523-1607," pp. 9-10, n. 16.

[2] 'Aphorisms on the Composition of the Primary History,' no. 3, in 'Preparative Towards an Experimental and Natural History,' *Spedding*, IV, p. 254.

[3] Coquillette, "Legal Ideology[..], I," p. 50; Coquillette, "Past the Pillars of Hercules," p. 571; Coquillette, "Legal Ideology[...], IV," p. 935, n. 359; preface to *Maxims of the Law, Spedding* VII, p. 311, HathiTrust, https://hdl.handle.net/2027/ucl.b3924335.

Before we give up scholarship, however, let us consider such a radical statement in light of other Baconian pronouncements. For example, he prefaced his law tract *The Elements of the Common Laws of England* with an "Epistle Dedicatory" to the Queen, in which he explains that he will be relying upon Justinian's Code that was being used in France, Italy, and Spain and had been invited into England by Edward I ("the lawgiver") — in his efforts to aid the Queen's reform of the laws. He wrote, "...as it cometh to pass in things so excellent, there being no precedent full in view but Justinian." *Montagu* III, pp. 219-220, HathiTrust, https://hdl.handle.net/2027/uc2.ark:/13960/t5v698p2n. Furthermore, he continued explaining that he did not "vouch the authorities" or "enforce or note upon them." He was "resolved not to derogate from the authority of the rules by vouching of the authority of the cases, though in mine own copy I had them quoted." He was going to be leaving out the citations, partly, it seems, so that people would not be swayed in their reasoning by the degree of authority of the person cited. *Montagu*, III, p. 222, HathiTrust, https://hdl.handle.net/2027/uc2.ark:/13960/t5v698p2n. HathiTrust has a 1639 version online. HathiTrust, https://hdl.handle.net/2027/osu.32437121660654 (also a 1741).

[4] This expression *legum leges (laws of the laws)* Bacon praises as "worthily and aptly called by a great civilian" in his law tract, "The Elements of the Common Laws of England," but he does not name that great civilian, which he, however, does name elsewhere as Azo. Bacon "did not affect to disguise into other words than the civilians use ...a matter of great authority and majesty." He makes it clear that he is going to be discussing civilian law, in a tract on the common law, without distinguishing the civilian contributions from the common. See *Montagu*, III, p. 221, HathiTrust, https://hdl.handle.net/2027/uc2.ark:/13960/t5v698p2n. On Bacon's "laws of laws," see Coquillette, FB, pp. 289-290.

---

recurring fact situations. Eventually, Chancery developed a body of its own case precedents, as "equity hardened into law."[1]

Prof. Daniel Coquillette credits Bacon's writings on equity with shaping the philosophical foundation for the flexible Federal Rules of Evidence in the United States.[2] Even our meaning of a "scientific fact" derives from Bacon's insistence, first in legal contexts, that a fact be narrowly defined.[3] There is so much we owe to Francis Bacon. Every four hundred years or so, perhaps it is a good idea to take stock of where we are.

Technology v. Memory

The printing of the old law reports was a two-edged sword. It made the law more accessible, but it increased the lawyer's memory burden by facilitating "information overload," just as legal search engines can do today. Something stage actors and lawyers had in common was the need to develop memory skills; in fact, it was a preoccupation of the times. Poetry could play a role in that.[4] Just as today, materials once converted to a new format were no longer kept. After they were printed, manuscripts we would consider valuable today would be discarded, once printed, or possibly recycled as "binder's waste." Parchment would last "forever," the monks had predicted, but not so paper. What would they think of a computer file?

Not surprisingly, errors could occur at all stages, from case reporting[5] through printing. One would assume that many printers could not read law French or Latin. The fonts they used in those days seemed designed to make the text as hard to read as possible. They mimicked handwriting. Imagine the eye strain in trying to read such texts, without modern lighting.[6] Coke, for one, was very nearsighted, but refused to wear spectacles.[7]

It should be kept in mind, as J. H. Baker warns, that the law then was not all found in the printed sources, but in oral and hand-written sources as well. Moreover, print sources were not considered superior to non-print sources.[8]

---

[1] Baker, *Intro*, p. 127.

[2] Coquillette, "Past the Pillars of Hercules," pp. 561, 564, 579.

[3] Barbara Shapiro, *A Culture of Fact* (Ithaca: Cornell University Press, 2003). http://www.cornellpress.cornell.edu/book/?GCOI=80140100453790.

[4] Richard J. Ross, "The Memorial Culture of Early Modern English Lawyers," pp. 229-326, 232 n. 3, 238 n. 23, 267, Digital Commons, http://digitalcommons.law.yale.edu/yjlh/vol10/iss2/1/.

[5] Ross, "The Memorial Culture," p. 278, 308, n. 261: "What hazard the truth is in when it passes through the hands of a report!" — Richard Hooker.

[6] Adam Max Cohen, *Shakespeare and Technology: Dramatizing Early Modern Technological Revolution* (New York: Palgrave MacMillan 2006, Digital 2008), p. 71.

[7] Bowen, *Lion*, p. 72.

[8] Abstract, J. H. Baker, *The Law's Two Bodies: Some Evidential Problems in English Legal History* (Oxford: Oxford University Press, 2001, Oxford Scholarship Online 2010), DOI:10.1093/acprof:oso/9780199245185.001.0001.

Another effect of printing was that the legal educational culture was changing, from a "gerontocratic culture," where the younger lawyers were trained and mentored by the older, experienced practitioners, to one in which law books were given a primary status for consultation.[1]

Mnemonic devices, including poetry such as Virgil's *Aeneid* and the idea of mapping, became even more important as the emphasis switched from learning principles of general application to memorization of case holdings.[2] This "culture of memorialization" among lawyers included an interest in history and antiquaries and a sense of an obligation to preserve the past by recording it.[3] Poetry with its rhyming structure aided memory. Bacon himself wrote about using "topics," an idea derived from Cicero's *Topica*, to spur remembrance.[4] Said Cicero, "It is easy to find things that are hidden if the hiding place is pointed out and marked."[5] Giordano Bruno had taught mnemonics, the art of memory.[6]

---

[1] Ross, "The Memorial Culture," pp. 271-272, 306.

[2] Ross, pp. 238, 270, 277; on mapping, see 282, 303. Mind-mapping is timely; see "How to Improve Memory with Mind Maps," iMindMap, https://imindmap.com/articles/how-to-improve-memory-with-mind-maps/.

[3] Ross, pp. 232, 238.

[4] Ross, "The Memorial Culture...," p. 284; on *Topica*, 280 n. 178.

[5] Ross, p. 280, n. 178.

[6] Michael White, *The Pope and the Heretic*, pp. 73-77, 196, 200, 205-7.

CHAPTER SEVEN: LAW SCHOOL HYPOTHETICAL

As Mark Edwin Andrews noted, in *Merchant*, the "strict adherence to legal forms and procedure" was one of Shakespeare's additions to his sources.[1] The art of using stories, parables, and fables for teaching purposes is ancient."[2] In law school, the "legal hypothetical" is a common teaching method. A narrative fact pattern is set out. Students are directed to spot all the legal issues therein, discuss the applicable law, and draw their conclusions. Ambiguities — multiple possible interpretations — are to be expected.

For example, was Portia a judge, advocate, *amicus curiae* — or imposter?[3] Mark Edwin Andrews identified Bellario and Portia as *amici curiae*, "friends

---

[1] MEA, foreword, xiii.

[2] Francis Bacon, preface to "The Wisdom of the Ancients," *The Works of Francis Bacon, the Wisdom of the Ancients and Other Essays*, 1609 (Roslyn NY: W.J. Black, 1932), p. 220; *Spedding*, VI, pp. 695-699.

In French, the word for an elderly person, *ancien*, is similar to the word for the pregnant state of a mother, *enceinte. Cassell's French-English Dictionary* (Collier Books, p.b., 1986), s.v. *enceinte*, pp. 344, 519.

Aesop's fables are "pregnant" with hidden meanings. Aristophanes quotes them in his comedies. Denison B. Hull, ed., trans., "Preface," *Aesop's Fables*, from the authentic third-century Valerius Babrius version (in verse), (Chicago: University of Chicago Press, 1960). (Might not "Valerius Babrius" have suggested the *persona* "Valerius Terminus" which Bacon used?) Traditionally, fables were actually used as "veiled political comment" with double meanings. Earle Toppings, "intro." *Aesop's Fables*, retold by Blanche Winder (New York: Airmont, 1965), p. 6. Prof. Coquillette explains that Bacon spoke through the *persona* of a "noble French philosopher" in the *Redargutio*. See Coquillette, FB, pp. 94-96 (on the *Redargutio*); 97-99 (on the *De Sapientia Veterum (Latin); Wisdom of the Ancients*, trans.); *Spedding*, VI, p. 607; *Spedding*, VI (trans.), p. 687.

[3] Sinsheimer, *Shylock*, p. 100.

---

of the court."[1] In a number of modern jurisdictions today, an amicus is an interested non-party which petitions for permission to file a brief advocating for a particular position or party. The term amicus is derived from the Roman *consilium*, a jurist, or even, in earlier times, any person who thought he had helpful information for the trier of fact. The consilium was a common figure in twelfth-century Italy.[2] Civilian lawyers advised judges in some late sixteenth-century and seventeenth-century English courts as well. These days, "it is the rare advocate who is a friend of the Court." Most are partisan.[3]

Hermann Sinsheimer explained that the fable of the pound of flesh had come to symbolize archaic law; therefore, it was apt for pedagogical purposes.[4] Edith Friedler has suggested the play would be a good vehicle for teaching comparative law in a law school survey course.[5] Daniel Kornstein calls Shakespeare "the greatest law school of all."[6]

As to Bacon, Prof. Coquillette has commented on his "comparativist philosophy," much like that of "contemporary English civilians...John Cowell, Alberico Gentili, William Fulbecke, and...Sir Julius Caesar," whereby he would pick and choose from the laws and customs he had learned abroad those best suited to transplanting and grafting into his own country's laws and customs.[7]

Kornstein says every lawyer eventually makes the pilgrimage to *The Merchant of Venice*. In looking at the play and its legal issues as if it were a hypothetical on a law school exam, at least initially, this would be my submission.

---

[1] Mark Edwin Andrews (MEA) quotes Lord Chief Justice Coke on the *amicus curiae*: "This custom cannot be traced to its origin but is immemorial in the English law. It is recognized in the Year Books, and it was enacted in 4 Hen. IV (1403) that any stranger as *"Amicus Curiae"* might move the court, etc. The custom included *instructing, warning,* and *moving* the court. The information so communicated may extend to any matter of which the court takes judicial cognizance." Coke, *Reports[...]*, 8, p. 15, "The Prince's Case," cited in MEA, p. 43, n. 21.

[2] The history and ambiguity of the *amicus curiae* is explored in S. Chandra Mohan, "The Amicus Curiae: Friends No More?" *Singapore Journal of Legal Studies* 2 (2010), pp. 352-374. Research Collection School of Law, http://ink/library.smu.sg/sol_research/975; Frank M. Covey, "Amicus Curiae: Friend of the Court," *DePaul L. Review* 9 (1959), pp. 30-37, 33-35, http://via. library.depaul.edu/law-review/vol9/iss1/5.

[3] Lee Epstein, "The Amicus Curiae Brief," *Constitutional Law for a Changing America: Institutional Powers and Constraints*, ninth ed. (Wash. D.C.: CQPress, 2016), 5.1.4.1, "Box 1-2.

[4] H. Sinsheimer, *Shylock*, pp. 75-76, Internet Archive, https://archive.org/details/ shylockthehistor01043lmbp.

[5] Edith Z. Friedler, "Essay: Shakespeare's Contribution to the Teaching of Comparative Law — Some Reflections on The 'Merchant of Venice,'" *LA L. Rev.* 60 (2000) http://digitalcommons. law.lsu.edu/cgi/viewcontent.cgi?article=5841&context, pp. 1087-1102.

[6] Daniel Kornstein, prologue, *Kill All the Lawyers?* p. xiii.

[7] FB, "Conclusion," p. 288.

A book published in Venice in 1587 revived the "pound of flesh" story. Its author, Gregorio Leti, relates how a Christian merchant told a Jewish merchant that Francis Drake had conquered San Domingo and taken much plunder. The Jewish merchant did not believe him and wagered a pound of his flesh that the report was false. The Christian merchant staked a thousand scudi on his story. The bet was duly recorded by a notary.[1] A 1754 translator thought this story could have been a source for *Merchant*.[2]

It was in 1587 that Pope Sixtus the Fifth created the position of "Promoter Fidei," commonly called the "Devil's Advocate." His job was to challenge the evidence for the canonization of particular saints.[3] The Council of Trent banned any writings by Gregorio Leti in 1667.[4]

Some Background on Chancery

It was said during this time that Chancery was a court not of law but of conscience. John Selden famously joked that equity varied like the size of the chancellor's foot.[5] Common law and equity had, over the past three and a half centuries, evolved as two distinct systems competing for business.[6]

Since the time of Henry VIII, England had been enveloped in religious upheaval. Thomas More, Henry's Chancellor, was not the first to use the equitable remedy of injunctions to prevent the enforcement of harsh judgments at common law, but he did make notable use of it. He told the common law judges he would keep issuing injunctions until they reformed their harsh laws.

Traditionally, change in the common law occurs slowly, often through the use of legal fictions such as the "straw man."[7]

---

[1] Sinsheimer, *Shylock*, pp. 75-76, from Leti's *Vita di Sixto Quinto*, an anecdotal biography of Pope Sixtus V.

[2] O. Hood Philips, *Shakespeare and the Lawyers*, pp. 100-102, 102; see also Edna Nahshon, ch. 2, "The Anti-Shylock Campaign in America," in Edna Nahshon and Michael Shapiro, eds., *Wrestling with Shylock: Jewish Responses to the Merchant of Venice* (Cambridge: Cambridge University Press, 2017), p. 38; Th. Niemeyer, "The Law against Shakespeare in *The Merchant of Venice*," *Michigan Law Review* 14, no. 1 (Nov., 1915), pp. 20-36.

[3] "History of the Devil's Advocate," *Unam Sanctam Catholicam*, www.unamsanctamcatholicam. com/history/79-history/351-devil-s-advocate.html.

[4] https://en.wikipedia.org/wiki/List_of_authors_and_works_on_the_Index_Librorum_Prohibitorum. A Dublin, 1766, edition of Leti's *Vita di Sixto Quinto* may be read at https://books.google. es/books?id=bgBgAAAAcAAJ.

[5] John Selden, *Table Talk of John Selden*, ed. for the Selden Society by Sir Frederick Pollock, together with an account of his life by Sir Edward Fry (London: Quaritch, 1927), p. 43, HathiTrust, https://hdl.handle.net/2027/wu.89094713427; Bowen, *Lion*, p. 360.

[6] MEA, pp. xi, 29-30, n. 13.

[7] A straw man or party: "a 'front,' a person who is put up in name only to take part in a deal ...." *Black's LD*, p. 1274.

The Jews

In Shakespeare's time, the Jews were not allowed to reside in England. They had not been allowed to reside there since 1290, and would not reside there again until 1655.[1]

Although Venice was a trading city teeming with foreigners, even in Venice Jews did not have the full rights of ordinary citizens. They were permitted to be in the city, but they were not allowed to permanently reside there until 1510.[2] They had to fight for a charter, which was finally granted in 1589. It gave them limited privileges and protection. For example, a merchant trader could bring his immediate family members with him into the city, so long as they stayed in the ghetto. They had to pay a fee even for these privileges, and their charter had to be renewed every ten years. They were only permitted to stay for a few months at a time. Even in Venice, Jews could not own real property.[3]

Because "j" was the same letter as "i" in Elizabethan England, the word "Jews" would have been pronounced as if the "j" were a "y,"[4] like the word *ius*.[5] In Elizabethan times, a capital "J" was used in place of a capital "I," or vice

---

For a discussion of "the Janus face of John Doe," see John C. Kleefeld, "From Brouhahas to Brehon Laws: Poetic Impulse in the Law," *Law and Humanities* 4 (2010), pp. 21-61, p. 41, n. 102, SSRN: http://ssrn.com/abstract=1937496.

Until 1868, the Japanese were still putting the "weightiest part of state documents" in verse. J. Huizinga, *Homo Ludens*, p. 126. Even Blackstone was a versifier. See, e.g., W. B. Odgers, Sir William Blackstone, *The Yale Law Journal* 28, no. 6 (April, 1919), pp. 542-566, JSTOR, www.jstor.org/stable/787211.

[1] "Exclusion Period for Jews," Oxford Jewish Heritage, http://www.oxfordjewishheritage.co.uk/english-jewish-heritage/174-exclusion-period-for-jews.

[2] Rena Lauer, "Jewish Law and Litigation in the Secular Courts of the Late MedievalMediterranean," *Critical Analysis of Law* 3, no. 1 (2016), pp. 114-132, 119.

[3] Baker, *Intro.*, p. 531; Aaron Kitsch, "Shylock's Sacred Nation," *Shakespeare Quarterly* 59, no. 2 (Summer, 2008), pp. 131-155, 132, 137. https://www.bowdoin.edu/faculty/a/akitch/pdf/sacred_nation.pdf. Writing in dialogue, Bacon recognizes "nations in name that are no nations in right" in "An Advertisement Touching an Holy War." *Spedding*, VII, p. 35, HathiTrust, https://hdl.handle.net/2027/ucl.b3924335. We all came from "one lump of earth," Bacon says, here, and in *Arguments of the Law, Case of the Post-Nati, Spedding*, VII, p. 664. *If you prick us, do we not bleed? Merchant*, III, 1, 1287.

[4] *Elizabethan Era Dictionary Usage*, http://www.elizabethanenglandlife.com/elizabethan-era-dictionary-english-usage.html. Note how Queen Elizabeth spelled "Jesus" in the prayer she wrote in French in her book of personal devotions: "Jhesus," (p. 87), "Jesus," (p. 93), and "Ihesus" (p. 96). William P. Haugaard, "Elizabeth Tudor's Book of Devotions: A Neglected Clue to the Queen's Life and Character," *The Sixteenth Century Journal* 12, no. 2 (Summer, 1981), pp. 79-106, 96.

[5] Ius was "the Latin word for law with an ethical, abstract sense, in contrast to *lex*, which was juridical, concrete. *Black's LD*, s.v. "jus" and "lex," pp. 770, 817. Ius could be defined, perhaps, as "law with the force of right." Mark Neustadt, "The Making of the Instauration: Science, Politics and Law in the Career of Francis Bacon," Ph.D. diss., 1987, Johns Hopkins University, 1990 (microfilm), p. 130.

---

versa, as in "John" spelled "Iohn."[1] Apparently, the pronunciation of "Jews" and *ius* would have been about the same.[2]

A Jew had no "nation"; rather, he was of his tribe and "the nation of traders."[3] One might, then, argue that any time a Jew was a party to a transaction or lawsuit, international law should apply. Alberico Gentili, a civilian jurist and member of Gray's Inn, considered English common law ill-suited for merchant cases or cases involving aliens, many of which, it seems, would have involved Jewish merchants or money lenders. In such cases, Gentili argued that the *ius gentium*, the law applicable to all peoples, would be better suited.[4] Originally, the *ius gentium* was the law applicable to non-Romans living within the Roman Empire.

Jurisdiction: Getting into an English Court of Law, ca. 1597

The Duke says he has jurisdiction. Ordinarily, that would tell you not to discuss jurisdiction in analyzing a hypothetical. As an academic exercise, this was my analysis under sixteenth-century English law.

- Debt: If Shylock had come to court pleading an Action for Debt, his recovery would have been limited to the amount of the debt.[5] One drawback of an Action for Debt was that a defendant could "wage his law" and call in eleven "oath-takers" to vouch for him,[6] thus defeating the lender's claim. Importantly, an action by or against a surety was not allowed under Debt.[7] Thus, even for a debt on an obligation under

---

[1] E.g., Bacon dedicated the third edition of his *Essays* to Sir Iohn Constable, *Spedding,* VI, p. 539, HathiTrust, https://hdl.handle.net/2027/ucl.31175002285222.

[2] See Marc Shell, ch. 3,"The Wether and the Ewe," *Money, Language and Thought,* for discussions of: the word "Jew" in *Merchant* (Shell, pp. 47-83, 48, 49 fn. 7) and two works by Bacon: his essay, "Of Usury," *Spedding,* VI, and his *Reading on the Statute of Uses, Spedding,* VII, (Shell, pp. 48-51, 54, 72 n. 45), https://books.google.ca/books?isbn=0520043790.

[3] Aaron Kitch, "Shylock's Sacred Nation," pp. 132-133.

In *Calvin's Case,* Polly Price finds Coke deriving his law of aliens from Protestant doctrine on Jews, itself derived from thirteenth century canon law on infidels. Scholars are "only beginning to explore the intersection of law and religion in the development of concepts of citizenship." Polly J. Price, "Natural Law and Birthright Citizenship in Calvin's Case (1608)," *Yale Journal of Law and the Humanities* 9, no. 1, pp. 89-90, 128, http://digitalcommons.law.yale.edu/yjlh/vol9/iss1/2/.

[4] Douglas M. Johnston, *The Historical Foundations of World Order: the Tower and the Arena,* (The Hague: Martinus Nijhoff, 2008), p. 387, https://books.google.ca/books?isbn=9004161678.

[5] Maitland, *Equity and the Forms of Action* (1916 ed.), lecture 5, "Debt," p. 357, HathiTrust, http://babel.hathitrust.org/cgi/pt?id=uc2.ark:/13960/t8ff3zj88;view=1up;seq=377.

[6] Maitland, p. 357.

[7] Baker, "Assumpsit in Lieu of Debt," *Intro.,* p. 390; R. H. Helmholz, R. H. Helmholz, "Assumpsit and Fidei Laesio," *Law Quarterly Review* 91 (1975), pp. 406-432, 411, n. 31.

---

seal,[1] it would seem that Shylock could not have brought his action under Debt.

- Covenant: It does not appear that Shylock could have brought his suit as an Action on the Covenant, although it was a sealed instrument, since Covenant excluded actions for recovery of a debt — "until some point in the seventeenth century."[2] Covenant as a remedy was falling into disuse[3] (Under Covenant, you could no longer get "specific performance" (an action to make a person do something — in personam — as opposed to an action for damages — in rem) after the fourteenth century. This is irrelevant, for Shylock was not seeking specific performance). Covenant would not have helped Shylock.[4]

- Assumpsit: *Indebitatus assumpsit*, to the best of my knowledge, did not apply where a document was under seal.[5] J. H. Baker says assumpsit *would* lie against a surety.[6] However, Maitland says that, after Slade's Case was decided (1602), assumpsit would lie where debt would lie,[7] and debt did not lie against a surety.[8] Antonio was Bassanio's surety. It appears that Shylock could not have brought the case under assumpsit — at least not before 1602. It is impossible to be sure what the actual practice was, from this remove. The written records may not tell the whole story.[9] One advantage of assumpsit, when applicable, was the availability of a jury trial rather than wager of law.[10] R. H. Helmholz has shown that the canon law action, *laesio fidei*, influenced the development of the action of assumpsit.[11]

---

[1] Baker, "Debt on an Obligation," *Intro.*, pp. 368-371, 368.

[2] Maitland, "Covenant," *Equity and the Forms of Action*, lecture 5, p. 358.

[3] Maitland, p. 357.

[4] Baker, "The Action of Covenant," *Intro*, pp. 361-365, 364.

[5] "Assumpsit," *Black's LD*, p. 112.

[6] Baker, *Intro.*, p. 390.

[7] Maitland, "Assumpsit," "Trover," *Equity and the Forms of Action*, lecture 6, p. 364.

[8] Maitland, p. 362, HathiTrust, http://hdl.handle.net/2027/uc2.ark:/13960/t8ff3zj88?urlappend=%3Bseq=382; "Assumpsit," *Black's LD*, p. 112.

[9] As A. W. Brian Simpson wrote about Slade's Case, "The conclusions advanced here can only be tentative." A. W. Brian Simpson, "The Place of Slade's Case in the History of Contract," *Law Quarterly Review* 74 (1958), pp. 381-396, 396.

[10] Although obsolete already in the seventeenth century, wager of law was not completely abolished until 1833. Maitland, "Trover," *Equity and the Forms of Action*, lecture 6, p. 364.

[11] R. H. Helmholz, "Assumpsit and Fidei Laesio," *Law Quarterly Review* 91 (1975), pp. 406-432, cited in Andrew Zurcher, ch. 2, "Consideration, Contract and The End of '*The Comedy of Errors*,'" in *Shakespeare and the Law*, ed. by Paul Raffield and Gary Watt (Oxford: Hart Publishing, 2008), p. 21, n. 6.

Other "Considerations"

Consideration: Under the Tudors, consideration or "good cause" was required for a binding contract. For *indebitatus assumpsit*, there had to be a *quid pro quo* ("this for that"),[1] but consideration was not required.[2] A rash deal, made recklessly, would be one made without consideration which originally meant just that, forethought.[3] Antonio had entered into a deal that was made in "merry jest," the very opposite of a serious undertaking. However, his bond was made under seal. Oral (parol) evidence extraneous to the writing under seal would have been inadmissible.[4] A sealed instrument predated the doctrine of consideration and required no consideration.[5] Its validity could not be challenged.[6] For these reasons, to the best of my knowledge, the consideration argument was foreclosed to Antonio.

Consideration must be both "good" and "valuable." Shylock calls Antonio a "good man."[7] Theological meanings aside, on the surface Shylock meant that Antonio was financially sufficient, "good for the money" — but was he, with all his ships at risk? Antonio thought he was in good shape financially (See Act I, Scene 1, his second speech). However, Shylock was more shrewd.

Bottomry was the earliest form of insurance, by which a loan made on the security of a ship and its cargo would only be payable if and when the ship and its cargo came safely into port.[8] While such an arrangement would have

---

[1] Baker, "The Doctrines of Consideration," *Intro.*, pp. 386-388.

[2] Simpson, "The Place of Slade's Case in the History of Contract," p. 392.

[3] Baker, p. 399.

[4] Baker, pp. 386-392, 386, 391, 396.

[5] "Contract under seal," *Black's LD*, p. 295.

[6] MEA, pp. 46-49 nn. 25, 27-28; p. 51 n. 34; p. 56-58, nn. 45-48.

[7] The Cathars had called themselves "good men" or "good Christians." See Antonio Sennis, ch. 1, "Good Men in the Languedoc...," pp. 1-20; Julien Thery-Astruc, ch. 4, "The Heretical Dissidence of the 'Good Men' in the Albigeois (1276-1329)...," pp. 79-111; and Clair Taylor, ch. 12, "Looking for the 'Good Men' in the Languedoc...," p. 242-256, all in *Cathars in Question*, ed. by Antonio Sennis (Rochester NY: York Medieval Press, 2016). See also Mark Gregory Pegg, "On Cathars, Albigenses, and good men of Languedoc," *Journal of Medieval History* 27, no. 2 (2001), pp. 181-195 (Abstract, as corrected by the pdf). http://www.sciencedirect.com/science/article/pii/S0304418101000082; "Albigenses," Encyclopedia Britannica, https://www.britannica.com/topic/Albigenses.

Languedoc Jews were persecuted as well. Whether by design or as collateral damage, "the culture of the troubadours was lost." See "Cathars and Cathar Beliefs in the Languedoc," copyright 2010-2016, http://www.cathar.info/ (twelfth par. It is nicely illustrated.); Michael Bryson and Arpi Movsesian, ch. 6.I, "The Death of Fin'amor, the Albigensian Crusade and its Aftermath," *Love and its Critics: From the Song of Songs to Shakespeare and Milton's Eden*, (Open Book Publishers, 2017), pp. 215-294, 232, https://www.openbookpublishers.com/htmlreader/978-1-78374-348-3/ch6.xhtml#_idTextAnchor025.

[8] Hartley Withers, "The Rise of Insurance," *The Cornhill Magazine*, ed. by George Smith and William Makepeace Thackeray, new ed., series 3, no. 22 (Jan.-June 1907), pp. 661-677, 662 (bottomry defined); p. 666. Marine insurance first developed between England and Venice

---

protected Antonio's life, his obligation to repay Shylock would have arisen when his ships came in.

As Luke Wilson points out, marine insurance was available in sixteenth-century London. Even so, there was still a great deal of uncertainty in insuring marine risks,[1] a state much remedied, however, by the passage of the Francis Bacon Act of 1601. In this Act, Queen Elizabeth acknowledged the underwriting of ships by groups such as the Hanseatic League.[2] A special Court of Assurances was also established for the remediation of insurance cases. Francis Bacon was highly instrumental in the passage of this Act.[3]

Note, however, that the play never tells us it is set in sixteenth-century London. I think it is set in twelfth-century Venice, for comparative purposes. While the early history of insurance is hazy, twelfth-century Venice did not have marine insurance. The first known marine insurance contract is from Genoa ca. 1350.[4]

in 1512. "Insurance Street" was a side street off of the Campo di San Giacomo, where trading took place. Withers, p. 672.

[1] Luke Wilson, ch. 8, "Drama and Marine Insurance in Shakespeare's London," in *The Law in Shakespeare*, ed. by Constance Jordan and Karen Cunningham (Houndsmills UK: Palgrave Macmillan, 2007), pp. 127-143, 128-130, 132.

[2] Withers, "The Rise of Insurance," p. 672. For Bacon's advice on risk management, see Alberto Feduzi and Jochen Runde, "Uncovering Unknown Unknowns: Towards a Baconian Approach to Management Decision-Making," in *Organizational Behavior and Human Decision Processes* 124, no. 2 (July 2014), pp. 268-283 ("building on ideas put forward by Bacon, 1620"); "Why Cambridge Academics Believe that Francis Bacon (1561-1626) May Hold the Key to Business Success," Brain Food, University of Cambridge, Aug. 27, 2014, https://insight.jbs. cam.ac.uk/2014/why-cambridge-academics-believe-that-francis-bacon-1561-1626-may-hold-the-key-to-business-success.

[3] "The Evolution of Reinsurance," Munich RE, https://www.munichre.com/site/marclife-mobile/get/documents_E1167439029/marclife/assset.marclife/Documents/Publications/Munich_Re_Evolution_of_Reinsurance.pdf ("Francis Bacon Act of 1601"); David M. Holland, "A Brief History of Reinsurance," article from *Reinsurance News*, no. 65, Society of Actuaries (February 2009), pp. 4-29, 4-12, https://www.soa.org/library/newsletters/reinsurance.../rsn-2009-iss65-holland.aspx; see also Guido Rossi, ch. 6, and A. B. Leonard, ch. 7, *Marine Insurance: Origins and Institutions, 1300-1850*, ed. by A. B. Leonard, https://books.google.ca/books?isbn=1137411384. For Bacon's notes, "Speech on the bringing in of a bill concerning assurances among merchants," see *Spedding*, X, p. 34, HathiTrust, https://hdl.handle.net/2027/ucl.b3618245.

[4] "History of Marine Cargo Insurance," Vazzano Ltd., International and Domestic Insurance Brokers, 2018 by Vazzano Ltd., http://www.cargoins.com/history; "The Evolution of Reinsurance," Munich RE, https://www.munichre.com/site/marclife-mobile/get/documents_E1167439029/marclife/assset.marclife/Documents/Publications/Munich_Re_Evolution_of_Reinsurance.pdf ("The Italians are credited with the first marine insurance policy," in 1350.); Samuel Marshall, *A Treatise on the Law of* Insurance, in Four Books, vol. 1 (Philadelphia, 1810), pp. 10-11 ("Maritime insurance is thought to have developed in the Italian states "about the end of the 13th century"; Yadira Gonzalez de Lara, *The Birth of Insurance Contracts*, work in progress, 2009, p. 1, http://citeseerx.ist.psu.edu/viewdoc/download?doi=10.1.1.557.8623&rep =repl&type=pdf; Florence Edler de Roover, "Early Examples of Marine Insurance," *Journal of Economic History* 5, no. 2 (Nov. 1945), pp. 172-200, 174-176, pub. online 2/1/2011, https://doi. org/10.1017/S0022050700112975; Cornelius Walford, *The Insurance Cyclopeadia* I (London, 1871),

Morally, a promise (in Italian, *polizza*, from which the word insurance *policy* comes) to pay money should be honored. Shylock, though, did not even care if he got his money, so long as he got his revenge. For Shylock, Antonio *himself* was the quid pro quo, just as possession of mankind was what Satan demanded of God in the *Processus Belial*. "Valuable" referred to monetary worth, market value, price. Antonio was neither "good" nor "valuable," as Shakespeare's characters acknowledge. Shylock's "interest" in the deal was not a financial percentage; it was Antonio himself.

Usury: A 1571 English statute created a common law offense supplemental to the ecclesiastical courts' long-standing jurisdiction over all usury. Under this statute, interest over ten per cent per annum was considered excessive and, categorically, usury. In 1625, King James reduced the rate to eight percent,[1] a reform for which Bacon had argued in his essay, "Of Usury." The Church courts had already divided usury into "grand" and "petit" usury before the statute, with proportionate penalties. Since Shylock did not charge any interest on his loan to Antonio, it would seem that he did not commit usury. A penalty for nonpayment of debt was not even considered "cloaked" usury."[2] However, although not delineated as interest, "part of the payment on a sea loan was clearly a risk charge," which ran afoul of the Church's prohibition on usury, especially after Pope Gregory IX banned sea loans in 1236.[3]

At any rate, we can see that Shylock would have problems getting his case before a common law judge in London ca. 1597.

If the play were set in the twelfth century in Venice, there would be some interesting historical facts at play. After 1166, the Jews had to sue in secular courts. First their Jewish-run court system was forbidden to them, and then the Byzantine-run system, dedicated to Jewish cases, was taken from them as well. Venice did not follow the *ius commune*, but rather, gave its judges a great deal of discretion. At least from 1350–1450, in Candia, Crete, a colony of Venice, in cases involving Jews, Catholic judges were charged with rendering justice "according to their perception of the normative rabbinical

---

pp. 486-487. "The earliest Chambers of Insurance appeared about the twelfth century in Mediterranean ports, of which Venice was probably chief." Walford, pp. 486-487.

[1] Sidney J. Low and F. S. Pulling, *The Dictionary of English History* (London, 1884), p. 603.

[2] Richard H. Helmholz, "Usury and the Medieval Church Courts," *Speculum* 61, no. 2 (1986), pp. 364-380: 366; 379-380 (Elizabethan period), http://chicagounbound.uchicago.edu/cgi/viewcontent.cgi?article=11246&context=journal_articles.

[3] David M. Holland, "A Brief History of Reinsurance," p. 6, https://www.soa.org/library/newsletters/reinsurance-section-news/2009/february/rsn-2009-iss65-holland.aspx, excerpted at *The Actuary*, http://www.theactuary.com/archive/old-articles/part-3/reinsurance-3A-a-brief-history/.

legal approach" (akin to a federal court applying the law of an individual state as if it were a state court, perhaps).[1]

Custom and Usage

Although it seems hard to comprehend, Sinsheimer wrote that it was not uncommon for contracts, until at least the fifteenth century, to contain "pound of flesh" penalty clauses dating back to the Twelve Tables of Rome, 450 B.C.[2] However, the language in medieval contracts was archaic, not enforced, and perhaps, even in ancient Rome, "never meant to be taken seriously."[3] Such language was hyperbole,[4] intended to reinforce the seriousness of the transaction.[5] The phrase *partis secanto* or *secare partis*, meaning "to cut apart," may have only ever meant "to divide up the debtor's goods among his creditors."[6] Still, a deal was a deal, and any oral understanding or misunderstanding was not part of a contract under seal.

The Court of Admiralty had for many years gotten away with ignoring law on the books restricting its jurisdiction. That changed when Coke began to enforce the law. "We didn't think you really meant it," Admiralty might have said, to which Coke probably laughed. In Antonio's case, though, his careless trust of someone he had no reason to trust very nearly cost him his life.

Francis Bacon wrote that there were certain things one did not joke about. One of them was a man's business matters. "As for jest, there be certain things which ought to be privileged from it; namely, religion, matters

[1] Rena N. Lauer, "Jewish Law and Litigation in the Secular Courts of the Late Medieval Mediterranean," *Critical Analysis of Law* 3:1 (2016), pp. 114-132, 119, 122, 127.

[2] H. Sinsheimer, p. 82;. Edward Wynne, *Eunomus: Or, Dialogues Concerning the Law and Constitution of England*, fifth ed. (London, 1822), dialogue 2, p. 269, https://books.google.ca/books?id=QgVNAQAAMAAJ.

[3] M. Radin, "Secare Partis: The Early Roman Law of Execution against a Debtor," *The American Journal of Philology* 43, no. 1 (1922), pp. 32-48, p. 33 (quoting A. Gellius), JSTOR, https://www.jstor.org/stable/289327. But see Roland Obenchain, "Roman Law of Bankruptcy," *Notre Dame Law Review* 3, no. 4, (1928), pp. 169-200, 174, 176-77 (disagreement among authorities), https://scholarship.law.nd.edu/ndlr/vol3/iss4/1/.

[4] "Hyperbolus," a politician, was lambasted in Aristophanes' comedy, *The Frogs*. A "bolus" is a ball, a rounded mass, a pill to be swallowed." *Webster's*, p. 116. "Laws be like pills all gilt over, which if they be easily and well swallowed down are neither bitter in digestion nor hurtful to the body." Francis Bacon, *Spedding*, X, p. 19, HathiTrust, https://hdl.handle.net/2027/ucl.b3618245, (notes for "Speech to repeal superfluous laws). How to persuade Parliament to pass legislation? Sugar-coat the plea in a play? In his "Speech on Bringing in a Bill Against Abuses in Weights and Measures," Bacon used the expression, "bandy bills like balls." *Spedding*, X, pp. 17-18, HathiTrust, https://hdl.handle.net/2027/ucl.b3618245.

[5] H. Sinsheimer, p. 82.

[6] Edward Wynne, *Eunomus: Or, Dialogues Concerning the Law and Constitution of England*, 5th ed. (London, 1822), dialogue 2, p. 269, https://books.google.ca/books?id=QgVNAQAAMAAJ; "Debt," *Conflict in Ancient Greece and Rome: The Definitive Political, Social, and Military Encyclopedia* (Santa Barbara CA: ABC-Clio, 2016), p. 853.

of state, great persons, any man's present business of importance, and any case that deserveth pity."[1]

Among the many practical lessons for law students in this play might be: don't gouge your opposing party in a negotiation. Leave him his dignity, or you may later wish you had.

Speaking of hyperbole, Tobie Matthew used that word in writing about his intimate friend Bacon: [He was] "a man so rare in knowledge of so many several kinds, endued with the facility and felicity of expressing it all, in so elegant, significant, so abundant, and yet so choice and ravishing a way of words, of metaphors, and allusions, as perhaps the world hath not seen, since it was a world. I know, this may seem a great Hyperbole, and strange kind of riotous excess of speech; but the best means of putting me to shame, will be for you (the reader) to place any other man of yours, by this of mine." [2]

Matthew also wrote to Bacon, in a postscript to an undated letter, a statement famously disputed as to its meaning: "The most prodigious wit that I ever knew of my nation, and of this side of the sea, is of your Lordship's name, though he be known by another."[3]

J. P. Feil attempted to prove that Tobie Matthew was praising a different Bacon, a Jesuit Thomas Bacon, instead of Francis Bacon. N. B. Cockburn points out the problems with his analysis. [4]

Bacon uses a word coined by Shakespeare, "transcendence" in the "now-obsolete sense of hyperbole" in his essay, "Of Adversity." Shakespeare had used the word just once, in *All's Well That Ends Well*.[5] "Tranect," a word which Shakespeare coined to refer to the ferry in *Merchant*, comes from the Latin *traicio (transicio)*, "to transport," which is related to *traiectio*, "a passing over, crossing over, hyperbole."[6]

Inadequate Remedy at Law

One is not entitled to equity jurisdiction unless his remedy at law is inadequate.[7] That was certainly Antonio's situation. Shylock's situation

---

[1] "Of Discourse," 'The Essays, or, Counsels, Civil and Moral' (1625 ed.) Spedding, VI, p. 455, HathiTrust, https://hdl.handle.net/2027/ucl.b3618242.

[2] John Donne, *A Collection of Letters Made by Sir Tobias Matthew Kt* ...1660, as cited in Nieves Matthews, ch. 2, "An Angel in Paradise," *The History of a Character Assassination*, pp. 13, 453 n. 2. For Matthew on Bacon, see also Spedding, XIV, p. 286, HathiTrust, https://hdl.handle.net/2027/ucl.31175012007947.

[3] See BSQ, ch. 22, "The Tobie Matthew Postscript," pp. 255-276. The Italian translation of Bacon's Essays was banned by the Holy Office of the Inquisition.

[4] J. P. Feil, "The Tobie Matthew Postscript," *Shakespeare Quarterly* 18, no. 1 (Winter, 1967), pp. 73-76, 75, JSTOR, http://www.jstor.org/stable/2868068; N. B. Cockburn, BSQ, ch. 22, "The Tobie Matthew Postscript," pp. 255-276.

[5] McQuain, *Coined by Shakespeare*, p. 225.

[6] *Cassell's Latin*, p. 225.

[7] For example, see Doug R. Rendleman, "The Inadequate Remedy at Law Prerequisite for an Injunction" (1981), Faculty Publications, paper 886, http://scholarship.law.wm.edu/cgi/viewcontent.cgi?article=2004&context=facpubs.

was more complicated. One equity maxim is "He that seeks equity must do equity." The equities, on balance, did not favor Shylock. What he sought was unconscionable, so wrong it shocks the conscience. Yet, by the end of the play, Shakespeare has us feeling sorry for him. Hermann Sinsheimer has observed that Shakespeare left Shylock his dignity, even when it seemed that all else was taken from him.[1] "A just man stands, though he fall seven times." Prov. 24:16.[2] When questioned before the Diet of Worms, Martin Luther had reportedly said, "Here I stand. I can do no other. God help me."[3] Shylock sought revenge, but in the end he was treated with compassion. His remedy at law turned out to be illusory, but his estate was preserved for his daughter and her husband.

Uses and Trusts

When the Duke tells Shylock that half his property is now Antonio's, but that Antonio's half could be remitted to a fine if Shylock were humble, Portia quickly says, "Let not Antonio's half be a fine, but the state's." Antonio then says he will waive his right to "his half" so long as he can have the use of "the other half" (the state's half) during the life of Shylock. That is some clever finagling but the Duke allows it. According to the deed of gift, at Shylock's death all of Shylock's property will go to his Christian son-in-law Lorenzo and the newly-converted Jessica.

As to trusts: essentially, the chancery courts came to distinguish two interests in any one piece of property: a legal interest (title), and a beneficial interest. In what became the modern law of trusts, one person might hold the bare legal title to property for the use or benefit, of another, still sometimes called the *cestui que trust*. The Statute of Uses of 1536 executed the use, bringing the legal interest over to the equitable interest, merging them into the same entity and thereby extinguishing the trust, so that the beneficiary of the trust was now the legal as well as the beneficial owner. The Statute of Uses had tax consequences.[4] However, there were exceptions. In the case of a "use on a use" *or* an active duty imposed on the trustee (feoffee), then the Statute of Uses did not extinguish the "use," and the legal and beneficial

---

[1] H. Sinsheimer, *Shylock*, p. 114.

[2] Stephan Kuttner discusses the ease with which the glossators moved back and forth between legal and biblical usages when they opposed Ulpian's "justice is a constant and enduring will" to Proverbs 24:16. Stephan Kuttner, "A Forgotten Definition of Justice." In *Melanges Gerard Fransen* 2, ed. by A. M. Stickler and S. Kuttner (Rome; Studia Gratiana 20, 1976). Reprinted in *The History of Ideas and Doctrines of Canon Law in the Middle Ages* 5 (London, 1980, Variorum reprint, 1992). pp. 75-109, 79.

[3] Dan Graves, "Here I stand, I can do no other, so help me God. Amen," Christian History Institute, Oct. https://christianhistoryinstitute.org/blog/post/here-i-stand-i-can-do-no-other/.

[4] Baker, "Trusts," *Intro.*, pp. 328-332.

interests remained separate.[1] Incidentally, the word "use" did not come from the word for law, "ius." Rather, it was the short version of the law French phrase *ad opus et ad usus*, meaning "for the benefit and use [of]."[2]

The earliest known "use on a use" situation was upheld by Francis Bacon's own father, Sir Nicholas Bacon, when he was the Lord Keeper of the Seal in the early years of Queen Elizabeth. Bertie, dowager duchess of Suffolk, had fled to Poland to escape religious persecution under Queen Mary. She sold her land to her lawyer, with the secret understanding that he would hold legal title for her equitable use (benefit). There was much religious-based opposition to the Statute of Uses 1536. In 1540, Crown lawyers were actually imprisoned in the Tower for advising clients on how to evade it.[3]

---

[1] Baker, *Intro.*, p. 288-295. See MEA, Table I, "The result of the creation of a *use after a use*," and Table II, "The result of the creation of the *Trust*," pp. 74-75.

[2] Baker, p. 286; F. W. Maitland, "The Origin of Uses," *Harvard Law Review* 8, no. 3 (Oct. 25, 1894), pp. 127-137, 127, JSTOR, http://www.jstor.org/stable/1321713.

For further reading on *ius*, see Charles J. Reid, Jr., "Thirteenth Century Canon Law and Rights: The Word *Ius* and its Range of Subjective Meanings," *Studia Canonica* 30 (1996), pp. 295-342.

[3] Baker, "Trusts," *Intro.*, p. 329, n. 46.

Chapter Eight: Characters, Counterparts, and Others — Part I

Portia

Portia appears in the Duke's court as Balthazar, the "young doctor of Rome."[1] There had been a "common medieval practice of a lay (non-church) court making use of professional advisers."[2] Shylock and Gratiano address Portia as "judge," actually.[3] Indeed, some of her first words in the play are in the pun "Good sentences, and well pronounced." (I, 2, 204). She identifies herself as a teacher, although, as a woman in love, she tells Bassanio she is an "unlesson'd, unschool'd, unpracticed girl."[4] At one point, Shylock is so sure she is on his side that he praises her, saying "A Daniel come to judgment." Then, she turns the tables on him.

Portia manages to save Antonio's physical life and Shylock's soul, in the Christian view, through his forced conversion and confession of faith.[5]

---

[1] *Merchant*, IV, 1, 2089. In III, 2, 1672, Bassanio praises Antonio as one "in whom the ancient Roman honour more appears than any that draws breath in Italy." www.opensourceshakespeare.org. As to "...whether you'll admit him" and the contemporaneous controversy over whether solicitors could practice law in the courts, which was resolved in 1597, see MEA, pp. 49-50, n. 29.

[2] Phillips, *Shakespeare and the Lawyers*, pp. 109-112, 111.

[3] *Merchant*, IV, 1: 2165, 2178, 2190, 2193, 2197, 2247, 2250 (Shylock); IV, 1, 2259, 2264, 2271 (Gratiano). www.opensourceshakespeare.org.

[4] Portia: "I can easier teach twenty what were good to be done, than be one of the twenty to follow mine own teaching...." (Merchant, I, 2 14-16; III, 2, 1529).

[5] Karl Elze explains St. Augustine's "Compel them to come in" forced conversion. Karl Elze, "*The Merchant of Venice*," in *Essays on Shakespeare*, trans. L. Dora Schmitz (London, 1874), essay 3, pp. 67-118, 106-107.

Instead of forfeiting all he owns to the State, Shylock is left with a life estate in half of all he possesses. Antonio has the use of the other half, for the duration of Shylock's life, with provision for all Shylock "dies possess'd of" to go to Shylock's heirs upon Antonio's death.

Portia did not draw up a will; rather, she drew up a deed of gift. Either would have been revocable.[1] Could the alien Shylock have made a will in England? I do not think so. Aliens could not inherit land,[2] own real property (land and whatever is erected or growing upon or affixed to it),[3] bring a real estate action,[4] sue for debts, or be sworn as witnesses, for Jews were not allowed to make an oath.[5] At the time Shylock "consented" to the decree, he apparently owned nothing of value, since Jessica had stolen his wealth. Jews maintained portable wealth, since they had no permanent residence. While his forced religious conversion gave him a better legal status, it shocks the collective conscience of those used to the protection by law of "certain inalienable rights."

Balthasar/Daniel

For a minor character, there is much to be said. Bellario vouched for Balthasar, saying never was there one so young with so old a head. Bacon wrote: "A man that is young in years may be old in hours, if he hath lost no time, but that happeneth rarely."[6]

The name Balthasar would have caught the Queen's attention since Balthazar Gerard, a fanatical French Catholic, had assassinated William of Orange in 1584, for which he was made to suffer an excruciatingly painful death by torture. "But Machiavel knew not of a friar Clement, nor a Ravaillac, nor a Jaureguy, nor a Balthazar Gerard....."[7] These men were all assassins.

Cf.: "Therefore, what shall we say if after joinder of issue he is not convicted by confesses? He must be treated more leniently" (D. 50.c.3). Bruce Brasington, *Order in the Court*, ch. 5, p. 236, (*Ordo Bambergensis*, provision for the payment of triple advocate's fees in the case of an overclaim).

[1] C. M. Brune, *Shakespeare's Use of Legal Terms* (London: Straker, Ltd., 1914), pp. 19-34.

[2] Polly J. Price, "Natural Law and Birthright Citizenship in Calvin's Case 1608," p. 93. http://digitalcommons.law.yale.edu/yjlh/vol9/iss1/2/.

[3] Baker, *Intro.*, ch. 26, p. 531.

[4] Baker, p. 107.

[5] Sheldon J. Godfrey, Judy Godfrey, *Search out the Land: The Jews and the Growth of Equality in British Colonial America 1740-1867* (Montreal: McGill-Queens University Press, 1995), pp. 6-7, fn. 18. On a Jew's inability to make an oath in sixteenth century, Venice, see Guido Rossi, *Insurance in Elizabethan England: The London Code*, Cambridge Studies in English Legal History (Cambridge: Cambridge University Press, 2016), pp. 232-233, n. 13.

[6] "*Of Youth and Age*," (3d. ed. 1625), p. 477; "Of Young Men and Age" (2d ed., 1612), *Spedding*, VI, appendix 2, p. 568, HathiTrust, http://hdl.handle.net/2027/ucl.31175002285222.

[7] "Of Custom and Education," in *Spedding*, VI, p. 470.

Besides Portia's servant, the name "Balthasar" is given to servants in *Romeo and Juliet, Much Ado About Nothing*, and a merchant in *The Comedy of Errors*.[1]

In April 1597, Bacon, as the Queen's "learned counsel extraordinary," was present during the interrogation of another Gerard, John Gerard, the Jesuit priest.[2] Coke spoke with frustration of "these boy priests and devilish good Fathers" and their equivocation.[3] After an interrogation in which Coke, Ellesmere, Bacon, and a few others were present, Bacon had gone back alone to see Gerard, after which Gerard escaped by boat, though weak from torture.[4] While the Queen appreciated the need for heightened security, she hated "this butchering [of] priests."[5] She realized that not every priest was a traitor bent on overthrowing England. Eventually, she declared she would "persecute no more as I have done."[6] Perhaps Bacon did help Gerard escape, under a tacit order of the Queen whom he served.

It is disturbing to think of Bacon signing orders, along with other members of the privy council, for examination of prisoners by torture.[7] It is natural for us to judge such actions harshly. Perhaps he felt compelled to take official actions which troubled him greatly. The record shows his involvement with state-sanctioned torture was more limited than what is commonly suggested.[8] Torture was technically illegal in Elizabethan England, but it was nevertheless employed.[9] Some would consider solitary confinement a form of torture, yet it is frequently allowed in United States prisons.

---

[1] Sandra Clark, *A Dictionary of Who, What, and Where in Shakespeare* (Chicago: NTC Publishing Group, 1997), pp. 97-98.

[2] Bowen, *Lion*, pp. 97-103; "English Mission," Central Intelligence Agency, last updated Jul. 1, 2008, https://www.cia.gov/library/center-for-the-study-of-intelligence/kent-csi/vol5no2/html/v05i2a12p_0001.htm.

[3] Bowen, *Lion*, p. 101.

[4] See John Gerard, *The Autobiography of a Hunted Priest*, trans. from the Latin by Philip Caraman (Garden City NY: Image Books, 1958; San Francisco: Ignatius Books, 2012); John Gerard, *The Condition of Catholics under James I*, ed., with his Life, by John Morris; *Father Gerard's Narrative of the Gunpowder Plot* (London, 1871), Project Gutenberg, http://www.gutenberg.org/ebooks/author/36738.

[5] Bowen, p. 85.

[6] *1 Calendar of State Papers Domestic*, 1601, as cited in Elizabeth Jenkins, *Elizabeth the Great* (New York: Coward-McCann, 1959), p. 295.

[7] Bowen, *Lion*, p. 92.

[8] David Jardine, *A Reading on the Use of Torture in the Criminal Law of England* (London, 1837), p. 52. See also pp. 51, 52, 42, 99, 100, 50, 66. On Peacham's Case, see Bowen, *Lion*, pp. 351-355, 287; cf. Nieves Matthews, ch. 24, "'With not a Trace of Pity for any Human Being,'" in Francis Bacon, *The History of a Character Assassination* (New Haven: Yale, 1996), pp. 283-294 (Bacon as a "tender-hearted prosecutor," p. 283). For further reading, see Coquillette, FB, notes to ch. 3, "The Theorist as Advocate," p. 184, fn 144; for Bacon's compassion, see "Of Tribute; or, giving that which is due," *Francis Bacon, a Critical Edition of the Major Works*, ed. by Brian Vickers, pp. 22-51, 23.

[9] Bowen, *Lion*, pp. 91-92

Bacon wrote, "In causes of life and death, judges ought (as far as the law permitteth) in justice to remember mercy; and to cast a severe eye upon the example, but a merciful eye upon the person."[1]

Spedding has explained several Baconian allusions that are not readily apparent. For example, Spedding says when Bacon used the phrase, "the Burgundian," he meant Balthasar Gerard.[2] In another instance, he implies that Bacon had in mind Giordano Bruno, at his execution, when he quoted Tacitus on the "wonderful composure and serenity at the point of death... displayed by many, as in the case of a centurion." The mention of Tacitus may signal a Tacitan taciturnity in Bacon. "Center-ion" might be a good name for a heliocentrist, as Bruno was.

Giordano Bruno reportedly told the judges who condemned him, "Perhaps your fear in passing this sentence upon me is greater than mine in accepting it."[3]

Tacitus wrote in a "condensed, pregnant" style, packing his text with meaning, as Bacon did as well.[4] In a famous anecdote, Bacon relates how, when the Queen sought his advice as to whether Dr. Hayward had committed treason, he told her, "The book of deposing King Richard the Second, and the coming in of Henry the Fourth, supposed to be written by Dr. Hayward" (who went to the Tower for it) did not contain treason but "very much felony," because "he had stolen many of his sentences and conceits out of Cornelius Tacitus."[5]

Shakespeare might have used the Italian form of Balthasar, "Baldassare," as in Baldassare Castiglione, author of *The Book of the Courtier*, which Bacon's cousin, Sir Thomas Hoby, had translated. Castiglione had taught the Queen her lovely handwriting.[6] The fact that he did not use the Italian form may be significant. The name "Balthasar" could be Spanish, German, or Dutch.[7]

---

[1] "Of Judicature," 'Essays,' third ed. (1625), *Spedding*, VI, p. 508 (for the second ed. (1612), see p. 583), HathiTrust, https://hdl.handle.net/2027/ucl.b3618242.

[2] 'De Augmentis,' iv, *Spedding*, IV, p. 375, nn. 2 and 3, HathiTrust, https://hdl.handle.net/2027/ucl.31175002901968; *Spedding*, I, p. 582, HathiTrust, https://hdl.handle.net/2027/ucl.b3618238.

[3] Michael White, *The Pope and the Heretic*, pp. 4-6, 6.

[4] "Tacitus, Agricola," *Loeb Classical Library* 35: 23-23. https://www.loebclassics.com/view/tacitus-agricola/1914/pb_LCL035.23.xml.

[5] "Apophthegms," in *The Essays, or Counsels, Civil and Moral of Francis Bacon, including also his Apophthegms, Elegant Sentences, and Wisdom of the Ancients, Spedding*, VII, p. 133, Hathitrust, https://hdl.handle.net/2027/ucl.b3924335; see also H.S., "Hayward's *Henry IV*" in Baconiana IV, Third Series (Jan. 1906), no. 13 (London: Gay & Bird, 1906), pp. 5-14.

[6] "Hoby, Thomas Posthumous," The History of Parliament (1964-2017), http://www.historyofparliamentonline.org/volume/1558-1603/member/hoby-thomas-posthumous-1566-1640).

[7] "Belshazzar and Bel(te)shazzar," Adventist Biblical Truths, http://dedication.www3.50megs.com/dan/belteshazzar.html; "Balthasar," British Baby Names (1/18/2014), http://www.britishbabynames.com/blog/2014/01/balthazar.html.

Shakespeare uses the name "Balthazar" as a character in four plays. "Balthazar" is also a character in Thomas Kyd's play, "The Spanish Tragedy."[1] Kyd died after torture, in a matter related to Christopher Marlowe.[2]

In Daniel 5, "Belshazzar," king of the Chaldeans (Babylonians), calls for Daniel (Beltshazzar) to come and read what the "hand" was writing on the wall: *Mene, mene, tekel, upharsin*. The words Daniel actually translates are *mene, tekel, peres* (Dan. :5:25–28). In an essay which Spedding calls "spurious," "Of a King," Bacon sums up Daniel's interpretation, saying, "He is found too light, his kingdom shall be taken from him."[3] Spedding provides only the first two words, *tekel, upharsin*, leaving off *Mene, mene*.[4] "Belteshazzar" may also be translated "one who lays up treasures in secret."[5] The Queen's brother, Edward VI is said to have written an "elegant" play in Latin, *De Meretrice Babylonia* (The Whore of Babylon), referring to the Catholic Church.[6]

Daniel is part of the "trial of mankind" literary tradition which "coalesced" in the twelfth century.[7] In more recent times, we see vestiges in Longfellow's "Golden Legend"[8] and Elie Wiesel's 1977–79 play, *The Trial of God*.[9] In the twelfth century, two liturgical plays of Daniel were performed. The first, in Latin, was by Abelard's pupil Hilarius, the *History of Daniel*, ca. 1140. Hilarius,

---

[1] "Balthasar," British Baby Names.

[2] Clare Asquith, ch. 2, "Secret Voices," *Shadowplay*, pp. 20-35, 24-25.

[3] Appendix 2 to "Of a King," in *The Works of Francis Bacon, The Wisdom of the Ancients and Other Essays* (New York: Walter J. Black, 1932), p. 209. Note: unlike the standard Longmans Spedding edition, Black's provides the full phrase, *mene, mene, tekel upharsin*. One wonders why Spedding omitted the words. Did he think they associated Bacon with Shakespeare's use of the name Balthazar?

[4] Cf. appendix 3 to 'Essays,' *Spedding*, VI, p. 595, HathiTrust, https://hdl.handle.net/2027/ucl.31175002285222. William F. Friedman, expert United States cryptologist, intriguingly called the biblical Daniel the "first cryptologist" for his interpretation of *mene mene tekel upharsim*. William Friedman, lecture 2, "Six Lectures on Cryptology," National Cryptologic School, National Security Agency (1965), pp. 15-37, 18. https://www.nsa.gov/news-features/declassified-documents/friedman-documents/assets/files/publications/ACC15281/41785109082412.pdf.

[5] "Belteshazzar," Bible Study Tools, from "Belteshazzar," *International Standard Bible Encyclopedia*, ed. by James Orr (1915), https://www.biblestudytools.com/dictionary/belteshazzar/.

[6] John Gough Nichols, preface, *Literary Remains of King Edward the Sixth*, vol. 1 (London, 1857), pp. xvii-xx.

[7] Hope Traver, "The Four Daughters of God, a Mirror[...]," pp. 44-92, 55-56, nn. 23, 24, JSTOR, http://www.jstor.org/stable/457268.

[8] Traver, "The Four Daughters of God, a Mirror[...]," p. 44-45, n. 4.

[9] Review of Elie Wiesel, *The Trial of God*, transl. by Marion Wiesel, *Kirkus Reviews* (New York: Random House, May 1, 1979, online Oct. 7, 2011), https://www.kirkusreviews.com/book-reviews/elie-wiesel/the-trial-of-god/; *God on Trial*, BBC Worldwide, online Jan. 8, 2012, https://www.youtube.com/watch?v=5caAug5n8Zk.

a goliardi, was thought to have been born in England.[1] There was also a *Play of Daniel* written by students of the school at Beauvais, ca. 1175.[2]

In Daniel 2, the Babylonians bound and threw three Hebrew youths, Shadrach, Meshach, and Abednego, into a fiery furnace because they refused to worship a golden image. However, God's angel protected them there from harm. In Daniel 6, Daniel was thrown into the lions' den because he openly prayed to his God, defying the king's decree. His enemies were amazed to discover that he had survived, alive and unharmed. After that, he became the King's trusted counselor.

In her book of private devotions, Queen Elizabeth recorded her prayers, but in foreign languages.[3] In the prayer she made before her coronation, she likened her imprisonment to God's protection of Daniel in the lion's den. In another prayer, writing in Italian, she compared herself to David the shepherd king whom God protected.[4]

The Biblical Daniel was an interpreter, not a judge. He was a righteous man who stood firm in his religious beliefs, as evidenced by his adherence to strict dietary laws. The same could be said of Shylock. Shakespeare repeats the ambiguous phrase, "A Daniel comes to judgment," three times, which seems significant (Shylock in IV, 1, 2164; Gratiano at IV, 1, 2281 and 2288). I think Shylock is a "Daniel" whose faith is being tried. Will he be "weighed in the balances and found wanting" A judge comes "to judge," not "to judgment." Sinners come to judgment.

Usually, however, "Daniel" in *Merchant* is thought to be a different Daniel: the Daniel in the apocryphal story of Susannah and the Elders. In that story, a youth named Daniel clears the good name of a woman, Susannah, who is wrongly accused of adultery, by questioning the two witnesses against her separately. He finds that their stories do not match.

For a long time, I had trouble seeing the relevance of the "Susannah" story to *Merchant*. For one thing, testimony would be irrelevant on a self-proving bond. However, as R. Blaine Andrus explains, this story became a justification for a change in procedure, beginning in the twelfth century and becoming standard in the thirteenth, in which the accused lost the right to confront and question the witnesses against him. The defendant could still see the witnesses being sworn in, *except* in matters of heresy before the

---

[1] E. K. Chambers, *The Medieval Stage*, vol. 2, pp. 107-108.
[2] Donnalee Dox, *The Idea of the Theatre in Latin Christian Thought: Augustine to the Fourteenth Century* (Ann Arbor: University of Michigan Press, 2004), p. 156, notes to p. 73; Haskins, *The Renaissance of the Twelfth Century*, p. 175.
[3] Haugaard, pp. 81-82.
[4] William Haugaard, "Elizabeth Tudor's Book of Devotions," pp. 79-106, 94(Daniel); 84 (David), JSTOR, http://www.jstor.org/stable/2539502.

Inquisition. This was to protect witnesses from retaliation. The testimony of any enemies of the accused might or might not be excluded.[1] As bizarre as it might seem, "The examination of witnesses was introduced neither through the civil law nor the canons, but by the apocryphal Daniel...."[2] Whether this Daniel was both judge and accuser was a topic for discussion, as was the number of witnesses required.[3] This last statement might help to explain the ambiguity in "A Daniel come to judgment." Is he judge or accuser?

Shylock's case on his bond, which he expected to win, was quickly converted into a criminal matter against him once Portia pointed out that he, as an alien, had committed the crime of making an attempt on the life of a citizen. I think of Giordano Bruno, languishing in a Venetian or Roman prison, from his arrest in 1592 on a charge of heresy until he was burned at the stake in 1600 by the Inquisition. The interrogation and torture of suspected heretics often took place in private villas similar to the fictional Belmont.

Did Bacon know him? Bruno knew Fulke Greville and Sir Philip Sidney,[4] as did Bacon, and they probably had other acquaintances in common. I have not found Bacon explicitly mentioning Bruno's name, but Shakespeare has preserved the hunting scene in a work by Giordano Bruno, "Spaccio de la bestia trionfante"— a dialogue set in England where it was published in 1584— by providing it verbatim in *Love's Labour Lost*.[5]

In the sixteenth century, the law no longer allowed a creditor to exact satisfaction from a debtor's body. However, under the Twelve Tables of Rome, a creditor had that right. The harsh Twelve Tables were softened by subsequent laws, such as the Poetelian law which abolished imprisonment for debt,[6] and by custom.

Shylock's "I am content" is reminiscent of Philippians 4:11 (KJV) where the Apostle Paul says, "For I have learned, in whatsoever state I am, therewith to be content." Bacon expresses a somewhat similar sentiment in closing a

---

[1] R. Blaine Andrus, ch. 4, "Daniel, 'Public Defender,' and the Art of Cross-Examination," *Lawyer: A Brief 5,000-year History* (Chicago: American Bar Association, 2009), pp. 35-42, 37-39, https://books.google.com/books?isbn=1604425989.

[2] Bruce Brasington, translation of cap. 15, "Concerning Witnesses," in ch. 5, "The Ordo Bambergensis," in *Order in the Court*, p. 245, n. 381.

[3] Brasington, ch. 5, "The Ordo Bambergensis," *Order in the Court*, p. 245, n. 381.

[4] For evidence that "Shakespeare" knew Bruno, see White, *The Pope and the Heretic*, pp. 205-207.

[5] Gilberto Sacerdoti, ch. 5, "'Self-Sovereignty' and Religion in 'Love's Labour Lost': From London to Venice via Navarre," in *Visions of Venice in Shakespeare*, ed. by Laura Tosi and Shaul Bassi (Farnham UK: Ashgate Publishing, 2011), pp. 83-105, esp. 87, 93-95, 99 n. 69.

[6] Gary Forsythe, *A Critical History of Early Rome: from Prehistory to the First Punic War* (Berkeley: University of California Press, 2003, p.b. 2006), pp. 313-314. https://books.google.com/books?isbn=0520249917.

letter to Buckingham: "Your grace will give me leave to be merry, however the world goeth with me."[1]

Tubal

What about the rights of poor Tubal who loaned Shylock the money he loaned Antonio? Is he out of luck?

While, according to *Use of the Law* (which is probably sufficiently accurate as to the law, even if it is not Bacon's[2]), a deed of gift which purports to give all that one has might be suspected of being a fraudulent transfer, one made to evade creditors.[3] However, the fact that the deed of gift Shylock signed was made under duress ought to dispel that concern.

Tubal may have gone looking for Jessica because he had a claim against Shylock and an interest in Shylock's wealth which Jessica stole. Shylock seems to trust him. Tubal had trusted Shylock. How will Shylock repay Tubal now?

Pertinent to our discussion may be the 1596 *Case of the Market Overt*.[4] A purchaser who in good faith buys stolen property in a market overt — one which openly trades in the same kind of merchandise as the stolen property, such as jewelry from a jeweler — on a regular market day, gains good title to it.[5]

If — though it does not seem likely — Jessica had taken the property "in jest," it would not be considered stolen.[6] Her name does sound like, and might suggest, "jest." Once an actual thief sold the property, however, in a market overt, the purchaser would gain good title. If, instead of selling it, she had kept it "for" her father to defraud the rights of Tubal or Antonio,

---

[1] Francis Bacon to Buckingham, prob. Jan. 1625-26, *Spedding*, XIV, p. 538, HathiTrust, https://hdl.handle.net/2027/ucl.31175012007947.

[2] Francis Bacon, "Use of the Law...," in *Spedding*, VII, pp. 451-505, p. 499, HathiTrust, https://hdl.handle.net/2027/ucl.b3924335. Note: The legal editor, D. D. Heath, thought the treatise was not "Bacon's," but might have been based on one of his "commonplace" books. *Spedding*, VII, pp. 302; preface, p. 453. Previously, it had been published as Bacon's; e.g., see *The Works of Lord Bacon: Philosophical Works*, I. (London: Henry G. Bohn, 1854), p. 586, https://books.google.com/books?id=ke43AQAAMAAJ. Originally published in 1629 with another tract anonymously [John Doderidge], it was printed in 1631 as part of a double tract called *The Elements of the Common Lawes of England* which also included *Maximes of the Common Lawes of England*. Coquillette, FB, appendix 3, p. 333.

As to fifty-four volumes of Bacon's "commonplace books," see Juan Schloch, "The Private Manuscript Library of Francis Bacon," http://www.sirbacon.org/Tottel.htm.

[3] *Spedding*, VII, p. 499.

[4] MEA, p. 28; "The Use of the Law," *Spedding*, VII, pp. 451-504, 500.

[5] "The Use of the Law," p. 500.

[6] "The Use of the Law," p. 500.

there would be a fraudulent trust. Bacon distinguishes fraudulent and good purposes of trusts in his *Reading on the Statute of Uses*.[1]

John Selden

While only a brief treatment will be given, John Selden's association to Shakespeare ought to be further explored. Among his many scholarly works, he had written six treatises on Jewish rabbinical law[2] which do not, however, pass Jewish scholarly muster in all respects.[3]

Why did Shakespeare choose the names Tubal and Chus for Shylock's Jewish friends (*Merchant*, V. III, 2, 1161)? Here is one theory: Tubal occurs in John Selden's first book of *Jani Anglorum Facies Altera* (*The Reverse or Back Face of the English Janus*), where he tells us that "Samothes was brother to Gomar and Tubal." First the Britons and then the Gauls were called "Samothei."[4] Bacon may have been familiar with this writing of Selden's. Tubal has the "bal" sound in it. We have seen "bel, bal" repeated in the play. "Tubal" could mean "world," or "world economy."[5]

Selden had worked for, and was friends with, Robert Cotton, the antiquarian with the wonderful library of old books and manuscripts.[6] When Bacon was banned from London, but writing *The History of the Reign of King Henry VII*, Selden helped him obtain the necessary documents from Cotton and even transcribed them for him.[7]

Selden dedicated one of his works to Bacon, *A Brief Discourse Touching the Office of Lord Chancellor of England....* and presented it to him upon his appointment to the office of Chancellor.[8]

---

[1] D. D. Heath, preface to *Reading on the Statute of Uses*, *Spedding*, VII, p. 391.

[2] Nathan Dorn, "John Selden as an Early Modern Maccabee," In Custodia Legis, Law Librarians of Congress (Dec. 27, 2011), https://blogs.loc.gov/law/2011/12/john-selden-as-an-early-modern-maccabee/. For a recent study, see Ofir Havrey, *John Selden and the Western Political Tradition* (Cambridge: Cambridge University Press, 2017), pp. 103-104 and part 5, "Selden and the "Universal Philosophy of Morals Drawn from the Hebrew Tradition," pp. 322-374.

[3] "John Selden," Jewish Virtual Library, 1998-2018, American-Israeli Cooperative Enterprise, http://www.jewishvirtuallibrary.org/selden-john-x00b0.

[4] John Selden, *Jani Anglorum Facies Altera, or, The Reverse or Back Face of the English Janus[...]* (London, 1682), http://name.umdl/umich.edu/A59098.0001.001.

[5] "Tubal meaning," Abarim Publications. http://www.abarim-publications.com/Meaning/Tubal.html#.WgZMqKK-Fq5. On "*bal and bel*," see Peter Dawkins, *The Wisdom of Shakespeare in 'The Merchant of Venice*,' pp. 157, 159.

[6] S. W. Singer, Esq., "Biographical Preface and Notes to *The Table Talk of John Selden*" (Cambridge: Cambridge University Press, 2015, first pub. London, 1847), p. xv.

[7] Intro., *The History of the Reign of King Henry VII*, ed. by Brian Vickers (Cambridge: Cambridge University Press, 1998), p. xiv.

[8] John Selden, *A brief discourse touching the office of Lord Chancellor of England[...]* (London, 1671), Early English Books Online: Text Creation Partnership, http://quod.lib.umich.edu/e/eebo/a59075.0001.001?view=toc; Ofir Haivry, *John Selden and the Western Political Tradition*, p. 222.

The names Cush (said to be for *Chus*), Tubal, Iscah (said to be for *Jessica*), and Salah (said to be reflected in *Shylock*), but not Samothes, are all found in Genesis 10: 2, 6, and 24 and Genesis 11: 14–15, 29 (KJV).[1] Samothes is a figure from Britain's early mythology.[2] According to Graham Parry, in his 1610 *Jani Anglorum Facies Altera*, Selden intentionally began with a myth to demonstrate his historical method,[3] a "first attempt to trace the development of the laws and constitution of England."[4]

Selden concluded that the early Britons did not place absolute power in their monarch. Rather, it was shared among assemblies of the people. He was careful not to state his strong Parliamentarian opinions outright, but to simply present facts from which readers could draw inferences. His contemporaries were more able to read between the lines than are readers today.[5] Finding Tubal and Chus in *Merchant* and in the *Jani Anglorum* makes me wonder what other connections there might be between Selden/Bacon/Shakespeare, and whether anyone has ever looked.

Shylock

Shylock is an alien, a non-citizen, under English law. Not only were his life and property at the mercy of the Duke for having threatened the life of a Christian, but an alien was not permitted to own land in England until 1870.[6] J. H. Baker notes that because England was a nation of traders, it was commercially expedient to extend protection to aliens, by means of "royal letters of safe conduct," for travel in and out of England. However, aliens were not allowed to stay indefinitely. While an alien could become a "friend" and thus receive the protection of the law, any alien who was not a friend would receive no protection.[7] An "infidel" (non-Christian) was, categorically,

---

[1] Cecil Roth, ch. 66, "Shylock the Venetian" (1933), *The Merchant of Venice: Shakespeare: The Critical Tradition* 5, edited by William Baker and Brian Vickers (London: Thoemmes Continuum, 2005), pp. 357–361, 357.

[2] John M. Ganim, *Medievalism and Orientalism* (New York: Palgrave MacMillan, 2005), p. 62.

[3] Graham Parry, ch. 4, "John Selden," *The Trophies of Time: English Antiquarians of the Seventeenth Century* (New York: Oxford University Press, 1995), pp. 95–130, 98–100.

[4] Parry, p. 106.

[5] Parry, pp. 98, 100, 106.

[6] Baker, *Intro.*, p. 531.

[7] Francis Bacon distinguishes "alien enemy" from 'alien friend" in "Articles Touching the Union of the Kingdoms," *Spedding*, X, *p.* 223, HathiTrust, http://hdl.handle.net/2027/hvd.32044105219539. In *Calvin's Case*, 77 Eng. Rep. 377 (K.B. 1608), Coke said an infidel was a perpetual enemy. Polly J. Price, "Natural Law and Birthright Citizenship in Calvin's Case (1608)," p. 128, n. 295. Until the Reformation, the restoration of civil rights for aliens and excommunicants under the canon law required an adjudication and oath of allegiance. Price, p. 124, n. 272; 126. http://digitalcommons.law.yale.edu/yjlh/vol9/iss1/2/. Shylock says he has an oath in heaven.

an enemy.[1] Shakespeare made the mutual hatred between Shylock and Antonio clear.[2]

The name "Shylock" sounds English, but also like the Hebrew "Shelach" ("Salah" in Genesis 10:24, 11:13-15, KJV), the grandson of Noah. The Hebrew language is written from right to left. In folklore, the devil does things "backwards." "Shylock" reversed, phonetically, is "collis." The Anglo-Saxon word for coal was *col*, while *collis* is Latin for "hill."[3] Perhaps a subtle sexual insult is at play.[4] "Collis" sounds like "collup," a thin strip of meat like *bacon*; also, it is a slang expression for "cook" (a pun on "Coke," perhaps.). In the "Twelve Days of Christmas" song, "four colly birds" means four black (coal-y) birds. One might "shie away" from a usurer. Coke had a protégé, James Whitelocke, called to the bar in 1601.[5]

"Like to like, quoth the Divel to the Collier," said Erasmus in *The Praise of Folly*, noting the affinity of young children and old men.[6] A debtor is to a creditor like a rasher is to the coals, or to a law student being "grilled on the hot seat." Brutus' wife Portia, from a family of Roman jurists, reportedly killed herself by swallowing hot coals, although this is contested.[7]

Shylock fared badly in court, representing himself, something even lawyers are cautioned against doing. He tells us he stands "for judgment" (IV, 1, 2035) and "for law" (IV, 1, 2077). His suit should have been easy, but he did not have the sympathies of the court. If he was a lawyer, the text did not hint broadly as to the fact. Antonio, on the other hand, shows that he is a lawyer by his skill and familiarity with common law and equity.[8] For example, he pointed out that the deed of gift needed to be recorded, and he demonstrated ease in manipulating the complicated law of uses.[9]

---

[1] Baker, *Intro.*, pp. 530-531.

[2] *Merchant*, I, 3: 439, 442, 457 ("spit"); IV, 1, 363, 862, 1991-92 ("hate"). A similar sentiment to Shylock's "I have my reasons" is expressed by King Antiochus in *Pericles*: "We hate the prince of Tyre and thou must kill him:/It fits thee not to ask the reason why,/Because we did it. Say is it done?" (*Pericles* I, 1, 212). In Roman property law, the one with possession had the preferred status. Here, Shylock had, or thought he had, the *right* to Antonio's body, his property. Thus, he thought he did not need to explain himself.

[3] *Webster's*, s.v. "coal," p. 192; *Cassell's Latin*, s.v. *collis*, p. 293.

[4] See Gordon Williams, "pillicock," in *Shakespeare's Sexual Language: a Glossary* (London: Continuum 2006), pp. 72, 235; *Lear* III, 4, 74-77 ("Pillicock sat on pillicock hill").

[5] Spedding, introductory remarks, "Note of my Lord Chancellor's Speech in Chancery to Mr. Whitlock, 29 June 1620...," *Spedding*, XIV, sec. 5, pp. 100-104, 100, HathiTrust, http://hdl.handle.net/2027/31175012007947.

[6] *The Praise of Folly*, by Desiderius Erasmus, with a life of Erasmus and illus. by Hendrik Willem van Loon (Roslyn NY: Walter J. Black, 1942), p. 111.

[7] "Life of Portia," http://portiacatonis.weebly.com/.

[8] Bacon's brother, Anthony Bacon, had studied law at Gray's Inn.

[9] In his talk on *The Merchant of Venice*, Simon Miles brought out the fact that Francis Bacon's brother, Anthony Bacon, freely loaned him money, just as Antonio, Bassanio's "kinsman," freely loaned Bassanio money. Simon Miles, lecture on *The Merchant of Venice*,' https://www.youtube.com/watch?v=KcQCljc1Mv8.

When Portia orders Antonio to bare his breast, we gasp. Then she adds that if Shylock spills one drop of Antonio's blood, he will owe triple damages for waste.[1] Initially, we might have assumed she was a non-lawyer "crash-briefed" for the case by Bellario. We might not have expected much from her, but she surprised us, in a stock formula for comedy. Shakespeare does not tell us explicitly whether she has legal training, but there are clues that she does. She tells Nerissa it is easier for her to teach than to follow her own teaching. We laugh at her quick-thinking resort to what seems like an illogical legal quibble. Yet, one of the powers of an equity judge was to enjoin the waste of an estate. Certainly the life of this man must be saved, even if it takes a procedural quibble to do it. There have probably been many lives saved by procedural quibbles over the ages.

More substantially, in the mid-thirteenth century, canon law held that, in an inquisition, Jews could not be tortured in ways that would draw blood.[2] Should a Christian be afforded less protection than a Jew?[3]

Perhaps Rule 34 of Bacon's *Ordinances in Chancery* will shed further light: "Decrees upon suits brought after judgment shall contain no words to make corrupt or weaken the judgment, but shall only correct the corrupt conscience of the party, and rule him to make restitution, or perform other acts, according to the equity of the cause."[4] With what seemed like a quibble about shedding blood, I believe Portia finally got through to Shylock's

---

[1] *Statute of Gloucester*, 6 Edward I, c. 5, 1278; MEA, p. 66 and n. 66. Only rarely would a court of equity award damages. More often, it would enjoin the waste. Baker, *Intro.*, p. 127, n. 63. "The punishment for waste is strict and severe, with treble damages," said Francis Bacon in *Arguments of the Law: The Case for the Impeachment of Waste. Spedding*, VII, p. 540, HathiTrust, https://hdl.handle.2027.ucl.b3924335. In *Merchant*, Portia would wish herself treble...a thousand times more fair, and would double and then treble the payment due on the bond (II, 2, 1523; III, 2, 1678).

[2] Kenneth Pennington, "Gratian and the Jews," *Bull. Medieval Canon L.* 31 (2014), pp. 111-124, http://scholarship.law.edu/scholar. p. 122, fn. 29.

Francis Bacon's Aphorism 39 in his *Treatise on Universal Justice*, regarding a "limitation for discretionary courts," which were to ameliorate the condition that equity did not apply in criminal cases, starts out, "Let there be no authority to shed blood, nor let sentence be pronounced in any court upon capital cases, except according to a known and certain law...." Coquillette, FB, ch. 5, "The Final Vision," p. 248, citing *Spedding*, V, p. 95, HathiTrust, https://hdl.handle.net/2027/ucl.b3618241.

[3] The words "merchant" or "merchandise" may have been code words for smuggling priests in and out of England, since merchants were granted safe passage. Clare Asquith, "Merchants," in "Glossary: A Selection of Coded Terms," *Shadowplay*, p. 295; Michael Srigley, ch. 1, "The Comedy of Errors," in *The Probe of Doubt: Skepticism and Illusion in Shakespeare's Plays* (Uppsala: Uppsala University 2000), p. 44. A search for the word "merchant" or "marcatant" in both Bacon and Shakespeare might be revealing.

[4] As discussed in Daniel R. Coquillette, "Past the Pillars of Hercules: Francis Bacon and the Science of Rulemaking," *University of Michigan Journal of Law Reform* 16, no. 2 (2012): 519-592, 575, n. 107; Francis Bacon, "Ordinances in Chancery," Rule 34, in *Spedding*, VII, pp. 755-775, 764, HathiTrust, https://hdl.handle.net/2027/ucl.b3924335.

---

conscience. No matter what man's law allowed, it was wrong to take a human life, according to a higher law, a universal law, *Thou shalt not kill*. This is stated plainly in the Ten Commandments; thus, it was also Jewish law.

> Could Portia have had legal training? While it is commonly assumed she had no legal education and was thus a rank imposter, there were a handful of famous women jurists in Italy, dating back to 1100. It is said that in twelfth-to-thirteenth century Bologna, a woman named Bettisia Gozzadini gave law lectures openly in the public square, because so many wanted to attend. From the twelfth century on, the University of Bologna had women teachers.[1]

> Novella d'Andrea, daughter of canonist Giovanni d'Andrea (d. 1348), gave lectures in law in her father's stead — from behind a curtain, so her beauty would not distract the male students.[2] So did Miriam Spiria-Luria, daughter of the learned rabbi Solomon Spira (1375–1453). In twelfth century Baghdad, a traveler reported that Bat ha-Levi, known only as the "daughter of Levi," would sit at an open window and lecture to male students below in the courtyard, so they would not be distracted by her beauty. Knowledge of Jewish law was part of the definition of an "educated Jew."[3]

> Maria di Filippo Strozzi, wife of lawyer Lorenzo di Piero Ridolfi, drew up the marriage contract for her relative Isabella di Pagnozzo Ridolfi and Benvenuto Olivieri, in late 1538–early 1539.[4] There were probably others whose names are now lost.

Jessica

In contrast with Portia, we are not told that Jessica was not educated. Various meanings have been given for the name "Jessica." "Iscah" means "she who looks forward, a spy, a lookout."[5] That meaning did not seem to fit. Peter

---

[1] University of Bologna, "Who We Are," http://www.unibo.it/en/university/who-we-are/our-history/famous-people-guests-illustrious-students.

[2] Isabella M. Pettus, "The Legal Education of Women," *Albany Law Journal*, 61 (Jan.-July 1900), pp. 325-331, 325-326

[3] Cheryl Tallan and Emily Taitz, "Learned Women in Traditional Jewish Society," *Jewish Women: A Comprehensive Historical Encyclopedia*, vol. 1 (March 2009), Jewish Women's Archive, https://jwa.org/encyclopedia/article/learned-women-in-traditional-jewish-society.

[4] Francesco Guidi Bruscoli, ch. 2, "The Ascent of the Olivieri Family," *Papal Banking in Renaissance Rome: Benvenuto Olivieri and Paul III, 1534-1549* (Aldershot UK: Ashgate 2007), p. 42, n. 79.

[5] Karl Elze, transl. by L. Dora Schmitz, essay 7, "The Supposed Travels of Shakespeare," *Essays on Shakespeare* (London, 1874), p. 283; "The name Iscah in the Bible," Abarim Publications, last updated 11-21-2017, http://www.abarim-publications.com/Meaning/Iscah.html.

If we have "one who looks forward," we might look for "one who looks backward" to continue the Janus theme. We have it in Shylock, for a "shy" person is called "backward." Also, Shylock "looks backward" in seeing his daughter as if she were still a little girl, not the woman she has become. Tevye sang, "Is this the little girl I carried?" Bock, Jerry, Joseph Stein, and Sheldon Harnick. "Sunrise, Sunset," from *Fiddler on the Roof*. New York: Times Square Music Publications, 1965.

Dawkins wrote that the name "Jessica" was related to "Jesse."[1] Jesse "holds a wide pallet of meaning." It means both "my husband" and "Yah/Yahweh exists....[It] contains the most profound notion that human marriage reflects divine revelation."[2] Given the beautiful moonlit garden scene with Jessica and Lorenzo, with the refrain, "In such a night..." reminiscent of the Easter Vigil liturgy,[3] this meaning seems to fit better than "spy or lookout."

In Shakespeare's time, the "J" in "Jessica" would have been pronounced "Y." Thus, "Jessica" would have been pronounced "Yessica." Thus, her name says "yes," if you will. The word for "yes" is *oc* in the langue d'oc (language of the Langue d'oc region of southern France, also called Occitania), as Dante observed in his writing on vernacular Romance languages, *De Vulgari Eloquentia*. Occitania, or the region where Occitan is spoken, is where the papally-authorized massacre of the Albigensians occurred. The Albigensians were the obliterated "heretical" sect whom the Catholics derogatorily called Cathars, in the early decades of the thirteenth century. Through Dante, Provençal language and the spirit and poetic style of the troubadours (from *trobar*, "to find") has been preserved and disseminated.[4] "Jessica" suggests the region of the Langue d'oc (Occitania), Dante, women's rights, and a "saying yes" to love.

Michel de Castelnau

Michel de Castelnau, French ambassador in London during Queen Elizabeth's reign, was from Occitania. He hosted Giordano Bruno during Bruno's years in London, 1583–85.[5] While still in France, Castelnau had escorted Mary Stuart from France back to Scotland after her husband Louis IX died. Castelnau-le-Lez is in southwestern France, Montpellier District, Languedoc, now part of the Occitanie administrative region.[6] De Castelnau

---

[1] Peter Dawkins, *The Wisdom of Shakespeare in 'The Merchant of Venice,'* p. 185.

[2] "The Name Jesse in the Bible," Abarim Publications, last updated 11-21-2017, http://www.abarim-publications.com/Meaning/Jesse.html.

[3] See Debra Murphy, "Cracking Shakespeare's Catholic Code: An Interview with Clare Asquith" *Godspy, Faith at the Edge,* Mar. 27, 2008. http://oldarchive.godspy.com/reviews/Cracking-Shakespeares-Code-An-interview-with-Clare-Asquith-author-of-Shadowplay.cfm.html.

[4] Cullen Murphy, ch. 2, "A Stake in the Ground: The Medieval Inquisition," *God's Jury: The Inquisition and the Making of the Modern World* (Boston: Houghton Mifflin Harcourt, 2012), p. 29; Maria Khodorkovsky, "Pays d'Oc, Pays d'Oil, "Pays de Si: a History of Romance Language Through the Word Yes," Beyond Words — Language Blog, ALTA Translation Services, 10/26/2009; "Dante and Occitania," Dante Poliglotta," 5/6/2016; "Oc Language," Provence and Beyond, copyright 1995-2017 Russ Collins, http://www.beyond.fr/history/oc.html.

[5] Michael White, *The Pope and the Heretic* (New York: William Morrow, 2002), pp. 80; 109-110; appendix 2, p. 214.

[6] "Castelnau-le-Lez," map-France.com, http://www.map-france.com/Castelnau-le-Lez-34170/.

---

left behind a book of his memoirs.[1] Like Bacon, de Castelnau was averse to universities, claiming they taught people what to believe rather than how to think.[2] Perhaps it is only a coincidence that there is a Belmont, France, in Gers, Occitania. Connections between de Castelnau and Bacon might be worth exploring in terms of the Shakespeare–Bruno connection.

Solanio

Solanio, who, with Salarino, was a friend to Antonio and Bassanio, might be a veiled reference to Giordano Bruno, "the Nolan" (from Nola, near Naples), a free thinker ahead of his time who was burned at the stake as a heretic. One of his "heretical" beliefs was that the earth revolved around the sun. Also, "Solon" (c. 630–560 B.C.) was an ancient law-giver who is said to have ameliorated the harsh laws of Drakon (c. 621 B.C.).[3] The word "solari" in Italian meant "stonemason."[4] Perhaps that word is closer to Salario (messenger from Venice) or Salarino.

Thoughts of "cormorant" being slang for a usurer led me on a "wild goose chase," — a phrase first used in *Romeo and Juliet* — after the *Sola or Sula Bassana*, a sea goose or gannet which is related to the cormorant and East Pacific booby. The booby was considered stupid because it was too trusting. It did not fly away when a human tried to catch it.[5] "Sola" was a hunting cry in *Love's Labor Lost* (IV, I, 1135),[6] and Launcelot Gobbo says it repeatedly (V, 1, 2491, 2493, 2496). Martin Luther had famously said that salvation comes "by faith alone," *sola fide.*[7]

A search at www.opensourceshakespeare.org found thirty-three instances of "sola" occurring alone, in the middle of the words "consolation" and "desolation," and in "solace."

Did "Shakespeare" know any "sitting ducks"? Perhaps Giordano Bruno became one when he returned to Italy after having been excommunicated.

---

[1] Michel de Castelnau, *Memoirs of the Reigns of Francis II and Charles IX of France,* in 7 books, 2 vols., trans. anon. (London, 1724, orig. pub. 1659). https://books.google.ca/books?id=nyBEAAAAcAAJ.

[2] Coquillette, FB, p. 32, citing *Spedding,* VIII, p. 124, HathiTrust, https://hdl.handle.net/2027/ucl.b3618243; Guido del Giudice, *Giordano Bruno: The Prophet of Infinite Universe* (n.p.: The Giordano Bruno Society 2013, 2014), p. 34. https://books.google.com/books?id=3PGLAwAAQBAJ.

[3] Sara Robbins, ed., *Law, a Treasury of Art and Literature* (n.p.: Hugh Lauter Levin Associates, 1990), p. 32.

[4] Linda Guzzetti, ch. 3, "Women in Court in Early Fourteenth Century Venice, in *Across the Religious Divide, Women, Property and Law in the Wider Mediterranean* (ca. 1300-1800), ed. by Jutta Gisela Sperling and Shona Kelly Wray (New York: Routledge 2010, Taylor & Francis e-book 2009), pp. 51-60, 58.

[5] "Northern gannet," (directory page), https://www.britannica.com/animal/northern-gannet.

[6] Eugene Shewmaker, *Shakespeare's Language,* 2d. ed. (New York: Facts on File, 2008), p. 504; Alexander Schmidt, *Shakespeare Lexicon and Quotation Dictionary* 2, s.v. "sola," p. 1083.

[7] "The Five Solas," Introduction to Protestantism, 2012-2018, http://protestantism.co.uk/solas.

His initial offense was secretly reading Erasmus in the privy.[1] He was arrested in Rome and taken to Venice for trial by the Inquisition. He had naïvely hoped for an audience with the Pope, to explain to him about his new theories.[2] Bruno was likely tortured, though there are no records of it. For a long time, the Catholic Church denied his existence. Because he would not recant his unorthodox theories, he was burned at the stake, with a metal bar through his mouth, after an eight year trial and imprisonment (1592–1600).[3] Bruno had been friends with Fulke Greville and Sir Philip Sidney, the nephew of Robert Dudley,[4] people Bacon knew. [5]

Launcelot Gobbo and Old Gobbo

Launcelot Gobbo is the only character in the play with both a first and last name. The name "Launcelot"[6] suggests Bishop Launcelot Andrewes, the Queen's own private chaplain, an Anglo-Catholic preacher, although the comparison would not be flattering. When Act II, Scene 2 opens, his conscience is plaguing him.[7] Later, he says, "The sins of the father are to be laid upon the children."[8] That could be taken as a rather harsh acknowledgement if it referred to the treatment of an illegitimate child. Young Gobbo rather outrageously parodies the Bible by saying, "I am your boy that was, your son that is, your child that shall be."[9] In *Theories of Comedy*, Theodor Lipps explains that it is "common to all comicality...that the comical object pretends to

---

[1] White, *The Pope and the Heretic*, p. 8.

[2] White, p. 171.

[3] White, p. 190; see also pp. 168-170, 172, 176; Famous Trials Website, Lawrence MacLachlan, *The Trials of Giordano Bruno 1592 and 1600*: Selected Links and Bibliography," http://law2.umkc. edu/faculty/projects/ftrials/brunolinks.html; Douglas O. Linder, Famous Trials, "Trials of Giordano Bruno 1592-1600," http://www.famous-trials.com/bruno; Frank Gaglioti, "Giordano Bruno, philosopher and scientist, burnt at the stake 400 years ago," 2/16/2000, https://www.wsws.org/en/articles/2000/02/brun-f16.html.

[4] White, pp. 205-206 (regarding Fulke Greville); 82-83, 110, 205 (regarding Sir Philip Sidney).

[5] Peter Dawkins, "The Life of Sir Francis Bacon," Francis Bacon Research Trust, https://www. fbrt.org.uk/pages/essays/Life_of_Sir_Francis_Bacon.pdf.

[6] *The New Oxford Shakespeare, Modern Critical Edition* (Oxford: Oxford University Press, 2016), gives "Lancelet" and "Iobbe" instead of "Launcelot" and "Gobbo." See pp. 1207. That is the spelling on four occasions in the "Heyes' Quarto; see *The Old Spelling Shakespeare: Being the Works of Shakespeare in the spelling of the best Quarto and Folio texts*, ed. F. J. Furnivall (New York: Duffield, 1909), pp. xi, xii, xvi. "Gobbo" is thought to be "Job." The Second Quarto uses "Gobbo," but the First Quarto and First Folio use "Iobbe." The Third Folio uses "Job." Peter Dawkins, *The Wisdom of Shakespeare in 'The Merchant of Venice,'* p. 194. On the Heyes' Quarto, see William Reynolds, intro., *The Merchant of Venice, The Bankside Shakespeare*, ed. by Appleton Morgan (New York, 1888), pp. 19-21.

[7] *Merchant*, II, 2, 566-596.

[8] *Merchant*. III, 5, 1841. It would be chilling to think of a spiritual advisor telling an illegitimate youth he was damned, but yet had a kind of bastard hope.

[9] *Merchant*. II, 2, 647-650.

---

be something great and then appears as an insignificant thing or a relative nothing."[1]

> In Bacon's letter (c. 1622) to Launcelot Andrewes, Bishop of Winchester, in view of their "ancient and private" friendship," Bacon explained why, despite a need for money, he did not seek republication of his essays and other works "of that nature," i.e., recreational. He did not believe a person should seek publication of his own writings while he was living.[2] If there was a secret about Bacon's birth, Andrewes, the Queen's personal chaplain, would likely have known of it. In a letter to his close friend Tobie Matthews, Bacon referred to Andrewes as his "Inquisitor," without explanation.[3]

> "Ancient" has referred to the Church of England, "an ancient church, catholic and reformed."[4] It has also referred to the Catholic church. Anthony à Wood used the word "antient," in the same paragraph, to refer both to the "antient religion" restored under Queen Mary and to the "ancient learning," in the universities.[5] Bacon in his Will referred to his "ancient" servants.[6] Perhaps he meant the writers who served him in "ancient endeavors." In dedications, writers might refer to themselves as the dedicatee's "servants."[7]

> In Queen Elizabeth's book of devotions, she had written a prayer, in French, in which she gave God undying thanks for "having done me the honor of being a mother and nurse to thy dear children." She asked God to "Preserve then the mother and the children whom thou hast given her for the good of thy poor church." One explanation is that she saw herself as the mother of her nation.[8]

Marc Shell has observed that Launcelot is the "major go-between for religion and sex" in the play.[9]

The next point needs a bit of background. Usually, a plaintiff in a legal action bears the burden of proving his case. In the *Ordo Bambergensis*, an

---

[1] "Theodor Lipps, from 'The Foundation of Aesthetics' (1903)," transl. by Lee Chadeayne, in Paul Lauter, ed., *Theories of Comedy*, (Garden City: Anchor Books, 1964), no. 41, pp. 393-397.

[2] *Spedding*, XIV, p. 374, HathiTrust, https://hdl.handle.net/2027/ucl.31175012007947.

[3] BSQ, p. 274 n. 2, citing: *Spedding* XI, p.144; *Spedding*, X, p. 256, HathiTrust, https://hdl.handle.net/2027/hvd.32044105219539; and *Spedding*, XIV, p. 371, HathiTrust, https://hdl.handle.net/2027/ucl.31175012007947.

[4] "History," The Church of England, https://www.churchofengland.org/about-us/history.aspx; see also http://www.anglican.org/church/ChurchHistory.html.

[5] Anthony à Wood, *History and Antiquities of the University of Oxford* 2, ed. by John Gutch (Oxford, 1796), part I, p. 235, as quoted in C. H. Conley, ch. 1, "The First Part of the Sixteenth Century," *The First English Translators of the Classics* (New Haven: Yale University Press, 1927), p. 8, HathiTrust, https://hdl.handle.net/2027/ucl.$b112274.

[6] *Spedding*, XIV, pp. 539-545, 543. https://hdl.handle.net/2027/ucl.31175012007947.

[7] See, e.g., Pierre Bayles' dedication to William Talbot on the title page, *A General Dictionary, Historical and Critical* 3 (London, 1735), https://books.google.com/books?id=oWBZAAAAYAAJ

[8] William P. Haugaard, "Elizabeth Tudor's Book of Devotions: A Neglected Clue to the Queen's Life and Character," *The Sixteenth Century Journal* 12, no. 2 (Summer, 1981), pp. 79-106, 96 97, 99, 102, JSTOR, http://www.jstor.org/stable/2539502.

[9] Marc Shell, ch. 3, "The Wether and the Ewe," *Money, Language and Thought*, pp. 24 to 47, https://books.google.ca/books?isbn=0520043790.

Anglo-Norman canon law procedural treatise dating from the late twelfth to thirteenth centuries (after 1186), there is a passage which concerns the rare situations in which a defendant has the burden of proof. Bruce Brasington, who translated the passage, tells us the passage has to do with the situation when a slave or serf has become a cleric. Here, we have Launcelot Gobbo, a servant, "becoming" a "cleric" — if he stands for Launcelot Andrewes.[1] This is the second clear reference to the *Ordo Bambergensis* in *Merchant*. The manuscript is English, not German, but was found at Bamberg.

Launcelot says, in an aside to the audience, "Oh heavens, This is my true-begotten father! Who being more than sand-blind, high-gravel blind, knows me not: I will try confusions with him."[2] It may be worth noting that, in determining compensation owed to another in the law, there is a situation called *confusio* in which an individual is both a debtor and a creditor, and it must be determined what each one owes the other.[3]

Another churchman whose writings may contain parallels with some lines in *The Merchant of Venice* is the canonist and civilian Gilbert of Foliot (1110–1187), who was trained in law. For example, there is a legal expression, *non mediocre firmamentum et robur*, translated "useful prop and stay." Gilbert of Foliot used it in arguing that natural law supported Empress Matilda's claim to rule England.[4] Where for Ulpian, "Justice is a steady and enduring will to render unto everyone his right," for Cicero, justice was "a disposition of mind preserved for the common good, attributing to each his dignity."[5] One of Gilbert's arguments, based on the Bible, was that, where there were no sons, a daughter could inherit, as had been determined with a Jew from the tribe of Manasseh. Queen Elizabeth's situation was analogous, since Edward VI, Henry VIII's only son, had not survived.

---

[1] Bruce Brasington, ch. 5, "The 'Ordo Bambergensis,'" *Order in the Court*, p. 250, fn. 421.

[2] *Merchant*, II, 2, 600-602.

[3] Bruce Brasington, ch. 5, "The '*Ordo Bambergensis*,'" *Order in the Court*, cap. 14, p. 236, n. 297.

[4] See Jason Taliadoros, ch. 6, "Law and Theology in Gilbert of Foliot's (c. 1105/10–1187/88) Correspondence in *Haskins Society Studies in Medieval History* 16, ed. by Stephen Morillo (Woodbridge UK: The Boydell Press, 2006), p. 82-84; 84, fn 35. The complete quotation is *si vero ius natural percurras, cause huic non mediocre firmamentum et robur invenies.* Dom Adrian Morey, ed., *The Letters and Charters of Gilbert Foliot, Abbott of Gloucester 1130-48, Bishop of Hereford (1148-1163) and London (1163-87)*, (Cambridge: Cambridge University Press, 1967), p. 62, lines 40-41.
For an interesting discussion of the history of natural law dating back to Heraclitus, as developed in the writings of medieval civilian lawyers (including Bassianus, Azo, and Placentinus), see Michael Bertram Crowe, IV.B, "The Medieval Civilians," *The Changing Profile of the Natural Law* (The Hague: Martinus Nijhoff, 1977), pp. 89-93. For Heraclitus's influence on Neoplatonism in the development of Renaissance poetry, see Bryson and Movsesian, ch. 7.I, "The Platonic Ladder of Love," *Love and its Critics, from the Song of Songs to Shakespeare and Milton's Eden*, pp. 295-352, p. 295 (Open Book Publishers, 2017), https://www.openbookpublishers.com/htmlreader/978-1-78374-348-3/contents.xhtml.

[5] Taliadoros, "Law and Theology[...]," pp. 82-83.

Mediocria firma was, of course, the Bacon family motto.

The ancient phrase *non mediocre firmamentum et robur* does not have an entry in *Black's Law Dictionary*. It reminded me of Old Gobbo's lines to Launcelot: "Marry, God forbid! the boy was the very staff of my age, the very prop," to which Launcelot responds: "Do I look like a cudgel or a hovel-post, a staff or a prop? Do you know me, father?" Another expression which Gilbert used was *ius suum cuique tribuere*, or "the law attributes to each his own." Jason Taliadoros wrote, "Stephen Kuttner's study of the origins and uses of this maxim indicate[s] that its meaning lies in the far more complex interstices of law and ethics, much like the phrase "useful prop and stay."[1]

Gilbert, a lawyer/theologian, applied the Roman law of the glossators and theology with a "speculative and flexible civilian's mind to find practical and fair solutions to cases." Like the English jurist Vacarius (1115/20–ca. 1200),[2] Gilbert applied the "learned law" to solve "everyday canonical and ecclesiastical problems" where there was no "immediate precedent." Jason Taliadoros found Gilbert to have been more practice-oriented than the theoretical Vacarius, still reliant on his Italian teachers; however, both men were concerned with "universality" in law.[3] For Gilbert, a "principled notion of what was fair or just, and a theoretical paradigm or brace in which to legitimate...positions of clemency, equity or conscience" was important.[4] His "ability to see beyond the confines of existing norms and adopt what was, for English litigants, a learned and foreign law" gave his use of law a degree of universality.[5]

Gilbert gives us both Ulpian's definitions of justice ("Justice is a steady and enduring will to render unto everyone his right") as well as Cicero's ("Justice is a disposition of mind preserved for the common good, attributing to each his dignity).[6] Did Bacon read Gilbert of Foliot? One would have to read more than this one play to be sure, perhaps.

---

[1] Taliadoros, "Law and Theology[...]," p. 84. See Stephan Kuttner, "A Forgotten Definition of Justice," pp. 75-109.

[2] For Vacarius, see Peter Landau, ch. 11, "The Origins of Legal Science in England in the Twelfth Century: Lincoln, Oxford, and the Career of Vacarius," in *Readers, Texts, and Compilers in the Earlier Middle Ages: Studies in Medieval Canon Law in Honour of Linda Fowler-Magerl*, ed. by Martin Brett and Kathleen G. Cushing (New York: Routledge, 2016); "Vacarius," Bio-Bibliographical Guide to Medieval and Early Modern Jurists, Ames Foundation, report 560a, last updated 4/14/2018, http://amesfoundation.law.harvard.edu/BioBibCanonists/Report_Biobib2.php?record_id=a560.

[3] Jason Taliadoros, "Law and Theology...," p. 80.

[4] Taliadoros, p. 94.

[5] Taliadoros, pp. 80, 93.

[6] Taliadoros, p. 84; "Cicero, *De invent.*, 2, 53, 160." Ulpian: "Iustitia est constans et perpetua uoluntas ius suum cuique tribuendi" is the opening sentence of Justinian's *Institutes* and, with *tribuens*, occurs in the first title of the *Digest*." Stephan Kuttner, "A Forgotten Definition of Justice," pp. 75-109, p. 75. The Stoic definition of justice is: "Justice is a virtue which gives

Launcelot Andrewes reportedly lacked compassion when trying to get Separatist leader Henry Barrow to recant. Barrow was imprisoned in 1587 for three years before being executed on religious grounds.[1] Obviously, any intended criticism of Andrewes would have needed to be extremely veiled.

Old Gobbo offered Lord Bassanius a dish of doves. The dove is often a symbol of the Holy Spirit, as well as a symbol of divine wisdom and reason.[2]

"Gobbo" was the code name writer Francis Davison gave Robert Cecil.[3] The "Il Gobbo di Rialto" is a statue of a hunchback in the center of Venice. It was a place for issuing decrees and sentences for petty offenders, whose punishment was to be made to run naked through the streets while being

---

everyone his due." Kuttner says it derived from Cicero's *De inventione*. Kuttner, p. 75. Kuttner traces a definition of justice as "an unspoken covenant of nature, devised for the aid of many" back through commentary on St. Augustine's *De Trinitate*, Seneca and St. Gregory, and Plato (Calcidius). Kuttner, p. 80. Other formulations of this "forgotten definition" are: "benefiting those most who have the least power" and St. Augustine's "acting for, or coming to, the relief of the wretched." Kuttner, p. 99. This definition is very different "in spirit" (as the Duke says in *Merchant*) from the usual one which equates law with the enforcement of rights.

If we are trying to understand how Portia came to be pleading with Shylock, who was, it had seemed, within his rights, to show mercy, we may find it worthwhile to consider this "forgotten" definition examined by Kuttner, pp. 94, 96. Some writers have speculated that Portia's quality of mercy speech was based on Seneca's "To the Emperor Nero on Mercy," "De Clementia." See "Seneca," *Stanford Encyclopedia of Philosophy*, first pub. 10/17/2007, https://plato. stanford.edu/entries/seneca/; "Of Clemency/Book I," Wikisource, from L. Annaeus Seneca, *Minor Dialogs Together with the Dialog 'On Clemency,'* transl. by Aubrey Stewart (London, 1900), ed. March 21, 2015, https://en.wikisource.org/wiki/Of_Clemency/Book_I.

[1] Welsby, Paul, *Lancelot Andrewes, 1555-1626* (London: SPCK, 1958), pp. 56-57, as cited in Jonathan Warren, "Lancelot Andrewes, the Star of Preachers." June 30, 2014. http:// anglicanpastor.com/lancelot-andrewes-the-star-of-preachers/, n. 2. On Launcelot Andrewes and Francis Bacon, see Welsby, pp. 225-227 (as cited in Peter McCullough, *Lancelot Andrewes: Selected Sermons and Lectures* (Oxford: Oxford University Press, 2005; online, 2012), http:// www.oxfordscholarlyeditions.com/view/10.1093/actrade/9780198187745.book.1/actrade-9780198187745-book-1), p. 357, fn. 22; blog, Chris Armstrong (church historian/educator), "The darker side of the chief King James Bible translator," *Grateful to the Dead, a Church Historian's Playground* (December 30, 2010), https://gratefultothedead.wordpress.com/2010/12/30/the-darker-side-of-the-chief-king-james-bible-translator-lancelot-andrewes/. See also Henry Barrow and John Greenwood, *A collection of certain letters and conferences lately passed betwixt certaine preachers and two prisoners in the Fleet* [Dordrecht?: s.n., 1590], Early English Books Online: Text Creation Partnership, http://name.umdl.umich.edu/A05036.0001.001; "A collection of certain sclandalous [sic] articles given out by the bishops against such faithful Christians [...] [Dordrech?:s.n., 1590], Early English Books Online: Text Creation Partnership, http://name. umdl.umich.edu/A05037.0001.001.

King James chose Launcelot Andrewes to debate Cardinal Robert Bellarmine on the oath of allegiance. Bellarmine presided over Bruno's trials and burning, and later, over Galileo's trial. *Spedding*, XI, p. 140, HathiTrust, https://hdl.handle.net/2027/uc1.31175012007939.

[2] E. Kantorowicz, *The King's Two Bodies*, p. 114. Kantorowicz describes a miniature in a "magnificent" gospelbook Henry II gave the Abbey of Monte Cassino which depicts the emperor as a mediator. He says the dove descending from heaven represents reason. *Iustitia, Pietas, Sapienta, Prudentia, Lex*, and *Ius*, are personified. E. Kantorowicz, pp. 113-114, fig. 20.

[3] E. K. Chambers, *William Shakespeare, A Study of Facts and Problems*, vol. 2 (Oxford: Clarendon Press, 1930), ch. 9, pp. 372-373.

---

beaten with sticks and then to kiss the statue at the finish line. The statue is across the street from the San Giacometto di Rialto Church, the "market church," under whose portico money lenders and bankers did business — just as in the play.

The Rialto was once the mercantile center of the world.[1] The Venetian painter Francesco Bassano, who had moved to Venice from the small nearby town of Bassano, painted a typical "Market Scene." (1580-85). Several of his paintings are in the San Giacometto church.[2] The family of Emilia Bassano Lanyer, mistress to Henry Carey, Lord Hunsdon,[3] were from Bassano.[4] She was well educated in the home of Susan Bertie, dowager Countess of Kent, a legal client of Sir Nicholas Bacon's. She wrote a long poem of merit.[5] Her descendant, Peter Bassano, argues that she played a part in writing the plays of Shakespeare.[6] Her name has been suggested as the inspiration for the name "Bassanio," which was not in Shakespeare's acknowledged sources.[7]

Attempts have been made to explain why "Gobbo" (soft "g") would be "Job" in the play. There was a Venetian cult of St. Job who is associated with patience and healing.[8] In the Biblical Book of Job, God allowed the devil to torment Job to see if Job's faith would remain true. While one might attempt to see Shylock as a Job, there is, perhaps, a clearer connection between *Merchant's* themes of love and hate, revenge and forgiveness and Bacon's writings on Job. For example, in his "Of the Exaltation of Charity" in his *Meditations Sacrae*, published in 1597, Bacon cites Job 31:29: "This also were an

---

[1] Chambers, p. 372. See chs. 5 and 6, Richard Roe, *Shakespeare's Guide to Italy* (New York: HarperCollins, 2011). For photographs, see also "Churches in Venice," http://www.slowtrav. com/blog/annienc/2007/10/san_giacometto.html.

[2] "Francesco Bassano," *World Gallery of Art*, http://www.wga.hu/index1.html.

[3] Lord Hunsdon (Henry Carey) became the patron of Shakespeare's theatrical company, called "the Chamberlain's Men" in 1594. Before that, it was called "Derby's Men." After Carey died, on July 22, 1596, the company was still called "Hunsdon's Men" for a time, and then "the Chamberlain's Men" again, when a new Chamberlain became patron. Henry Carey is Mary Boleyn (Carey)'s son, conceived while she was mistress to Henry VIII. He was the nephew of Anne Boleyn and Henry VIII and possibly the son of Henry VIII. If Francis Bacon were the son of Elizabeth and Dudley, then Hunsdon (Carey) would be his cousin. If he were the son of Henry VIII, he would be Bacon's uncle. By his theatre patronage, Hunsdon protected the acting profession from prosecution, as Robert Dudley had done before him with his patronage of Leicester's Men. On Hunsdon, see Charles Boyce, *Shakespeare A to Z*, s.v. "Hunsdon (2)," Henry Carey, Baron (1524-1596) p. 303; "Henry Carey, 1st Baron Hunsdon," Geni.com 2018, https://www.geni.com/people/Henry-Carey-1st-Baron-Hunsdon/5259940388980072787.

[4] Peter Bassano, "Shakespeare," *Peter Bassano*. http://peterbassano.com/shakespeare.

[5] Aemilia (Bassano) Lanyer, 1569-1645, https://www.poetryfoundation.org/poets/aemilia-lanyer (2018).

[6] P. Bassano, "Shakespeare."

[7] Boyce, *Shakespeare A to Z*, s.v. "Bassanio," p. 52.

[8] Julia Reinhard Lupton, "Job in Venice: Shakespeare and the Travails of Universalism," in Laura Tosi and Shaul Bassi, eds., *Visions of Venice in Shakespeare*, with foreword by Stanley Wells (London: Routledge, 2016), pp. 105-125, 121. https://books.google.com/books?isbn=1317001303.

iniquity to be punished by the judge: for I should have denied the God that is above, if I have rejoiced at the overthrow of him that hated me, or took pleasure when adversity did befall him (verses 28-29)."[1]

According to Bacon, we are not to rejoice at the destruction of our enemy or lift ourselves up when evil finds him. We are to pardon, forgive, forbear — do good to them that hate us, even though our enemy may be "obstinate." The mark of true charity, says Bacon, is when evil overtakes your enemy, and you are grieved and distressed, taking "no joy in the day of revenge."[2] Portia begs Shylock to apply these principles, but it is Antonio who demonstrates them in his treatment of Shylock. Shylock had tried to kill him, and so, by law, Antonio was entitled to all of Shylock's property. He did not have to give Shylock anything, but he agreed to do so. The cycle of revenge, a theme in classical Greek tragedies as well, had to be broken in order for England to heal from its religious wars.

Like Job, Shylock was righteous in his own eyes (Job 32:1).

Bacon mentions the book of Job as having "great aspersion of natural philosophy." He remarked that the Bible praised Job for his wisdom and knowledge. He ranked Job with Moses, Solomon, and the prophets as men worthy of esteem.[3] He mentions Job in his writing numerous times.[4]

Launcelot Andrewes preached a sermon using Job 19:23-27 as his main text, "before the King's Majesty at Whitehall on Easter, April, 8, 1610, in addition to making reference to Job in other sermons."[5] In a sermon on

---

[1] Cf. the KJV, Job 31: 28-30: "This also were an iniquity to be punished by the judge: for I should have denied the God that is above/If I rejoined at the destruction of him that hated me, or lifted up myself when evil found him; /Neither have I suffered my mouth to sin by wishing a curse to his soul."

[2] Francis Bacon, "Of the Exaltation of Charity," *Meditationes Sacrae, Montagu,* I, p. 68, HathiTrust, https://hdl.handle.net/2027/umn.31951002094295e.

[3] F. Bacon, *Filum Labyrinthi, Montagu,* I, p. 98, HathiTrust, https://hdl.handle.net/2027/umn.31951002094295e.

[4] Bacon's references to Job may be found in: (1) *Montagu,* I: pp. xciv, xxviii, ixxxix, 14, 82, 68 (love your enemies, op. cit.); pp. 98 (*Filum Labyrinthi,* op. cit.); 163, 175 (Book of Job is "pregnant and swelling" with natural philosophy. Cf. "swelling port," *Merchant* I, 1, 131); book 1, *Adv. Of Learning,* pp. lxxxix, 249. *Montagu,* I: HathiTrust, https://hdl.handle.net/2027/umn.31951002094295e; (2) *Montagu,* II, p. 413 ("Job, speaking of the magnity and gravity of a judge in himself"). *Montagu,* II: HathiTrust, https://hdl.handle.net/2027/umn.31951002094294g; and (3) *Montagu,* III, pp. 25, 135 ("Job himself, or whoever was the justest judge"); 351; 480; 547 (Atalanta). *Montagu,* III: HathiTrust, https://hdl.handle.net/2027/umn.31951002094297a. After his "fall," Bacon said he had been the "justest judge," but that the censure was also just, recalling the words of Job.

[5] "A Sermon Preached before the King's Majesty at Whitehall on the Eighth of April, MDCX A.D." *Ninety-Six Sermons by the Right Honorable and Reverend Father in God, Lancelot Andrewes . Sometime Lord Bishop of Winchester. Pub. by his Majesty's special command* vol. 2, ed. by John Henry Parker (Oxford, 1841, orig. pub. 1629) pp. 252-269. For all references to Job in this volume, see pp. 30, 68, 75, 90, 101, 104, 127, 139, 194, 198, 207, 262, 278, 320, 327, 373, 374, 400, 411. HathiTrust, https://hdl.handle.net/2027/nyp.33433068270721. Useful also may be the Online Books Page for Launcelot Andrewes, http://onlinebooks.library.upenn.edu/webbin/book/lookupname?key=Andrewes%2C%20Lancelot%2C%201555%2D1626.

riches, Launcelot Andrewes gets much mileage from Job 8:14[1] ("Whose hope shall be cut off, and whose trust shall be a spider's web," in the KJV, not published until 1611) when he writes, "Job's simile verified, that riches are like a cobwebb, that which a man shall be weaving all his life long, and with great adoe and much travail, ther comes me a souldier, a barbarous souldier, with his broome, and with the turning of a hand, sweeps it clean away." In his Easter Day sermons, Andrewes particularly examined faith as a way of knowing.[2]

Andrewes was apparently a secret follower of the doctrines of Martin Luther.[3] Luther had also made a special study of Job, relevant to *Merchant* and Launcelot Andrewes' sermons on Job.

As to knowing, a kind of fish called the "goby," the gudgeon fish, *Gobio gobio*, was common to the Thames; it would "swallow anything; hence, it was gullible.[4]

Was Launcelot really Old Gobbo's son? They both thought so. The goby prefers the shoals[5] — shallows or sand banks (e.g., the "Goodwins"—

---

[1] *Ninety-Six Sermons* V, sermon 1, "A Sermon preached at St. Mary's Hospital on the 10th of April, being Wednesday in Easter week, A. D. MDLXXXVIII [1588]", pp. 3-53. This at least suggests the story of St. Felix, serving under Bishop Maximus, whose life was saved by a spider's web over the well [variation: doorway] in which he hid, which tricked the Roman soldiers who hunted him into thinking it was deserted. Grace Hall, "Felix and the Spider," Stories of the Saints, The Baldwin Project, http://www.mainlesson.com/display.php?author=hallg&book=saints&story=felix.

[2] See Joseph Ashmore, "Faith in Lancelot Andrewes's preaching," The Seventeenth Century 32:2 (May 3, 2017 online), pp. 121-138. Abstract: http://www.tandfonline.com/doi/full/10.1080/0268117X.2017.1293559?scroll=top&needAccess=true.

[3] Peter McCullough, Lancelot Andrewes: *Selected Sermons and Lectures*, Intro., p. xx; p. 367; Kenneth Stevenson, ch. 7, "The Sacraments," in *The Vocation of Anglican Theology: Sources and Essays*, ed. by Ralph Carmichael (Norwich, UK: SCM Press, p. 2014), pp. 244-279, 247 ("not politic to acknowledge Lutheran sources").

[4] *The Shorter Oxford English Dictionary*, ed. by C. T. Onions, vol. 1 (Clarendon Press: Oxford, 1933), s.v. "Gudgeon," p. 841. Shakespeare uses the word "gudgeon" just once, in *Merchant* I, 1, 108. www.opensourceshakespeare.org/.

[5] "Gudgeon," *McLane's Standard Fishing Encyclopedia*, ed. by A. J. McClane (New York: Holt, Rinehart & Winston, 1965), pp. 390-391.
In an "imperfect piece, found among the posthumous *scripta* published by Gruter" after Bacon's death, Bacon says, "Again from the nursing and tutoring of this man (Aristotle) have arisen a shoal of cunning triflers." *The Works of Francis Bacon* ...Vol. the Eleventh, containing ...A Critique on the more Ancient Philosophers (London, printed for M. Jones, 1815), p. 263., HathiTrust, https://books.google.com/books?id=9HMNAAAAYAAJ.
As to publication dates and places of Bacon's posthumous works, see *The Cambridge History of the Book in Britain* 4. 1557-1695, ed. by John Barnard and D. F. MacKenzie (Cambridge: Cambridge University Press, 2002), p. 736; Sarah Hutton, *British Philosophy in the Seventeenth Century*, (Oxford: Oxford University Press, 2015), p. 102.
On Bacon's executor Rawley's arrangement with the philologist Janus Gruter to have Bacon's works published in the Netherlands, see Peter Langman, "'I Give Thee Leave to Publish,' *New Atlantis* and Francis Bacon's Republic of Knowledge," in *Centres and Cycles of Accumulation in and Around the Netherlands during the Early Modern Period*, ed. by Lissa Roberts (Zurich: Lit Verlag,

Goodwin Sands), *Merchant* III, 1, 1242)[1] — dangerous for ships and a favorite image with Bacon when speaking of, for instance, the ship of state.[2] In a memorable quotation, Bacon compares "letters" to ships passing through vast seas of time.[3] The gudgeon, which is found in the Thames River, also has an association with ancient Jews who, during their Captivity in Babylon, began to eat fish on Fridays, says Jessie Weston, in her discussion of the Fish–Fisher King symbolism in the literature of the Holy Grail.[4] In a fascinating chapter which describes how the concept of the holy grail, which incorporated both mystical and practical thought, evolved as the concept of money itself evolved, Marc Shell observes, "The grail was the sign of an age not only of impoverished aristocrats who, like the sinner/fisher king, seemed to await redemption, but also of a new merchant class, which created graceful mercy and money (*merces*) as its special emblems."[5]

2011), pp. 53-73, 66-72. http://www.academia.edu/946407/Centres_and_cycles_of_accumulation_in_and_around_the_Netherlands.

In the third person, Bacon wrote: "He thought, also, that knowledge is almost generally sought either for delight and satisfaction, or for gain or profession, or for credit and ornament, and that every one of these are as Atalanta's balls, which hinder the race of invention." *Scala Intellectus sive Filum Labyrinthi*, part I, no. 5, *Montagu*, I, p. 97, HathiTrust, https://hdl.handle.net/2027/uc2.ark:/13960/t6zw1952d.

[1] *Chambers Encyclopedia*, vol. 5, ed. by W. and R. Chambers, s.v., "Goodwin Sands" (London, 1890), p. 296 (2d. col., 2d par.).

[2] Continuing the ship of state analogy, see Bacon's essays: "Of Vicissitudes of Things, p. 61 ("great shoals of great alterations in states"); "Of Goodness and Goodness of Nature, p. 21 (Dispositions of "natural malignity" in some men, while seeming to be" errors of human nature," are the fittest timber to make great politics, like knee timber, that is good for building ships that are ordained to be tossed, but not for houses that are made to stand firm"); "Of Nobility" p. 22 (A fair timber tree is like a noble family that has "stood against the weathers and waves of time"); and "Of Seditions and Troubles, p. 22 (Tempests of state are like tempests at sea). *Montagu*, I, HathiTrust, https://hdl.handle.net/2027/uc2.ark:/13960/t6zw1952d.

[3] Francis Bacon, *The Advancement of Learning*, book 1, in *Spedding*, III, p. 318, HathiTrust, https://hdl.handle.net/2027/ucl.b3618240.

[4] Jessie L. Weston, *From Ritual to Romance*, pp. 108-129, esp. 121-129.

[5] Marc Shell, ch. 2, "The Blank Check: Accounting for the Grail," *Money, Language and Thought*, pp. 24 to 47, https://books.google.ca/books?isbn=0520043790.

Chapter Nine: Characters, Counterparts, and Others — Part II

Bassanio

Bassanio is a lawyer. He uses lawyerly language in speaking to his beloved; e.g., "until confirm'd, sign'd, ratified by you."[1] That strikes me as ridiculous but sweet, something only a lawyer would ever say. He also says, "In law what plea so tainted and corrupt/But, being seasoned with a gracious voice/Obscures the show of evil?" (III, 2, 1440–1444). Bassanio praises Antonio as one "in whom the ancient Roman honour more appears than any that draws breath in Italy." (III, 2, 1672–73). That phrase could be interpreted to mean that he was no longer living, but that would not make sense, unless Antonio was a ghost. By a slight stretch, Antonio might be considered an "honorary Roman."

There was a famous Bolognese twelfth-century jurist and law professor called in Latin Bassianus (sometimes just Johannes; Giovanni Bassiano in Italian).[2] He is one of the "glossators" who wrote glosses and other works

---

[1] *Merchant*, III, 2, 1482, www.OpenSourceShakespeare.org. In the 1616 *"Per Ipse Regum,"* the commission headed by Bacon to resolve the dispute between the courts of law and equity did "approve, ratify, and confirm" the practice of Chancery. MEA, p. 40.

[2] Francis de Zulueta and Peter Stein, *The Teaching of Roman Law in England around 1200*, Selden Society Supplement Series, 8, (Selden Society: London, 1990), pp. xviii to xx, xxxix, xl-xli, xlix-li, lxvii; p. xviii. Johannes Bassiano was "something of a mystery" to us today, but in his own time known as a "down-to-earth teacher who sought to clarify and make understandable the entire *corpus juris*" (body of the law). De Zulueta, p. xviii. His procedural works and method were influential in England. In fact, manuscripts of all of his works have been found in England. De Zulueta, p. l (the letter "el.").

expounding upon the *Corpus Iuris Civilis*, the compilation of ancient Roman law the Byzantine emperor Justinian commissioned in the sixth century. The glossators have been largely forgotten by all but legal historians. Bassianus had been taught law by Bulgarus at the University of Bologna. Bulgarus is considered the most influential of the "Four Doctors" whom Irnerius[1] taught: Bulgarus,[2] Martinus, Hugo de Porta Ravennate, and Jacobus de Boragine.

Bassianus's works were known in England; in fact, it is believed he went to England in the 1190s and may have even died there.[3] He had also taught at Mantua.[4] He was a popular, practice-oriented teacher who illustrated his lectures with stories and fables, such as an Aesop's fable told by Marie de France (1140–1200).[5] His best-known works include lectures on Justinian's Institutes (*Lectura Institutionum*) and the *Arbor Actionem* (*The Tree of Legal Actions*),[6] used for teaching legal procedure.[7] His positions on the law were

According to Manlio Bellomo, Bassianus was brilliant, but his personal life was not exemplary. It seems that, like Bassanio in *Merchant*, he gambled. Manlio Bellomo, *The Common Legal Past of Europe 1000-1800*, p. 167; see "Johannes Bassianus, last half of the twelfth century," report no. c015, Bio-Bibliographical Guide to Medieval and Modern Jurists, last updated 4/14/2018, http://amesfoundation.law.harvard.edu/BioBibCanonists/Report_Biobib2.php?record_id=c015. A canonist named Bazianus may be the same person as Bassianus; see "Bazianus,"report no. a053, d. 1197, last updated 4/14/2018, http://amesfoundation.law.harvard.edu/BioBibCanonists/Report_Biobib2.php?record_id=a053.

[1] Haskins, ch. 7, "The Revival of Jurisprudence," *The Renaissance of the Twelfth Century*, pp. 198-200; F. de Zulueta, *The Teaching of Roman Law in England around 1200*, p. xiii.

[2] "Bulgarus," c. 1100-1166, report no. c001, Bio-Bibliographical Guide to Medieval and Early Modern Jurists, last updated 5/5/2018, http://amesfoundation.law.harvard.edu/BioBibCanonists/Report_Biobib2.php?record_id=c001.

[3] Charles Donahue, Jr., "Bassianus, that is to say, Bazianus? Bazianus and Johannes Bassianus on Marriage," *Rivista international di diritto commune* 14 (2003) 41-82, 43. http://www.law.harvard.edu/faculty/cdonahue/writings/RIDC14_41_82.pdf; F. de Zulueta, *The Teaching of Roman Law in England around 1200*, p. I.

[4] Magnus J. Ryan, "Corporate Theory," *Encyclopedia of Medieval Philosophy: Philosophy Between 500-1500*, vol. 1, ed. by Henrik Lagerlund (Dordrecht, Netherlands: Springer, print and electronic bundle 2011), p. 236. The writings of Bassanius, his student Azo, and Azo's student Accursius helped to develop the modern theory of the corporation. Id.

[5] Zulueta, *The Teaching of Roman Law*, pp. xx, xxxix.

Marie de France was "the first poetess in a European vernacular and the first person to translate Aesop into such a language." She retold Aesop's fables in verse in a popular collection of 102 fables. She lived in England at the court of the French-speaking Henry II (1154-1189) and, after him, the troubadour king Richard I (1189-1199). Howard Needler, intro., to *Fables from Old French, Aesop's Beasts and Bumpkins*, trans. Norman R. Shapiro, (Middletown, CT: Wesleyan University Press, 1982), pp. xxv-xxvii; "Marie de France," *The Northeastern Dictionary of Women's Biography*, 3d ed., compiled and edited by Jennifer S. Uglow, revised by Maggy Hendry (Boston: Northeastern University Press, 1998), p. 358; Pierce Butler, *Women of Medieval France*, 5, *Woman: In All Ages and in All Countries*, (Philadelphia: Rittenhouse Press, 1907-1908), pp. 128-133; see bibliography, *Archives de litterature Du Moyen Age*,Arlima.net, *derniere mise a jure* (4/5/2018), https://www.arlima.net/mp/marie_de_france.html.

[6] Howard Needler, intro., *Fables from Old French*, p. xix.

[7] For links to Bassianus's *Arbor actionem*, see Otto Vervaart, "A mosaic of digitized medieval legal manuscripts," Rechtsgeschiedenis Blog, last updated 5/5/2018, https://rechtsgeschiedenis.

often opposed to those of another jurist, Placentinus, in the writings of Bassianus' famous pupil, Azo.[1] The writings of Bassanius are thought to have influenced the legal procedural tract, the *Ordo Bambergensis*.[2]

The glossators "glossed," or gave their interpretation of, the meaning of the Roman law texts. They did not sign with their names but with their *sigla* (sign), often an initial or initials.[3] When called upon by the courts to give their opinions, they were not above giving their interpretations on the texts they glossed the full force of law. They glossators did more than just gloss (interpret) texts, however. They wrestled with the "big questions" about law and theology and justice — higher law, such as Francis Bacon associated with equity in the quote with which this book begins, from his unpublished manuscript, the *Aphorismi*.[4]

Andrea Padovani, who is currently studying their writings, observes, "Whereas the Roman jurists of Antiquity, in line with the pragmatism of their law, were not inclined to address complex questions of natural philosophy, the glossators and commentators of late medieval jurisprudence displayed a radically different attitude. In doing so, they implemented a change of greatest importance in the history of juridical thought."[5] Perhaps every four hundred years or so is not too soon to revisit the glossators. The problem is, they did not write in English.

Despite his brilliant legal accomplishments, Bassianus had difficulties in his personal life. He seems to have been both a gambler and an alcoholic.[6] It would be relatively easy for such a person to soon find himself heavily in debt, as Bassiano was, in fact, when the play began. Gambling is represented with the casket lottery. Is Bassanio really worthy of Portia? Her first attraction for

---

wordpress.com/2012/04/21/a-mosaic-of-digitizedmedieval-legal-manuscripts/.

[1] Mario Ascheri, ch. 4, "The Beginning of University Teaching and Groundwork for 'Corpus Iuris Canonici,'" in *The Laws of Late Medieval Italy (1000-1500)*, pp. 107-135. 114.

[2] Bruce Brasington, ch. 2, "The Early Romano-Canonical Process: The Worlds of Hariulf and Bulgarus," *Order in the Court*, p. 97, n. 251.

[3] On sigla, see Otto Vervaart, "A personal touch: Chasing autograph manuscripts of medieval lawyers," Rechtsgenschiedenis Blog, Feb. 27, 2017, https://rechtsgeschiedenis.wordpress.com/?s=February+27%2C+2017.

[4] "Certainly it partakes of a higher science to comprehend the force of equity that has suffused and penetrated the very nature of human society." Francis Bacon, *Aphorismi de Jure gentium maiore, sive de fontibus Justiciae et Juris*, transl. by Mark Neustadt, appendix to Mark Neustadt, "The Making of the Instauration: Science, Politics and Law in the Career of Francis Bacon," Ph.D. diss., 1987, Johns Hopkins University, 1990 (microfilm).

[5] Andrea Padovani, foreword, ch. 2, "The Metaphysical Thought of Late Medieval Jurisprudence," in Michael Lobban, *The Jurists' Philosophy of Law from Rome to the Seventeenth Century*, vol. 7, ed. by Andrea Padovani and Peter G. Stein, Treatise Of Legal Philosophy And General Jurisprudence (Dordrecht, Netherlands: Springer, 2007), 2.1, p. 31.

[6] Charles Donahue, Jr., "Aggadic Stories About Medieval Western Jurists?" https://cardozo.yu.edu/sites/default/files/Charles%20Donahue%2C%20Jr.%2C%20Aggadic%20Stories%20About%20Medieval%20Western%20Jurists.pdf, pp. 209 to 215, 209.

---

him is that she has been "richly left" (*Merchant*, I, 1, 168). Once they marry, all her fortune will become his. Surprisingly, the word "heiress" never appears in the play. While it is assumed her father left her his estate, her wealth may have come from a deceased husband. The terms "heir" or "heiress" would apply if the decedent had died intestate. We are told that Portia's father left a will. The word "widow" does appear in the play. Portia says, "My maid Nerissa and myself meantime/Will live as maids and widows.... (III, 2, 1688).

A Closer Look at Portia

We assume that Portia is a first name, because women are not generally called by their last names. Portia, wife of Marcus Junius Brutus, friend of Julius Caesar, was of the *gens* Portia, a family of distinguished Roman jurists.[1] The Portia Basilica was the place where legal and business matters were historically transacted in Rome.[2] *Porcius* in Latin means "pig," so there could be a pun on "bacon."[3] Other explanations for the meaning of the name "Portia" have been proposed.[4] There is not necessarily just one right answer, of course.

When I saw the name "Azzolinus Portius" (c. 1140–possibly 1220 or 1230)[5] in an article by Professor R. H. Helmholz,[6] the similarity of "Portius" to "Portia" caught my eye. Who was Azzolinus Portius, or "Azo," as he was commonly known?[7] Azo was the most famous pupil of Johannes Bassianus. He became a famous teacher of the law at the University of Bologna.[8] Azo

---

[1] William Smith, ed., *Dictionary of Greek and Roman Biography and Mythology*, vol. 1, s.v. "Brutus" (London, 1844), p. 512.

[2] Smith, *Dictionary*, vol. 1, s.v. "Cato, Portius," p. 646; *Dictionary*, vol. 2, s.v. "Roma," p. 653. For an image of an engraving of the Portia Basilica from Giacomo Lauro, *The Wonders of Ancient Rome* (1641), Harvard Art Museums, no. M24967.56, https://www.harvardartmuseums.org/art/176129.

[3] Simon Miles' lecture on *The Merchant of Venice* before the Francis Bacon Society, https://www.youtube.com/watch?v=KcQCljc1Mv8.

[4] See Gary Watt, ch. 6, "The Law of Dramatic Properties in *The Merchant of Venice*," in *Shakespeare and the Law*, p. 240.

[5] The date of Azo's death is uncertain. See Manlio Bellomo, *The Common Legal Past of Europe*, p. 167, n. 24.

[6] R. H. Helmholz in *Roman Canon Law in Reformation England* (Cambridge: Cambridge University Press, 1990), p. 15 n. 52, http://catdir.loc.gov/catdir/samples/cam034/89035785.pdf (sample).

[7] D. Izzo, "Azo of Bologna," *History of the Izzo, Ezzo, and Azzo Surname*, lulu.com (2014, 2015). He also went by Porcius, Porcus, Azzo, Azzone, Azolenus, and Azo Soldanus or Soldani, after his father's surname Izzo.

[8] De Ferriere says Azo taught at Montpellier before going back to Bologna, but perhaps he is confusing him with Placentinus. Cf. M. Claude Joseph de Ferriere, ch. 14, "Of the most celebrated interpreters of the civil law," in *The History of the Roman or Civil Law, to which is added Dr. Duck's Treatise of the Use and Authority of the Civil Law in England*, trans. into English by J. B. Esq. (London, 1724), p. 144. https://books.google.ca/books?id=3do2AAAAIAAJ with "Azo," report no. c023, c. 1160-1230, Bio-Bibliographical Guide to Medieval and Modern Jurists, last

has been called the most distinguished jurist of the thirteenth century.[1] Tradition has it that he married Bassianus's widow.[2]

Azo had written a famous handbook for lawyers, the *Summa Codicis*, part of a larger collection called the *Summa Aurea*. The Goliardi quipped, "If you don't have Azo, don't go to court."[3] Azo used a Ciceronian scheme of philosophical classification.[4] In matters of controversy, Azo would present both sides, often the conflicting views of Placentinus and Azo's teacher, Johannes Bassianus.[5]

Azo coined the term *interesse* (in Latin, "to be between"), from which our modern word "interest" derives, in order to distinguish the compensation a lender was legally entitled to upon default from usury, as defined and prohibited by the Church.[6] The *as* in Latin was a pound weight; hence, there is a pun with the "pound of flesh." "As if" are words which open the doors to the imagination.

Azo and his famous pupil Accursius both held the chair at the University of Bologna that had been established by Irnerius.[7] Azo did not write every word of the legal treatises which bear his *sigla*.[8] He reworked glosses written by other glossators and put his *sigla* on them. This made it difficult to tell which works he actually wrote. John Selden believed that the last three books of one of Azo's *Summa* were actually written by Placentinus.[9]

Azo's summaries were relied upon by the nearly-contemporary Henry de Bracton in the treatise which bears his name, *Bracton*. Bracton tried to

---

updated 5/5/2018, http://amesfoundation.law.harvard.edu/BioBibCanonists/Report_Biobib2.php?record_id=c023.

[1] Zulueta and Steen, *The Teaching of Roman Law*, pp.xiv, xviii, xx.

[2] Charles Donahue, Jr., "Aggadic Stories About Medieval Western Jurists," https://cardozo.yu.edu/sites/default/files/Charles%20Donahue%2C%20Jr.%2C%20Aggadic%20Stories%20About%20Medieval%20Western%20Jurists.pdf, pp. 209-215, 209.

[3] Manlio Bellomo, *The Common Legal Past of Europe*, 1000-1800, p. 168, n 27.

[4] Bellomo, p. 168.

[5] Emmanuele Conte, ch. 2.2, 'Summa Aurea,' in Serge Dauchy, *The Formation and Transmission of Western Legal Culture : 150 Books That Made The Law in the Age of Printing* (Cham, Switzerland: Springer International, 2016), pp.22-24, 23. For an illustration of Azo's *Summa codicis*, AD 1482, see Dauchy, *The Formation and Transmission*, p. 484.

[6] Lawrin David Armstrong, *Usury and Public Debt in Early Renaissance Florence: Lorenzo Ridolfi on the Monte Commune*, p. 62.

[7] Constant van de Wiel, *History of Canon Law* (Louvain: Peeters Press, 1991), p. 131.

[8] "Azo," *Biography: Or, Third Division of "The English Encyclopedia,"* Supp., ed. by Charles Knight (London, 1872), pp. 140-141.

[9] *The Dissertation of John Selden Annexed to Fleta*, translated with notes by [Robert Kelham] editor of Britton, 1771, p. 165, HathiTrust, https://hdl.handle.net/2027/nyp.33433008667663. John Selden writes that Odofredus labelled those before Azo and Johannes Bassianus "antients" and those after them "moderns." Selden, pp. 160-165, 160. Selden thought Rogerius might have been Vacarius, but modern scholars disagree. Sir Thomas Edward Scrutton, *The Influence of the Roman Law on the Law of England*[...] (London, 1885), p. 68.

"graft" the writings of Azo and the other Roman jurists into the English common law "tree,"[1] but it was not always a good fit.[2] *Bracton* was relied upon by Blackstone in his *Commentaries on the Laws of England* which became the standard reference on the common law of England. In the United States, every state save Louisiana has passed a statute of reception adopting the common law of England.[3]

In *Merchant*, Portia tells her new husband Bassanio that she will learn from him.[4] This is a hint that he, like she, is a teacher. Azo had learned from his teacher, Bassianus. Some of Bassianus's writings concern marriage.[5] What a clever way to hide the hint of "Azo": under the skirts of a woman!

When the real-life Azo married the real-life widow of Johannes Bassianus, as the story is told, she would have assumed the name of her new husband.

My search indicates that, in all of Volume VII of Spedding, where Bacon's legal works are found, Bacon mentions Azo by name just once, in his *Reading on the Statute of Uses*, where he calls him "a civilian of great understanding." He goes on to provide Azo's definition of a trust, in Latin.[6] *Fides est obligation conscientia unius ad intentionem alterius.* "A trust is an obligation of one's conscience to carry out another's intention" (close translation).[7] The

---

[1] Apparently, Bracton did not write all of the treatise which bears his name, *Bracton*, but surely this is not surprising. See Frederick Bernays Wiener, "Did Bracton Write Bracton?" *American Bar Association Journal* 64, no. 1 (1978), pp. 72-75, JSTOR, http://www.jstor.org/stable/20745182. For an overview of Bracton in context, see Kenneth Pennington, "Roman and Secular Law in the Middle Ages" (under "English law"), first published in *Medieval Latin: an Introduction and Biographical Guide.* Edited by F. A. C. Mantello and A. G. Rigg. Washington D.C.: Catholic University Press of America, 1996. pp. 254-266, http://legalhistorysources.com/Law508/histlaw.htm. Even today, legal treatises often continue for years in the names of their original authors, though edited by successors.

[2] *Select Passages from the Works of Bracton and Azo*, ed. for the Selden Society by F. W. Maitland (London, 1895), HathiTrust, https://hdl.handle.net/2027/coo.31924032664025.

[3] Of interest may be R. H. Helmholz, "Natural Law and Human Rights in English Law: From Bracton to Blackstone," *Ave Maria Law Review* 3 (2005), pp. 1-22. http://chicagounbound.uchicago.edu/cgi/viewcontent.cgi?article=2480&context=journal_articles; Bryan A. Garner, "common law," *A Dictionary of Modern Legal Usage* (Oxford; Oxford University Press, 2001, p.b.), pp. 177-178.

[4] *Merchant*, III, 2, 1519. http://opensourceshakespeare.org/.

[5] Charles Donahue, Jr., 'Bassianus, that is to say, Bazianus? Bazianus and Johannes Bassianus on Marriage,' *Rivista international di diritto commune* 14 (2003) pp. 41-82, 66-82, http://www.law.harvard.edu/faculty/cdonahue/writings/RIDC14_41_82.pdf.

[6] *Spedding*, VII, p. 401, HathiTrust, https://hdl.handle.net/2027/hvd.32044069750248 (parallel, "*Montagu*, III, p. 298, first col., third par., HathiTrust, https://hdl.handle.net/2027/nyp.33433084718513).

[7] Albert Gibson, *Intermediate Law Examination Made Easy: A Complete Guide to Self-preparation in Mr. Sergeant Stephen's New Commentaries of the Laws of England*, 3d ed. (London, 1882). Albert was "Honors, Easter term, 1874," and there is a "shameless plug" for the bar review course his brother is teaching.

---

definition of a trust today includes: "a right of property, real or personal, held by one party for the benefit of another."[1]

Black's Law Dictionary (fifth ed., 1979) translates a similar quotation which gives all appearance of being derived from Azo's: *Fides est obligation conscientiae allicujus ad intentionem alterius*: "A trust is an obligation of conscience of one to the will of another."[2] No ascription to Azo is given in either the 1882 or 1979 (fifth) editions. In the current, tenth edition, I searched for, but did not find, that Latin quotation. The word "conscience" survives, though, in the definition of a constructive trust. Here is the illustration: "A constructive trust is the formula through which the conscience of equity finds expression. When property has been acquired in such circumstances that the holder of the legal title may not in good conscience retain the beneficial interest, equity converts him into a trustee."[3]

Another example of a constructive trust is in *Shylock v. Antonio*, but I believe the Court, not Shylock, became the trustee, holding the legal title for the life of Shylock, with beneficial interests in Antonio and Shylock for the life of Shylock, and then to Jessica and Lorenzo.[4]

While there are fifty-four references to "conscience" in *Black's Law Dictionary* (tenth edition, 2014, online), the name "Azo" does not come up in a search at all. One wonders whether his name was in even the 1882 edition. But we still have Portia, the constructive trust, and "conscience."

Later in his *Reading on the Statute of Uses*, Bacon simply refers to Azo (presumably) as "a civilian of great understanding,"[5] the term he had used for Azo before. In his epistle dedicatory to the Queen to his *Maxims*, he again writes that such maxims are "...called by a great civilian '*legume leges*',," but he does not mention any name.[6] In the *Case De Rege Inconsulto*, he quotes in Latin, "as the Civilian saith," again without naming a name.[7] I assume he means Azo each time. Perhaps it is hard for us to understand the risk he perceived if he

---

[1] *Black's LD*, p. 1352.

[2] *Black's LD*, p. 563.

[3] *Beaty v. Guggenheim Exploration Co.*, 122 N.E. 378, 380 (N.Y. 1919). *Black's Law Dictionary*, tenth ed., ed. by Bryan A. Garner, Thomson Reuters Westlaw, 2018, s.v., "trust, --constructive trust." Online.

[4] Tables prepared by Prof. William Arthur, School of Law, University of Colorado, MEA, p. 75.

[5] Spedding, VII, p. 407, HathiTrust, https://hdl.handle.net/2027/nyp.33433081627360.

[6] Spedding, VII, p. 320, HathiTrust, https://hdl.handle.net/2027/nyp.33433081627360 (*Montagu* III, pp. 219-220, HathiTrust, https://hdl.handle.net/2027/uc2.ark:/13960/t5v698p2n).

[7] Spedding, VII, p. 701. This expression, *legum leges* (*laws of the laws*), Bacon praises as "worthily and aptly called by a great civilian" in his "Law Tracts, "The Elements of the Common Laws of England," but he does not name that great civilian, which he elsewhere, however, names as Azo. Bacon "did not affect to disguise into other words than the civilians use ... a matter of great authority and majesty." Yes, he tells us, he is going to be giving us civilian law in a tract on the common law, in the civilians' own words! Cheeky devil. See *Montagu*, III, p. 221. On the "laws of laws," see Coquillette, *Francis Bacon*, pp. 289-290.

were to cite a civilian authority by name. Perhaps he truly wanted to ensure sure his writings were not destroyed, so that later generations would have them.

Nerissa

Beginning to see a pattern, I wondered whether the name "Nerissa" might suggest "Irnerius,"[1] the man credited with "establishing Roman law as a field of study in Bologna" in the twelfth century.[2] Nerissa was "ne're an heiress," but then, technically, neither was Portia. Irnerius's actual contribution may have been relatively small, just as Nerissa's role in the play was small.[3] He was, apparently, primarily a teacher. It is not such a small thing, though, that he had four famous pupils, the "Four Doctors" who went on to teach other famous pupils, who went on to teach others....Kenneth Pennington writes that, besides teaching in Bologna, he advised Emperor Henry V between 1106–1125 and served as a judge in Tuscany.[4]

Gratiano

Another character whose name has a real-life embodiment is Gratiano. Gratian, author of the *Decretum Magistri Gratiani*, also known as the *Concordia discordantium canonum* or simply the *Decretum*, is one of the most well-known of canon lawyers. That being said, little is known of his life. He taught at a monastery in or near Bologna around 1130–1140, possibly as early as 1120, where he wrote the *Decretum*, ca. 1140. While there is no proof he was a monk, he may have been a bishop. In fact, Chiusi (Chus! *Merchant* III, 2, 1662) claims him as its former bishop. He initially wrote anonymously. He organized and harmonized the canon law decrees in his *Decretum*, which helped make canon law a respectable discipline for study. He was known as a good teacher and is given credit for inventing the teaching hypothetical.[5]

---

[1] Haskins, ch. 7, "The Revival of Jurisprudence," *The Renaissance of the Twelfth Century*, pp. 198-200; F. de Zulueta and P. G. Stein, *The Teaching of Roman Law in England around 1200*, p. xiii.

[2] Kenneth Pennington, ch. 4.1, "Politics in Western Jurisprudence," in *A Treatise of Legal Philosophy and General Jurisprudence*, ed. by A. Padovani and P. G. Stein (Dordrecht: Springer International, 2007), pp. 157-211, 158.

[3] James Gordley, *The Jurists: A Critical History* (Oxford: Oxford University Press, 2013), pp. 28-31; Christopher Kleinhenz, *History of Canon Law* (Louvain: Peters Press, 1991), p. 131.

[4] Pennington, "Politics in Western Jurisprudence," p. 158.

[5] De Zulueta and P. Stein, *The Teaching of Roman Law in England around 1200*, pp. xvii, xxiv, lxxxiv; Bellomo, *The Common Legal Past of Europe*, p. 66.

Gratian "legitimized" the canon law, which the civil lawyers until then had tended to think of as unscientific, by reconciling inconsistencies between it and the civil law, harmonizing discordant canons. Zulueta and Steen, *The Teaching of Roman Law*, p. xvi.

The *Decretum* was a book in its time "known to every educated person in Europe," studied by all law students. Gratian organized the canon law in a way that made it accessible to students. He was the first to outline the natural, or human, rights of man. He was the "Christopher Columbus Langdell of the twelfth century," using the Socratic method based on his hypothetical *causa* (cases) which were "wonderful teaching tools ... exciting and compelling teaching material."[1]

Although Gratian's rules could be seen as harsh, his guidelines were more lenient than those in a prior *Decretum*, a handbook on penances for priests by Burchard. For example, where Burchard would require a priest who had been possessed by a demon to spend ten years demon-free before returning to the priesthood, Gratian would allow him to return after only one year.[2] Not long after he had written the *Decretum*, others began to gloss on his writings, often softening his interpretations. The first to do so was Paucapalea with his *Summa decretorum*.[3]

In Act II, Scene II, Gratiano says to Bassanio, "I have a suit to you. You must not deny me. I must go with you to Belmont." Bassanio says, fine, but curb your boisterous spirit.[4] Gratiano then says, "Signior Bassanio, hear me:/ If I do not put on a sober habit,/talk with respect, and swear but now and then,/Wear prayer-books in my pocket, look demurely,/Nay more, while grace is saying, hood mine eyes/Thus with my hat, and sigh, and say 'amen,'/ Use all the observance of civility,/Like one well studied in a sad ostent[5]/To please his grandam, never trust me more" (II, 2, 755).

---

[1] Kenneth Pennington, "The Biography of Gratian, The Father of Canon Law," *Vill. L. Rev.* 59, no. 4 (2014), pp. 679-706, 689, 706. http://digitalcommons.law.villanova.edu/vlr/vol59/iss1/5.

[2] Kenneth Pennington, "The Biography of Gratian," p. 701. For further discussion of Burchard's *Decretum* as it applied to medieval marriage, ca. 1007-1012, see Georges Duby, ch. 3, "Marriage According to Bourchard," in *The Knight, the Lady, and the Pries[t...]*," pp. 59-65.

Images of the *Decretum* may be found at http://amesfoundation.law.harvard.edu/BioBibCanonists/ImageDescr.htm; in addition, for eighteen lovely images from an illuminated manuscript of Gratian's *Decretum* showing the "Tree of Consanguinity" (relationship by blood) and "Tree of Affinity" (relationship by marriage), see http://www.fitzmuseum.cam.ac.uk/gallery/law/.

[3] Stephan Kuttner, "A Forgotten Definition of Justice," pp. 79-82.

[4] Bassanio also tells Gratiano to allay his skipping spirit (II, 2, 751-52). Bacon described one overcome by passions as "uncomely, unsettled, skipping, and deformed." *Spedding*, IV, p. 496. HathiTrust, https://hdl.handle.net/2027/hvd.hn6e7y. "Skipping" is used in this sense also in *Henry IV, Part I*, III, 2, 1883; *Love's Labor Lost*, V, 2, 2701; *Macbeth*, I, 2, 49; and *Twelfth Night*, I, 5, 93. Anyone who did not understand the meaning of "skipping" in the Shakespeare passages now has them explained by Bacon.

[5] In Latin, *ostendere* or *ostentare* meant "to hold out, show, reveal." *Ostentum* means a prodigy, a portent. *Ostentui* means "for a show, merely for show, as a sign or proof." *Ostentatio* meant showing, revealing, showing off, or a display, deceitful show, pretense. *Cassell's Latin*, s.v. *ostendo, ostento, ostentum, ostentui, ostentation*, p. 157.

Interestingly, modern legal scholars have only relatively recently discovered that *a* Gratian, thought to be *the* Gratian, is recorded as having been in Venice in 1143, in the company of two other Bolognese jurists, as a legal adviser in a court case in which a cardinal sat as judge.[1] There is also a record of *a* Gratian being in Venice in 1150 to advise a judge in a court case.[2] Did Shakespeare know? Is it not more likely that Bacon would have discovered this fact than that Shaxpere did? How very clever to place *a* Gratiano, *a* Portia, and *a* Bassianus in court in Venice at the same time! What a way to preserve the memory of these men!

It should be mentioned that Mario Ascheri writes that Venice rejected the Roman law, the *ius commune* system, preferring to rely on a more "amorphous" system of judicial discretion called *arbitrium iudicis*.[3]

"Until recently, we knew little of the growth of legal ideas in the period from Irnerius to Accursus."[4] And yet, the author of *Merchant* seems to have known more than most individuals about the twelfth-century glossators.

This is not the first time I have wondered whether a Catholic priest in hiding might have collaborated on the writing of Shakespeare's plays. Anthony Munday reported that Catholic priests hid as actors within the theatre, in costumes, touring with theatre groups, holding masses after performances.[5] There would likely be an abundance of secrecy surrounding such endeavors.

It was Gratian who first clearly stated a rule that a priest could enter the clergy if he had married prior to taking sacred orders; however, if he married after taking sacred orders, he could not be ordained.[6] Many priests made

---

[1] Anders Winroth, "Where Gratian Slept: The Life and Death of the Father of Canon Law." https://classesv2.yale.edu/access/content/user/haw6/Law/KA03_Winroth_Gratian_K2-1.pdf, (7/04/2013), pp. 105-106, 124 n. 58, 125, 127; Kenneth Pennington, "The Biography of Gratian," pp. 680, 698, 704-705. http://digitalcommons.law.villanova.edu/vlr/vol59/iss1/5.

[2] Pennington, "The Biography of Gratian," pp. 704-705, fn. 81; Antonia Fiori, ch. 2.1, "*Concordia discordantium canonem*, also known as *Decretum*," in Serge Dauchy, ed., *The Formation and Transmission of Western Legal Culture: 150 Books That Made the Law in the Age of Printing* (Chaum, Switzerland: Springer International, 2016), pp. 20-21, 20.

[3] Rena N. Lauer, *Jewish Law and Litigation in the Secular Courts of the Late Medieval Mediterranean, Critical Analysis of Law* 3, no. 1 (2016), p. 127, citing Mario Ascheri, *The Laws of Late Medieval Italy (1000-1500)*, pp. 276-78, 329-30.

[4] F. de Zulueta and Peter G. Stein, *The Teaching of Roman Law*, p. xxi.

[5] Clair Asquith, ch. 2, "Secret Voices," *Shadowplay*, pp. 20-35, 27. For a "good read" on the hunted priests, see Alice Hogge, *God's Secret Agents*, (New York: HarperCollins, 2005).

[6] Bruce Brasington, ch. 5, *Order in the Court*, pp. 200, n. 18; 226, n 206; "The Catholic Sacrament of Holy Orders," Dummies, a Wiley brand, http://www.dummies.com/religion/christianity/catholicism/the-catholic-sacrament-of-holy-orders/.

---

secret marriages prior to ordination. In the latter part of the Council of Trent (1545–1563), the marriage of priests became entirely forbidden.[1]

Throughout the play, Gratiano speaks of religious matters, hinting at his being a churchman. Portia proposes to Bassanio that he go with her to the church to be married, and we assume they marry; however, the play is silent about where, how, or when the other couples marry.

At the end of the play, Portia says, "Let us go in; And charge us there upon inter'gatories/And we will answer all things faithfully" (V, 1, 2771). Peter Dawkins has pointed out that Gratiano's response, "Let it be so," is like saying "Amen" in church.[2] Presumably, the wedding night would now commence. Did the *quaestio montes* suggest "inter'gatories" (rhymes with "purgatory)?[3] What a contrast between the Inquisitional inter'gatories and those contemplated here!

In W. H. Auden's "Love and Usury in *The Merchant of Venice*," Auden points out that in Shakespeare's source for this play, *Il Pecorone*, it was Ansaldo, not Gratiano, who married the counterpart of Nerissa.[4] Sometimes, it can be revealing to ask why an author has changed the story from his source. What if the marriage of Gratiano/Gratian and Nerissa/Irnerius "stood for" the marriage of the civil and canon law?

If the character Gratiano were a jurist summoned to advise the Duke on the case, then his speaking out in the courtroom would make more sense, although even commoners were allowed to speak in court as consilia at one time.

Gratian wrote about marriage, and he wrote about the Jews. In fact, he wrote about at least three issues in the play: forced conversion (Shylock), interfaith marriage (Jessica and Lorenzo), and the fact that Christians should not be servants to Jews (by which token Launcelot Gobbo should not be Shylock's servant).[5] Gratiano is the one who urges the harsh treatment of Shylock. Some have blamed the canonist Gratian's *Causa 23* of the Decretum, which defends a "just war" against heretics, for providing "justification" for the historical mistreatment of the Jews.[6]

---

[1] Gratiano says, "I have a wife .... I would she were in heaven, so she could entreat some power to change this currish Jew." *Merchant* IV, 1, 2235. www.opensourceshakespeare.org.

[2] Peter Dawkins, *The Wisdom of Shakespeare in 'The Merchant of Venice,'* p. 135.

[3] The *quaestio montes* will be discussed, supra, this chapter.

[4] W. H. Auden, "Love and Usury in *The Merchant of Venice*," in *Four Centuries of Shakespeare Criticism*, ed. by Frank Kermonde (New York: Avon Books, 1965, p.b.), pp. 240-252, 245.

[5] See Pennington, "Gratian and the Jews," *Bull. Medieval Canon L.* 31 (2014), pp. 111-124, 114, http://scholarship.law.edu/scholar.

[6] Brian Moynahan, *God's Bestseller: William Tyndale, Thomas More, and the Writing of the English Bible — A Story of Martyrdom and Betrayal* (New York: St. Martin's Press, 2002), p. 202.

The character structure in *Merchant* might be a variation on the *Commedia dell'Arte*. The stock characters, ca. 1492, were: a Director who was also an actor; two old men; Pantalone, also called "Magnifico"; a clown, an old pedant in a wine-stained academic gown called "Gratiano" or "Dottore"; a pair of male lovers; a pair of female lovers; two comic valets — one "deceitful and cunning" and one "oafish"; one or two "soubrettes" ("coquettes, frivolous young women"); incidental characters; a stock narrator; and singers, dancers, or acrobats.[1]

One might imagine Bacon in the role of Director at an Inns of Courts production, just as Bellario could be seen to direct the court action, at least from "behind the scenes," in *Merchant*. Shylock has been recognized as a Pantalone type,[2] and there are "Magnificos" listed in the cast list. *Merchant* has a character named Gratiano, but the clown is now Launcelot Gobbo, with a name similar to that of a Reformation theologian. The pair of male lovers could be Antonio and Bassiano, while Portia and Nerissa represent the two female lovers. We might find Launcelot Gobbo to be a cunning valet, while his father, Old Gobbo, was oafish. Jessica was a heedless young woman, a "soubrette."

Peter Dawkins of the Francis Bacon Research Trust lists twelve Shakespeare plays in which the influence of the *Commedia dell'Arte* is evident (not including *Merchant*).[3] It is possible that Bacon may have seen a performance of the *Commedia dell'Arte* when he was in France with Ambassador Amyas Paulet between October 1576 and February 20, 1579.[4] The Gelosi, a professional Venetian family troupe, performed in Blois(e) in February 1577 before the Estates General. They also performed in Paris on May 13, 1577 and July 27, 1577, with the express permission of Henry III of France (1551–1589).[5]

In his essay "Of Travel," Bacon names "comedies, such whereunto the better sort of persons do resort" in his list of "things to be seen and observed" in a foreign place. Bacon's comment suggests he knew that the *Commedia dell'Arte* was of two types, one more learned and the other more rustic.[6]

---

[1] *The Great Parade: Portrait of the Artist as Clown*, ed. Jean Clair (New Haven: Yale University Press, 2004), p. 350. See also See Hope Traver, "I Will Try Confusions with Him," *The Shakespeare Association Bulletin* 13, no. 2 (April, 1938), pp. 108-120, 113, JSTOR, http://www.jstor.org/stable/23675765; "The *Commedia dell'Arte*," characters, http://www.tim-shane.com/Commedia-Dottore.htm; Faction of Fools Theatre Company, Inc., copyright 2010 by Matthew R. Wilson, http://www.factionoffools.org/history. Another book which may be of interest is *Commedia dell'Arte in Context*, ed., Christopher B. Balme (Cambridge: Cambridge University Press, 2018).

[2] See Artemis Preeshl, *Shakespeare and Commedia dell' Arte: Play by Play* (Taylor & Francis: print, July 2017; ebook, June 2017), pp. 90-92, http://www.tandfebooks.com/action/showBook?doi=10.4324%2F9781315624907&.

[3] "Francis Bacon's Life," *Francis Bacon Research Trust*, p. 4, fn. 7, p. 28. http://www.fbrt.org.uk/pages/essays/Life_of_Sir_Francis_Bacon.pdf.

[4] Brian Vickers, ed., "Principal events in Bacon's life," *The History of the Reign of King Henry VII*, p. xxxvi. The embassy was in Blois, France, in December 1576. Peter Dawkins, "The Bacon Brothers and France," http://fbrt.org.uk/pages/essays/Bacon_Brothers_and_France.pdf, p. 4.

[5] J. Clair, *The Great Parade*, p. 350.

[6] *Spedding*, VI, pp. 417, HathiTrust, https://hdl.handle.net/2027/hvd.32044058286733.

Accursius

If Portia "is" Azo, Bassanio "is" Bassiano, and Irnerius "is" Nerissa, then who might Shylock "be"? I think he is supposed to be Accursius, "the most important jurist of Roman law in the thirteenth century.[1] He was Azo's most famous pupil. Accursius compiled the *glossa magna* or "Great Gloss," a collection of 96,940 glosses from all the glosses that had been written on the *Corpus iuris civilis*. Accursius is Latin for Accorso or Accurro, but he is known only as Accursius. Shylock is called a "devil" numerous times in the play.[2] Dante in his *Inferno* relegated the *son* of Accursius, jurist Francesco d'Accorso, to the seventh level of hell for sodomy.[3]

The *glossa magna*, together with Accursius' own annotations, made up the *glossa ordinaria*.[4] Glosses not preserved in the 96,940 eventually fell into disuse.[5]

The elder Accursius took his glosses from the writings of Bassianus, Pillius, Placentinus, and their teachers, including Rogerius, ("Frogerius")[6] Martinus, Bulgarius, and Irnerius.[7] The glossators were not above giving their own writings the force of law or even refashioning it to suit the time and place. After all, the *Corpus iuris civilis* had been written some five centuries before. For example, Accursius "updated" the Justinian law relating to the citizenship of a foreign bride.[8] Later, Bartolus revisited that law, further modernizing it.[9]

In 1724, Claude Joseph de Ferriere gave an unflattering opinion of the elder Accursius, saying that he "sometimes reports laws that are nothing to

---

[1] Kenneth Pennington, ch. 4.2, "Politics in Western Jurisprudence," in *A Treatise of Legal Philosophy and General Jurisprudence*, ed. by A. Padovani and P. G. Stein (Dordrecht: Springer International, 2007), pp. 157-211, 174.

[2] Launcelot: "I should stay with the Jew, my master,/who (God bless the mark!) is a kind of devil; and, to/run away from the Jew, I should be ruled by the/fiend who, saving your reverence, is the devil/ himself. Certainly the Jew is the very devil incarnal; ...." (II, 2, 597-602).

[3] Dante, "canto XV," *The Divine Comedy* vol. II, *Inferno*, transl. with intro., notes, and commentary by Mark Musa (New York: Penguin Books, 1985), p. 208, 212 n. 110, 173.

[4] For an image of the *glossa ordinaria*, see "Codex, with gloss of Accursius," see Luna, a Collaboration between ARTstor and the Bodleian Library, Collections, Medieval and Renaissance Manuscripts, MS Canon. Misc. 495, http://bodley30.bodley.ox.ac.uk:8180/luna/servlet/detail/ODLodl-1-1-1808-101837:Codex,-with-gloss-of-Accursius-.

[5] de Zulueta and Steen, *The Teaching of Roman Law in England around 1200*, p. xiv.

[6] "Rogerius," 1110-1162, report no. c007, Bio-Bibliographical Guide to Medieval and Modern Jurists, Ames Foundation, last updated 5/5/2018, http://amesfoundation.law.harvard.edu/BioBibCanonists/Report_Biobib2.php?record_id=c007.

[7] Bellamo, *The Common Legal Past*, p. 172.

[8] Julius Kirschner, ch. 7, "Women Married Elsewhere: Gender and Citizenship in Medieval Italy," *Marriage, Dowry, and Citizenship in Late Medieval and Renaissance Italy* (Toronto: University of Toronto Press, 2015) pp. 161-189, 165.

[9] Kirschner, p. 166.

the purpose, and gives others a very wrong meaning; but all that, as well as the contradictions for which he is blam'd, proceeds, possibly, from his having too hastily collected an Heap of his Predecessors' opinions. Besides, there are many decisions taken to be his, which are reported from others...."[1]

By standardizing the glosses into a great gloss, Accursius has been accused of stifling what had been a fluid, creative process of legal interpretation, causing the natural evolution of the law to stagnate.[2] "The vast number of manuscripts and complexity of Accursius's apparatus may explain why no critical edition of his *apparatus*, or a systematic compilation of glosses,[3] is available."[4]

Bartolus's teacher Cina, whom Franciscus Accursius, son of Accursius, had taught at the University of Bologna, is given credit for breaking the study of law free from Accursius's glossorial method, the "status quo," one might say. "Standing," or "standing for," is an important representational concept, inherent in acting as well as in law. The word "stand" or "stand for" is appears thirty times in the play, if you count the times it can be found within other words, such as "understanding." Whereas Portia tells us she stands for sacrifice (IV, 1, 1422), Shylock tells us he stands for judgment (IV, 1, 2035) and the law (IV, 1, 2077). *Stare decisis* (from L. *sto*, to stand), means to abide by or adhere to decided cases, to stand on precedent (*Black's LD*, p. 1261).

Like Shylock, the elder Accursius, known just as "Accursius," had amassed considerable wealth from his professional endeavors. In 1291, his son Franciscus Accursius (1225–1293) petitioned Nicholas IV for absolution, confessing the sin of usury. Both father and son had lent money to students at interest and taken bribes. Like his father, Franciscus Accursius was a lawyer trained at the University of Bologna. He had spent time in England serving Edward I as a diplomatic envoy and legal counselor. He had served on Edward's commission regarding a complaint of the Jews, alleging they were being extorted by a sheriff. A few years later, in 1290, Edward I expelled the Jews from England. Legal historian von Savigny found that most of the

---

[1] de Ferriere, Claude Joseph, ch. 30, "Of the Most Celebrated Interpreters of the Civil Law," *The History of the Roman or Civil Law[...]*, transl. by J. B. Esq. (London, 1724), pp. 143-157, 144.

[2] Alain Wijffels, ch. 2, "Accursius, Standard Gloss," in Serge Dauchy, ed., *The Formation and Transmission of Western Legal Culture: 150 Books That Made the Law in the Age of Printing* (Cham, Switzerland: Springer International 2016), pp. 24-28, 27. For a lovely color illustration of a page from a 1468 glossa ordinaria, see *The Formation and Transmission of Western Legal Culture*, p. 485.

[3] '*Glossa Ordinarium*,' *New Catholic Encyclopedia*, Encyclopedia.com, copyright 2003 The Gale Group, http://www.encyclopedia.com/religion/encyclopedias-almanacs-transcripts-and-maps/glossa-ordinaria.

[4] Wijffels, ch. 2, pp. 24-28, 27.

works attributed to the son, Franciscus Accursius, were actually written by other authors.[1]

Accursius might suggest "cur" or "dog," insults which Graziano[2] and Solanio[3] hurl at Shylock. In addition, Shylock complains that Antonio treats him like a cur.[4]

Stephano

The name *Stephano* might be intended to represent the twelfth-century jurist Stephen, Bishop of Tournai (1128–1203), who was credited with spreading the Roman law from Bologna to Northern France. Like Bassianus, he studied law under Bulgarus. Stephen wrote a famous *Summa* on Gratian's *Decretum*.[5] He gave a dramatic sermon in which the devil accused mankind before God, in the tradition of the "four daughters of God" allegory.[6]

Lorenzo

Lorenzo, Jessica's beloved, twice uses the word "beshrew." That might be a clue as to whom Lorenzo might "stand for." There was an important twelfth-century canonist named Laurentius Hispanus (1190–1248).[7] He was the "first to look upon the will of the prince as a primary source of law."[8] Following clues in the play, however, my research took me in a different direction.

Lorenzo says, speaking of Jessica, "Beshrew me but I love her heartily/For she is wise, if I can judge of her/and fair she is, if that mine eyes be true/and true she is/as she hath proved herself,/ and therefore, like herself, wise, fair, and true,/shall she be placed in my constant soul" (II, 6, 965ff). In the second

---

[1] *Medieval Italy, an Encyclopedia*, vol. 1, ed. by Christopher Kleinhenz, s.v. "Accursius, Franciscus" (Oxford: Routledge 2016, first pub. 2004), p. 364; Conway Robinson, *History of the High Court of Chancery and other Institutions of England [...]*(Richmond, 1882), ch. 16: "1272-1307," pp. 382-384;William Senior of the Middle Temple, Barrister-at-Law, *Doctors' Commons and the Old Court of Admiralty; a Short History of the Civilians in England* (London: Longmans, 1922), p. 4. https://archive.org/stream/doctorscommonsol00seniiala/doctorscommonsol00seniiala_djvu.txt.

[2] *Merchant*, IV, 1: 2068, 2237.

[3] *Merchant*, I, 3: 438, 445, 448-449.

[4] *Merchant*, III, 2, 3.

[5] Ronald G. Witt, *The Two Latin Cultures and the Foundation of Renaissance Humanism in Medieval Italy* (Cambridge: Cambridge University Press, 2012), p. 343.

[6] Traver, "The Four Daughters of God, a Mirror....," (1925), p. 72; Stephen of Tournai, *Die summa über das Decretum Gratiani*, ed. by Johann Friedrich von Schulte (Giesen, 1891; Aalen: Scientia, 1965), http://works.bepress.com/david_freidenreich/12.

[7] Kenneth Pennington, "Politics in Western Jurisprudence." In *A Treatise of Legal Philosophy and General Jurisprudence*. Edited by A. Padovani and P. G. Stein. Dordrecht: Springer International, 2007. First published online, March 13, 2015. pp. 157-211.

[8] Pennington, "Politics in Western Jurisprudence," pp. 165-166.

---

instance, he says, "In such a night/Did pretty Jessica, like a little shrew/ Slander[1] her love, and he forgave her" (V, 1, 2469ff). "Savvy" and "shrewd" are words used to describe a prudent man of good judgment "informed by world experience normally associated with high social standing.[2] Lorenzo may think he is a man of good judgment, but is he?

There were two famous men named Lorenzo Ridolfi. Lorenzo di Piero Ridolfi (1503–1576) served for a time as Apostolic Secretary. He was the younger brother of Niccolò Ridolfi (son of Contessina, sister to Pope Leo), who had been made Cardinal at the age of twelve (and died, poisoned, in 1550).[3] Lorenzo was married to Maria di Filippo Strozzi, daughter of Filippo Strozzi the Younger, a prominent Florentine banker, whose wife was Clarice, sister of Duke Lorenzo di Medici (1492–1514).[4] The Ridolfi family was wealthy and prominent. Robert Ridolfi (1531–1612), head of a banking house in London, is famous for his participation, as agent of Pope Pius V,[5] in the "Ridolfi plot," sometimes called the "casket plot," to put Mary, Queen of Scots on the throne of England.[6]

Lorenzo di Piero Ridolfi was a humanist and patron of the arts. Among other works of patronage, he commissioned a statue of Mercury.[7]

More pertinent to *Merchant*, perhaps, is Lorenzo di Antonio Ridolfi (1462–1443; in Latin *Laurentius*), an "outstanding Florentine lay canonist, diplomat, and savvy government lawyer, author of well-known and often-

---

[1] In the twelfth century, those "convicted of composing a slanderous poem" were disqualified from testifying as witnesses, due to wickedness. In cases where any witness might be admitted, they might be permitted to testify, "but not without torture." Brasington, ch. 2, "The Early Romano-Canonical Process: The Worlds of Hariulf and Bulgarus," *Order in the Court*, pp. 52-112, 96, 97, nn. 246-248, 254.

[2] Lawrin Armstrong, intro., *Usury and Public Debt*, p. 27, fn. 83.

[3] Cristina Acidini Luchinat, *The Medici, Michelangelo, and the Art of Late Renaissance Florence* (New Haven: Yale University Press, 2003), pp. 214-215 https://books.google.com/ books?isbn=0300094957; Janet Ross, *Florentine Palaces and their Stories* (London: J. M. Dent, 1905), pp. 270-272, 271. https://books.google.com/books?id=u4BoAAAAMAAJ.

[4] Machiavelli presented the engaged couple with a manuscript of his play *La Clizia*, based on Plautus's *Casina*, in honor of their marriage. *Niccolò Machiavelli: An Annotated Bibliography of Modern Criticism and Scholarship*, Bibliographies and Indexes in Law and Politics no. 13, compiled by Silvia Ruffo Fiore (New York: Greenwood Press, 1990), p. 172 .

[5] Lawrence P. Buck, *The Roman Monster: An Icon of the Papal AntiChrist in Reformation Polemics*, Early Modern Studies 13 (Kirksville MO: Truman State University Press, 2014), p. 205 (providing the text of the papal bull for excommunication of Elizabeth).

[6] Susan Ronald, *Heretic Queen: Queen Elizabeth I and the Wars of Religion* (New York: St. Martin's Press, 2012), pp. 153-154; Janet Ross, *Florentine Palaces and their Stories* p. 271. On the Ridolfi plot, see Charlotte Mary Young, *Cameos from English History: England and Spain*, 5th series (London, 1895), cameo 10, "The Ridolfi Plot (1571-1572)," pp. 83-93. https://books.google.com/ books?id=cYnWAAAAMAAJ.

[7] Luchinat, *The Medici, Michelangelo, and the Art of Late Renaissance Florence*, pp. 214-215. https:// books.google.com/books?isbn=0300094957.

---

cited tracts on usury and morality."[1] His most important work is the *Treatise on Usury*, which he finished writing in 1404.[2] Prof. Lawrin David Armstrong has translated and edited the most historically important part of Ridolfi's *Treatise on Usury*, the "Quaestio Monte," Question of the Public Debt, which comprises about one-third of the treatise.[3]

Lorenzo Ridolfi has been called a "civic humanist," focused on the "common good."[4] Since the Medici ran Florence,[5] it is tempting to suggest that "what was good for the Medici was good for Florence."

In the *Treatise on Usury*,[6] Lorenzo Ridolfi argued in favor of allowing interest on loans to government entities and speculation on the government debt market.[7] Whereas, in canon law and theology, no charge on a loan was permitted, Lorenzo argued that interest, but not excessive interest (usury), ought to be allowed.[8] This also was Francis Bacon's position, espoused in his essay "On Usury." In Roman law, delay, or a space of time, in returning payment, *mora*, was distinguished from a penalty for nonpayment or late payment, *poena*.[9] In *Antonio v. Shylock*, the issue was the penalty. Shylock charged no interest. With interest, time has a price.[10]

One might wonder what marriage has to do with debt, but in Ridolfi's Florence, the growing public debt, the *Commune Monte*, was accumulating interest and becoming a real headache, just as it does in modern times. The Florentine government had tripled the tax rate between 1384 and 1412, and loans had been forced on the commonwealth.[11] Ridolfi's defense of the

---

[1] Julius Kirshner, "A Critical Appreciation of Lauro Martinez' Lawyers and Statecraft in Renaissance Florence," in *The Politics of Law in Late Medieval and Renaissance Italy, Essays in Honor of Lauro Martinez*, ed. by Lawrin Armstrong and Julius Kirshner (Toronto: University of Toronto Press, 2011), pp. 7-39, 10, n. 12.

[2] Lawrin David Armstrong, Intro., *Usury and the Public Debt in Early Renaissance Florence: Lorenzo Ridolfi on the Monte Commune* (Toronto: Pontifical Institute of Medieval Studies, 2003), p. 1, https://books.google.ca/books?isbn=0888441444.

[3] Armstrong, preface, p. x; ch. 6, "The Edition," *Usury and the Public Debt in Early Renaissance Florence.*

[4] Armstrong, ch. 5, "Law, Politics, and Public Debt," pp. 100-111, 103-104, 107-108.

[5] On Cosimo's behavior as "officer of the Monte," see Katharine Dorothea Ewart, *Cosimo De' Medici* (London, 1899), ch. 5, "The Domestic Policy of Cosimo De' Medici and the Consolidation of His Power," pp. 140-183; 110, 150-151.

[6] Lawrin David Armstrong, *Usury and Public Debt*, p. 261. Lorenzo Ridolfi begins his treatise with a formal "Proemium," utilizing the Roman or papal "cursus" style. Armstrong, p. 261.

[7] Luciano Pezzolo, ch. 8, "Bonds and Government Debt in Italian City-States, 1250-1650," in *The Origins of Value, the Financial Innovations that Created Modern Capital Markets*, ed. by William N. Goetzmann and K. Geert Rouwenhorst (Oxford: Oxford University Press, 2005), p. 159.

[8] See L. Armstrong, front cover, *Usury and Public Debt*.

[9] Armstrong, ch. 3, "Usury and the Public Debt Controversies," p. 62.

[10] Armstrong, p. 95. There are 34 references to "time" in *Merchant*, made by: Lorenzo: I, 1, 75; I, 1, 160; II, 6, 972; V, 1, 2538; and Shylock: I, 3, 413; I, 3, 433, and IV, 1, 2243. www.opensourceshakespeare.org.

[11] Armstrong, ch. 2, "The Public Debt," pp. 28-52, 42.

public debt in his *Treatise on Usury* was "the most influential contribution to the debate and quickly became the standard canonical authority on the problem."[1]

The public debt was largely financed by the *monte delle doti*, a kind of insurance plan for dowries. One could pay in over a period from seven and a half to fifteen years for coverage for a daughter. The fund would pay you a predetermined set amount for a dowry when your daughter either married or entered the convent. In the latter case, the dowry would be returned to the family patrimony upon the daughter's death. If she neither married nor entered the convent, the family would not collect. Shares could be purchased in the fund's stock.[2]

Lorenzo Ridolfi was a serious student of sacred learning who called St. Jerome his mentor. In fact, he donated a book of the *Epistles of S. Jerome* to Santo Spirito Church for its library, for the use of all.[3] One manuscript of his *Treatise on Usury* bears a dedication to Christ, the Virgin Mary, and four patron saints (Jerome, Lawrence, Bernard, and Catharine).[4]

Prior to concentrating on law, Lorenzo had studied rhetoric under Salutati, after which he had lectured and written on the art of rhetoric. He had an interest in Latin poetry; in fact, his Proem to the *Treatise on usury* employs a poetic style. He taught law at the Studio Fiorentino.[5] His four sons, one of whom was named Antonio, were all "Gonfaloniers of Justice," the highest legal post, akin to being Chancellor of England. They were also all friends of the Medici.[6]

His father, Antonio Ridolfi, had been a wealthy merchant, like Antonio in *Merchant*. He had met with great misfortune when his palazzo was sacked and burned during riots in 1378.[7] However, the family regained its wealth just three years later by prospering in the wool business.

Lorenzi Ridolfi was one of the busiest jurisconsults of the early fifteenth century.[8] He was active in politics, representing Italian and foreign governments and advising judges.[9] Unusually, he had been betrothed "by

---

[1] Armstrong, front cover.

[2] Michael Veseth, *Mountains of Debt: Crisis and Change in Renaissance Florence, Victorian Britain, and Postwar America* (New York: Oxford University Press, 1990), pp. 44, 67-68.

[3] Lawrin Armstrong, *Usury and Public Debt*, p. 261.

[4] Armstrong, p. 117.

[5] Jonathan Davies, ch. 6, "The Studio Fiorentino and Florentine Culture," *Florence and its University during the Early Renaissance* (Leiden: Brill, 1998), pp. 107, 118 fn. 60.

[6] Janet Ross, *Florentine Palaces and their Stories*, p. 270.

[7] Armstrong, intro., *Usury and Public Debt*, p. 13.

[8] Lauro Martinez, *Lawyers and Statecraft in Renaissance Florence*, Studies and Texts 144 (Princeton: Princeton University Press, 1968), p. 107. Ten-years of education were required to master both canon and civil law. Martinez, pp. 78-91.

[9] Martinez, p. 106.

proxy," since he had been completing his law studies in 1388 and could not appear in person.[1] His second marriage was to Caterina di Luigi Guicciardini. Brian Vickers says Bacon followed the historical writing style of Francesco Guicciardini (1483–1540), Tacitus and Machiavelli which focused on observation and analysis rather than on moralizing and idealization.[2]

Because of Robert Ridolfi's implication in a conspiracy on behalf of Mary, Queen of Scots (the 1571 Ridolfi plot), the dramatist might have considered it unwise to make any reference by name to Ridolfi or his *Treatise on Usury* which might be relevant to the themes of *Merchant*. "Catholic" books were banned in 1573 — but not all of them.[3] I do not know whether Ridolfi's *Treatise on Usury* was banned in England, but it seems likely that Bacon as a statesman would have made it his business to obtain and read the book.

The marriage of Jessica and Lorenzo might signify the concept of forward-thinking worldly expedience, where religion can be changed without qualm and the law is starting to concern itself more with commerce than theology. One has to stop somewhere, but interesting questions arise as to dowry. How did the Jewish law on dowry differ from the Venetian law? Did Jessica forfeit rights to dowry by stealing from her father and/or eloping? What portion of what she stole would have been a dowry portion? Once she married Lorenzo, did ownership, in whole or part, pass to him? Was there intrafamily immunity? Would a twelfth-century Venetian court have heard a suit of Jew versus Jew? And on and on....

I have not identified any Italian jurist from the twelfth century or later whom Jessica could be said to represent. The letters in her name might suggest "Isaac." Jewish women of the time were not educated, unless they were taught at home. Jessica represents the "heedless coquette," one who acts "without consideration," even selling her father's wedding ring. In Jewish law, the exchange of rings was an essential act. It was the consideration for the marriage contract.[4]

Records survive of two learned Jewish women who were related to men named Isaac, "Bellette" in the eleventh century and an unnamed widow in

---

[1] Martinez, p. 19; Julius Kirschner, *Marriage, Dowry, and Citizenship in Late Medieval and Renaissance Italy* (Toronto: University of Toronto Press, 2015), p. 30.

[2] Francis Bacon, *The History of the Reign of King Henry VII*, ed. by Brian Vickers, intro., p. xxi; see also pp. xv, xviii, xxi, xxiif, xxv, xl, 225 n. 1, 239.

[3] See Deborah Shuger, ch. 1, "That Great and Immoderate Liberty of Lying," *Censorship and Cultural Sensibility: The Regulation of Language in Tudor-Stuart England* (Philadelphia: University of Pennsylvania Press, 2006), nns. 14-16. https://books.google.com/books?isbn=0812203348.

[4] Rena N. Lauer, "Jewish Law and Litigation in the Secular Courts of the Late Medieval Mediterranean," p. 130.

the twelfth century (d. ca. 1185). To be considered an educated Jew, one had to be learned in the Jewish law.[1]

Carmagnola

Around 1342, Lorenzo Ridolfi had appeared before the Doge, Francesco Foscari, in Venice, making a speech advocating for his city of Florence, pleading for the military aid of Venice against Florence's attacker, Philip (Filippo Maria Visconti, d. 1447), prince of Milan.[2] Francesco of Carmagnola, "the most famous of all Italian soldiers of fortune," had been treated so poorly by the ungrateful Philip, whom he had previously served as *condottiero* (mercenary), that he transferred his services and allegiance to the Doge of Venice, Francesco Foscari.

Francesco's first official duty was to perform an assassination. Nice guy. In time, the Duke and those in power in Venice began to fear him. After he had failed in an important mission, he was ordered to return to Venice "in order to give his good masters advice as to the peace." Unsuspecting of any trap, "no more suspicious than Othello in the same circumstances might have been,"[3] he was tricked into going to the Doge's palace. He had considered the Doge his friend. However, the Doge was not there. False friends, pretending to be showing him another way out of the palace, led him into the prisons inside the Doge's palace, from which he never escaped.[4] He was "examined by torture before the secret council" — chilling words — after which he was executed by beheading.

Shylock, like Carmagnola, was brash and arrogant, "harsh and haughty." Giordano Bruno, "the Nolan" (from Nola, near Naples), had also been brash and arrogant. Bruno was also tricked and betrayed by a supposed friend, Mocinego, into the clutches of the Venetian Inquisition. Like Carmagnola, Bruno was tortured before being executed. Both men died gagged.[5] At least Shylock survived with his life. Dr. Roderigo Lopez, a possible prototype for Shylock, had not been so lucky.

Inquisitional imprisonment and torture did take place in private villas in Italy during medieval and Renaissance times. Galileo was held for a week at the Villa Medici after his sentence had been pronounced, in 1633, but

---

[1] Cheryl Tallan, "Learned Women in Traditional Jewish Society," Jewish Women's Archive, https://jwa.org/encyclopedia/article/learned-women-in-traditional-jewish-society.

[2] Lawrin Armstrong, intro., *Usury and Public Debt*, p. 25; "A Soldier of Fortune," *Blackwood's Edinburgh Magazine* 137, no. 183 (April, 1885), pp. 460-484, 469. https://books.google.com/books?id=6Vg2AQAAMAAJ.

[3] "A Soldier of Fortune," p. 482.

[4] "A Soldier of Fortune," p. 483.

[5] "A Soldier of Fortune," pp. 460-484, *https://books.google.com/books?id=6Vg2AQAAMAAJ.*

he was only threatened with torture.[1] Torture is part of the history of the Doge's Palace in Venice.[2] Bruno was not held in a villa but in a prison, the San Domenico di Castello.[3]

Based on distance and travel time to Padua, Richard Roe suggests that the Villa Foscari-La Malcontenta corresponds geographically to Portia's Belmont and, thus, is likely the very villa Shakespeare had in mind. It was built in 1559–60[4] by Andrea Palladio. Shakespeare could have chosen any of a number of beautiful villas along the Brenta, but he chose this one. There are numerous reasons why it was particularly apt.[5]

Due process of law: St. Jerome, mentor of Lorenzo Ridolfi, had been denied due process in his trial for heresy. The trial of Savonarola was also noted for its lack in due process, being allegedly based on false charges. Lorenzo Ridolfi, a lawyer in the case, argued the matter should be taken away from the Chamber, for the process went against "every law of equity."[6] One wonders whether due process was also lacking in Bruno's or Dr. Roderigo Lopez' case (d. 1594). Perhaps the play felt like a safe(r) outlet for the playwright to express his strong feelings about state-condoned torture. One must guard against the tendency, however, to make Bacon, at least, the mouthpiece for one's own thoughts or feelings, as Prof. Coquillette has warned.

Leonardo

Francis Bacon had reminded us that sometimes it is the little things that are the most important, like the magnetized needle that guides the compass. When we read a mystery novel or watch a mystery movie, we are constantly on the lookout for the little things that would give away the culprit. We cringe when the escaped prisoner of war, incognito, gives himself away to the Gestapo by such a simple thing as saying "thank you" in his own language, as in the 1963 movie "The Great Escape."

---

[1] Maurice A. Finocchiaro, ed. and transl., *The Trial of Galileo: Essential Documents* (Indianapolis: Hackett, 2014, ebook), sec. 0.1, p. 1; on threats of torture, see pp. 9 n. 11, 11, 27, 39, 133-134.

[2] Melanie Renzulli, "What to See at the Doge's Palace," last updated 3/19/18, https://www.tripsavvy.com/doges-palace-highlights-1548017; "The Doge's Palace Secret Itineraries Tour," https://www.tripsavvy.com/doges-palace-secret-itineraries-tour-1548020; "The Doge's Palace, Venice," last updated 12/12/17, https://www.tripsavvy.com/doges-palace-history-1548018 .

[3] Monica Cesarata, blog, "The Ghost of Ca' Mocenigo, 10/1/2014, https://www.monicacesarato.com/blog/2014/01/10/the-ghost-of-ca-mocenigo/.

[4] "Villa Foscari, 'La Malcontenta,'" *Il Burchiello*, http://www.ilburchiello.it/en/villa-foscari-la-malcontenta.

[5] Richard Paul Roe, ch. 6, "The 'Merchant of Venice,'" *The Shakespeare Guide to Italy* (New York: Harper Perennial, 2011), pp. 141-157, 144-152, 152.

[6] John Browning, *The History of Tuscany from the Earliest Era* 3, trans. from Ital. by Lorenzo Pignotti (London, 1826), pp. 365-366. https://books.google.com/books?id=3boUAAAAYAAJ.

I had thought the character "Leonardo" was just a minor "extra," an unimportant servant, but a search for "Leonardo jurist" revealed a Leonardo who had done much to promote the modernization of the law on debt in Florence. Mantuan jurist Leonardo Legge was a prolific writer/editor who had published at least seventeen editions of theological and legal works in just four years, between 1570 and 1574.

A 1572 work of his was "expurgated" by order of the Holy Inquisition in 1575. His writing demonstrated "philological precision" and "anti-heterodoxical zeal." He is a "figure still entirely to be studied."[1] "Legge" sounds like it could have been a pseudonym, from the Latin word for law, *lex, legis*. Some works by him show up on WorldCat, but most information on him is in Italian. What better way to hide/preserve the name of a blacklisted author than to give it to a lowly servant! That would, of course, not be the only way. Francis, the "puny drawer" in *The First Part of Henry IV*, was also a lowly servant.

During the latter part of the Council of Trent, a commission was put in place to draw up a new index of banned books. From 1568 on, law books were especially targeted, with three separate institutions "vetting" them after 1571.[2] "Correcting" Machiavelli's works was discussed,[3] and Boccacio's works were "suspected."[4] Since books on marriage crossed boundaries between law and religion, they were given especially strict scrutiny.[5] Jean Hotman and Jacob Spiegel's *Lexicon* was cited in the *Avviso* of 1574.[6] Nicholas Cusanus' writings were banned[7]; Jean Bodin's *Republique* and *Methodus* were banned "until corrected."[8] The commission never gave reasons for banning a particular book.[9]

The works of Charles Du Moulin, "the most eminent learned commentator on French customary law,"[10] were unconditionally prohibited.[11] In fact, Gigliola Fragnito calls him the "jurist who personified the object of

---

[1] Rodolfo Savelli, ch. 8, "The Censoring of Law Books," transl. by Adrian Belton, in *Church, Censorship, and Culture in Early Modern Italy*, ed. by Gigliola Fragnito (Cambridge: Cambridge University Press, 2001), pp. 223-254, pp. 237-238. https://books.google.ca/books?isbn-0521661722.

[2] Saveli, p. 239.

[3] Saveli, p. 248.

[4] Saveli, p. 239.

[5] Saveli, p. 250.

[6] Saveli, p. 241.

[7] Saveli, p. 242.

[8] Saveli, p. 247.

[9] Saveli, p. 239.

[10] R. C. van Caenegem, *An Historical Intro. to Private Law*, transl. by D. E. L. Johnston (Cambridge: Cambridge University Press, 2003), p. 40.

[11] Saveli, p. 231.

censorship in law."[1] Venetian publishers had resorted to removing his name from publications or disguising his annotations as the publisher's own. One, Gaspare Cavallini, published three of Du Moulin's works under his own name, and that included the *Tractatus commerciorum et usuranum*.[2] Publishers tried omitting Du Moulin's name or using initials, but the censors always detected the ruse.[3] One might wonder why Leonardo would be chosen over Charles. One answer might be that Leonardo was an Italian name. It might make one think of Leonardo da Vinci, who, however, had nothing to do with usury or, for that matter, banned books.

In Venice, a purged edition of Gratian's *Decretum* annotated by Du Moulin was published. This was of particular concern to the censors, since the *Decretum* was being officially revised under Popes Pius V and Gregory VIII, a task not completed until 1582.[4] In 1588, an edition of Justinian's *Institutiones* (*Institutes*) was published which contained some content from two writers who were on the blacklist. The censors caught it.[5]

In determining whether or not to censure, ban, or expurgate a book, the book's "usefulness" or "uselessness" was taken into consideration.[6] However, law books, although "useful," were closely scrutinized if they concerned law and religion, as was the case with books on marriage.[7] The Talmud was ruled "useful," only because of the advocacy of the University of Basle.[8] Part of the satire going on in *Merchant* may be a protest in frustration against the unavailability of useful treatises to scholars and statesmen, such as Bacon, seeking to benefit from them.

---

[1] Saveli, p. 247.

[2] Saveli, p. 234-235. Du Moulin also authored the *Indici dei Tractatus universi iuris*. Saveli, pp. 234, 248.

[3] Saveli, p. 236.

[4] Saveli, pp. 229, 236.

[5] Saveli, p. 242-243; see also 245.

[6] Saveli, p. 231.

[7] Saveli, p. 250.

[8] Saveli, p. 173. On "useful," see also pp. 39, 134, 150, 202, 230.

Chapter Ten: Characters, Counterparts, and Others — Part III

Portia may "stand for" Azolinus Porcius and Bassanio for Johannes Bassianus. Does Bellario have a twelfth century juristic counterpart? Initially by process of elimination — having tentatively accounted for Irnerius, Azo, Bassanius, Gratian, and Stephan of Tournai — I wondered if it might be Placentinus (early 12th century–c.1182),[1] a jurist trained by Bulgarus, student of Irnerius, in Bologna. Not much is known about him, and his date of death is uncertain (perhaps as early as 1180, although there is a tombstone dated 1192), but he was one of the most important and influential of the twelfth-century Italian jurists.

Placentinus wrote his serious legal works in a poetic style which included verse and allegory, a style which his colleague in Montpellier, Rogerius — also trained by Bulgarus — employed as well. H. Kantorowicz speaks of a Rogerius-Placentius-Pillius school. While Placentinus' pupil, Pillius de Medicina (d. 1210 or after 1213),[2] continued to write in the poetic style of his teacher, Pillius does not seem to have trained a poetic legal protégé. Perhaps the Albigensian Crusade, followed by the Inquisition, had a chilling effect on the writing of law in verse, as it did on the poetry of the troubadours. Incidentally, the name "troubadour" comes from *trobar*, "to find."

---

[1] Placentinus, report c013, http://amesfoundation.law.harvard.edu/BioBibCanonists/Report_Biobib2.php?record_id=c013, last updated 5/5/2018.

[2] "Pillius," report #c016, Bio-Bibliographical Guide to Medieval and Modern Jurists, last updated 5/5/2018, http://amesfoundation.law.harvard.edu/BioBibCanonists/Report_Biobib2.php?record_id=c016.

Pillius was the "first jurist to write a Commentary on the *Liber feudorum*" of Obertus de Orto, a judge in Milan, on the feudal law.[1] In 1187, Pillius is found advocating on behalf of the monks of Canterbury in 1187.[2]

Pillius claimed the ghost of Placentinus appeared to him once in a vision, urging him to complete Placentinus' unfinished works. While Pillius is our main source of information about Placentinus,[3] Placentinus also wrote about himself. In fact, he was the first glossator to write about himself, in a Prooemium. The poetry of the troubadours re-emerged in Sicily with the legally-trained Cino, Dante,[4] Petrarch, and Boccaccio.

Other Bolognese glossators had tried to write in verse, but Placentinus' verse, in Latin, was vastly superior, according to Hermann Kantorowicz. In classical Latin, a *pilum* was a "spear," or the "heavy javelin of the Roman infantry." *Pilus, -a, -um* was "a single hair, a trifle."[5] Thus, one seeking to revive the tradition of writing law poetically might have seen a punning potential in *pilum*.

An edition of Placentinus's writings was published in Venice in 1584–86 by F. Ziletti, in a collection called the *Tractatus Universi Iuris.*[6] Placentinus, or

---

[1] Kenneth Pennington, ch. 4, "Politics in Western Jurisprudence," p. 174.

[2] Sir Travis Twiss, 'The Pseudo-Ulpian, the Latter Days of Ricardus Anglicus,' part 2, "The Twelfth Century, The Age of Scientific Judicial Procedure," in *The Law Magazine and Law Review*, fourth series, no. 19, ed. by T. P. Taswell-Langmead (London, 1893), p. 191. https://books.google.com/books?id=z2gvAQAAMAAJ; Everett U. Crosby, *Bishop and Chapter in Twelfth Century England: A Study of the Mensa Episcopalis*, Cambridge Studies in Medieval Life and Thought (Cambridge: Cambridge University Press, 2003), p. 101. https://books.google.com/books?isbn=052152184X.

[3] H. Kantorowicz, "The Poetical Sermon of a Medieval Jurist: Placentinus and his 'Sermo de Legibus,'" *Journal of the Warburg Institute* 2, no. 1 (Jul., 1948), p. 25.

[4] Lorenzo Valterza, "Dante's Justinian, Cino's Corpus, The Hermeneutics of Poetry and Law," in *Medievalia et Humanistica, Studies in Medieval and Renaissance Culture*, new series, no. 37, Literary Appropriations, ed. by Paul Maurice Clogan (Lanham MD: Rowman & Littlefield, 2011), pp. 89-110, 89.

[5] Edwin Bormann, *Francis Bacon's Cryptic Rhymes*, p. 212; *Cassell's Latin*, p. 169. Nestor," statesman, ruler, judge," was the wise, elderly King of Pylos, a hero of the Trojan War. Language on the Shakespeare Monument calls Shakespeare "A Pylus in judgment, a Socrates in genius, a Maro in art." Peter Dawkins, intro., *The Wisdom of Shakespeare in 'The Merchant of Venice'* (Warwickshire UK: I. C. Media Productions, 2015), p. vii. There are 31 references to "Nestor" in *Shakespeare*, including *Merchant* I, 1, 59.

[6] "Placentinus," report # c013, early twelfth century, c. 1182, last updated 5/5/2018, http://amesfoundation.law.harvard.edu/BioBibCanonists/Report_Biobib2.php?record_id=c013.

The *Tractatus* is said to include the writings of a jurist named Lancellottus (d. 1583), brother of canonist Giovanni Paolo Lancellotti. "Robertus Lancellottus," report # t140, d. 1583, last updated 5/5/2018, http://amesfoundation.law.harvard.edu/BioBibCanonists/Report_Biobib2.php?record_id=t140 (viewed at http://pds.lib.harvard.edu/pds/view/44452197?n=18&oldpds). There is also "Politi, Ambrogio Catarino ('Lancellotto de,' Siena 1484, d. Napoli 1553)," no. 92, whose name shows up next to Placentinus' in the authors' list for the *Tractatus*, and Gallia Lancellotus, no. 43 (not in numerical order), last updated 7/31/14, http://amesfoundation.law.harvard.edu/digital/TUI1584/TUI1584Metadata_Authors.html. Perhaps the playwright had

Piacentino ("of Piacenza"), a toponym, is the only name by which Placentinus is known. None of the twelfth-century Bolognese jurists ever referred to his teacher by name. Placentinus referred to Bulgarus only as *Os aureus*.[1] The jurists signed their writings by their *sigla*; in the case of Placentinus, the capital letter "P." H. Kantorowicz surmises that his first name may have been the same as his grandson's, "Savinus," since Italians were often named after their grandfathers.[2] Piacenza is located about twenty-five miles from Bassanius's town of origin, Cremona. The "Pi" in "Piacenza" becomes "pl" when Latinized. The patron saint of Piacenza was St. Anthony (d. 303 A.D.), known, among other things, for his desire for martyrdom,[3] a trait which Antonio in *Merchant* seems to possess.

Placentinus was peripatetic. Trained in Bologna by Bulgarus and, perhaps, Martinus,[4] Placentinus first taught law in Mantua in the early 1160s.[5] After that, he may have taught in Bologna briefly, or he may have gone directly to Montpellier, where he taught for ten to seventeen years. There was an

---

obtained a copy of the *Tractatus*, published in Venice in 1584. If so, perhaps "Lancellottus" suggested "Lancelot" to him.

[1] H. Kantorowicz, "The Poetical Sermon of a Medieval Jurist," pp. 22-26. Where there is discrepancy as to dates for Placentinus, the modern Ames Foundation Reports will be used.

[2] Placentinus' grandson's name was "Savinus nepos magistri Placentini, filius Albertus Vallis de Placentia." Placentinus' family seems to have come from a "distant, high fortified place high up in the mountains," its oldest name being "Torresana, the "strong tower," H. Kantorowicz, "The Poetical Sermon of a Medieval Jurist," p. 23. "Savinus" may refer to the savin tree, the red cedar, a form of cypress that grows in Lombardy (Savin Rock in West Haven, Connecticut was named for the red cedar. Marlene Clark, "The Amusing History of Savin Rock, from 1870 to now," *Hartford Courant*, 7/18/2007, http://articles.courant.com/2007-07-18/news/0707180261_1_hot-dog-beach-street-new-haven.

[3] Piacere, Piacenza. https://www.comune.piacenza.it/welcome/the-city/the-story-of-piacenza; Umberto Benigni and C.F. Wemyss Brown, "Piacenza," *The Catholic Encyclopedia* 12 (New York: Robert Appleton, 1911); online, 15 Nov. 2017, http://www.newadvent.org/cathen/12069a.htm.

There was also St. Anthony of Padua (1195–1231), a friend of St. Francis, patron saint of lost articles. He taught occasionally at the universities in Montpellier and Toulouse in Southern France: "St. Anthony of Padua," Catholic Online, https://www.catholic.org/saints/saint.php?saint_id=24; St. Anthony of Padua, https://www.stanthony.org/st-anthony-of-padua/; Dal-Gal, Niccolò, "St. Anthony of Padua," *The Catholic Encyclopedia*, vol. 1, (New York: Robert Appleton, 1907); http://www.newadvent.org/cathen/01556a.htm; Paul Burns, ch. 13, "St. Anthony of Padua," *Butler's Lives of the Saints* (Collegeville MN: Liturgical Press, 2003), pp. 272-273.

[4] Hermann Kantorowicz, *Studies in the Glossators*, p. 126.

[5] Placentinus, "early 12th c.-1182," Bio-bibliographical Guide to Medieval and Modern Jurists, Report No. c013, last updated 5/5/2018, http://amesfoundation.law.harvard.edu/BioBibCanonists/Report_Biobib2.php?record_id=c013.

According to a source which is a "work in progress," five of the seven texts attributed to Placentinus are in the *Tractatus Universi Iuris* which was published in Venice 1584-86 by Francesco Ziletti. "Placentinus," The Ames Foundation, *Tractatus Universi Iuris (Venice 1584-86 Authors,)* ed. by Charles Donahue, item no. 91, copyright 2014, http://amesfoundation.law.harvard.edu/digital/TUI1584/TUI1584Metadata_Authors.html. Placentinus taught at Piacenza, Mantua, Bologna, and Montpellier. H. Kantorowicz, "The Poetical Sermon of a Medieval Jurist," pp. 22-26, JSTOR, www.jstor.org/stable/750022.

increasing demand for teachers of Justinian's *corpus* throughout Europe during that time. Either he founded his own school or taught in Rogerius's school ca. 1165–70. Kantorowicz thinks he was also a pupil of Rogerius'.[1] After his first period in Montpellier, he spent two months back in Piacenza. He then lived with the Castelli family in Bologna, giving law lectures at their home before returning to Piacenza. He probably went back to Montpellier in 1179–80 and died in the early eighties. Although the date on "his" tombstone has been questioned,[2] many sources give the date of his death as 1192.[3]

He is credited by Peter Goodrich with "giving birth" to the satirical critique of law. He writes, "the first work of satirical legal studies is a critique of Justinian's *Corpus*, Placentinus' *Sermo de legibus*.[4] Satire itself did not begin with Placentinus, of course, or end with him. We surely would find satire in Aesop's fables or in the Greek and Roman dramas. Horace had written satirical critiques, and François Hotman, the Reformation jurist whose son probably tutored Bacon in civil law, had written a satirical critique of Justinian's law.[5]

While teaching law at the University of Bologna, Placentinus was honored by being asked to give a sermon at the start of the new school term. His sermon would follow that of a theologian, so it was a serious occasion.[6] Placentinus gave his *Sermo de legibus*, "sermon on the laws," a satirical, "polemical" poem criticizing the way law was taught at that very school, the University of Bologna. It was an outrageous thing to do.

Word had gotten around that his text would include the "*initium* of the lex C, 3, 1, 14" which begins *Rem non novam...aggredimur*. Bulgarus, Placentinus's own teacher, had begun a talk on this text the morning after his second wedding, making a personal anecdote of it, to the reported amusement of

---

[1] H. Kantorowicz, ch. 7, "Rogerius," *Studies in the Glossators*, pp. 122-144, 126-127.

[2] "Placentinus," report # c013, early twelfth century–c. 1182, last updated 5/5/2018, http://amesfoundation.law.harvard.edu/BioBibCanonists/Report_Biobib2.php?record_id=c013.

[3] See, e.g., Ioannis Seldeni, *Ad Fletam Dissertatio*, transl. by David Ogg, (Cambridge: Cambridge University Press, 1925), p. 121; Hermann Kantorowicz, *Studies in the Glossators*, p. 8; Mari Ascheri, *The Laws of Late Medieval Italy (1000–1500)*, p. 211; Germain Sicard, *The Origins of Corporations: The Mills of Toulouse in the Middle Ages* (New Haven: Yale University Press, 2015), p. 326.

[4] Peter Goodrich, "Satirical Legal Studies, From the Legist to the *Lizard*," *Michigan Law Review* 103, no. 3 (2004), pp. 397-517, 419-422, 419, https://repository.law.umich.edu/mlr/vol103/iss3/1.

[5] Peter Goodrich, "Satirical Legal Studies," pp. 410, 415, 438, 515 (Horace); pp. 418, n. 108 (Hotman, *Antitribonian*—Tribonius being the person Justinian commissioned to compile the *Corpus iuris civilis*).

[6] Manlio Bellomo, *The Common Legal Past of Europe 1000-1800*, p. 197.

the students.[1] With this advance publicity, the house was packed with anticipating students.[2]

Placentinus' satirical critique took the form of a dialogue in verse between two women, a lovely country girl called "Ignorantia" and an old, ugly, deformed woman called "Jurisprudentia."Hermann Kantorowicz provides the Latin text which Peter Goodrich explains.[3] Placentinus also personified Jurisprudentia in another allegorical work, his *Libellus de actionum varietatibus.*[4]

Placentinus was more popular with the students than with his colleagues. In fact, he had so alienated one of them, Henricus de Baila, by openly criticizing his work that de Baila, a nobleman, had him attacked during the night. Placentinus fled but afterwards lived in fear of another attack.[5]

The *Merchant of Venice*, among other things, is a satire on the state of the law. It would make sense for an Elizabethan satirist of the law to pay homage to Placentinus, the first modern legal satirist (if he knew of him). Who better to write such a satire than a man who had been expected since birth to use his tremendous talents in the service of the commonwealth and his fellow man, who had been charged by the Queen herself to reform the laws of England, who had studied them and knew what a sorry state they were in, and who had the literary skills, aptitude, and inclination towards theatrical endeavors to write such a play? If you think I am trying to describe Francis Bacon, you are right.

Placentinus had taught at Mantua in the 1160s.[6] It has been thought a mistake — printer's or otherwise — when, in the first and second Quarto and even in the First Folio, the play has Balthasar meeting Bellario at Mantua instead of Padua, because — it is said — the University of Padua was where Elizabethan young men would go to study the civil law.[7] However, what

---

[1] Pierre Bayles recounts it in "Bulgarus," *A General Dictionary, Historical and Critical: In which a New and Accurate Translation of that of the Celebrated Mr. Bayle[...],* (London, 1735), pp. 65-66, 66, https://books.google.com/books?id=oWBZAAAAYAAJ.

[2] H. Kantorowicz, "The Poetical Sermon of a Medieval Jurist," pp. 22-41, 26, JSTOR, http://www.jstor.org/stable/750022.

[3] Goodrich, "Satirical Legal Studies," pp. 419-422; H. Kantorowicz, "The Poetical Sermon of a Medieval Jurist," pp. 22-41.

[4] H. Kantorowicz, *Studies in the Glossators*, p. 203.

[5] Id.; Peter Goodrich, *Law in the Courts of Love, Literature, and other minor Jurisprudences* (London: Taylor & Francis e-Library 2003, prev. pub. by Routledge, 1996), pp. 129-131; Peter Goodrich, *Oedipus Lex: Psychoanalysis, History, Law* (Berkeley: University of California Press, 1995), p. 244-247.

The medieval glossators sometimes wrote their legal material in rhymed prose or verse which they called *carmen*, such as a "series of eleven would-be classical hexameters" describing a lawsuit. Placentinus' carmen far surpassed those of the other glossators in quality, according to Hermann Kantorowicz, *Studies in the Glossators*, p. 222.

[6] H. Kantorowicz, *Studies in the Glossators*, pp. 145, 190, 202, 207.

[7] *The Merchant of Venice*, ed. by M. M. Mahood (Cambridge: Cambridge University Press, 2012), commentary to notes for Act III, scene 4, line 51 (III, 4, 1799 in www.opensourceshakespeare.

if the change were deliberate? Had something happened that made Padua more personally significant to the playwright? We assume that by Padua is meant the University. However, the play does not say Bellario was affiliated with a university, or even that the play is clearly set in the sixteenth century.

Giordano Bruno taught at the University of Padua from Nov. 1591 to March 1592, prior to his arrest in Venice in May 1592 for heresy.[1] Like Placentinus, he had lived a peripatetic life after his excommunication, as a Dominican friar, for heresy in 1576. He lived and taught at numerous places, in Germany, France, Switzerland, England, and of course, Italy, never staying too long in one place, since he was not popular with religious authorities of any persuasion.[2]

Other famous alumni of the University of Padua include Nicholas Copernicus (1473–1543)[3] and Dr. William Harvey, who discovered the circulation of the blood.[4] Galileo began teaching mathematics there in 1592; in fact, Bacon corresponded with him.[5]

There were two men named "Placentinus" who lived or taught at Padua in the sixteenth century: Rusticus Placentinus, editor in 1515 of the first Latin edition of Galen's works,[6] and Giulio Casserio (Julius Casserius Placentinus), Harvey's anatomy teacher.[7]

Portia sends Balthazar to meet Bellario "at Padua." While the records do not show that Placentinus ever taught law in Padua, there are very few records in general on the early study of law there. However, it does appear

---

org; see also, in OSS: IV, 1, 2042, 2053, 2355; V, 1, 2738); *The Pelican Shakespeare*, ed. by A. R. Braunmuller (New York: Penguin Books, 2017), p. lii; *A New Variorum Edition of Shakespeare: 'The Merchant of Venice*,' ed. by Horace Howard Furness (Philadelphia, 1888), p. 176; *Staunton's Shakespeare*, I, ed. by Howard Staunton (London, 1858), p. 422.

[1] Michael White, *The Pope and the Heretic, The True Story of Giordano Bruno, the Man Who Dared to Defy the Roman Inquisition* (New York: William Morrow, 2002), on Padua: see pp. 37, 40-41, 102-103, 214, 218; on Bruno in England (1583-1585) and acquaintance with "Shakespeare," see pp. 205-207. For Bruno's influence on modern physics and literature, see White, ch. 10, "Encore!" pp. 186-210.

[2] White, appendix 2, "A Brief Chronology of Bruno's Life," *The Pope and the Heretic*, pp. 213-214.

[3] "Nicolaus Copernicus," *Stanford Encyclopedia of Philosophy*, https://plato.stanford.edu/entries/copernicus/.

[4] "Eminent Alumni," Università Degli Studi di Padova. http://www.unipd.it/en/university/history/eminent-alumni.

[5] "Galileo Galilei," *Stanford Encyclopedia of Philosophy*, https://plato.stanford.edu/entries/galileo/.

[6] Owsei Temkin, *The Double Face of Janus and Other Essays in the History of Medicine* (Baltimore: Johns Hopkins University Press, 1977), pp. 179-180; William Osler, M.D., F.R.S., *Thomas Linacre* [transl. Galen's Greek into Latin] (Cambridge: Cambridge University Press, 1908), p. 46.

Galen's *De Temperamentis* and the smaller treatise *De inequali in temperie* were published in England in 1521 in Greek type by the German immigrant publisher John Siberch. E. Gordon Duff, *The English Provincial Printers, Stationers and Bookbinders to 1557* (Cambridge: Cambridge University Press, 2010, p. b.), pp. 77, 80-81. John Selden had once owned the rarest of all of Siberch's books, a sermon of St. Augustine's. Duff, p. 78.

[7] Nicholas McDowell and Nigel Smith, *The Oxford Handbook of Milton* (Oxford: Oxford University Press, 2009), p. 655.

---

that law *was* being taught in the city of Padua prior to the thirteenth century, before the University of Padua opened in 1222, just as it had been taught in Bologna, in private *schola*, before the founding of the University in 1088.[1] It appears that Padua had been a satellite school of Bologna staffed by itinerant faculty from the University of Bologna. Thus, Placentinus could have been "at Padua" when Portia sent Balthazar to him.

It is as if the playwright gleefully worked out a historical puzzle of "rule, exclusion, exception" for future generations to solve, in search of Bellario.

Padua did not produce its own eminent jurist until the mid-fourteenth century.[2] Odofredus, a student of Accursius who taught at Padua from 1229 on, was more remembered for his discursive chronicles than for his commentaries. Marsilius (1275 to 1342), a doctor of medicine and lay canonist, taught at Padua. His most famous work is *Defensor pacis*, for which he was branded as a heretic. His ideas were considered precursors to those of Martin Luther.[3]

Bacon's great-nephew, the son of Sir Julius Caesar, had been killed in a street brawl in Padua, similar, perhaps, to the street brawl in which Mercutio was slain, in Mantua, *Romeo and Juliet*.[4]

While we will never know for sure, I am inclined to believe the playwright chose to change "Mantua" to "Padua," for personal reasons.

If Jean Hotman tutored Bacon in civil law when he was in France, Bacon might have first learned of Placentinus then. Placentinus was one of, if not the, preeminent jurist(s) of his time. Like Bacon, Placentinus "would not submit to the mere authority of texts."[5] Like Bacon-Shakespeare, Placentinus

---

[1] A. J. Carlyle, A. J. Carlyle, *The Political Theory of the Roman Lawyers and Canonists from the Tenth Century to the Thirteenth Century, A History of Medieval Political Theory in the West* 2 (New York: G. P. Putnam's Sons, 1909), p. 6.

[2] John Kenneth Hyde, *Padua in the Age of Dante* (New York: Barnes & Noble, 1966), p. 284. https://books.google.com/books/about/Padua_in_the_Age_of_Dante.html?id.

[3] Louis Salembier, "Marsilius of Padua," *The Catholic Encyclopedia*, vol. 9. (New York: Robert Appleton, 1910). http://www.newadvent.org/cathen/09719c.htm.

[4] "Caesar, Sir Julius," Crown copyright and the History of Parliament Trust, 1964-22017, http://www.historyofparliamentonline.org/volume/1604-1629/member/caesar-sir-julius-1558-1636.

[5] Peter Goodrich, *Oedipus Lex*, pp. 244-245, citing H. Kantorowicz, "The Poetical Sermon." Ronald Witt disagrees with some of Kantorowicz's attributions and dating in *The Two Latin Cultures and the Foundation of Renaissance Humanism in Medieval Italy* (New York: Cambridge University Press, 2012), pp. 340-342.

The *Sermo de legibus*, attributed to Placentino, was an orientation address for incoming students, delivered either in 1185 or 1189, in *prosimetron*, a genre of prose alternating with poetry. (However, these dates do not work if he died in the early 1180s.) Ronald G. Witt, ch. 2, "The Birth of the New Aesthetic," *In the Footsteps of the Ancients: The Origins of Humanism from Lovato to Bruni* (Leiden: Brill Academic Publishers, 2003), p. 34.

Shakespeare wrote in prosimetry, interspersed prose, poetry, and rhyming verse. See, e.g., Kim Ballard, "Prose and Verse in Shakespeare's Plays," The British Library, Discovering Lit-

was a poet and classical scholar, more so than the other jurists of his time.[1] Placentinus addressed contemporary legal problems through poetical satire. Bacon — I mean Shakespeare — did too. Both Placentinus and Bacon were frustrated with the way law was being taught. Like Bacon, who believed the university would teach you what to believe, not how to think,[2] Placentinus was critical of a university education.

Like Bacon, Placentinus had an enemy who was a thorn in his side, Henricus de Baila (Bayles).[3] For Bacon, it was Coke. Virgil was admired by both men. Bacon frequently quoted him, and Placentinus was proud of being a fellow Lombard.[4] Perhaps most important is their similar thinking on higher law. For Placentinus, equity was integral to justice.[5] Bacon phrased it similarly, that equity was supplied to every law.[6]

Placentinus was the first glossator to write an autobiographical sketch of himself — in his Proemium to his commentary on *Summa Trium librorum*, books 10–12 of Justinian's Code. He also wrote a *materia* or *proemium* to his *Summa Institutionum*.[7] It seems likely that Bacon himself drafted "Rawley's" "Life of Bacon."[8] Lawyers draft things. For example, he had drafted writings for the Earl of Essex; and, as the king's counselor, he drafted the decree in the

---

erature: Shakespeare. https://www.bl.uk/shakespeare/articles/prose-and-verse-in-shakespeares-plays.

Peter Goodrich in his *Law in the Courts of Love : Literature and other Minor Jurisprudences*, called Placentinus "the most remarkable and eloquent ...proponent of legal poetics" (pp. 129-131, 129). Elsewhere, he writes, "The dramatic form of the satire, of genre that combines vehemence, conceit, and polemic is entirely appropriate and historically exemplary of the critique of law." Peter Goodrich, ch. 8, "Conclusion: A Legality of the Contingent," *Oedipus Lex: Psychoanalyses, History, Law* (Berkeley: University of California Press, 1995), p. 244-246, 244.

[1] Ronald G. Witt, ch. 2, "The Birth of the New Aesthetic," *In the Footsteps of the Ancients[...]*, pp. 34-35, n. 5 (Placentinus used more references to classical literature than any other jurist before or after him).

[2] *Spedding*, VIII, p. 124; *Spedding*, IV, p. 288 ('Novum Organum'); Guido del Giudice, *Giordano Bruno: The Prophet of Infinite Universe*, p. 34.

[3] "Henricus de Baila," fl. 1160's, report no. c014, fl. 1160s, Bio-bibliographical Guide to Medieval and Early Modern Jurists, http://amesfoundation.law.harvard.edu/BioBibCanonists/Report_Biobib2.php?record_id=c014, last updated 5/5/2018).

[4] H. Kantorowicz, "The Poetical Sermon of a Medieval Jurist," p. 25.

[5] See ch. 12, infra.

[6] Marginal notation in Sicardus' *Summa decretorum* to Placentinus' *Summa Institutionum*. Stephan Kuttner, "A Forgotten Definition of Justice," pp. 84-85; "For there is no law under heaven which is not supplied with equity." Francis Bacon, *The Jurisdiction of the Marches, Spedding*, VII, p. 602, HathiTrust, https://hdl.handle.net/2027/ucl.b3924335.

[7] "Placentinus," report no. c013, Bio-Bibliographical Guide to Medieval and Early Modern Jurists, last updated 5/5/18, http://amesfoundation.law.harvard.edu/BioBibCanonists/Report_Biobib2.php?record_id=c013.

[8] *Opuscula varia posthuma, philosophica civilia, et theologica Francisci Baconi, Baronis de Verulamio, Vice-Comitis Sancti Albani, Nunc primum Edita. Cura & Fide*, Guilielmi Rawley, *Sacrae Theologiciae Doctoris*, *primo Dominationi suae postea Serenissimae Majestati Regiae, á Sacris, Una cum Nobilissimi Auctoris Vita* (London, 1658). https://books.google.ca/books?id=AS2blDnlkPIC.

1616 Glanville case. Others who wrote proems are Dante, Cino, and Bartolus, and William Caxton to his 2d edition of Chaucer's (1343–1400) *Canterbury Tales*.[1]

A *prooemium* is a preface, introduction, or prelude,[2] with features of poetry.[3] Bacon wrote a proem for his *Instauratio Magna*,[4] in addition to its *Praefatio* (preface).[5] The *Instauratio Magna* was very special to him. He also wrote a beautiful, moving proem to a planned treatise, *Of the Interpretation of Nature*.[6] Soldier-poet Gilbert Hay (1397–1465) has been said to be the first "in modern times" to write a proem,[7] but Cino (d. 1336–37) predates him. Cicero had used *prooemium* to mean an "overture, a song before the song."[8] The Byzantine John Tzetzes (c. 1110–180)[9] had written a "First Proem to Aristophanes."[10]

I have not found Placentinus's *Proemium* to *Summa Trium librorum* in translation. His works were printed in Mainz, 1535 (*Summa Institutionum*); Pavia, 1506 (*Summa Trium librorum*); and Venezia (Venice), 1584 (*Libellus de actionum varietatibus*, c. 1160; *De expediendis iudiciis; De iudiciis et de traditione eorum in quovis iudico estimantur; De senatusconsultis tractatus*). Perhaps Bacon was able to obtain the Venice 1584 edition. Would Shaxpere have been able to obtain

---

[1] William Caxton, "Proem to Chaucer's *Canterbury Tales*," 2d ed., 1484, repr. in "Famous Prefaces," The Harvard Classics. 1909-14, http://www.bartleby.com/39/18.html.

"Chaucer" is close to one of the related spellings of Shakespeare: "Chaucsper." See E. K. Chambers, *William Shakespeare[...]*, vol. 2, pp. 374-5; David Kathman, "The Spelling and Pronunciation of Shakespeare's Name," http://shakespeareauthorship.com/name1.html.

[2] "*Prooemium*," *Cassell's Latin*, p. 182 (with two "o's.").

[3] The word comes from Old French, from Latin, from a Greek word meaning "song, poem." *Webster's*, p. 792; the Greek meaning "prelude" came from a word meaning "way, road." William Little and C. T. Onions, eds., "Proemium," *The Oxford Universal Dictionary on Historical Principles*, 3d ed. rev. (Oxford: Clarendon Press, 1955), p. 1592. A song "for the road" sounds very goliardic. It makes me think of "The Road is Calling...," a lovely round, and the wonderful Swarthmore tradition of singing rounds in the Bell Tower, in which I was once privileged to participate. See "music, rounds," John Krumm.com, https://www.johnkrumm.com/music/rounds/pdfs/.

[4] "Francis Bacon," Proemium to *Instauratio Magna*, in "Prefaces and Prologues to Famous Books," *The Harvard Classics*, 1909-1914, 39, selected by Charles W. Eliot, Bartleby.com (2001), http://www.bartleby.com/39/18.html.

[5] Spedding, IV, "Proemium" to *The Great Instauration*, p. 5, HathiTrust, https://hdl.handle.net/2027/mdp.39015057080239; *Selections from the Works of Lord Bacon, comprising the prefaces to the Instauratio magna[...]*, transl. and illus. with notes and appendix by Thomas W. Moffett (Dublin, 1847), pp. 1; 103, https://hdl.handle.net/2027/umn.31951001600483h.

[6] Spedding, X, p. 84, HathiTrust, https://hdl.handle.net/2027/ien.35558005316951.

[7] *Oxford Living Dictionaries*, English, s.v. "proemium," Oxford University Press, 2018, https://en.oxforddictionaries.com/definition/prooemium.

[8] *Oxford Living Dictionaries*, s.v. "proemium."

[9] "John Tzetzes," Britannica.com, https://www.britannica.com/biography/John-Tzetzes.

[10] See "John Tzetzes, from *First Proem to Aristophanes* (c. 1110-80 C. E.)" transl. by Lane Cooper, in Paul Lauter, ed., *Theories of Comedy*, (Garden City: Anchor Books, 1964), pp. 33-41, 33-34.

such a volume? Maybe the fictional, hybrid Shaxpere that is so dressed up in Bacon's clothes that you cannot tell him apart from Bacon could have.

Placentinus might suggest "Placentia Palace." First called "Bella Palace," it had been the home of Humphrey, the Duke of Gloucester. After his death, Queen Margaret enlarged it and changed its name to Placentia Palace, *placentia* meaning "pleasures" in Latin.[1] Renamed Greenwich Palace, it was the family home of Henry VII and Henry VIII, the birthplace of Mary and Elizabeth Tudor.[2]

If I am right that *chez sphere* lies behind "Shakespeare" as a pseudonym, it might seem fitting that the meaning of the French word *chez* has to do with place, as if to subtly reassert the point, if only to himself, that there was some ambiguity as to whether he was born at York Place or York House.

---

[1] *Placeo*, infinitive *placens*, "to please," *Cassell's*, p. 170.
[2] Ben Johnson, "the Palace of Placentia, Greenwich, Historic UK, https://www.historic. uk.com/HistoryUK/History of England/The-Palace-of-Placentia-Greenwich/; "Greenwich," London, BBC Home, Archived (28 Oct. 2014), BBC, www.bbc.co.uk/london/content/ articles/2005/04/20/royal_history_feature.shtml.

Chapter Eleven: Glosses, *Glanvill*, and Pre-Gratian Marriage Law

The Use of "Gloss" in Bacon and Shakespeare

In trying to ascertain to what extent Bacon was interested in the civil law, I did a search for the word "gloss" in the works of both Bacon and Shakespeare. *Glossa* in Latin was a foreign word requiring explanation.[1] I used www.onlineshakespeare.org and the HathiTrust (https://www.hathitrust.org) search function in the three-volume *Montagu* edition of Bacon's *Works* to search "gloss(es, ed)" and "gloze."

I found that Shakespeare uses "gloss" as a noun fifteen times and as a verb, "gloze, glozed, or glozes" five times. He also uses the word "glose" once, in the sense that one should listen to what an old man (the dying John of Gaunt) says; his words are few, and he is less prone to flatter (or "glose," which he rhymes with "close") than a young man.[2]

"Gloss" can mean: n., "brightness, luster or 'specious appearance/superficial quality or show'; "interpretation, as of marginal or interlinear words; a note of explanation, commentary"; or v., "to furnish with glosses, explain by notes." [3]

---

[1] *The American Heritage Dictionary of the English Language*, fifth ed. online, s.v. "gloss, 2" (New York: Houghton Mifflin Harcourt, 2017, online 2018), https://www.ahdictionary.com/word/search.html?q=gloss; *Webster's*, p. 425.

[2] *Richard II*, II, 1, 692.

[3] The *American Heritage Dictionary of the English Language*, https://www.ahdictionary.com/word/search.html?q=gloss; *Webster's*, p. 425.

Shakespeare uses "gloss," as a noun, to describe: a beauty that will fade (*Passionate Pilgrim*, lines 170, 177), like the bloom on a rose (*Venus and Adonis*, line 958), or the good opinions of others (*Macbeth*, I, 7, 510; *Timon of Athens*, I, 2, 355).

Other uses of gloss are: "the over-daring Talbot hath sullied all his gloss of former honour" (*The First Part of Henry VI*, IV, 4, 2091); "flattering gloss" (*Henry VI*, Part Two, I, 1, 172); a new finish on clothes (*Macbeth*, I, 7, 510 and *Tempest*, II, 1, 766); and the shine of recent good fortune (*Othello*, I, 3, 576). More uses are: the soil of virtue (*All's Well*, I, 1, 154); virginity a commodity that will lose the gloss with lying (*Much Ado*, III, 2, 1203-1205: "Nay that would be as great a soil in the new gloss of your marriage as to show a child his new coat and forbid him to wear it'); virtue like fair fruit that will rot (*Troilus and Cressida*, II, 3, 1337); "if virtue's gloss will stain with any soil" (*Love's Labor Lost*, II, 1, 533-534); a phony exterior (*Henry VIII*, V, 3, 3130); and a slanted version of facts (*The First Part of Henry VI*, IV, 1, 1868).

"Gloze" as a noun meant "explanation or flattery" in Old English, from Old French; archaically: "a note or gloss." Rare: "specious; show; gloss." As a verb: to shine, glow, gleam; obsolete: "to make glosses on; to explain; to smooth over, palliate, gloss, to make a gloss, comment."[1]

Shakespeare uses "gloze" in five instances: (1) French legal: the French "unjustly gloze," as above (*Henry V*: I, 2, 185); (2) set in France, "flatteries," as in: "Now to plain dealing; lay these glozes by" (*Love's Labor Lost*, IV, 3, 1716); (3) to legally interpret: e.g., King Antiochus said he would "gloze" with Pericles regarding the "tenor of our strict edict" (*Pericles*, I, 1, 161); (4) "to talk smoothly and speciously, use fair words or flattering language," as in Tamora's: "Why thus it shall become high-witted Tamora to gloze with all" (*Titus Andronicus*, IV, 4, 2045); and (5) to comment upon, expound: "Paris and Troilus, you have both said well,/And on the cause and question now in hand/Have glozed, but superficially, not much/Unlike young men, whom Aristotle thought Unfit/to hear moral philosophy" (*Troilus and Cressida*, II, 2, 1163).[2]

As for the "gloze" spelling, in *Henry V* (I, 2, 185), the Archbishop tells King Henry,

---

[1] "Gloze," *Webster's*, p. 426.

[2] http://opensourceshakespeare.org/search/search-results.php. See "Gloss," *A Shakespeare Glossary*, ed. by C. T. Onions (Oxford: Clarendon Press, 1911), http://www.perseus.tufts.edu/hopper/text?doc=Perseus%3Atext%3A1999.03.0068%3Aentry%3Dgloss.

> "But this, which they produce from Pharamond,[1]
> 'In *terrem Salicam mulieres ne succedant*':
> 'No woman shall succeed in Salic land':
> Which Salic land the French unjustly gloze
> To be the realm of France, and Pharamond
> The founder of this law and female bar...."

Shakespeare also used the word "smooth" sixty times, often as a synonym for "gloss." Neither Bacon nor Shakespeare used the modern expression "to gloss over," but Shakespeare used "smoothe" or "soothe" to mean, inter alia, "to gloss over" or "to flatter," as seen in *Henry VI* (III, 1, 48), *Richard II* (II, 1, 3); and *Richard III* (six uses). "Sooth" also meant "truth."[2] The first words in the play are Antonio's "In sooth, I know not why I am so sad."

Two Francis Bacon Aphorisms on the Salic Law

"There was a French gentleman speaking with an English[man] of the law Salique; that women were excluded from inheriting the crown of France. The English said, "Yes, but that was meant of the women themselves, not of such males as claimed by women." The French gentleman said, "Where do you find that gloss?" The English[man] answered, "I'll tell you, sir: look on the back side of the record of the law Salique, and there you shall find it endorsed: implying there was no such thing as the law Salique, but that it is a mere fiction."[3]

There was a friar in earnest dispute about the law Salique, that would needs prove it by Scripture; citing that verse of the gospel, *Lilia agri non laborant neque nent*; the lilies of the field do neither labour nor spin; applying it thus: That the flower-de-luces of France cannot descend, neither to the distaff nor to the spade: that is, not to a woman nor to a peasant.[4]

---

[1] Pharamond is considered the first king of the Franks, ca. A.D. 420. Harriet Willoughby, *The History of France, in Rhyme, From the Accession of King Pharamond, A.D. 420, to the Revolution of 1830* (London, 1846), p. 1, https://books.google.ca/books?id=eKVhAAAAcAAJ.

[2] See *Shakespeare's Non-Standard English: A Dictionary of His Informal Language*, ed. Norman Blake and Norman Francis Blake (London: Continuum, 2006), pp.77, 134, 154, 156, 271, 357, 392.

[3] *Montagu*, I, p. 117, aphorism no. 184, HathiTrust, https://hdl.handle.net/2027/hvd.32044098248545. Peter Goodrich suggests that in Selden's *Jani Anglorum Facies Altera*, the "back side of the English Janus" meant, well, what the back side of a human might be called. Perhaps Bacon was suggesting something similar with his aphorism. See Genealogies of Legal Vision, ed. by Peter Goodrich and Valérie (Abingdon: Routledge, 2015), p. 6, https://books.google.ca/books?isbn=1317683897.

[4] *Montagu*, I, p. 117, aphorism no. 185, HathiTrust, https://hdl.handle.net/2027/hvd.32044098248545. On that same page, does not aphorism 173 brings to mind the similar scene in *Henry V*?

Shakespeare also coined the word "anothanize."[1] It never caught on, but it seems to mean the same thing as gloss, "to explain, explicate." Since he did use the word "gloss" with this meaning, one wonders why he felt he needed to coin a new word.

No examples of Bacon using "gloze" came up in my search of Montagu. As for gloss(es, ed), I began to suspect that when Bacon used the word "gloss," it might signal a need to read between the lines. In *Montagu*, I, Bacon used "gloss" three times: (1) in an Apophthegm" (anecdote) on the Salique law; [2] (2) to refer to the "gloss and softness" of a silkworm's thread;[3] and (3) to refer to "variety and particularity" as a "gloss or paraphrase that attendeth upon the text of natural history."[4]

In *Montagu*, II, there are five uses of "gloss" and two of "glosses," all but one by Bacon: (1) In his "Charge against Mr. Lumsden," he says that he does not wish to "set the gloss before the text";[5] (2) There is a use by Rawley;[6] (3) In speaking of Parliament's changing the law of the succession regarding "natural heirs of the queen's body," Bacon writes: "they do maliciously, and indeed villainously gloss, that it was the intention of the parliament, in a cloud to convey the crown to any issue of her majesty's that were illegitimate...";[7]

---

[1] In some versions of the induction to 2 *Henry IV*, 1, Rumour, painted with tongues, says, "Rumour is a pipe ...But what need I thus My well-known body to "anothomize" (The Globe version's prologue says "anatomize"), meaning to analyze, break down into parts in order to explain. Bacon's essay, "On Fame" (meaning rumor) expresses his often-repeated warning about the dangers of rumor (*Spedding*, VI), HathiTrust, https://hdl.handle.net/2027/ucl.b3618242.

The *New Oxford Shakespeare* defines "annothanize" as "seemingly a mixture of anatomize and "annotate." Gary Taylor, ed., *The New Oxford Shakespeare, Modern Critical Edition* (Oxford: Oxford University Press, 2016), p. 801. It is interesting that the words "atom" (from Greek for "uncut") and "anatomy (from Greek for "to cut") are related ("atom," "anatomy," *Webster's*, pp. 39, 68). Atoms, of course, were part of the atomists' (Democritus, etc.) explication of the world, that everything was made up of tiny particles. In the *New Organum*, Bacon wrote that founding a "real model of the world in understanding" could not be done without "dissecting and anatomizing the world." *Montagu*, III, p. 369 (first col., at no. 124), HathiTrust, https://hdl.handle.net/2027/hvd.hwkblf.

[2] Montagu, I, p. 117, HathiTrust, https://hdl.handle.net/2027/hvd.32044098248545.

[3] *The Interpretation of Nature*, Montagu, I p. 432, HathiTrust, https://hdl.handle.net/2027/hvd.32044098248545.

[4] *Advancement of Learning* II, Montagu, I, p. 196, HathiTrust, https://hdl.handle.net/2027/hvd.32044098248545.

[5] *Montagu*, II, p. 310, HathiTrust, https://hdl.handle.net/2027/uiug.30112112501439.

[6] William Rawley, "To the Reader," *Sylva Sylvarum*, Montagu, II, p. 6, HathiTrust, https://hdl.handle.net/2027/ucl.b3618254.

[7] F. Bacon, "Observations on a Libel," Spedding, VIII, pp. 146-208, HathiTrust, https://hdl.handle.net/2027/ucl.b3618243; Montagu, II, pp. 242-265, 265, HathiTrust, https://hdl.handle.net/2027/ucl.b3618254.

The text of William Allen's biting allegations, against the Queen, in "Admonition to the Nobility and People of England and Ireland Concerning the Present Warres Made for the Execution of his Holines Sentence, by the high and mightie King Catholike of Spaine," are set

(4) "I dare not scan upon her majesty's actions, which it becometh me rather to admire in silence, than to gloss or discourse upon them, though with never so good a meaning";[1] (5) any man may discern the treasons, etc., of Robert, Earl of Essex, "without any gloss or interpreter";[2] (6) re: preachers calling for reformation: "For, though I observe in one of them many glosses, whereby the man would insinuate himself into their favours, yet I find it to be ordinary, that many pressing and fawning persons do misconjecture of this humour of men in authority...";[3] and (6) "Steel glosses are more resplendent than the like plates of brass would be."[4]

In *Montagu*, III, there is one use of "gloss," but it is not Bacon's. It is in a 1616 letter *to* Bacon *from* the University of Cambridge to him, asking for his assistance.[5]

In modern meaning, to "gloss over" is to ignore, as in the way the twelfth-century glossators have been "glossed over," as if they had nothing to contribute to modern legal discussions. What if that assumption were wrong?

The treatise *Glanvill* was primarily concerned with "civil litigation by writ before the King's justices." The treatise is known as the first common law textbook. Its two major themes were the king's court at Exchequer and writs.[6]

Just out of curiosity, I did a search within *Glanvill* for the names of these twelfth-century jurists: Irnerius, the four doctors he trained (Bulgarus, Martinus, Hugo, Jacopus), and in the next generation: Bassanius/Johannes, Azo, Placentinus, Pillius, Rogerius, and Vacarius. I did not find them, except in the introduction (p. xvi) written by the editor, Hall, in 1965. The only reference to a "Hugo" I found was to a "Hugo Bardolf," a man who had been

---

forth in Deborah Shuger, ch. 1, "That Great and Immoderate Liberty of Lying," *Censorship and Cultural Sensibility: The Regulation of Language in Tudor-Stuart England* (University of Pennsylvania: Philadelphia, 2006), pp. 12-55, 16-18, http://www.upenn.edu/pennpress/book/14246.html.

[1] F. Bacon, "A Speech in Parliament, 29 of Elizabeth, upon the Motion of Subsidy," *Montagu*, II, p. 287 (before the first full paragraph), HathiTrust, https://hdl.handle.net/2027/uc1.b3618254.

[2] F. Bacon, "A Declaration of the Treason of Robert, Earl of Essex. *Montagu*, II, p. 348 (just before the last paragraph).

[3] F. Bacon, "Of Church Controversies," *Montagu*, II, p. 413. "There is no greater confusion than the confounding of jest and earnest" (first col. 2d. par.).

[4] F. Bacon, "Physiological Remains, Inquisitions Touching the Compounding of Metals," *Montagu*, II, p. 456 (2d to the last par., first column).

[5] University of Cambridge to Sir Francis Bacon, "Letters from the British Museum," *Montagu*, III, p. 166, HathiTrust, https://hdl.handle.net/2027/hvd.hwkb1f.

[6] *The Treatise on the Laws and Customs of the Realm of England Commonly Called Glanvill* [in Latin and English], ed. and transl. with intro. by G. D. G. Hall (Oxford: Clarendon Press, 2002), p. xi, https://books.google.com/books?isbn=0191585181.

sheriff under Henry II, Richard I, and John I.[1] There is a character named "Bardolph" in *Henry IV*. There was a Lord Thomas Bardolph (1368–1408), "one of the baronial leaders under Simon de Montfort."[2] He was alive during the reign of Henry IV (1399–1413).

Whoever wrote the procedural text *Glanvill*, "formerly attributed to Glanvill,"[3] had some knowledge of Roman law,[4] but his knowledge was not deep, according to Maitland.[5] While *Glanvill* does mention "the Roman law" and cites to the *Institutes* in his preface,[6] the citations in my edition appear to have been added by their modern editor, Hall.[7]

Ranulf de Glanville (1130?–d. 1190) started his career as a sheriff. He then served as justiciar, the king's right-hand man under Henry II. Later, he was a Crusader. Maitland thought it more likely that a clerk wrote *Glanvill*.[8]

Pre-Gratian Marriage Law, Briefly Touched Upon

Professor Charles Donahue has studied marriage law in the time of the glossators (from Irnerius through the *Great Gloss* of Accursius) up to the time of the undated pronouncements of Pope Alexander III which changed the longstanding Roman law to remove ceremony and parental consent as

---

[1] *Treatise on the Laws and Customs of the Realm of England*, ed. by G. D. G. Hall (New York: Oxford 2002), pp. 63-64, https://books.google.com/books?isbn=0191585181; see also appendix 4, *The Thirty-first Annual Report of the Deputy Keeper of the Public Records*, Oxford Medieval Texts, ed. by D. E. Greenway (London, 1868), pp. 272-273, 321, 353, 356.

[2] "Bardolf, Lord Thomas," *Dictionary of National Biography*, ed. by Sidney Lee (London, Elder, 1901), p. 123, Online Books Page, http://onlinebooks.library.upenn.edu/webbin/metabook?id=dnb.

[3] See Jason Taliadoros, ch. 6, "Law and Theology in Gilbert of Foliot's Correspondence," pp. 77-94, 78, n. 6.

[4] Hall, intro., *Treatise on the Laws and Customs of the Realm of England*, p. xviii, https://books.google.com/books?isbn=0191585181.

[5] F. W. M. [Frederick Maitland], "Glanvill, Ranulf de," *Dictionary of National Biography* 21, ed. by Leslie Stephen and Sidney Lee (New York, 1885-1900), pp. 413-415, 414-415, https://books.google.com/books?isbn=0191585181; Online Books Page, http://onlinebooks.library.upenn.edu/webbin/metabook?id=dnb. Modern writers generally concur that his knowledge of Roman law was not deep. E.g., see Ralph Turner, ch. 4, "Roman Law in England Before the Time of Bracton," pp. 45-71, 59, and ch. 5, "Who was the Author of Glanville?" pp. 71-103, 82 in D. J. Ibbetson, *Judges, Administrators, and the Common Law* (London: The Hambledon Press, 1994); D. J. Ibbetson, *A Historical Intro., to the Law of Obligations* (Oxford: Oxford University Press, 1999), sect. I.1, pp. 17-21, 19.

[6] See William Stubbs, ch. 8, "The History of the Canon Law in England," in *Select Essays in Anglo-American Legal History* 1, ed. by John Henry Wigmore (Boston: Little, Brown, 1907), pp. 448-289, 260.

[7] See. e.g., *Treatise on the Laws and Customs of the Realm of England*, ed. by G. D. G. Hall, p. 69, https://books.google.com/books?isbn=0191585181.

[8] "Glanvill," Maitland, *Dictionary of National Biography* 21, pp. 413-415, https://books.google.com/books?id=rN01XoJVG7AC; Online Books Page, http://onlinebooks.library.upenn.edu/webbin/metabook?id=dnb.

---

requirements.[1] According to Donahue, a history of the Roman law of marriage in the Middle Ages does not yet exist.[2] There was nothing explicit in the *Corpus Juris Civilis* itself that spelled out, beyond dispute, the requirements for a valid marriage.[3]

Donahue's working hypothesis, however, was that, prior to Alexander, it was "virtually unanimous" among the glossators that a valid marriage was created by mutual consent/acceptance of one another as husband and wife and a *ductio*, a "leading home" or handing over of the bride, usually from the house of the father to the house of the groom.[4] Here, the possibility of a pun on "lead" with the casket and "duke" (*ductio*) instead of "doge" suggest themselves to me; maybe I have been doing this too long. Punning and word play — even rhyming, were appreciated more in Elizabethan times than they are today.

Under pre-Gratian Roman law, interspousal gifts, such as the rings Portia and Nerissa gave to Bassanio and Gratiano, were not required to create a valid marriage; nor was a father's consent.[5]

Bulgarus and Martinus substituted *affectio* for *consensus* as the requirement,[6] as did Martinus.[7] Neither he nor Placentinus, in continuing to compose the *Summa* of Rogerius after his death, required a "bedding" (consummation), nor did Bassianus, although Gratian did. Thus, when an espoused woman, having been sent for by her espoused husband and having been led to his house by his friends, never lived with her groom because he fell into the Tiber and drowned prior to consummation, they were not married, under Gratian's *Decretum*.[8]

Thus, Bulgarus, Martinus, Bassianus, Rogerius, and Placentinus, it seems, pretty much agreed that a valid marriage required the agreement to marry (affection or consensus) and some "outward manifestation of a change in status," such as a *ductio*, either by the bride or groom.[9] As Martinus pointed out, they did not even have to have a home.[10] Portia had a home; Nerissa led Gratiano to Portia's home, which may have been her home; but Jessica and

---

[1] Charles Donahue, Jr., "The Case of the Man who Fell into the Tiber: the Roman Law of Marriage at the Time of the Glossators," *The American Journal of Legal History* 22, no. 1 (Jan. 1978), pp. 1-53, 12.

[2] Donahue, p. 11.

[3] Donahue, p. 11.

[4] Donahue, pp. 7, 20, 26.

[5] Donahue, p. 8.

[6] Donahue, p. 14.

[7] Donahue, p. 16.

[8] Donahue, p. 15, 18, 19 fn. 80.

[9] Donahue, p. 16.

[10] Donahue, p. 16.

Lorenzo were mere guests and house sitters at Belmont. It did not matter, pre Gratian's *Decretum*.

In *The Merchant of Venice*, we have three couples: Bassanius and Portia, Nerissa and Gratiano, and Jessica and Lorenzo. Portia's father is dead, Nerissa's father is not mentioned, and Jessica has refused to acknowledge her father's authority over her; however, a father's consent to marriage was not required, under Roman law. I do not know what Jewish law would have required. In Portia's case, though, the "casket test" was a condition of her father's will, an issue not explored herein. Interspousal gifts were not part of the marriage requirements, so it was of no consequence that Bassanio and Gratiano gave their rings back to the givers. Gratiano, consistent with Gratian, is the one who hints at consummation in the last lines of the play. However, all three couples are already referring to one another as husbands and wives before that point.[1]

For what it is worth, my very brief analysis leads to a tentative conclusion that there is nothing in the wedding arrangements described in the play that is inconsistent with mid-to-late twelfth-century marriage law, as found in the writings of the twelfth-century Bolognese glossators and Gratian.

With Bassanio and Portia we have represented a real-life marriage between Bassianus the jurist and his wife who married Azo after Bassianus' death.

With Gratiano (Gratian) and Nerissa (Irnerius), we have, figuratively, the marriage of canon and civil law, as they began to meld.

Finally, with Launcelot and the Moor, we may have, figuratively, two who will never "marry," an accommodating "Anglo-Catholic" (Launcelot Andrews) and a man who would die rather than swear to an oath he did not believe (Sir Thomas More). "Pregnancy" may signal a hidden meaning, as is said of the style of Tacitus.

Or not. As Freud said, "Sometimes a cigar is just a cigar."

Portia's Ring, Marital Debt, and Drama

Prof. R. H. Helmholz, a scholar of medieval civil and canon law, writes that the medieval ecclesiastical courts, which had jurisdiction over marriage, were not shy about ordering married parties to honor their "marital debt."[2]

---

[1] For example, see *Merchant*, III, 5, 1867 (Lorenzo), 1908, 1920; IV, 1, 2218 (Antonio); IV, 1 2227, 2229, 2396 (Bassanio); IV, 1, 2235 (Gratian); IV, 1, 2632 (Portia).

[2] Richard Helmholz, "Canonical Remedies in Medieval Marriage Law: The Contributions of Legal Practice Founding," *University of St. Thomas Law Journal* 1 (2003), pp. 647-655, p. 651, http://chicagounbound.uchicago.edu/cgi/viewcontent.cgi?article=2479&context=journal_art.... See also Charles Reid, Jr., "Conjugal Debt," in *Women and Gender in Medieval Europe, an Encyclopedia*,

This concept may be reflected in language in several Shakespeare plays. In *Troilus and Cressida*, Hector says, "What nearer debt in all humanity than wife is to the husband?" (II, 2, 176-177). In *Taming of the Shrew*, Katharina says: "Too little payment for so great a debt. Such duty as the subject owes the prince, Even such a woman oweth to her husband (V, 2, 2262).

In *Merchant*, there are two major themes, debt and marriage. According to Helmholz, the canon law on the formation of marriage did not change much from 1200 to the Council of Trent (1545–1563) and remained stable "even longer in England."[1]

The Church used drama as a teaching tool; more particularly, the Church used the play *Jeu d'Adam* (*Play of Adam*, ca. 1150–1170) to teach its ideas on marriage and adultery, at a time when women were gaining ground "too quickly" towards equality. That was a heresy that could not prevail.[2]

In the *Jeu d'Adam*, Adam, Eve, God, and Satan were the main actors, with plenty of devils running around, even making sallies among the spectators.[3] A major theme in this play of church propaganda was that husbands needed to control their wives. Women represented the "weakness in human nature, its irrational and sensuous aspect." In this cosmology, Adam's downfall was caused by his seeing his wife as an equal.

Interestingly, the Latin feminine, *Sathana*, was used for Satan. As time went on, the serpent in the mystery plays was often portrayed as having a female head or fair virgin face and, at times, as wearing a blonde wig.[4] The *Jeu d'Adam* dates from the twelfth to thirteenth centuries. Georges Duby thinks it was probably first composed between 1150 and 1170, "near the court of Henry Plantagenet, then the most outstanding center of literary creativeness."[5] It was in the twelfth century that these Church plays, having grown in length and requiring more detailed settings, began to outgrow the

---

ed. by Margaret Schaus (New York: Routledge, 2006), p. 164, https://books.google.ca/books?id=aDhOv6hgN2IC&printsec=frontcover&redir_esc=y#v=onepage&q&f=false..

[1] Helmholz, "Canonical Remedies in Medieval Marriage Law," p. 655.

[2] See Georges Duby, *The Knight, the Lady, and the Priest, the Making of Modern Marriage in Medieval France*, trans. Barbara Bray (New York: Pantheon Books, 1983), pp. 213-216, 218. For stage directions for the *Jeu d'Adam*, see E. K. Chambers, ch. 20, "The Secularization of the Plays," *The Medieval Stage*, vol. 2 (Oxford: Oxford University Press, 1925, first pub. 1903), p. 80-82.

[3] Chambers, p. 85.

[4] John K. Bonnell, "The Serpent with a Human Head in Art and in Mystery Play," *American Journal of Archaeology* 21, no. 3 (Jul.-Sept., 1917), pp. 255-291, JSTOR, www.jstor.org/stable/497250. In the Norwich Manuscript of 1565, the serpent says to Eve, "Oh lady of felicite, beholde my voice so small" (Bonnell, pp. 286-287). In a York Manuscript of 1583, the Fifth York Play, the serpent is depicted as a lizard with a female face (Bonnell, pp. 287-288). And, in a 1611 Cornwall "Creation" play by Jordan, Lucifer is played as a "fine serpent with a virgin face and yellow hair upon her head" (Bonnell, p. 289; Chambers, *The Medieval Stage*, vol. 2, p. 142).

[5] Duby, p. 214.

Church performing space and moved outdoors, into market places, "church precincts," or even graveyards."[1] See the modern skit — for serious literary discussion purposes only, you understand.[2] The last words of the *Jeu d'Adam* warned play-goers to "beware of poets."[3]

---

[1] Chambers, *The Medieval Stage*, vol. 2, pp. 71, 79.

[2] "Betty White and Johnny Carson in Funny Skit as Adam and Eve...," (1979, online Feb. 22, 2011), https://www.youtube.com/watch?v=Ih6LxwdwvlA.

[3] Duby, p. 216.

CHAPTER TWELVE: "FOR THERE IS NO LAW UNDER HEAVEN…"

"For there is no law under heaven which is not supplied with equity,"[1] said Francis Bacon. From whence did Bacon derive such an interesting idea? According to Prof. Daniel Coquillette, Bacon developed his theory of equity during his chancellorship. He sets it out in book 8 of the *de Augmentis*.[2]

Sir Philip Sidney's words in his "Apologie for Poetrie" seem to express a similar arrangement between art and nature: "There is no Arte delivered to mankind that hath not the works of Nature for his principal object…without which they could not consist, and on which they so defend, as they become Actors and Players, as it were, of what Nature will have set forth.[3]

In his article "A Forgotten Definition of Justice," Stephan Kuttner traced the development of the idea of a justice which includes a conception of equity, after Bulgarus's observation that Ulpian had defined justice more narrowly than the "rhetorical tradition" had done. Ulpian had "made the aim of justice identical with the aim of law, while in the non-legal texts *suum* or *dignitas sua* for everyone transcended that which is merely legal. Hence, *ius* had here to be construed more broadly, including all that is deserved (*meritum*), all that is due (*debitum*) to God, self, and neighbor."[4] *Merchant* could be viewed as concerning these themes.

Glossators, including Paucapalea, the first to gloss Gratian's *Decretum*, and those "in the Bulgarus tradition," viewed justice much more broadly than

---

[1] Francis Bacon, *The Jurisdiction of the Marches*, in *Spedding*, VII, p. 602, HathiTrust, https://hdl.handle.net/2027/ucl.b3924335.
[2] Coquillette, FB, p. 211.
[3] Sister Miriam Joseph, *Shakespeare's Use of the Arts of Language*, p. 6.
[4] Stephan Kuttner, "A Forgotten Definition of Justice," p. 77. The parentheses are Kuttner's.

had Ulpian.[1] Kuttner translated a marginal gloss to a manuscript (Vienna MS 2125) which reminded me of the quotation from Sidney, supra. In the marginal gloss, dialectical pairs are drawn between *iustitia–ius* and *natura–ars*. Kuttner translates: "In like manner, nature encompasses more than art (science). Every art is a sum (collection) of precepts while nature includes what has not yet been discovered but can be turned into precepts once it becomes known."[2]

Placentinus wrote that justice and equity differ "...because justice has its place (*consistit*) in the minds of men, equity in their words and deeds; hence, properly speaking we should call a man 'just', but his judgment 'equitable'."[3] A definition of justice which Kuttner attributes to Plato reads, in Latin:

> "...Restat ut exponamus quid sit iustitia. Iustitia est secundum Platonem uirtus que plurimum prodest his (al. potest in his) qui minimum possunt, nempe in personis miserabilibus euisdentius clarescit iustitia. Vel ut Tullius ait...."[4]

I do not have a translation of the entire phrase, but *que plurimum potest... qui minimum possunt* describes the function of justice "which can do the most for those who can do the least." Stephan Kuttner believes Placentinus derived it from the Commentary of Calcidius to Plato's *Timaeus*, through an introduction by William of Conches (1090–1154) to his gloss on the *Timaeus*.[5]

The Latin word *tacita* is part of a definition of justice, outside the mainstream dichotomy of mercy/justice, in an early gloss on Gratian by Paucapalea. The definition is attributed to Gregory the Great but is actually derived from a treatise, *Formula honestae vitae*, on four virtues (justice, fortitude, modesty, prudence[6]) by St. Martin of Braga (ca. 520–580),[7] although it was usually ascribed to Seneca: *Iustitia est nature tacita conuentio in adiutorium multorum inuenta.*[8]

---

[1] Kuttner, pp. 77-78.

[2] Kuttner, p. 84.

[3] Kuttner, "A Forgotten Definition of Justice," pp. 84-85.

[4] Kuttner, p. 96.

[5] Kuttner, p. 96-98. The passage in Placentinus is set out in fuller detail, in Latin, in A. J. Carlyle, ch. 1, "The Theory of Law: Aequitas and Justice," in R. W. and A. J. Carlyle, *The Political Theory of the Roman Lawyers and Canonists from the Tenth Century to the Thirteenth Century, A History of Medieval Political Theory in the West*, 2 (New York: G. P. Putnam's Sons, 1909), p. 10 fn. 2. For more on William of Conches, see "About William of Conches," Stanford Libraries, https://exhibits. stanford.edu/mss/feature/about-william-of-conches.

[6] Istvan Bejczy, ch. 1, "Patristic Era and Early Middle Ages (c. 400- c. 1100), *The Cardinal Virtues in the Middle Ages, a Study in Moral Thought: From the Fourth to the Fourteenth Century*, Brill's Studies in Intellectual History 202, ed. by Han Van Ruler (Leiden: Brill, 2011), pp. 11-68, 54-55.

[7] "Martin of Braga, Saint," https://www.catholic.com/encyclopedia/martin-of-braga-saint.

[8] Kuttner, "A Forgotten Definition of Justice," pp. 81-85, 93, 104-106. Stephen Pennington translates Paucapalea's definition: "Justice is the tacit contract of nature discovered to help

I was struck by the word *tacita* because of Bacon's tendency to refer to Tacitus in certain contexts in which I thought he was invoking the kind of "pregnant" taciturnity that Tacitus is known for. Perhaps there was more to it, in Bacon's private schema. Perhaps for Bacon, a reference to Tacitus invoked a plea for *tacita*, an otherwise unspoken plea for mercy, for justice to do its bidding in secret, and that this was a secret understanding between the Queen and himself. When Bacon recounts how he told Queen Elizabeth that the dramatist Dr. John Hayward, who was in trouble with the Queen, had gotten his plot from Tacitus, and thus, should be prosecuted for felony, not treason,[1] a tacit plea for mercy seems implicit.

The twelfth- and early-thirteenth-century jurists searched for the "justice intrinsic to every law" as they explored the relationship between *sistema legum* (law) and *sistema iuris* (rights), writes Professor Manlio Bello. Post-glossator Lucas of Penna, who was responsible for the education of Henry II, boldly stated that, where the will of the prince deviated from equity, justice or reason, it was not law.[2]

The work of Bacon's which Spedding renamed "A Conference of Pleasure," a copy of which was found at Northumberland House in 1867, was headed, "M'ffra [Master Francis?]: Bacon of tribute or giving that which is due" (and elsewhere, "Tribuit or Giving that wch [*sic*] is due (BcF 320)."[3] In Bacon's "In Praise of Knowledge," he writes, "But why do I in a conference of pleasure enter these great matters, in short that pretending to know much, I should forget what is seasonable?...Let me give every man his due, as I give time his due, which is to discover truth."[4]

In the Bible, Jesus tells his disciples to "Render therefore unto Caesar that which is Caesar's; and unto God the things that are God's" (Matt. 22:20-

---

many people." Kenneth Pennington, "Lex Naturalis and Ius Naturale," in *Crossing Boundaries at Medieval Universities* (Leiden: Brill, 2011), pp. 227-254, 234. There are probably entire books that could or have been written just on that sentiment.

[1] "Sir John Hayward," *Chalmers 1811-1818 Dictionary of Biography* 17, p. 270; Words from Old Books, http://words.fromoldbooks.org/Chalmers-Biography/h/hayward-sir-john.html.

[2] Manlio Bellomo, *The Common Legal Past of Europe, 1000-1800*, p. 180. On Lucas of Penna ("before 1345 to after 1382"), see Walter Ullmann, *"The Medieval Idea of Law as Represented by Lucas de Penna* (London: Routledge Revivals, 2010, first pub. 1946). This seems to be a return to a pre-Laurentius Hispanus view. Canonist Laurentius (died 1248) had asserted that the will of the prince alone could be a source of human law, whether or not it was reasonable. Previous to this, there had been a consensus that a law that was not reasonable was null and void. Kenneth Pennington, ch. 4, "Politics in Western Jurisprudence," pp. 165-166.

[3] *Francis Bacon, A Critical Edition of the Major Works*, ed. by Brian Vickers (Oxford: Oxford University Press, 1996), p. 514 (notes to pp. 21-51), discussed in Svetozar Y. Minkov, *Francis Bacon's Inquiry Touching Human Nature: Virtue, Philosophy, and the Relief of Man's Estate* (Lanham MD: Lexington Books, Rowman & Littlefield, 2010), pp. ix, 44-48, 63, 69.

[4] *Montagu*, I, p. 80, HathiTrust, https://hdl.handle.net/2027/umn.31951002094295e.

22, KJV). Ulpian (d. 228 A.D.) had famously stated that tribute should be given where tribute was due.[1]

Tudor–Stuart common law lawyers would have been exposed to some civil law as it was incorporated by Bracton (d. 1268) into the legal treatise which bears his name. Bracton had derived most of his civil law from Azo (d. 1220–1230?). However, Bracton, a cleric without much civilian legal training, was no match for Azo's erudition. Maitland finds him struggling in his attempts to reconcile Azo with English situations, such as when Bracton tried to incorporate Azo's teaching on contract law, but England did not yet have a general theory of contract.[2] Even as late as 1458, the state of English law on contract was not clear.[3] There is a long-standing debate about the degree of Bracton's learning.[4]

Because one simply cannot cite every case, legal writers will drop earlier cases from a citation in favor of newer ones, since currency is important. However, significant citations, such as those to landmark cases, are retained. Similarly, Maitland described how Coke, in his *Third Institute*, dropped off a reference to the Roman jurist Ulpian (d. ca. 228 A.D.) when citing the Englishman Bracton, who had included the citation to Ulpian.[5] Ulpian was, of course, much more of an authority on Roman law than Bracton, but Coke was a common law lawyer who preferred the common law to civilian law. That may be an understatement.

Bacon rarely cited authorities, but I suspect part of his motivation was that he wanted to shield foreign-derived ideas from prejudice. He did refer or allude to Ulpian at times, such as when he pronounced the Earl of Essex, after his downfall, "almost a *praefectus praetorio*." Ulpian, as *praefectus praetorio* in charge of the Roman army, was murdered by his own rebelling troops. Ulpian had fled to the feet of the emperor, Severus Alexander, who revered him. Alas, this time the emperor could not save him by throwing his purple

---

[1] Joseph Bingham, *Origines Ecclesiasticae: Or, The Antiquities of the Christian Church and other works* 1 (London, 1834), p. 439; Charles Donahue, Jr., "'Ius' in the Subjective Sense in Roman Law: Reflections on Villey and Tierney, in Domenico Maffei, Italo Birocchi, Mario Caravale, Emanuele Conte, and Ugo Petronio," edited by A. Ennio Cortese (Rome: Il Cigno Edizioni, 2001), 1:506-35, p. 507.

[2] *Select Passages from the Works of Bracton and Azo*, Publications of the Selden Society 8, ed. by F. W. Maitland for the Selden Society (London, 1894), intro., pp. 9-38, 9, 15, 17-19, 22-23, HathiTrust, https://hdl.handle.net/2027/coo.31924032664025. In addressing law students at Gray's Inn, in his *Reading on the Statute of Uses*, Bacon remarked that the Latin in the phrase *ad opus* was "barbarous," "like some chaplain's that was not much past his grammar." *Spedding*, VII, p. 410.

[3] Baker, *Intro.*, ch. 18, "Covenant and Debt," pp. 360-374, 367.

[4] Coquillette, *FB*, p. 8.

[5] Maitland, appendix 2, "Bracton and Bernard of Pavia on Homicide," *Select Passages from the Works of Bracton and Azo*, pp. 233-234, HathiTrust, https://hdl.handle.net/2027/coo.31924032664025.

cloak around him. It is an apt analogy for how "this time, the Queen did not save Essex."[1]

Bacon seems to have accepted foreign law more readily than Coke did. Bacon said, "That our laws are as mixed as our language; and as our language is so much the richer on that account, so are the laws more complete."[2] Perhaps he was also guided by the way in which Ulpian, who was Greek, deliberately incorporated Greek words into his legal writings so as to make the Roman rule of law more understandable and palatable to his own countrymen who had come under Roman rule.[3]

Another source of definitions of justice is the *Ordo Bambergensis*, the medieval procedural treatise discussed previously (chapters six and twelve). It defines justice as "the power granted to another, with permission to deliver the law, and the faculty of establishing equity." Prof. Bruce Brasington believes this quotation may be a citation from Placentinus's *Quaestiones de iuris subtilitatibus*. Also, "Placentinus's *Summa* on the Codex was clearly a source for this *Ordo*, he says. This *Ordo* concerns itself with both civil and canon law, much more so than previous ordos. It frequently cites canon law, Gratian in particular.[4]

In the *Ordo Bambergensis*, at "Concerning Arbiters" (cap. XVIII), as translated by Brasington, we find: "Jurisdiction is the power granted to another, with permission to deliver the law and the ability to establish equity," which Brasington says follows Placentinus's treatise, *Summa Codicis* 3.13.3.[5] This is very similar to the language in the definition of "justice" in the preceding paragraph. This could be read as defining "justice" in terms of "jurisdiction" over both law and equity.

---

[1] "A Declaration of the Treason of Robert, Earl of Essex," *Spedding*, IX, pp. 245-275, p. 248, HathiTrust, https://hdl.handle.net/2027/ucl.b3618244; *Montagu*, II, p. 348, HathiTrust, https://hdl.handle.net/2027/umn.31951002094294g (The information was found by searching "gloss" in *Montagu*); John S. McHue, *Emperor Alexander Severus: Rome's Age of Insurrection, A.D. 222-235*, with color illus. (South Yorkshire: Pen & Sword Military, 2017), pp. 107-110, 113-115, 325, 245, 184. https://books.google.com/books?isbn=1473845823.

[2] Conway Robinson, preface, *History of the High Court of Chancery and other Institutions of England [...]* (Richmond, 1882), p. iv.

[3] Jill Harries, "Triple Vision: Ulpian of Tyre on the Duties of the Proconsul," in *Roman Rule in Greek and Latin Writing, Double Vision*, ed. by Jesper Majbom Madsen (Leiden: Koninklijke Brill NV, 2014), pp. 193-209, 203, 206, 209.

[4] Brasington, ch. 5, "The Ordo Bambergensis," *Order in the Court*, pp. 198-199.

[5] Brasington, p. 259, fn. 490.

Chapter Thirteen: Semi-Final Arguments

We set out to look at the character of Bellario, to see whether he might represent Francis Bacon and, if so, the implications of that fact vis-a-vis the Shakespeare authorship controversy. At the outset, it must be conceded that the case for William Shaxper is constructed from very few facts.[1] O. Hood Phillips, writing in 1972, said, "What we need, however, is more evidence linking the Stratford man with the plays and poems."[2] Similarly, James Shapiro concedes: "Shakespeare's biography hasn't changed much in the past 100 years."[3]

We have "his" six signatures; at least, we think they are all his.[4] We have the name "William Shakespeare" printed on the title pages of his plays. We have contemporary references to "Shakespeare," dating from Francis Meres' *Palladis Tamia*, entered in the Stationer's Register in 1598. Much has been conjectured from the few facts that are known.

---

[1] See, e.g., Robert Gore-Langton, "The Campaign to Prove Shakespeare Didn't Exist," *Newsweek*, 12/26/14. Retrieved from *Stage Voices*, 1/1/2015, http://www.stagevoices.com/stage_voices/2015/01/the-campaign-to-prove-shakespeare-didnt-exist-.html.

[2] *Shakespeare and the Lawyers*, p. 22.

[3] James Shapiro in "Toward a New Shakespeare Biography," *Shakespeare Survey* 58 (2005), ed. by Peter Holland, excerpted at "Into the Intro, Toward a New Shakespeare Biography," Academic Perspectives from Cambridge University Press, blog (1/19/16), http://www.cambridgeblog.org/2016/01/into-the-intro-toward-a-new-shakespeare-biography/.

[4] Five of the alleged signatures may be viewed in H. C. Beeching, D.Litt., *William Shakespeare, Player, Playmaker, and Poet, A Reply to Mr. George Greenwood, M.P.*, 2d ed. (London: Smith, Elder, 1909), pp. 20, facing p. 20, and 75 (from Sir Sidney Lee's *Life of Shakespeare*), HathiTrust, http://hdl.handle.net/2027/wu.89101414944. On the various spellings of "Shakespeare," see E. K. Chambers, *William Shakespeare, a Study of Facts and Problems*, vol. 2 (Oxford: Clarendon, 1930), pp. 371-373.

A pseudonym would make sense if the works were collaborative.[1] During the McCarthy era in the 1950s, blacklisted Hollywood script writer Dalton Trumbo edited the movie scripts of others *sub rosa* and ghost-wrote scripts sold under the names of other writers.[2] Robert Greene was a notorious "ghost-writer," depicted in contemporaneous art sitting at his desk in his shroud.[3] There was a fair amount of ghost-writing going on during that time. It is not out of the question that the name "William Shakespeare" was a cover.

In his essay "Of Vain-Glory," Francis Bacon wrote, "They that write books on the worthlessness of glory, take care to put their names on the title page." Cicero had said, "What do our philosophers do? Do they not, in those very books which they write on despising glory, set their names in the title-page?"[4]

> "The best temper of minds desireth good name and true honour; the lighter, popularity and applause."[5] When King James as a new judge went to Scotland, leaving Chancellor Bacon as second in command, in charge of the country until his return, Bacon gave a speech in which he addressed the judges serving under him: "Plaudites are fitter for players than for magistrates...And therefore you are not fit to be copies, except you be *fair written without blots or blurs* (italics mine), or anything unworthy your authority: and so I will trouble you no longer for this time."[6]

> Perhaps Ben Jonson had this speech in mind when he wrote, "Would he had blotted out a thousand!" in his *Timber, or Discoveries.*[7] With the "timber motif" in

---

[1] Even Russian Shakespearean scholar Ilya Gililov, whose book espoused the theory that Roger Manners, the fifth Earl of Rutland, and his wife Elizabeth wrote much of *Shakespeare*, ascribed an editorial role to Bacon. Ilya Gililov, *The Shakespeare Game: The Mystery of the Great Phoenix* (New York: Algora Publishing, 2003). On Roger Manners, see http://www.luminarium.org/encyclopedia/rutland5.htm. Spedding believed Bacon wrote two letters to the Earl of Rutland and one to Fulke Greville that were signed "E" for Essex, on behalf of the Earl. *Spedding*, IX, pp. 6-26, and "Commentary," pp. 1-6; 28-29. Bacon was the wise, older, "brotherly" mentor, advising the rash young hothead Essex.

[2] "Dalton Trumbo, Biography," updated 2/18/2016, http://www.biography.com/people/dalton-trumbo-9511141; Elizabeth Day and Mitzi Trumbo, "Hollywood blacklisted my father, now I'm proud they've put him on screen," *The Guardian*, 1-16-16, https://www.theguardian.com/film/2016/jan/16/dalton-trumbo-hollywood-blacklist-mitzi-trumbo-bryan-cranston.

[3] Robert W. Maslen, ch. 8, "Greene and the Uses of Time," in *Writing Robert Greene: Essays on England's First Notorious Professional Writer*, ed. by Kirk Melnikoff and Edward Gieskes (Aldershot UK: Ashgate, 2008), pp. 157-188, 160. Note the cover art. https://books.google.ca/books?isbn=1409474925.

[4] Cicero's '*Tusculanae Disputationes*,' b. i. c. 15, *The Works of Francis Bacon, The Wisdom of the Ancients and other Essays* (Roslyn NY: Walter J. Black, 1932), p. 187, n. 6; *Spedding*, VI, p. 504.

[5] Francis Bacon, "Natural History," century X, *Sylva Sylvarum*, #1000, in *Spedding*, II, p. 672, HathiTrust, https://hdl.handle.net/2027/ucl.31175012007822.

[6] "The Speech which was used by the Keeper of the Great Seal in Star Chamber before the Summer Circuits, the King being then in Scotland, 1617," *Spedding*, XIII, pp. 211-214, 214, HathiTrust, https://hdl.handle.net/2027/ien.35558005316928.

[7] "Timber: or, Discoveries Made Upon Men and Matter," ed. with intro. and notes by Felix E. Schelling (Boston, 1892), HathiTrust, https://catalog.hathitrust.org/Record/000589020. Discussed in E. K. Chambers, *William Shakespeare: A Study of Facts and Problems*, vol. 2 (Oxford: Clarendon Press, 1930), p. 210.

---

mind, consider that, in his essay "Of Suspicion," Bacon wrote, "Certainly, the best mean, to clear the way in this same wood of suspicions, is frankly to communicate them with the party that he suspects...."[1] In *The History of the Reign of King Henry VII*, regarding the matter of Perkin Warbeck, Bacon speaks of King Henry VII being "lost in a wood of suspicions."[2]

In the late sixteenth and early seventeenth century, a list of those who wrote or translated works anonymously includes: William Cecil (Lord Burghley);[3] Anne Cooke, mother to Francis Bacon;[4] a translator of Francis Hotman's 1574 *Franco-Gallia* in 1711;[5] an anonymous tract concerning Bacon's alleged bribery and corruption;[6] an editor of Bacon's *Works* in 1734;[7] a legal handbook, "I.D."[John Dodderidge] to which was attached "The Use of the Law," a treatise associated with Bacon;[8] a historical discourse by Nathaniel Bacon in 1647;[9] *The History of the Reigns of Henry the Seventh, Henry the Eighth, Edward the VI, and Queen Mary: the first written by the Right Honorable Francis [Bacon] Lord Verulam...: the other three by...Francis Godwyn, Lord Bishop of Hereford;*[10]

"Every charge brought against Bacon was thoroughly refused over a century ago by his master biographer, James Spedding, editor of his complete works." Nieves Matthews, ch. 3, "The Horrible Old Rascal," *History of a Character Assassination*, pp. 16-24, 19-20 and all of part 2, "The Corrupt Chancellor," pp. 89-217.

[1] "Of Suspicion," *Spedding*, VI, p. 454-455, HathiTrust, https://hdl.handle.net/2027/hvd. 32044058286733.

[2] *Spedding*, VI, p. 144.

[3] *A Dictionary of the Anonymous and Pseudonymous Literature of Great Britain*, vol. 2, ed. by Samuel Halkett and John Laing [librarians] (Edinburgh, 1883), p. 1265, https://books.google.ca/book s?id=bwgDAAAAYAAJ&source=gbs_book_other_versions.

[4] *Dictionary of the Anonymous*, vol. 2, *Fourtene sermons of Barnardine Ochyne, concerning the predestinacion and eleccion of God ...translated out of Italian into our natyue tongue by A. C.*," p. 951; See also *Lady Anne Bacon*, ed. by P. Demers, pp. 7-12.

[5] *Dictionary of the Anonymous*, vol. 2, translated by the author of the *Account of Denmark* [Robert Molesworth, Lord Molesworth]," p. 955.

[6] *Dictionary of the Anonymous*, vol. 2, "Francis, Lord Bacon: or, the case of private and natural corruption, and bribery, in part consider'd. Address'd to all South-Sea directors etc. By an Englishman [Thomas Gordon]," p. 955.

[7] *Dictionary of the Anonymous* 2, vol. 2, an introduction, with no author's name given, "ed. J. Locker," p. 1423.

[8] *Dictionary of the Anonymous*, vol. 2, "[Sir John Doderidge or Dodderidge or Dodridge] "...to which is annexed for the affinitie of the subject, another treatise called *The Use of the Law* [Francis Bacon] (London 1629)," p. 1329 (librarians' insertion of bracketed material). Heath, Bacon's legal editor, believed the work was not Bacon's, but that it may have been based on one of his commonplace books. See *Spedding*, VII, pp. 302, 453. Doderidge was co-counsel for the defendants with Bacon in *Slade's Case*, 4 Co. Rep. 94b, 76E.

[9] *Dictionary of the Anonymous*, vol. 2 p. 1115.

[10] *Dictionary of the Anonymous*, vol. 2, "anonymously translated [Morgan Godwyn, son of Bishop Francis Godwyn, in 1676]," p. 1163. Interestingly, Bishop Francis Godin (Godwyn) wrote the first science fiction work in English, *'The Man in the Moone'* (1638, pub. posthumously), and a book on cryptology, *Nuntius Inanimatus* (1629). William Poole, "Nuntius Inanimatus. Seventeenth-Century Telegraphy: The Schemes of Francis Godwin and Henry Reynolds," *The Seventeenth Century* 21, no. 1 (Spring, 2006), pp. 45-72, https://www.questia.com/library/ journal/1P3-1182305391/nuncius-inanimatus-seventeenth-century-telegraphy, discussed

a tract attacking popery by Nathaniel Bacon,[1] and, last but not least, a playwright in the 1700s whose real name was, intriguingly enough, "Phanuel Bacon."[2] It was William Cecil, later Lord Burghley, who encouraged John Jewel, whose *Apologia* Bacon's mother translated (and which was initially published anonymously), to write his 1561 Latin *Epistola* under a pseudonym, "Nicholaus N. Anglus."[3]

Let us pause to briefly compare Bacon, Shaxpere, and Bellario, in 1597. Was Bacon, like Bellario, a jurist-teacher whose legal opinions and authority were highly respected? In 1597, he was more aspiring than actual, but he had written his *Maxims*. I believe he did see himself as a teacher. Public office would elude him until after the death of Elizabeth.

How about Shaxpere? Not even aspiring.

Was Bacon, like Bellario, frequently ill? Yes. Was Shaxpere? Not that we know of.

Can we think of any good reason why Shaxpere would have inserted into "his" play a cameo non-appearance by Francis Bacon; or, at any rate, of a learned jurist who could not publicly appear in the theatre, who was known for being of poor health but wise beyond his years, and who had a greater interest in Roman law than he could comfortably let on, who was a cousin in some way to Portia who may represent the Queen?

There are numerous reasons why *Bacon* might hide his authorship.[4] First, Bacon and his brother, Anthony Bacon,[5] were involved in running an intelligence network for the government,[6] an undertaking which required secrecy. Second, Bacon was a lawyer for the Crown, with state secrets and

---

in Katherine Ellison, "Early Modern Cryptology as Fashionable Reading," *Journal of the Northern Renaissance*, no. 6 (2014), digital only, par. 21, http://www.northernrenaissance. org/1144000727777607680000-wayes-early-modern-cryptography-as-fashionable-reading/.

[1] *Dictionary of the Anonymous*, vol. 1, s.v. "REL," "Relation (a) of the Fearful Estate of Francis Spira, in the Year 1548 (first pub. anon. 1638; with name "Nathaniel Bacon;" published as by Nathaniel Bacon 1665; pub. as anon., with other titles in 1815, 1845; pub. with the given title as anon. [Nicholas or Nathaniel Bacon] (Glasgow, 1761) p. 56.

[2] *Dictionary of the Anonymous*, vol. 2, pp. 1189, 1233, 1307, 1657 (1729 A. D., 1757-58, and other dates).

[3] *Lady Anne Bacon,[...],* ed. by Patricia Demers, pp. 1-35, 16.

[4] See Roderick L. Eagle, "Why Bacon Suppressed His Name," http://www.sirbacon.org/links/suppressedname.htm; N. B. Cockburn, BSQ, ch. 4, "Bacon's Reasons for Anonymity," pp. 40-54, excerpted at http://www.sirbacon.org/anonymous.htm.

[5] http://www.historyofparliamentonline.org/volume/1558-1603/member/bacon-anthony-1558-1601.

[6] Patrick Martin, *Elizabethan Espionage, Plotters and Spies in The Struggle Between Catholicism and the Crown* (Jefferson NC: McFarland, 2016).

On John Dee's teaching Francis Bacon an ancient Hebrew cipher, the Gematria, see "A Bond for all the Ages: Sir Francis Bacon and John Dee: The Original 007." http://www.sirbacon.org/links/dblohseven.html.

personal confidences to keep.[1] Third, Bacon as a statesman had powerful enemies jealous of his abilities. He had seen the political downfall of those around him and would experience his own. Fourth (relatedly), he needed to protect his literary progeny. He had seen the writings of people he knew censored/destroyed, including Spenser's by Burghley.[2] Perhaps the world was not quite ready for all he had to say, but he envisioned future generations that would be.

Fifth, creative work requires quiet and time alone for gestation. Like any artist, Bacon wrote about personal matters, things of which he could not speak plainly. Sixth, he may have been protecting others. Certain subjects were taboo, such as the succession. Seventh, he was giving a gift to the world for which he wanted no personal acclaim. He once stated that an author's works should only be published after he has died, although he did break his own rule. Eighth, if any of the works were collaborations, it would be wrong for one writer to take the credit, or the "heat," in case of repercussions. Ninth, it may have been great, recreational fun to design giant literary puzzles, burying names and literary treasures for others to rediscover, re-creating the past so it would not be forgotten. Tenth, what was permitted to say one year might be forbidden the next. For example, when England was at war with Spain, Spanish proverbs might be considered "politically incorrect."

Eleventh, Bacon had not been pardoned by King James after he was relieved from duty as Chancellor when the First Folio came out. England was on the verge of a civil war. Perhaps this was not a good time for revelation.

Twelfth, under Kuttner's "forgotten definition of justice," Bacon may have thought he was helping justice "do its work in secret" by writing the Shakespeare plays *sub rosa*. There are mysteries connected with these plays and there are mysteries connected with Francis Bacon's philosophies. In other words, he may have had his own reasons, about which we still remain in the dark.

For Bacon's explanation on ciphers, including the biliteral cipher he invented when he was a young man serving the Queen in France, see Francis Bacon, (transl.) *De Augmentis*, vi, ch. 1,"Organ of Discourse," in *Spedding*, IV, p. 444-447, HathiTrust, https://hdl.handle.net/2027/hvd.hn6e7y and "Appendix on the Art of Writing in Cipher," *Spedding*, I, p. 841, HathiTrust, https://hdl.handle.net/2027/ucl.b3618238.

In the *De Augmentis* passage, Bacon comments that the biliteral cipher is capable of being utilized by anything capable of making two sounds, such as "bells, trumpets, torches, gunshots, and the like." *Spedding*, IV, p. 445.

[1] "Therefore set it down, that a habit of secrecy is both politic and moral." Bacon, "Of Simulation and Dissimulation," *Spedding*, VI, pp. 387-389, 388, HathiTrust, https://hdl.handle.net/2027/ucl.31175002285222.

[2] For Spenser's retaliation, see Bruce Danner, *Edmund Spenser's War on Lord Burghley*, Early Modern Literature in History, Cedric C. Brown, gen. ed. and Andrew Hatfield, ed. (Houndsmills, Basingstoke, Hampshire: Palgrave MacMillan, 2011), pp. 17, 97, 215-216, 228.

The frontispiece to Jessie L. Weston's book *From Ritual to Romance* bears two quotations worth noting. In the first, Francis M. Cornford writes, "Many literary critics seem to think that a hypothesis about obscure and remote questions of history can be refuted by a simple demand for the production of more evidence than in fact exists. But the true test of a hypothesis, if it cannot be shewn to conflict with known truths, is the number of facts that it correlates, and explains."[1]

The second quotation is by Francis Bacon, *Animus ad amplitudinem Mysteriorum pro modulo suo dilatetor, non Mysteria ad angustias animi constringantur.* Spedding translates, "But here we ought by no means to be wanting to ourselves; for as God uses the help of our reason to illuminate us, so should we likewise turn it every way, that we may be more capable of receiving and understanding his mysteries; *provided only that the mind be enlarged, according to its capacity, to the grandeur of the mysteries, and not the mysteries contracted to the narrowness of the mind.*"[2]

Spedding, in his preface to the third book of the *Novum Organum*, discusses how, in "Valerius Terminus" and "Temporis Partus Masculus," Bacon revealed how he intended for his new doctrine to be veiled in an abrupt and obscure style, hidden from the "vulgar" who would not understand it, but providing a treasure hunt for his "filios" or disciples, in the tradition of the magi and alchemists.[3] While Brian Vickers once asserted that Bacon was never intentionally obscure, in his introduction to *Francis Bacon, A Critical Edition of the Major Works,* Bacon himself said, "For I do not endeavor either by triumphs of confutation, or pleadings of antiquity, or assumptions of authority, or even by the veil of obscurity, to invest these inventions of mine with any majesty; which might easily be done by one who sought to give luster to his own name rather than light to other men's minds."[4] It is difficult to reconcile these two statements. Perhaps Vickers has written something more recently that would shed further light on his statement, above.

Why do we study history, anyway? The great Roman orator and statesman Marcus Tullius Cicero wrote, "To be ignorant of what occurred before you were born is to remain always a child. For what is the worth of human life unless it is woven into the life of our ancestors by the records of history?"[5]

The Roman god Janus, which faced both forward and back, was also identified with Prudence. Prudence requires "consideration of the past

---

[1] F. M. Cornford, *The Origin of Attic Comedy* (first pub. Cambridge: Cambridge University Press, 1914), frontispiece to Jessie L. Weston, *From Ritual To Romance* (Mineola NY: Dover Publications 1997, first pub. 1920).

[2] *De Dignitate et Augmentis Scientiarum*, ix, in *Spedding*, V, p. 114.

[3] *Spedding*, I, pp. 85-86, 113, HathiTrust, http://hdl.handle.net/2027/nyp.33433081627303.

[4] Francis Bacon, preface to *The Great Instauration, Spedding*, IV, p. 19, HathiTrust, https://hdl.handle.net/2027/hvd.hn6e7y.

[5] Cicero, *Orator* 120, quoted in Kate Wintrol, "The Intrinsic Value of the Liberal Arts: Cicero's Example," *Journal of the National Collegiate Honors Council* 15, no. 1, paper 131 (Spring/Summer 2014), pp. 129-134, 133.

and foresight of the future."[1] By definition, jurisprudence requires looking backward and forward. Did Jessica only look forward? Burning her bridges behind her?

> Titian painted "An Allegory of Prudence," 1565, depicting the forward and backward-looking faces of Janus.[2] In *Merchant*, Act I, Scene I, Salarino swears: "Now, by two-headed Janus...."[3] The jurist William Fulbecke likened the civil, canon, and common law to *three* sisters holding hands, looking at one another, yet also facing away from each other.[4] Bacon described the "Janus of the Imagination" as having a face towards Reason — with the print of truth, and a face towards Action — with the print of Good.[5]

> In a letter, Bacon wrote that King James must be "Janus bifrons" with a face towards Scotland and one towards England.[6] Bacon opposed *ex post facto* laws, those with retroactive effect, saying "we approve not of a Janus in laws."[7]

Bacon wrote to Launcelot Andrewes that he studied Seneca, Cicero, and Demosthenes to learn how to cope with adversity.[8] Queen Elizabeth studied the classics, translating works such as Boethius[9] and Cicero to help keep her mind sharp for statecraft.[10]

At the time in which Francis Bacon was writing, England was lagging behind the Continent in terms of culture, education, and modernity. It still had one "foot," so to speak, in the Middle Ages. To a large extent, it was Bacon

---

[1] Frank J. Fabozzi, ch. 2, "The Theory and Practice of Investment Management after the Crisis: Need for Change?" in *Investment Management: a Science to Teach or an Art to Learn?* CFA [Chartered Financial Analysts] Research Foundation Publications, ebook May 2014), p. 28, n. 10, http://www.cfapubs.org/doi/pdf/10.2470/rf.v2014.n3.1.

[2] See Jeremiah S. Pam, "Prudence in International Strategy: From Lawyerly to Post-Lawyerly, GWU Law School Publications Law Research Paper no. 2017-64; GWU Legal Studies Research Paper no. 2017-64, pp. 199, 219, https://scholarship.law.gwu.edu/faculty_publications/1304/; available at SSRN: http://ssrn.com/abstract=3036566; *De Augmentis*, in *Spedding*, IV, p. 406, HathiTrust, HathiTrust, https://hdl.handle.net/2027/hvd.hn6e7y.

[3] It was Simon Miles' talk, "Francis Bacon and The Merchant of Venice" on YouTube which first alerted me to the significance of the "Janus" mask in connection with *The Merchant of Venice*.

[4] Coquillette, "Legal Ideology ...I," p. 67, n. 336.

[5] *De Augmentis*, in *Spedding*, IV, p. 406, HathiTrust, HathiTrust, https://hdl.handle.net/2027/hvd.hn6e7y.

[6] "A Letter to Mr. Foules," March 28, 1603. *Spedding X*, p. 65, HathiTrust, https://hdl.handle.net/2027/ucl.b3618245.

[7] Aphorism 47, 'Example of a Treatise on Universal Justice,' (transl.) *De Augmentis*, viii, *Spedding*, V, p. 97, HathiTrust, https://hdl.handle.net/2027/ucl.b3618241, discussed in Coquillette, FB, pp. 250, 271 fn. 157.

[8] *Spedding*, XIV, p. 372, HathiTrust, https://hdl.handle.net/2027/ucl.31175012007947.

[9] Terttu Nevalainen, ch. 2.5, "Sources For the Study of Early Modern English," *An Introduction to Early Modern English* (New York: Oxford University Press, 2006), pp. 23-25, 25.

[10] The learned Queen Elizabeth owned a worn, leather-bound copy of Cicero, from which she translated passages. See "Lot 53, Elizabeth I, Queen of England. Cicero, Marcus Tullius. *Orationem volume primum* 1543. Bound for Queen Elizabeth. Live auction April 9, 2015: *sold*." http://www.invaluable.com/auction-lot/elizabeth-i,-queen-of-england.-cicero,-marcus-tu-53-c-5da482eb94.

who brought the Renaissance to England. He was attempting to shake not just England but the whole world of thought loose from its moorings. He set the world on a modern course, but not without caution.

While he proposed reforms in law and education, he believed laws should be rooted in "nature, manners, and policy," lest they become mere "wallflowers" which would not withstand the passage of time.[1] As to "wall flowers," Bacon related how the Roman Emperor Constantine called the Emperor Hadrian a "wall flower" for having his name emblazoned on so many walls.[2]

Paul Kocher explained thus: The broader the knowledge base a judge has, the more equipped he/she will be to generate general principles, by induction, "to the yet broader principles of *Philosophia Prima*," and to apply them, by deduction, to individual cases."[3] Important to Bacon was *cultura animi*, the cultivating of your mind.[4] Although he realized the limitations of fame — reputation — and discouraged the seeking of glory, he exhorted those he counselled to, above all else, preserve their good names.[5] (This was the advice the presiding judge gave to a whole roomful of new lawyers when I was sworn in to the bar.)

Four hundred years ago, the challenges wrought by the printing press were as monumental in their own way as those we face today with digital technology.[6] Then, the courtesy of a gentleman circulating among friends a manuscript he had written (or making a private gift of it) was giving way to a need to protect one's work from piracy.[7] Moreover, in those times of repression, the threat of censorship loomed.[8]

---

[1] Francis Bacon, dedication of *The Arguments in Law of Sir Francis Bacon* to the law students of Gray's Inn. *Spedding*, VII, p. 524, HathiTrust, https://hdl.handle.net/2027/hvd.32044069750248.

[2] "An Offer to be Made of a Digest of the Laws of England," *Spedding*, XIV, p. p. 359, HathiTrust, https://hdl.handle.net/2027/ucl.31175012007947; *Apophthegms New and Old* (1625), *Spedding*, VII, p. 140, HathiTrust, https://hdl.handle.net/2027/ucl.b3924335.
For Barry R. Clarke's research on the frequency of "wall flower" and other uncommon words, found by computer analysis in the writings of both Shakespeare and Bacon, see Barry R. Clarke, *Francis Bacon's contribution to three Shakespeare plays*, Ph.D Thesis, 2010-2013, Brunel University, p. 87, http://barryispuzzled.com/PhDThesis.pdf.

[3] Paul H. Kocher, "Francis Bacon on the Science of Jurisprudence," *Journal of the History of Ideas* 18, no. 1 (Jan. 1957), pp. 3-26, p. 26. http://www.jstor.org/stable/2707577?seq=1#page_scan_tab_contents.

[4] Matthew Sharpe, "Not for personal gratification...," p. 37, quoting Bacon, 'Advancement of Learning,' *Spedding*, III, p. 432; "Advice to the Earl of Rutland on his Travels," (1595-1596), *Spedding*, IX, pp. 6-15, 7, HathiTrust, https://hdl.handle.net/2027/ucl.b3618244.

[5] "Dedication to the Duke of Buckingham of the 3d edition of his *Essays*" (1625), *Spedding*, VI, p. 373.

[6] See preface, *Spedding*, VIII, p. viii.

[7] Before the printing press, medieval monks or scribes did not use title pages. They would instead sign and date the last pages of their works. http://www.hrc.utexas.edu/educator/modules/gutenberg/books/legacy/.

[8] For an overview of press restrictions in England from William Caxton (ca. 1477) through the 17th century, see Nancy C. Cornwell, *Freedom of the Press: Rights and Liberties Under the Law* (Santa

Religious persecution was also a real threat.[1] One might wonder about the suicidal tendencies of any playwright who openly proclaimed his authorship.[2]

Why was Shakespeare virtually the only playwright of his time who was never in trouble with the authorities? Clare Asquith has suggested he was protected by powerful people.[3] If so, why was he special? The Bishop's Ban of 1599 banned satires, naming Hall, Marston, John Davies, Thomas Nashe, Gabriel Harvey, and others. "Shakespeare" was not named, though a printer who printed his works in quarto, Valentine Sims (Symmes), was racked and his type was melted down.[4]

Had Bacon (for I do think it was Bacon) broadly proclaimed his authorship role in the Shakespeare plays, we might not even have them today. Manuscripts were frequently confiscated (e.g., Thomas Nashe and Gabriel Harvey's satires and Coke's legal manuscripts,[5] with the king's men carting away his manuscripts as he lay dying[6]) or burned (John Cowell's legal dictionary, *The Interpreter*, ruled "unconstitutional" for drawing upon Roman law[7]). No one seems to know what happened to Selden's manuscript, *Life of Roger Bacon*.[8] On account of their writings, authors suffered royal disfavor

---

Barbara: ABC-Clio, 2004), pp. 20-24; 4 Holdsworth, *A History of English Law* 296-307, 302 (Boston: Little Brown, 1924); "Primary Sources on Copyright (1450-1900)," Commentaries, http://www. copyrighthistory.org/cam/commentary/uk_1538/uk_1538_com_972007121733.html.

[1] In 1593, *An Act Against Popish Recusants* had passed, "for the better discovering dangerous conspiracies by sundry wicked and seditious persons terming themselves Catholics ...." A second bill targeted Puritan Separatists and other nonconformists who refused to take the Oath of Supremacy. Bowen, *Lion*, pp. 39-41, 40.

[2] William S. Niederkorn, "To Be or not To Be Shakespeare," *New York Times*, Learning Network, Student Connections (August 21, 2004), http://www.nytimes.com/learning/students/pop/20040823snapmonday.html.

[3] Clare Asquith, *Shadowplay*, p. 29. Yet, see "H. S.," "Hayward's Henry IV," *Baconiana* 4, 3d series (Jan., 1906), no. 13, pp. 5-14, p. 13, https://books.google.ca/books?id=8wEdYDaZt8sC.

[4] Cliff Forshaw, "'Cease to bawle, thou wasp-stung Satyrist': Writers, Printers and the Bishops' Ban of 1599,' *Entertext* 3, no. 1 (May 22, 2003; online, June 12, 2004), pp. 101-131, 117-119. https://www.brunel.ac.uk/__data/assets/pdf_file/0005/111020/Cliff-Forshaw,-Cease-Cease-to-bawle,-thou-wasp-stung-Satyrist-Writers,-Printers-and-the-Bishops-Ban-of-1599.pdf.

For more on Sims, see Frank G. Hubbard, ed., "The First Quarto Edition of Shakespeare's Hamlet," *University of Wisconsin Studies in Language and Literature* 8 (Madison: University of Wisconsin, 1920), p. 17

[5] W. F. Swindler, *Magna Carta: Legend and Legacy* (Indianapolis: Bobbs-Merrill, 1965) pp. 166-191, p. 187.

[6] Boyer, *Sir Edward Coke*, p. 27.

[7] John Stone, "John Cowell's *Interpreter*: Legal Tradition and Lexicographical Innovation," *Sederi* X (1999), pp. 121-129, p. 121. www.sederi.org/wp-content/uploads/2016/12/10_12Stone.pdf; Polly J. Price, "Natural Law and Birthright Citizenship in Calvin's Case (1608)," p. 94. http://digitalcommons.law.yale.edu/yjlh/vol9/iss1/2/.

[8] Ofir Haivry, John Selden and the Western Political Tradition (Cambridge: Cambridge University Press, 2017), p. 230.

(Bacon's father, Nicholas Bacon);[1] imprisonment (playwrights Chapman, Marston, and Jonson in 1605 for writing *Eastward Ho*[2] and Peter Wentworth for speaking and writing about the succession[3]); maiming (John Stubbs, for writing about the succession[4]); torture (printer of Shakespeare plays Valentine Simms), and/or death (William Tyndale).[5]

As facts build upon facts, it can be easy to lose the forest for the trees. There may not be one linchpin argument upon which this case of mysterious identity rests. It is more about all the little daubs of paint that make up one portrait.

The burden of proof in a civil case is a mere preponderance of the evidence. Just a feather's weight[6] to tip the scales is all that is required.[7] Perhaps, in this case, that feather is a *nom de plume*.

---

[1] "Sir Nicholas Bacon (1509-1579)," *Luminarium Encyclopedia Project*. http://www.luminarium. org/encyclopedia/nicholasbacon.htm.

[2] "George Chapman," https://www.britannica.com/biography/George-Chapman.

[3] "Peter Wentworth (1524-97), of Lillingstone Lovell, Oxon." http://www.history ofparliamentonline.org/volume/1558-1603/member/wentworth-peter-1524-97. See also "Freedom of Speech in Elizabethan Parliaments," http://www.historyofparliamentonline. org/periods/tudors/freedom-speech-elizabethan-parliaments. By comparison, Henry VIII had been very clear in naming the order of those who would succeed him in ruling England. See Michel de Castelnau, *Memoirs of the Reigns of Francis II and Charles IX of France*, I, transl. anon. (London, 1724), ii, ch. 4, p. 62. https://books.google.ca/books?id=nyBEAAAAcAAJ.

[4] Deborah Shuger, ch. 1, "That Great and Immoderate Liberty of Lying," *The Censorship and Cultural Sensibility: The Regulation of Language in Tudor-Stuart England* (University of Pennsylvania Press: Philadelphia, 2006), pp. 14, 19, 23, 74, 278; William Howitt, *John Cassell's Illustrated History of England* (London, 1858), p. 491.

[5] See, e.g., P. H. Ditchfield, *Books Fatal to their Authors* (New York, 1895), pp. 19-20, HathiTrust, http://hdl.handle.net/2027/uc2.ark:/13960/t84j0jh8z.

[6] The feather is significant as an Egyptian symbol for justice. The Egyptian goddess Maat, goddess of truth, justice, cosmic law, and related concepts, wore an ostrich feather in a band on her head. The feather was sometimes depicted alone, on a pedestal, "denoting foundational importance," At death, a person's heart ("will, feelings, thought, character") was weighed against a feather to determine where that person would spend the afterlife. See Judith Resnik and Dennis Curtis, chs. 2 and 4, *Representing Justice* (New Haven: Yale University Press, 2011), pp. 20, 21, 77.

[7] In a 1916 case, a judge ruled, based on the evidence presented, that Bacon was the author of the Shakespeare plays. http://www.sirbacon.org/links/nytimes.html; Robert Loerzel, "Judge: Bacon Wrote Shakespeare Plays" (2003), http://www.alchemyofbones.com/stories/ shakespearehtm, citing the *Chicago Tribune* (April 22, 1916); the *New York Times* (Aril 22, 1916); and an Associated Press article (June 13, 2001). The decision was, however, rescinded by a new judge who dismissed the case on jurisdictional grounds. *The Morning Oregonian* 46, no. 17, 368 (July 22, 1916), p. 1. http://oregonnews.uoregon.edu/lccn/sn83025138/1916-07-22/ed-1/ seq-1.pdf.

Chapter Fourteen: Encore

From the time the first baby played peek-a-boo, people have loved secrets and mysteries, treasure hunts, games of hide-and-seek. But when it comes to secrets of state, different rules apply. Winston Churchill famously said, "In war-time,...truth is so precious that she should always be attended by a bodyguard of lies."[1] In his roles as counsellor to sovereigns, Bacon kept secrets of state which protected the not just the realm but the Queen's very life. In his unfinished fragment, *The Beginning of the History of Great Britain*, Bacon spoke twice of the succession of Queen Elizabeth as a "secret of estate."[2] What is that secret?

---

[1] Winston Churchill, *The Second World War* Vol. 5: *Closing the Ring* (Boston: Houghton Mifflin, 1951), p. 383.

[2] Francis Bacon, "The Beginning of the History of Great Britain," fragment, in *The History of the Reign of King Henry VII and Selected Works*, ed. by Brian Vickers (Cambridge University Press: Cambridge, 1998), pp. 215-221, 218-219; *Spedding*, VI, p. 271. See also Rawley's *Life of Francis Bacon* in *Spedding*, I, p. 5, HathiTrust, http://hdl.handle.net/2027/nyp.33433081627303. *Webster's*, p. 341, gives as an archaic meaning of "estate": "social standing or rank, especially of a high order; also pomp, state."

Shakespeare wrote plays about Henry IV, V, VI, and VIII of England, skipping Henry VII. Francis Bacon completed one history of a King Henry, that of Henry VII (1622), although he had begun a history of Henry VIII. In *The History of the Reign of King Henry VII*, he invented speeches for several main characters, including Perkin Warbeck. John Ford's play, ca. 1630, about Perkin Warbeck, was based on Bacon's *The History of Henry VII*. John E. Curran, Jr., *Character and Individual Personality in English Renaissance Drama, Tragedy, History, Tragicomedy* (Newark: University of Delaware Press, 2014), pp. 272-276, 280-281, 289-290. Robert Cotton had written a history of Henry III of England (a thinly-veiled political commentary paralleling King James' reign), and John Selden's *Jani Anglorum* takes the history of England through the decease of Henry II. Graham Parry, *The Trophies of Time*, pp. 105, 87-88. Among the three of them, they had covered the history of the English kings through Henry VIII. Planned or coincidence?

Knowing who authored the Shakespeare plays is important to help us understand the plays. If Bacon is Shakespeare, understanding one will help us understand the other.

I have been asking myself, how does mercy "season" justice? Salt or another condiment (from *condo, condere,* with all its delicious possible meanings[1]) pickles, seasons, and preserves food. It becomes a part of the dish. Meat without salt has no flavor, no savor. Is justice without mercy like meat without salt, in Cordelia's analogy in *King Lear*? Is it like Bacon without Shakespeare?

Some things we may never know for sure; the sands of time obscure.[2] Bacon acknowledged the power of myth and fable to improve a true story. The belief that a largely self-taught actor— who paradoxically exhibits the education and culture of a Renaissance prince—wrote the plays certainly has had staying power.

To borrow Bacon's signature three-part structure,[3] there are those who are sure they know who wrote the plays, those who do not question the status quo, and those who keep an open mind, finding treasures as they explore.

One of those treasures, for me, was finding the "forgotten definition of justice," in Kuttner's article, that goes beyond legal rights and incorporates a conception of equity or fairness. In 1948, a United States law school "hornbook" author warned that "The only hope for the preservation of equity

---

[1] "To build, found, form, establish, of a literary work, to compose, write, to put up, put away safely, store, to hide, withdraw, of corpses, to bury, of time, to pass, dispose of." *Cassell's Latin,* p. 46.

[2] Italian Renaissance painter Francisco Pacheco (1564-1654) advises tempering pigment with oil and white, for "time will darken it." Quoted in frontispiece, William Maxwell, *Time Will Darken It* (Random House: New York, 1962).

[3] E.g., "Some books are meant to be tasted, others to be swallowed, and some few to be chewed and digested; that is, some books are to be read only in parts, others to be read, but not curiously, and some few to be read wholly, and with diligence and attention." Francis Bacon, "Of Studies," in *Spedding,* VI, pp. 497-498, HathiTrust, https://hdl.handle.net/2027/hvd.32044058286733.

On the tripartite structure in *Merchant,* see Alice Benston, "Portia, the Law, and the Tripartite Structure of 'The Merchant of Venice'" *Shakespeare Quarterly* 30, no. 3, pp. 367-385; on the tripartite structure in Bacon, see Thomas Wheeler, ed., *The Merchant of Venice: Critical Essays* (London: Routledge, 2015), p. 163. JSTOR, http://www.jstor.org/stable/2869472.

Ulpian is known for his tripartite structure. See Christopher N. Warren, *Literature and the Law of Nations, 1580-1680* (Oxford: Oxford University Press, 2015), p. 116 (Ulpian distinguished laws of nature, nations, and civil laws). Placentinus used a tripartite structure when he distinguished three categories of ignorant sellers of products with latent defects. John W. Cairns and Paul J. de Plessis, *Creation of the Ius Commune, from Casus to Regula,* Edinburgh Studies in Law (Edinburgh: Edinburgh University Press, 2010), pp. 185-187, JSTOR, www.jstor.org/stable/10/3366/j.cttlr28k7.

lies in a continuous study of it as a system based on fundamental conceptions, but applied in all of the various fields of the law."[1]

Is equity in danger of distinction? It might depend how we define equity; there are different contexts. At heart, equity is a basic concept of fairness, but in court, it is dependent upon procedure and knowledge of procedure.

Equity was important to Francis Bacon. It was equally important to the author of *The Merchant of Venice*.

Bacon liked to tell stories as part of his teaching. It is said that, through hearing and telling stories, we develop empathy and a sense of our own human frailties. In perhaps his best-known speech, former United States Supreme Court Justice Learned Hand even defined the Spirit of Liberty as the state of being "not too sure we are right."[2] Scientific objectivity requires humility, as Erich Fromm wrote in *The Art of Loving*.[3] Virgil's rustic shepherd Corydon saw his reflection in the water and thought he looked pretty good. He did not see his faults. In the best of circumstances, "To err is human, to forgive is divine."[4] These words, carved into the masonry of the old Rochester Public Library, slated for extinction but preserved by the Landmark Society, are worthy of remembrance: "And what doth the Lord require of thee, but to do justly, and to love mercy, and to walk humbly with thy God?" Micah 6:8.

---

[1] Henry L. McClintock, *Handbook of the Principles of Equity*, 2d. ed., Hornbook Series (St. Paul: West, 1948), pp. 18-19.

[2] Speech, "The Spirit of Liberty" (1944), *The Spirit of Liberty, Paper and Addresses of Learned Hand*, collected with intro. and notes by Irving Dilliard (New York: Vintage Books, 1959), pp. 143-145, Digital History, 1199, http://www.digitalhistory.uh.edu/disp_textbook. cfm?smtID=3&psid=1199.

[3] Erich Fromm, *The Art of Loving* (New York: Harper & Row, Perennial Library ed., 1956), p. 101.

[4] Alexander Pope.

Appendix I. Musings on the Name *Bellario*

In Latin, the word for "bell" was either *tintinnabulum* or, sometimes, *aes*. *Aes, aeris* meant copper, bronze, or things made of bronze. Money was *aes signatum*. Debt was *aes alienum*.[1] The genitive (possessive) singular of *aes*, which is *aeris*, is the same as the word for "air" (*aer, aeris*.) As (*as, assis*, m.) could mean "the whole, a small coin, a weight. The *as* or *libra* was the Roman pound, which weighed twelve ounces.[2] *Heres ex asse* meant "sole heir."[3] Shakespeare used "airie", the nest of an eagle or other bird of prey, figuratively, to mean a "noble stock of children."[4] In *Midsummer Night's Dream*, he wrote, "The poet's pen... gives to airy nothing a local habitation and a name."[5]

"Belarius" is the name of an ancient Roman character in Shakespeare's play *Cymbeline*. In revenge, he stole the two sons of the king Cymbeline.[6]

In Beaumont and Fletcher's play *Philaster, or Love Lies Bleeding*, "Bellario" is a prince's messenger boy who turns out to be a girl in disguise.[7]

---

[1] Cassell's, p. 10.

[2] "Roman weights and measures," Site Seen Ltd., 2017, http://www.tribunesandtriumphs.org/roman-life/roman-weights-and-measures.htm; Philip Smith, "Libra or As," *A Dictionary of Greek and Roman Antiquities*, ed. by William Smith (London, 1875), p. 706, http://penelope.uchicago.edu/Thayer/E/Roman/Texts/secondary/SMIGRA*/Libra.html, last updated 5/8/2018.

[3] *Aer, aes, as*, and "bell," *Cassell's Latin*, pp. 10, 21, 251. The word "estimate" comes from *aes*.

[4] *The Oxford Universal Dictionary on Historical Principles*, 3d ed., rev. (1955), s.v. "airie," p. 30.

[5] *Merchant*, V, 1, 1845-1846, www.opensourceshakespeare.org.

[6] "Belarius," in *Cymbeline, King of Britain*, Schmoop University, copyright 2018, https://www.shmoop.com/cymbeline/belarius.html.

[7] Francis Beaumont and John Fletcher, "Philaster: or Love Lies a-Bleeding," Harvard Classics, vol. 47, Bartleby.com, http://www.bartleby.com/47/3/.

Bellaria is the name of the queen in Robert Greene's novel *Pandosto*.[1] She is thought to be a source for Shakespeare's Queen Hermione in *The Winter's Tale* (V, 2, 3202).[2] Similarity has been noted between the "review of suitors" scenes in Greene's *The Anatomie of Love's Flatteries* and *The Merchant of Venice*.[3] Like other Shakespeare's heroines such as Desdemona and Hero, and like Anne Boleyn, giving her the benefit of the doubt, Queen Hermione was unjustly accused of adultery.

In *The Winter's Tale*, "Gent. 3" tells us the lifelike statue of Hermione was created by Italian artist Giulio Romano, also known as Giulio Pippi (ca. 1492/99 to 1546).[4] Romano created painted, realistic, wax funeral statues.[5] He was the only sixteenth-century artist Shakespeare ever praised by name.[6]

Romano had made a red and black chalk drawing of the goddess "Justice" with her hand on the neck of an ostrich, a symbol of justice as well as Christ and his mercy.[7] Romano had been Raphael's chief assistant. After his death, Romano helped to complete Raphael's unfinished projects before going to Mantua to serve Duke Federico II Gonzaga whose death was thought to have inspired the "Mousetrap play" in *Hamlet*. Romano was friends with Baldesarre Castiglione, author of *The Book of the* Courtier, translated by Bacon's cousin by marriage Sir Thomas Hoby. It was Castiglione who taught Queen Elizabeth her lovely, "spidery" handwriting.[8] It was in Mantua that Romano worked as a sculptor and architect.[9]

Old Gobbo's blindness made me think of "Belisarius, Justinian's real-life general who attained mythical status.[10] One was that Justinian had blinded him out of jealousy. A people Belisarius had conquered wanted to make him their king. But he could not be their king unless he overthrew Justinian, so

---

[1] "Pandosto, the Triumph of Time," Internet Shakespeare Editions, The University of Victoria, http://internetshakespeare.uvic.ca/Annex/DraftTxt/Pandosto/pandosto/.html.

[2] "*Pandosto*, the Triumph of Time."

[3] "The Life of Robert Greene (1560-1592)," *Encyclopedia Britannica*, vol. 12, eleventh ed., (Cambridge: Cambridge University Press, 1910), *http://www.luminarium.org/renlit/greenebio.htm.* For further reading, see *Writing Robert Greene, Essays on England's First Notorious Professional Writer*, ed. by Kirk Melnikoff and Edward Gieskes (London: Taylor & Francis, 2016).

[4] Karl Elze, trans. L. Dora Schmitz, "The Supposed Travels of Shakespeare," in *Essays on Shakespeare* (London, 1874), pp. 284-289, 288.

[5] See John Hamill, "The Ten Restless Ghosts of Mantua, Part 1," in *Soul of the Age, Edward de Vere as Shakespeare Stimulates a Golden Era of English Literature*, 9, ed. by Paul Hemenway Altrocchi, M.D (iUniverse 2014), pp. 134–149, p. 138, n. 147.

[6] Resnick and Curtis, ch. 4 and pp. 76-77, 105, 387, 438-39, 540, 661.

[7] Resnik and Curtis, ch. 4, *Representing Justice*, pp. 76-77, 105, 387, 438-39, 540, 661.

[8] Elizabeth Jenkins, *Elizabeth the Great*, p. 20.

[9] See Armelle Sabbatier, *Shakespeare and Visual Culture, A Dictionary* (London: Bloomsbury ebook 2017), pp. 98-99.

[10] "Belisarius and Antonina," from Procopius, *Secret History*, website of P. Atkinson, A Theory of Civilization, copyright March 9, 2018, http://www.ourcivilisation.com/smartboard/shop/procopius/blsrs.htm. Note "Antonina," similar to the name "Antonio" in the play.

---

he deceived them. Belarius had an unfaithful wife whose behavior caused him much humiliation. Was Launcelot *really* Old Gobbo's son? "Father, don't you recognize me?"

Shakespeare seems to be playing with the sound *bel* or *bal* in *Merchant*. Balthazar, which comes from the name of the god "Baal," is a form of Belshazzar.

Antonio calls himself a "wether," a castrated ram. A bell-wether is a belled, but not castrated, sheep that leads the flock — or the leader of a thoughtless crowd.[1] In modern French, a *beliere* is a sheep bell.[2]

Belial is not a Biblical name, but its etymology implies a negative state. It comes from two roots to the Hebrew form *bala* that convey meanings of either something that is "used up, obsolete, wasted, or "instilling terror upon people."[3] The forms appear sixteen times in the Bible. One form, *bal*, is an adverb meaning "not," negation (uncommonly). Bell-ario (bal-heir) could be interpreted to mean "without — or not — an heir."

One form of *bal*, *belima*, which sounds a little like "Belmont," means "nothingness." It occurs only in Job 26:7. Job's statement that the "earth is suspended on nothingness" has been the source of speculation.[4]

Hyperbole, or exaggeration, is a word that is associated with Shakespeare. It comes from the Greek *hyperballein*, to throw, as in throwing a ball, over or beyond.

"Bellario" might also bear translation as "beautiful spirit or song," while the word "comedy" comes from the Greek *komos* (festal procession) + *aidein* (to sing); hence, an ode sung at a festal procession.[5] Perhaps the name is, at least in part, intended to embody or invoke the original Greek spirit of comedy.[6]

---

[1] "Bell-wether," *Webster's*, p. 96. The term "Bell-wether" is also found in *As You Like It*, III, 2, 1192 (Touchstone) and *Merry Wives of Windsor* III, 5, 1847 (Falstaff). www.opensourceshakespeare. org.

[2] *Cassell's French and English Dictionary* (Collier Books, p.b., 1986), s.v. "beliere," p. 42.

[3] Arie Uittenbogaard, Abarim Publications' *Online Biblical Hebrew Dictionary*, s.v. "Belial meaning," first pub. Dec. 26, 2010, http://www.abarim-publications.com/Meaning/Belial.html#.V5cAk-Bf3IU.

[4] Uittenbogaard, "Belial meaning."

[5] "Comedy," *Webster's*, p. 200.

[6] "Air," "beau, bel," *Cassell's French and English Dictionary*, pp. 13, 41.

Appendix II. *The Tragedy of Anne Boleyn*

Interestingly, Robert Greene's play *Pandosto* with the queen named Bellaria is one of several texts to which Elizabeth Wells Gallup and her team applied Francis Bacon's bi-literal cipher[1] to retrieve an actual, entire play, *The Tragedy of Anne Boleyn.*[2] Indeed, several lines in *Anne Boleyn* are found verbatim in *The Merchant of Venice*.

I was not looking for ciphers. In fact, I only found out there was such a play by doing a Google search for Portia's line, "For the intent and purpose of the law hath full relation to the penalty." The only two places that line came up were in *The Merchant of Venice* and in *The Tragedy of Anne Boleyn.*[3] Needless to say, I was intrigued.

Gallup explains that deciphering involves following keys which lead the decipherer on a treasure hunt, from one work to the next, retrieving text that eventually makes up the body of a narrative play. The "playing field" (my term) for this play is made up of the works of William Shakespeare, Francis Bacon, Robert Greene, and other writers. This is explained in detail in Gallup's appendix to *The Tragedy of Anne Boleyn*.

---

[1] For Bacon on ciphers, see *De Augmentis*, in *Spedding*, IV, p. 444, HathiTrust, https://hdl.handle. net/2027/hvd.hn6e7y; Spedding, "Appendix on the Art of Writing in Cipher," in *Spedding*, I, p. 841, HathiTrust, https://hdl.handle.net/2027/ucl.b3618238.

[2] *The Tragedy of Anne Boleyn, a Drama in Cipher Found in the Works of Sir Francis Bacon, from original editions in the British Museum 1579 to 1590, as. Deciphered by Elizabeth Wells Gallup from the Novum Organum of Sir Francis Bacon by means of the Biliteral Cipher, described in his 'Advancement of Learning'* (Geneva Illinois: Riverside Laboratories, 1916), pp. 148-161, 148-150, HathiTrust, https://hdl. handle.net/2027/hvd.hnlczc. For further reading, see bibliography, infra.

[3] *Merchant*, IV, 1, 2910; *The Tragedy of Anne Boleyn*, p. 131.

In *Anne Boleyn*, the lines "For the intent and purpose of the law hath full relation to the penalty" are spoken by Thomas Cromwell. Only someone quite astute and "in-the-know" would compare Portia's sly, intentional maneuvering of Shylock's case into the penal arena with Thomas Cromwell's reputation for craftiness and brutal punishments under the 1534 Act of Supremacy. Does it not enhance our appreciation of both situations to have this comparison?

On page 130 of *Anne Boleyn*, Cromwell is speaking to the doomed Queen Anne: "The law hath many grounds and positive learnings which are not of the highest rule of reason — which are *legume leges* — yet are learning received, yet with such maxims will the law dispense, rather than crimes and wrongs should be unpunished." This is the opening sentence of Bacon's "Regula 12" in his *Maxims of the Law*![1] This maxim is discussed by legal historical scholar Andrea Padovani and by Prof. Coquillette in his book on Bacon's jurisprudence.[2]

On just page 130 of *Anne Boleyn* alone, the line-by-line references are to these works of Francis Bacon's: *Chudleigh's Case, Gray's Inn Epistle, Case de Rege, Charge upon Commissioners for the Verge, Union of the Laws, Maxims of the Laws,* and Shakespeare's *Henry VIII* and *Henry IV, Part Two.*

In the invaluable appendix to *Anne Boleyn*, there are references to the works of Shakespeare, Greene, Peele, Marlowe, Jonson, Burton, Spenser, Bacon, and the editions used for all 147 pages of the play. According to Elizabeth Gallup, Bacon explained that he had used ciphers in his intelligence work for the Crown for so many years that he had no difficulty in producing such a work. It is a little like writing a research paper, taking a bit of text from here, a bit from there, and making a coherent whole of it.

On page 131, Cromwell ends with these lines: "In treason no witness shall be received upon oath for the party's justification. These be the very words of the civil law which cannot be amended."

"These be" the exact words found in Bacon's "A Preparation for the Union of Laws"[3] and *Maximes of the Law,* "Regula XI"![4]

On page 131 of *Anne Boleyn*, the Queen says to Cromwell, "You know the law. Your exposition hath been most sound." Shylock says these very words to Portia.[5]

---

[1] *Spedding*, VII, p. 358, HathiTrust, https://hdl.handle.net/2027/hvd.32044069750248. Bacon was writing these Maxims in 1596-97. *Spedding*, VII, p. 310.
[2] Andrea Padovani, ch. 2, "The Metaphysical Thought of Late Medieval Jurisprudence," in A Treatise of Legal Philosophy and General Jurisprudence, vol. 7 (Dordrecht, Netherlands: Springer, 2007), pp. 31–78, 31–44, 40; FB, pp. 35-48 et al.
[3] *Spedding*, VII, p. 735, HathiTrust, https://hdl.handle.net/2027/ucl.b3924335.
[4] *Spedding*, VII, p. 357. HathiTrust, https://hdl.handle.net/2027/ucl.b3924335.
[5] *Merchant*, IV, 1, 2179, www.opensourceshakespeare.org.

Cromwell's statement, "It is true I could have wished some abler person had begun," is what Bacon says to the Gray's Inn students in his dedication of "The Arguments of the Law"[1] — a sentiment with which this author can definitely relate. Isn't it funny, though, to put those words in Cromwell's mouth!

Another line in *Anne Boleyn* is, "These things are but toys to come amongst such serious observations." This line is verbatim from Bacon's essay 37, "Of Masques and Triumphs."[2]

In the play, Henry VIII recites an eloquent soliloquy upon seeing his infant daughter Elizabeth for the first time:

> The government of a woman at all times hath been a rare thing,
> and felicity in such a government is rarer still,
> Felicity and long continuance the rarest thing of all.
> Her opening prospects Fortune hath chequer'd with uncertainty.[3]

Five pages or so later, Henry says:

> If all the pens that ever poets held,
> Had fed the feeling of their masters' thoughts,
> And every sweetness that inspir'd their hearts,
> Their minds, and Muses on admir'ed themes,
> If all the heavenly quintessence 'still'd,
> From their immortal flowers of poesy,
> Wherein as in a mirror we perceive,
> The highest reaches of a human wit,
> If these had made one poem's period,
> And all combin'd in beauty's worthiness,
> Yet should there hover in their restless heads,
> One thought, one grace, one wonder, at the least,
> Which into virtue wonder can digest, Ho messenger![4]

If one compares each line in this speech with its source (see appendix to *Anne Boleyn*), one cannot help but be impressed — mind-boggled, even — at the genius of mind which could produce such eloquence for mere normal mortals to decipher.

Spedding could not understand why Bacon had focused on Anne Boleyn so much in his elegy for Queen Elizabeth, *In Felicem Memoriam Elizabethae, Anglicae Regiae*. The state-sanctioned murder of her mother by her father

---

[1] *The Tragedy of Anne Boleyn*, p. 129; *Spedding*, VII, p. 523, HathiTrust, https://hdl.handle.net/2027/ucl.b3924335.

[2] *The Tragedy of Anne Boleyn*, p. 66; *Spedding*, VI, p. 467, HathiTrust, https://hdl.handle.net/2027/ucl.b3618242.

[3] *The Tragedy of Anne Boleyn*, pp. 90-91.

[4] [William Shakespeare et al.?] *The Tragedy of Ann Boleyn*, beginning at line 95.

certainly had affected her greatly in her personal choices which ultimately affected the course of history.

Bacon's "writer's prayer" suggests he used it in leading a writer's group, a "ring" of writers and of poesy. Gratiano spoke of the "posy" (or "poesy") or motto on the ring Nerissa gave him.[1] According to William J. Rolfe, in the First Folio the word was spelled "poesy" only two times when speaking of a motto on a ring: with Gratiano in *Merchant* and when Hamlet says, "Is this a prologue, or the poesy of a ring?"[2] That very line appears also in *The Tragedy of Anne Boleyn*.[3]

Counterargument

Paul Edmonson and Stanley Wells, in *Shakespeare Beyond Doubt, Evidence, Argument, Controversy,* write that Dr. Owen's and Mrs. Gallup's "cipher theories... sounded ridiculous to most."[4] Did he mean, to most Stratfordians? Virtually all "Orthodox" Shakespeare scholars, including Edmonson and Wells, cite William F. and Elizebeth S. Friedman's 1957 book, *The Shakespearean Ciphers Examined*, as authority for putting to rest for evermore any and all claims that there are codes or ciphers in the works of Shakespeare.[5]

Reply

Fairly early on, a cipher in the plays was claimed. Thomas Tennison wrote in *Baconiana*, "The fairest, and most correct Edition of this Book (*de Augmentis*) in Latine, is that in Folio, printed at London, Anno 1623. And whosoever would understand the Lord Bacon's Cypher, let him consult that accurate Edition. For, in some other Editions, which I have perused, the form of the Letters of the Alphabet, in which much of the Mysterie consisteth, is not observed: But the Roman and Italic shapes of them are confounded."[6] Francis

---

[1] *Webster's*, s.v. "posy," "poesy," pp. 766, 776.

[2] *Merchant*, III, 2, 162; Rolfe, *Shakespeare's Comedy of The Merchant of Venice*, p. 164, fn. 146, HathiTrust, https://hdl.handle.net/2027/nyp.33433074919121.

[3] *The Tragedy of Anne Boleyn*, p. 15; see also line 95.

[4] Paul Edmonson and Stanley Wells, *Shakespeare Beyond Doubt, Evidence, Argument, Controversy* (Cambridge: Cambridge University Press, 2013), pp. 27-28, 246. See also William Sherman, "How to Make Anything Signify Anything," *Cabinet Magazine*, no. 40, Winter 2010/11, pp. 1-15, http://www.cabinetmagazine.org/issues/40/sherman.php.

[5] William and Elizebeth Friedman, *The Shakespeare Ciphers Examined* (Cambridge: Cambridge University Press, 1957). See also Samuel Shoenbaum, *Shakespeare's Lives* (Oxford: Clarendon Press, 1991), p. 415. https://books.google.com/books?isbn=0198186185; Helen Hackett, *Shakespeare and Elizabeth, The Meeting of Two Myths* (Princeton: Princeton University Press, 2009), p. 156, 158.

[6] Tennison, Thomas, *Baconiana[...]*, pp. 27-28, Early English Books Online: Text Creation Partnership, http://tei.it.ox.ac.uk/tcp/Texts-HTML/free/A28/A28024.html, also http://name.

Bacon had invented the Bi-Literarie Cipher, a two-letter cipher, based on "a" and "b," upon which binary code modern computer technology and Morse Code is based.[1]

That Francis Bacon wrote in ciphers in his intelligence work, invented the bi-literal cipher, and *could* have written a play in the fashion claimed for *The Tragedy of Anne Boleyn*, the Friedmans have as much as conceded in their book. They did not think, however, that Mrs. Gallup, Dr. Orville Ward Owen, and the team at the Riverside Lab had proven such a cipher by rigorous scientific standards. Their results had not been reproduced by another cryptologist working independently.[2] Their method, said the Friedmans, left too much room for choice. It allowed a decipherer to produce any answer he liked.[3] In their early years in cryptology, the Friedmans had themselves met and worked at the Riverside Lab.

The Friedmans begin the final paragraph of their book with: "It must be remembered that the biliteral cipher is the one reputable system among all those proposed so far in support of anti-Stratfordian theories — that is, it is the only cipher which the professional cryptologist could admit as a valid system in itself. Yet, we think we have shown decisively that it was not used."[4]

Granted, the Friedmans were expert cryptologists who helped to end World War II by decoding enemy messages.[5] That being said, the Friedmans were writing seventy years ago, before the current advancements in computer technology existed. Surely cipher-finding capabilities must have improved since Mrs. Gallup's work was published. A hypothesis is always susceptible of being disproven with new evidence. "Confirmation bias," or finding the result you are seeking, is a problem in *all* scientific research.[6]

---

umdl.umich.edu/A28024.0001.001.

[1] The Friedmans, *The Shakespeare Ciphers Examined*, p. 32.

[2] The Friedmans, pp. 188-287, 287.

[3] The Friedmans, ch. 5, pp. 63-76, 74; ch. 2, "Cryptology as a Science," pp. 15-26, pp. 19-25. On Francis Bacon's ciphers, see also William F. Friedman, lecture 2, "Six Lectures on Cryptology," National Cryptologic School, National Security Agency (1965), pp. 15-37, 30-36, https://www.nsa.gov/news-features/declassified-documents/friedman-documents/assets/files/publications/ACC15281/41785109082412.pdf. For more information on the Friedmans, search "William F. Friedman" at https://www.nsa.gov.

[4] Friedmans, p. 287.

[5] See, e.g., "Release of the William and Elizebeth Friedman Collection" *Crytologic Quarterly*, Center for Cryptologic History 34, no. 1 (2015), https://www.nsa.gov/about/cryptologic-heritage/historical-figures-publications/publications/cryptologic-quarterly/assets/files/cryptologic-quarterly-2015-01.pdf. Seven thousand declassified documents in the "Friedman Collection" were released by the National Security Administration in 2015. See https://archive.org/details/nsa-friedman.

[6] Nassim Nicholas Taleb, ch. 5, "Confirmation Schmonfirmation!" in *The Black Swan, The Impact of the Highly Improbable* (New York: Random House, 2007), pp. 51-61.

However, William Friedman did not say a cipher in the plays was ruled out entirely, only that it had not been proven, according to his exacting scientific standards. He conceded that "the fact that Bacon invented this cipher and described it in such detail lends plausibility to a theory entertained by many persons that Bacon wrote the Shakespeare plays and that he inserted secret messages in those plays by using his cipher."[1]

The Tragedy of Anne Boleyn, though, was not about looking for "secret messages" in the plays as much as it was a treasure hunt among a number of literary works — not just the plays of Shakespeare, and not just the works of Bacon and Shakespeare. Were all those writers in on the game? If there was one mastermind, one would presume it was Bacon. In the end, a lovely work of art was produced by a very unusual method.

Kenneth R. Patton takes the honesty, motivation, and impartiality of the Friedmans to task.[2] Penn Leary's chapter, "Friedman," in his book, *The Cryptographic Shakespeare*, is a good overview, setting out the Friedmans' tests for assessing the scientific validity of a cryptographic system.[3]

Many have been discouraged from looking for ciphers or codes in the works of Shakespeare. The theory and its proponents have been much derided. Many, this author included, do not understand the specific methodology Mrs. Gallup employed. N. B. Cockburn, author of *The Bacon Shakespeare Question, The Baconian Theory Made Sane*, does not believe there are ciphers in the works of Shakespeare.[4] There was a deep interest in cryptology in the seventeenth century, though, as Katherine Ellison describes.[5]

---

[1] The Friedmans, *The Shakespearean Ciphers Examined*, p. 33.

[2] Patton, Kenneth R. www.SirBacon.org Presents *Setting the Record Straight: an Expose of Stratfordian Anti-Baconian Tactics. Book One: The Vindication of William Stone Booth, a Detailed Critical Analysis of Chapter IX: The String Cipher of William Stone Booth in Elizebeth S. and William F. Friedman's The Shakespearean Ciphers Examined*. San Diego: September, 2000. Internet. http://www.sirbacon. org/pattonstrs.htm.

[3] Penn Leary, ch. 7, "Friedman," The Cryptographic Shakespeare, https://www.baconscipher. com/chapter-seven-friedman.

[4] See, e.g., BSQ, ch. 24, "Cryptomania," p. 280.

[5] For example, see Katherine Ellison, "Early Modern Cryptology as Fashionable Reading," *Journal of the Northern Renaissance*, no. 6 (2014), digital only, esp. pars. 15-27 and bibliography for further reading.

Appendix III. "Just Deserts" or "Just Desserts"?

In Latin, *bellaria* means "dessert."[1] A man's "desserts" were his wages, his payment for what his services were worth.[2] "Dessert" was served after the table was cleared: a *mensa secunda*, or "second table."[3] Both meanings of "desserts" come from the same Latin root *deservire*, meaning "to serve."[4] Who among us would not prefer "just dessert" to his "just deserts?" Hamlet, replying to Polonius, said: "God's bodykins, man, much better! Use every man after his desert, and who should 'scape whipping?" (*Hamlet II*, 2, 1601). The Princes of Aragon (*Merchant* III, 9, 1180) and Morocco (*Merchant* II, 7, 1018) each thought they deserved to win Portia, however, their "just deserts" were a fool's head and a skull, respectively.

A search of www.opensourceshakespeare.org brought up 160 uses of "deserve" in thirty-three plays and four sonnets, plus the poems "Passionate Pilgrim," "Rape of Lucrece," and "Venus and Adonis." I found "desert" sixty-eight additional times, adding one new play to the list and five additional sonnets. . My search found no instances of the word "dessert" in Shakespeare. It was a French word in use in 1539, first seen in English around 1600.[5] Bacon had spent time in France in his youth, and he would have been associated with French diplomats at Court.

The word "ambiguous," a useful word for lawyers arguing contract terms, comes from another French word, *ambigu* that was known in the 17th century.

---

[1] See *Cassell's Latin*, p. 26.
[2] *Cassell's Latin*, p. 349.
[3] *Cassell's Latin*, p. 269.
[4] *Cassell's Latin*, p. 65.
[5] Lynn Oliver, "Dessert," Food Timeline Library, http://www.foodtimeline.org/foodfaq7.html.

It referred to the style of serving all the courses at the same time, on the same board, as the Danish do with their smorgasbord.

"Banquet" was the English word for dessert, a light repast of sweets, fruits, and drinks the ancient Romans would have had, following dinner. The word was thought to come from *banc* (perhaps *banquette*, a little bench), the French word for bench which derives from the Germanic *benc*.[1] Charles Mackay, however, suggests it may come from the Keltic *ban* (woman, lady) and *cead* (hard "k," leave or permission), because the women often were invited to join the men for this part of the evening.[2] "The bench" also refers to the judiciary, because English judges sat on benches.

It is thought that the word "bank" derives from the bench the medieval Italian money lender would sit upon when engaged in his business. I believe this word also comes from the German *benc*. There was no similar word in Latin.

The upper classes used special, beautifully decorated wooden trenchers for the serving of cheese and delicacies after dinner.[3] The trenchers, which evolved into wooden "roundels," were served face down. After the dessert was eaten, one would turn over the trencher to recite or act out the verse or poem inscribed on it, in the center or around the rim, sort of like a fortune cookie. Later, the decorations were printed instead of hand-painted, and the practice, now affordable, spread to the middle and merchant classes, ever eager to copy their "betters." The blogger calls the Tudor-into-Elizabethan-and-Jamesian age "one of magnificent subtleties." "Gilded eggs" or "walnuts containing gifts" might be served. Guests loved the idea of being fooled by objects which seemed to be one thing but turned out to be something else.[4] Perhaps *The Merchant of Venice* is like a gilded egg. Today, an "Easter egg" is slang for an intentional inside joke, an idea for which I am indebted to Simon Miles and his talk, again.[5]

---

[1] "Bench," *English Oxford Living Dictionaries*, https://en.oxforddictionaries.com/definition/bench.

[2] Charles Mackay, *A Glossary of Obscure Words and Phrases in Shakespeare and his Contemporaries* (London, 1887), pp. 18-19. https://books.google.ca/books?id=wKXTAAAAMAAJ.

[3] Blog of "Louise," Twenty-first Century Renaissance Printmaker, "Recreating a set of Elizabethan Trenchers: an Introduction" (November 12, 2014), https://21stcenturyrenaissanceprintmaker.wordpress.com/2014/11/12/recreating-a-set-of-elizabethan-trenchers-an-intro./.

[4] Blog of "Louise," citing Bridget Ann Henisch, Fast and Feast: Food in Medieval Society (University Park: Pennsylvania State University Press, 1976). https://books.google.ca/books?id=mIbfAAAAMAAJ.

[5] Simon Miles talk on *The Merchant of Venice*, https://www.youtube.com/watch?v=KcQCljc1Mv8.

Appendix IV. Handwriting on the Wall

Discussion

> It is possible that someday, during rebinding of an old book from Shakespeare's time, one of his manuscript pages might accidentally be discovered under the spine, or glued as reinforcement under one of the binder's boards.[1]

To prove authorship of a writing in a court of law, one would need to submit the best available evidence. We do not have signed manuscripts. We do, arguably, have acrostics embedded in the printed plays.[2] Actually, a buried acrostic might actually be considered more reliable than a printed name. Bacon had experienced the pirated printing of his works.[3] However, the acrostics that have been found in the plays have been discredited by William and Elizebeth Friedman in their 1957 book, *The Shakespearean Ciphers Examined*, although some, including myself, still find William Stone Booth's book, *Subtle Shining Secrecies*, convincing.[4]

---

[1] Andrea Mays, *The Millionaire and the Bard*, p. 26.

[2] See, e.g., Booth, William Stone, *Subtle Shining Secrecies Writ in the Margents of Books* (Boston: Walter H. Baker, 1925), pp. 3-9; *Technique*, pp. 27-50; in *The Merchant of Venice*, pp. 124 to 132, devices ##82 to 92, including INIBUI or INIBUIT on the opening lines of the play ("I or he have suppressed"); pp. 279-282. The techniques include acrostics, mesostics, acro-telestic, telestic, and gallows (French *potens*). Booth, p. 30-31. While the first edition of Bacon's *Essays* had no name on the title page, his name is found in acrostic in the dedication to his brother Anthony Bacon. Booth, p. 32; *Spedding*, VI, p. 523.

[3] Spedding's prefatory remarks to early editions of the *Essays*, *Spedding*, VI, p. 521-523, HathiTrust, https://hdl.handle.net/2027/ucl.b3618242.

[4] For more on ciphers, codes, and acrostics, see infra, appendix 2

In 1921, Amelie Deventer von Kunow wrote, "In general it is demonstrated that there exist no handwritten MSS of the individual plays except the speeches in the Gray's Inn Christmas play of 1595, which were found later in the Northumberland MSS.[1] Giles E. Dawson and Laetitia Kennedy-Skipton concur, with the "possible exception" of the 148 lines of "Hand D" in the play, *The Booke of Sir Thomas More*, first printed in 1844, which are "believed to be Shakespeare's."[2]

In 1924, printer Edward Des Moineaux printed a side-by-side handwriting sample comparing the handwriting of Francis Bacon to that in "Hand D."[3] It is appended herein.

What is interesting is that "striking coincidences" have been found between "the famous three pages in Hand D in the manuscript *Booke of Sir Thomas More*, the only document of any length in what is believed to be Shakespeare's handwriting" and the only quarto ever made of *Henry IV, Part Two*, printed by Valentine Simmes, entered in the Stationer's Register 1600.

> What matters is that, from a whole series of unequivocal signs —
> such as permissive stage directions, the presence of ghost characters,
> peculiar spellings, etc. — it appears that Quarto was set from authorial
> manuscript (often called 'foul papers'), and it should therefore reflect
> Shakespeare's original writing and composition more closely than
> most other texts in the canon.... The quarto therefore offers a rare
> opportunity of speculating on Shakespeare's spelling habits, and its
> evidence is reinforced by some striking coincidences....[4]

Stratfordian Shakespeare scholar Stanley Wells has "offered into evidence" ten paleographers to corroborate his statement that "Hand D" is

---

[1] Amelie Deventer von Kunow, *Francis Bacon, Last of the Tudors*, p. 87. https://www.sirbacon.org/vonkunow.html.

[2] Giles E. Dawson and Laetitia Kennedy-Skipton, "Survival of Manuscripts," Elizabethan Handwriting: 1500-1650: A Manual (New York: W. W. Norton, 1966), https://shakespeareauthorship.com/survival.html.

[3] Edward J. Des Moineaux, *Manuscript Said to be Handwriting of William Shakespeare Identified as Penmanship of Another Person. Mystery of "Sir Thomas More Document" Unravelled, an Entirely New Phase of the Baconian-Shakespeare Controversy* (Los Angeles: printed for the author by Phillips Printing, 1924), pp. 1-31; "Directory of 'Sir Thomas More, Document Unravelled.'" SirBacon.org Presents Directory of Sir Thomas More, Documents Unraveled, by Edwin J. Des Moineaux, www.SirBacon.org/stmcontents.htm; Walter Saunders, "The Northumberland Manuscript and a Remarkable Discovery by Simon Miles," 2007, http://www.sirbacon.org/nmsaunders.htm.

[4] George Melchiori, ed., "Textual Analysis," *The Second Part of Henry IV* (Cambridge: Cambridge University Press. 1989), pp. 189-203, 189 (noting, however, some unreliability in the text). See also Grace Iopolo, "Manuscripts Containing Texts by Shakespeare," in *The Cambridge Guide to the Worlds of Shakespeare*, ed. by B. Smith (Cambridge: Cambridge University Press, 2016), p. 131-132.

"Shakespeare's" own autograph.[1] He and ten others makes eleven, sufficient for "proof" by archaic wager of law (That is a joke).

But, by "Shakespeare," does he mean William Shaxpere the Stratford man or the "real author" who has taken Shakespeare as a pen name? The problem is that the six signatures which purport to be Shaxpere's do not constitute a very good writing sample for comparison. They do not even match themselves. Granted, they are the only writing examples which exist for him. They all date from the last four years of his life, 1612–1616. Some or all may have beem made by law clerks.[2] "Signatures, even six of them, are not reliable in comparisons of this sort because they tend to be stylized and formal, bearing little observable relationship to a man's ordinary working hand."[3] Independent Shakespearean researcher Diana Price concurs."[4]

There is one other handwriting sample which should be mentioned. In 1988, a handwritten scene that is thought to be an early version of the robbery scene, Act II, Scene 1 of Shakespeare's *The First Part of King Henry IV*, was found in "binder's waste," in an old copy of Homer's *Odyssea* (Geneva, 1586). The fifty-seven-line fragment was offered for sale by Sotheby's, July 21–22, 1992. At the request of the late British barrister Francis Carr, forensic handwriting expert Maureen Ward-Gandy compared the handwriting in that play scene fragment to the handwriting of Francis Bacon, as well as to that of twenty-nine other seventeenth-century persons.[5]

With Ms. Ward-Gandy's permission, Lawrence Gerald (SirBacon.org) provided a copy of the report to me for inclusion in this book. It is appended herein.

In her 25-page report, Ms. Ward-Gandy concluded that it was "highly probable" that the writing in the Henry IV handwriting sample was Francis

---

[1] See Stanley Wells and Gary Taylor, *William Shakespeare: A Textual Companion* (New York: W. W. Norton, 1997, corrected from 1987 ed.), p. 125.

[2] Alfred W. Pollard, W. W. Greg, and E. Maunde Thompson, *Shakespeare's Hand in the Play of Sir Thomas More* (New York: Cambridge University Press, 2010, first pub. 1967), p. 71.

[3] Giles E. Dawson and Lisa Kennedy-Skipton, "The Survival of Manuscripts," from their book, Elizabethan Handwriting, 1500-1650: A Manual (New York: W. W. Norton, 1966), http://shakespeareauthorship.com/survival.html.

[4] Diana Price, "Hand D and Shakespeare's Unorthodox Literary Paper Trail," *Journal of Early Modern Studies* 5 (2016), pp. 329-352. DOI: http://dx.doi.org/10.13128/JEMS-2279-7149-18095.

[5] Arthur Freeman, "The Tapster Manuscript: an Analogue of Shakespeare's 'Henry the Fourth Part One,'" *English Manuscript Studies 1100-1700*, 6, ed. by Peter Beal and Jeremy Griffiths (1997): pp. 93-105, 93, 99, 104; Heather Purchase, "Writing's on the Wall for Shakespeare," *London Evening Standard* (July 30, 1992), http://www.sirbacon.org/links/handwriting1.html; http://www.sirbacon.org/links/gandy.htm.

Bacon's.[1] A second graphologist concurred.[2] This evidence has never been refuted. Orthodox Shakespeare scholars have acknowledged the existence of the manuscript fragment. [3]

In 1997, Arthur Freeman, a bookseller, examined the manuscript and provided his observations. In the scene, a Tapster in an Inn is telling two guests how they can rob a patron of his gold. The guests offer the Tapster a pipeful of tobacco, which he has never tried. He takes a puff and chokes on it.

Freeman compared the handwriting in the manuscript to "a large number of literary hands of the period, including (I think) every named professional dramatist whose penmanship survives, and nearly all playhouse scripts—many in multiple hands—without finding a credible match." Francis Bacon is, of course, not generally thought of as a dramatist. Freeman does not tell us whether he compared the manuscript to a sample of Bacon's handwriting.

In "four short lines of notes, partly torn away in a minute script at the top left-hand corner of the recto, written vertically and apparently under the beginning of the dramatic text...," Freeman read, "with some difficulty and doubt," these words: "...or fiddle/fiddle E/Italian Catlins/mysteria.verbi ad popul[um?]." Catlins are "fine lute strings" (cat-gut?).[4] The name "Isaac" appears twice at the bottom of the page. The words "care I had and labor" are written in another hand, along the top right-hand edge of the "recto" side of the manuscript. Richard Proudfoot observed that the manuscript resembles in some ways that of a c. 1611 Gray's Inn play, *Tom a Lincoln*, in that both plays have stage directions "boxed," with no dividing lines between speeches.[5] The

---

[1] See Heather Purchase, "Writing's on the Wall for Shakespeare," *London Evening Standard* (July 30, 1992), http://www.sirbacon.org/links/handwriting1.html; http://www.sirbacon.org/links/gandy.htm.

[2] http://www.sirbacon.org/graphics/sothebys.jpg.

[3] See, e.g., Alan Stewart, *Shakespeare's Letters* (Oxford: Oxford University Press, 2008), pp. 97, 331-332; Graham Holderness, *Textual Shakespeare: Writing and the Word* (Hertfordshire: University of Hertfordshire, 2003), pp. 151-152, https://books.google.ca/books?isbn=1902806212; *King Henry IV Part 1*, third series, ed. by David Scott Kastan (London: Arden Shakespeare, 2002), pp. 349-353, 352 on M. Ward-Gandy; Graham Holderness, Bryan Loughrey, and Andrew Murphy, "What's the matter? Shakespeare and textual theory," in *Textual Practice*, ed. by Lindsey Smith, 9:1 (Taylor and Francis e-book Spring 1995), pp. 87-113, 98-99; see also Grace Iopolo, "Some Recent Dramatic Manuscript Studies," in Leeds Barroll, ed., *Shakespeare Studies* 30, (Cranbury NJ: Associated University Press, 2010), pp. 129-130. But see Barry R. Clarke, *The Shakespeare Puzzle: A Non-Esoteric Baconian Theory*," (2010 online), pp. 150-151; http://barryispuzzled.com/shakpuzz.pdf; "Police and Home Office Handwriting Expert Thought it was in Francis Bacon's Hand," http://barryispuzzled.com/HenryMS02.pdf.

[4] Arthur Freeman, "The Tapster Manuscript: an Analogue of Shakespeare's '*Henry the Fourth Part One*,'" *English Manuscript Studies 1100-1700*, vol. 6, ed. by Peter Beal and Jeremy Griffiths (1997): pp. 93-105, 100.

[5] Freeman, "The Tapster Manuscript," p. 100.

---

manuscript is currently in the Schoyen Collection of Martin Schoyen, Oslo and London, catalogued as Manuscript 1627.[1]

I am not aware that any scholar has attempted to solve the mystery of the mysterious words "mysteria verbi." Here is a possibility:

In Latin, *mysteria* means "mysteries, secrets, especially of worship." In a Google search, *mysteria verbi. ad popul[um]* shows up in theological settings. The first two words and the last two words, with words in between, were used as part of an epitaph on the tombstone of a seventeenth-century Scottish minister, Robert Langlands, d. 1696.[2] St. Thomas Aquinas used *mysteria verbi* when referring to the mystery of the Incarnation of Christ, the "Word made flesh."

In a letter to Januarius, St. Augustine (A.D. 354–430 wrote *ad mysteria verbi Dei, similitudinum signa.* He was discussing how signs from God's creation (the visible, temporal world) could be used, through the "eloquence of teaching," to "turn" listeners toward the invisible, eternal, incorporeal things of God.[3] St. Augustine was one of the "three great Late Antique Latin Fathers" who were "against the pagan world of fiction," along with Ambrose (ca. 340–397) and Jerome (ca. 347–420). St. Augustine, who had loved the theatre in his youth, disparaged its "depraved pleasures" in his later years.[4] And yet, he realized the educational potential of signs and symbols used in the Bible itself, such as doves and serpents in Matt. 10:16.[5]

---

[1] "Shakespeare, Henry IV, Part 1," The Schoyen Collection, https://www.schoyencollection. com/literature-collection/modern-literature-collection/shakespeare-henry-fourth-4-ms-1627; "Play of Thieves and a Gullible Tapster," https://www.lostplays.org/lpd/ Play_of_Thieves_and_a_Gullible_Tapster (with excerpt from: Arthur Freeman, "An Analogue of Shakespeare's *Henry the Fourth Part One*"[...](website maintained by David McInnes, University of Melbourne, last updated 5/20/16); Arthur Freeman, "The Tapster Manuscript[...], pp. 93-105.

[2] *Collections of Epitaphs and Monumental Inscriptions: Chiefly in Scotland* (Glasgow, 1834), pp. 253-254 ("...a faithful preacher, opening mysteries; not slothful, but was teaching ev'rywhere His people, with sedulity and care...." This sounds like a quotation. Tracing it to its source might prove fruitful. The marginal words written in another hand on the binder's waste fragment were "care I had and labor.").

[3] Anders Cullhed, "The Figures of the Spirit," *The Shadow of Creusa, Negotiating Fictionality in Late Antique Latin Literature* (Berlin: Walter De Gruyter, 2015, e-pub. www.jouve.com), II.3, pp. 207-262, 210, citing St. Augustine's letter to Januarius, 55.7.12-13, 55.6.11. See also pp. 211-213; "Letters of St. Augustine," transl. by J. G. Cunningham, no. 55.6.11, 55.7.12, 13, *Nicene and Post-Nicene Fathers*, vol. 1, first series, ed. by Philip Schaff (Buffalo, 1887), rev. and ed. for New Advent by Kevin Knight, http://www.newadvent.org/fathers/1102055.htm.

[4] St. Augustine, *Confessions*, book III, 2.2-4; book VIII.10.23, transl. by J.G. Pilkington, *Nicene and Post-Nicene Fathers*, vol. 1, first series, edited by Philip Schaff (Buffalo, 1887), rev. and ed. by Kevin Knight, http://www.newadvent.org/fathers/110103.htm; St. Augustine, ch. 29, *On Christian Doctrine*, transl. by James Shaw, *Nicene and Post-Nicene Fathers*, vol. 2, first series, ed. by Philip Schaff. (Buffalo, 1887.), rev. and ed. for New Advent by Kevin Knight, http://www. newadvent.org/fathers/12021.htm.

[5] Cullhed, pp. 211-213. See also ch. 1, "Fictionality: Theoretical Considerations" which discusses *Hamlet.*

Ad popul could be short for a thought Bacon once expressed: "Everything should be more fully explained, and pointed out, as it were with the finger, to the capacity of the people."[1]

In Bacon's beautiful proem to the planned treatise "Of the Interpretation of Nature," he explained that he hoped by his writings to help men improve the state of their souls.[2] Elsewhere he wrote, "Did not one of the fathers in great indignation call poesy 'vinum daemonum,' because it increaseth temptations, perturbations, and vain opinions?"[3] Is there not morally permissible and justifiable fictive art?

R. E. Hughes described how Bacon's theory of education shows evidence of the influence of St. Augustine.[4] Bacon based his argument that man has free will on St. Augustine, following his line of reasoning over Calvin's.[5] Bacon read St. Augustine.[6] Bacon, too, was concerned with the mysteries of divine wisdom.[7]

What does all this have to do with a scene in which a tapster, or drawer of ale, is helping robbers plan the robbery of a guest? The author of this draft may have been having similar thoughts, asking himself whether this particular application of his art was relevant to his higher purposes.

In the *First Part of King Henry IV*, Act II, Scene 1, the Tapster of the early analog scene has been replaced by the Chamberlain. In Act II, Scene 4, the "puny drawer," Francis, is introduced, perhaps in place of the Tapster.

Might not "puny" signal "pun?" The beer would have been kept in the cellar. Thus, this Francis was analogous to the ancient Roman "cellarius," or "promus," who brought up the provisions from the cellar. St. Augustine said Creation was a "storehouse of figures for presentation of the mysteries."[8] The Promus was, of course, Bacon's private literary notebook, his "storehouse" of literary expressions, many of which are found in the Shakespeare plays.

---

[1] Aphorism 68, '*Example of a Treatise on Universal Justice*,' (transl.) *De Augmentis*, viii, *Spedding*, V, pp. 88-110, 102-103, HathiTrust, https://hdl.handle.net/2027/ucl.b3618241, mentioned infra, ch. 4.

[2] *Spedding*, X, p. 84, HathiTrust, https://hdl.handle.net/2027/ien.35558005316951.

[3] *Spedding*, III, p. 440, HathiTrust, https://hdl.handle.net/2027/ucl.b3618240.

[4] See R. E. Hughes, "Francis Bacon, The Renaissance State, and St. Augustine: A Chapter in the History of Education," *History of Education Journal* 9, no. 2 (Winter, 1958), pp. 32-36, JSTOR, http://www.jstor.org/stable/3692579.

[5] See, e.g., Steven Matthews, *Theology and Science in the Thought of Francis Bacon* (Aldershot: Ashgate, 2008)

[6] For other references to Bacon and St. Augustine, see *Spedding*, VII, p.. 227; *Spedding*, VIII, pp. 211-214; Montagu, II, p. 437 ("Of a Holy War"); *The Essays or Counsels, Civil and Moral, of Francis Bacon*, edited by Samuel Harvey Reynolds (Oxford, 1890), pp. xxxi; 10; 26; 77; 343 (on poetry) (editor's notes).

[7] For example, see *Spedding*, V, p. 114. See ch. 13, infra, for the full quotation (side bar).

[8] Cullhed, *The Shadow of Creusa*, p. 211.

"To draw or draft" also means "to write" and "of a hound, to attract game by the scent, and to approach the game cautiously after pointing." Was Francis the puny drawer a hint?

In his 1997 article, Freeman notes Shakespeare's "notorious refusal to mention smoking tobacco in all his extent work."[1] In the "tapster manuscript," the robbers offer the Tapster a smoke of tobacco, which he takes, and chokes, comically. Peter Dawkins discusses how Shakespeare meant "tobacco" when he spoke of writing in a "noted weed," under which he hid his authorship. The letters "bacco" hint at Bacon. "Weed" meant both a garment and an herbaceous plant.[2]

Perhaps one reason this draft scene was not used was because it portrayed smoking. Bacon had written, "The use of tobacco is growing greatly and conquers men with a certain secret pleasure, so that those who have once become accustomed thereto can later hardly be restrained therefrom."[3] However, he was not vehemently against tobacco smoking. He dealt with tobacco as a business interest and allowed that, mixed with other herbs, a small amount of tobacco might even be beneficial.[4]

Perhaps, for him, the theatre gave as much "addictive" pleasure as tobacco gave to others, too much to give it up entirely. And yet, his writings on poetry are witness to an ambivalence about its worth and place in his schema of knowledge.[5]

In Shakespeare's plays, there is no mention of St. Augustine of Hippo, but Queen Hippolyta is a character in *Midsummer Night's Dream*, thought to have been written in 1595–1596. Bacon tells us in his elegy to her that she read St. Augustine. "In the reading of the Scriptures, and the writings of the fathers, especially of Saint Augustine, she was very frequent; she composed certain prayers herself on emergent occasions." "Emergent" is an interesting word.[6] It was in those prayers that she thanked God for her children.[7] On the other

---

[1] Freeman, p. 103.

[2] Sonnet 76, line 1056; see also *Romeo and Juliet* V, 1, 2846; Peter Dawkins, *The Shakespeare Enigma*, ch. 8, "The Great Artist," p. 223

[3] 'History of Life and Death,' transl., *Spedding*, V, p. 265 (*Montagu*, III, p. 491-492).

[4] For other references to Bacon and tobacco, see *Montagu*, III, pp. 87, 179 (tobacco business), 105, 109, 122; *Montagu*, II, pp. 117, 127).

[5] Robert Schuler, "Francis Bacon and Scientific Poetry," *Transactions of the American Philosophical Society* 82, no. 2 (1992): pp. 1-65, 8-15, JSTOR, http://www.jstor.org/stable/3231921; Reynolds, notes to *Essays*, p. 343.

[6] *Montagu*, I, p. 398.

[7] In Queen Elizabeth's book of devotions, she had written a prayer, in French, in which she gave God undying thanks for "having done me the honor of being a mother and nurse to thy dear children." She asked God to "Preserve then the mother and the children whom thou hast given her for the good of thy poor church." William P. Haugaard explains that she was seeing herself as the mother of her nation. William P. Haugaard, "Elizabeth Tudor's Book of

hand, Francis himself plainly states: the Queen "left no issue of her own."[1] Where not all the evidence fits the dogma, there is a paradox. Perhaps Bacon would take this matter out of the court of public opinion. However, in the matter of Shakespeare's authorship, the court of reason ought to hold sway over the court of blind faith. While the Stratfordians may continue to hope evidence will turn up to prove their case,[2] no court of reason can afford to ignore competent evidence that disproves it.

Exhibit List

1. Six signatures purporting to be those of William Shaxpere, claimed to be those of William Shakespeare. From Des Moineaux.

2. Fragment of the manuscript of the play "Sir Thomas More" attributed to William Shakespeare (commonly known as "Hand D"), and "The Fragment Deciphered," a readable transcript.

3. Private Report of Maureen Ward-Gandy, forensic document and handwriting specialist. "Elizabethan Era Writing Comparison for Identification of Common Authorship. For Francis Carr. Originally examined 24 July 1992. Reviewed for Mr. Lawrence Gerald 2 July 1994. Published with permission of Maureen Ward-Gandy and Lawrence Gerald, 25 pages. Redacted.

Devotions: A Neglected Clue to the Queen's Life and Character," *The Sixteenth Century Journal* 12, no. 2 (Summer, 1981), pp. 79-106, 96 97, 99, 102, JSTOR, http://www.jstor.org/stable/2539502.

[1] 'In Felicem Memoriam,' *Spedding*, VI, p. 310, HathiTrust, https://hdl.handle.net/2027/ucl.b3618242.

[2] See, e.g., Robert Gore-Langton,"The Campaign to Prove Shakespeare Didn't Exist," *Newsweek*, 12/26/14. Retrieved from *Stage Voices*, 1/1/2015, http://www.stagevoices.com/stage_voices/2015/01/the-campaign-to-prove-shakespeare-didnt-exist-.html.

Signatures

The signatures below are said to be those of William Shaxpere, claimed to be "the" Shakespeare.

They are reproduced from *Manuscript said to be Handwriting of William Shakespeare Identified as Penmanship of Another Person, Mystery of "Sir Thomas More" Document Unravelled*, which appears on the following pages.[1]

---

[1] Printed for Edwin J. Des Moineaux, the author, Los Angeles, 1924, pp. 7-8. At Sir Francis Bacon's New Advancement of Learning, http://www.sirbacon.org/stmcontents.htm. See also Ilya Gililov, *The Shakespeare Game, The Mystery of the Great Phoenix* (New York: Algora, 2003), pp. 111-114.

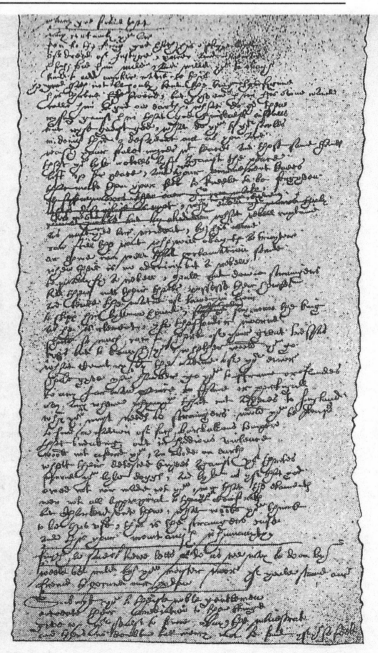

Fragment of manuscript of the play "Sir Thomas More." now Harlein MS. No. 7368, in the British Museum, claimed by some controversialists to be in the handwriting of Will Shakespeare of Stratford-on-Avon.

THE FRAGMENT DECIPHERED

marry god forbid that

nay certainly yo^u ar
for to the king god hath his offyc lent
of dread of Iustice, power and Comaund
hath bid him rule, and willd yo^u to obay
and to add ampler matie to this
he (god) hath not (le) souly lent the king his figure
his throne (hys) & sword, but gyven him his owne name
calls him a god on earth, what do yo^u then
rysing against him that god himsealf enstalls
but ryse against god, what do yo^u to yor sowles
in doing this o desperat (ar) as you are.
wash youre foule mynds w^t tears and those same hande
that yo^u lyke rebells lyft against the peace
lift vp for peace, and your vnreuerent knees
(that) make them your feet to kneele to be forgyven
(is safer warrs, then euer yo^u can make)
                              (in in to yor obedience) s
(whose discipline is ryot; why euen yor (warre) hurly)
        tell me but this
(cannot pceed but by obedienc) what rebell captaine
as mutynes ar incident, by his name
can still the rout who will obay (th) a traytor
or howe can well that pclamation sounde
when ther is no adicion but a rebell
to quallyfy a rebell, youle put downe straingers
kill them cutt their throts possesse their howses
and leade the matie of lawe in liom
                        (alas alas)
to slipp him lyke a hound; (saying) say nowe the king
as he is clement, yf thoffendor moorne
shoold so much com to short of your great trespas
as but to banysh yo^u, whether woold yo^u go.
what Country by the nature of yor error
shoold gyve you harber go yo^u to ffraunc or flanders
to any Iarman pvince, (to) spane or portigall
nay any where (why yo^u) that not adheres to Ingland
why yo^u must neede be straingers, would yo^u be pleasd
to find a nation of such barbarous temper
that breaking out in hiddious violence
woold not afoord yo^u, an abode on earth
whett their detested knyves against yor throtes
spume yo^u lyke dogge, and lyke as yf that god

owed not nor made not yo^u, nor that the elamente,
but Charterd vnto them, what woold yo^u thinck
wer not all appropriat to (ther) yor Comforte.
to be thus vsd, this is the straingers case
and this your mountanish inhumanyty.
fayth a saies trewe letts us do as we may be doon by
weele be ruld by yo^u master moor yf youle stand our
freind to pcure our pdon

Submyt yo to theise noble gentlemen
entreate their mediation to the kinge
gyve vp yor sealf to forme obay the maiestrate
and thers no doubt, but mercy may be found yf yo^u seek

ELIZABETHAN ERA
WRITING COMPARISON
FOR
IDENTIFICATION OF
"COMMON AUTHORSHIP"

ELIZABETHAN ERA
WRITING COMPARISON
FOR
IDENTIFICATION OF
"COMMON AUTHORSHIP"

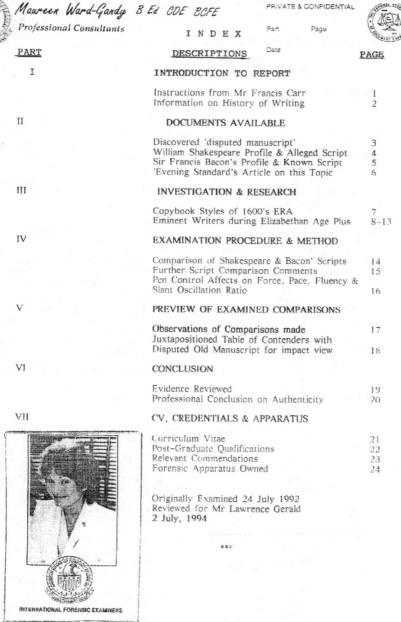

Maureen Ward-Gandy B Ed CDE BCFE

Professional Consultants

PRIVATE & CONFIDENTIAL

I N D E X

Part   Page

Originally Examined 24 July 1992
Reviewed for Mr Lawrence Gerald
2 July, 1994

***

INTERNATIONAL FORENSIC EXAMINERS

Registered Business as required by Section 20 of the Companies Act 1981

249

**FORENSIC DOCUMENT &
HANDWRITING SPECIALISTS**

Maureen Ward-Gandy B Ed CDE BCFE

FSBT FABFE NADE NFC RMGA
Professional Consultants

PRIVATE & CONFIDENTIAL

SHAKESPEARE vs. BACON 1992

MS DALYA ALBERGE

FORENSIC WRITING REPORT:
Submitted as evidence for:

COMPARISON OF ELIZABETHAN
WRITING TO ESTABLISH COMMON
AUTHORSHIP LIKELIHOOD

FOR THE "INDEPENDENT"

Case no:
Court: (Via Francis Carr)

AUTHENTICITY OF DISPUTED HANDWRITING

Mr Francis Carr first wrote to ask if I would compare two exemplars
of writing from the Elizabethan Age to assess if they were of a
common authorship

He did not reveal the identity until he telephoned in response to
my reply to his letter; my reply enclosed evidence of my Law Society and Lord Chancellor connections for fee regulation, and my
forensic equipment for verifying authenticity scientifically if
the writing were original: With original writing the pen flow,
number of pen lifts and variances of stroke can be finely defined
and add credibility to the personal professional opinion

After a discussion over the telephone, it was established that
the writing I had given a cursive glance to before replying, was
suspected to be of Francis Bacon rather than William Shakespeare

On Wednesday 23rd July, The Independent newspaper journalist called
regarding the above matter and wanted a more definite opinion, and
asked if I had compared the writing with other samples of that Era
as Sotherbys had declared it to be typical of Elizabethan writing

After promising to make a fuller investigation; I searched through
my writing collection and reference books for evidence of the Era
and famous writers involved with the writing of those times

Also searching for more writing of Francis Bacon and William Shakespeare for further scrutiny and main style comparisons

There were similarities and differences as in all comparisons, but
some peculiarities of style recurred more often in the Francis
Bacon known writing and the 'Disputed' script, than from comparison of William Shakespeare's writing and the 'Disputed' script:

It must be noted that the 'Disputed' script was not clear owing to
parchment age and blurred photocopy, but the small, angular middle
zone and extra long and heavy DOMINANT downstrokes, especially 'f'
in Francis Bacon & the 'Disputed' writing were very similar: The
fact that Bacon's writing was more carefully penned, and Shakespeare's
known writing and the 'disputed' were rapidly drafted, made parallels
more definite—My findings are presented

FSBT (Dip) MRMG (Dip) AHAF
(Registered with the British Law Society as Handwriting Expert)

National
Forensic
Center

Part I   Page 2

Date   July 1992

FORENSIC WRITING REPORT: COMPARISON OF ELIZABETHAN   INDEPENDENT
WRITING FOR COMMON
AUTHORSHIP

CASE NUMBER: INFORMATION:

HISTORIC PREVIEW OF HANDWRITING EXPERTISE

As with fingerprints, no two different person's handwriting samples are
identical: Encyclopaedia Britannica claims that the chance of parallel
handwriting from two people is ONE CHANCE IN EIGHTY-TWO MILLION without doubt,
and during my 25 years experience in analysing, examining and comparing writing, I have not found any two samples exactly the same

Resemblances occur where writers have followed precisely a copybook style
taught in their country or school, but there are always individual peculiarities of pen strokes which make one person's writing distinguishable from
another's, making the writing recognisable when the style becomes familar

Whenever signatures are made, they are normally faster than the written text
of letters or documents, and often are illegible: As one person signing
several times at one time can have natural VARIANCES in their formation
of name letters, it is more suspect of tracing if an absolute 'match'
is found, although there is always an involuntary or automatic style charac-
teristic in everyone's writing of which, even the writer may not be aware

When a person tries to DISGUISE his writing, the commonest change is slant,
yet slant is the first noticeable change normally found when writing is
affected by mood, health or circumstances at the time of writing: Spacing
between letters, words, lines, baseline evenness and area and strength of
pen pressure are the most identifiable aspects of writing, and they change
least of all with changes of the mind and body: Size of writing changes in
cases of ill health, ageing, stress and influence of alcohol or drugs: The
rhythm and pen flow varies according to circumstances and mood very quickly

The actual 'motor action' of writing appeals to some from infancy, whilst it
remains a laborious, tedious task to others for ever, unless help is found:
(This does not necessarily indicate a brighter mind with appealing script);
the mind with rapid thought cannot move at the slower pace of the hand, so
illegibility is more often in intellectuals (remember the Doctor's prescrip-
tions), and most people find they can write more fluently at some times than
others: When children are taught to write and reach the 'cursive' stage,
they are encouraged to 'join their letters' in a complete word before adding
the diacritics and punctuations; some start early adding them before the end

As each child matures his handwriting becomes more flowing as he develops
individual pen movements of his own; as a former school teacher, I soon
recognised the author of unnamed work, even of school wall graffiti and
suspect excuse notes for absence: Lifting a pen remains an involuntary act
and the omitting of diacritics or stopping as the word progresses to add a
dot or dash affects the style and speed of all writing: Each movement makes
the spontaneous writing into the writer's unique style: Hence the amateur
forger has little chance when faced with an excellent Forensic Writing Expert,
but the genius forger could be a challenge and foreign styles need studying too

This particular case requires the study of writing in the Elizabethan Era and
consideration for the general style used not just in England, but in Europe
as many formations are similar to writing I have studied of Italian, Spanish
and French forms of earlier Centuries; and thus a finer perception can be drawn

FORENSIC WRITING REPORT **AUTHENTICITY** DISPUTED SCRIPT

DOCUMENTS EXAMINED (Shakespeare or Bacon?)

OLD MANUSCRIPT DISCOVERY   DISPUTED AUTHORSHIP

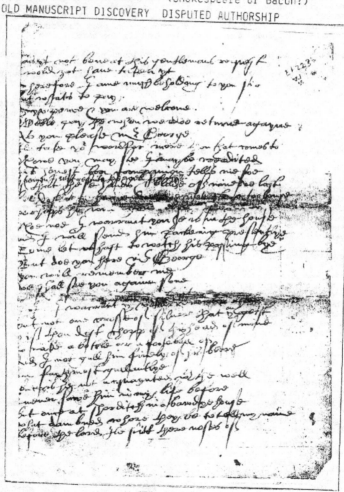

Maureen Ward-Gandy
Professional Consultants

Part III Page 4

July 1992

COMPARISON OF ALLEGED & KNOWN GENUINE

SHAKESPEARE, William (1564–1616), English dramatist and poet, was born at Stratford-on-Avon, Warwickshire, son of John Shakespeare, a glover and husbandman, and Mary Arden, of an ancient family

WILLIAM SHAKESPEARE. *The frontispiece to the folio of 1623 engraved by Martin Droeshout, probably an authentic portrait. (By courtesy of the National Portrait Gallery.)*

of well-to-do farmers. John Shakespeare was a local burgess from 1557 and rose to be bailiff (i.e. mayor) in 1568. From 1576, however, his position much declined: he may (discreetly) have been a Catholic recusant. William was probably educated at the Stratford grammar school and shortly after November 1582 married Anne Hathwey or Hathaway, then aged twenty-six. The next years are obscure, but by the late 1580s he was probably working somewhere in the London theatre and by 1592 he was known as an actor who had successfully tried his hand at writing plays or at adapting them. During the plague years of 1592–4, acting ceased in London and he was probably in the personal service of Henry Wriothesley, earl of Southampton, to whom he dedicated his two long narrative poems *Venus and Adonis* (1593) and *The Rape of Lucrece* (1594). At the subsequent reorganisation of the acting companies, he became a leading member of the company of the (Lord) 'Chamberlain's Men', after

BELOW RIGHT: Known signatures of William Shakespeare

SHAKESPEARE, William 1564–1616. English dramatist and poet. The most famous name in English literature. Autographically, it must be said, Shakespeare is very unsatisfactory! Here shown are the only *two of six* extant signatures fully accepted as genuine. Shakespeare's autograph has been frequently forged, in particular by William Ireland (1777–1835).

Trembling signature

BELOW: Last Will & Testament

LEFT: Allegedly believed manuscript (extract) by William Shakespeare (?)

NB: The signatures are so unstable, they do not bear any resemblance to the rest of writing on this page nor to DISPUTED SCRIPT

253

Maureen Ward-Gandy B Ed CDE BCFE

Professional Consultants

Registered with The British Law Society as
Forensic Handwriting / Document Expert

AUTHENTICITY DISPUTED SCRIPT

FORENSIC WRITING REPORT:

DOCUMENTS EXAMINED

Bacon: the focus of a
50-year controversy

Sir Francis Bacon was
a renowned very clever
gentleman of substance
& talented academic:

He was popular in some
Court Circles

His wide travels &
activity in Politics
enhanced his image &
insight into Humanity: A much more
likely author of the alleged Shakespeare Works of Art: Perhaps he used
a pseudonym for self-security as some
parts were considered treasonable kind

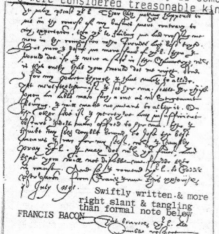

Swiftly written & more
right slant & tangling
than formal note below

FRANCIS BACON

BACON, Francis, 1st Baron Verulam and Viscount St Albans (1561–1626), English statesman,
essayist and philosopher, was the youngest son of Sir
Nicholas Bacon (q.v.), lord keeper. A member of Parliament, he became confidential adviser to the earl of
Essex, Queen Elizabeth's favourite. One of his essays,
published after the execution of Essex, and thoroughly
edited by the queen and her council before being
printed, endeavoured to remove popular misgivings
regarding the queen's conduct in the Essex affair.
Knighted by King James, Bacon became attorney-
general in 1613 and as such was closely associated with
the struggle between Coke and Ellesmere. He was
appointed lord chancellor five years later, introducing many important reforms in the procedure of the
chancery, and by 1620 had been created Viscount
St Albans. In the same year he was tried by his peers
on charges of bribery, convicted and fined £40,000,
excluded from court and all public offices and sent to
the Tower. The king, however, remitted the fine and
ordered his release from the Tower after four days. He
devoted his remaining years to writing literary, philosophical and legal works.

His first *Essays*, only ten in number (published 1597,
with *The Colours of Good and Evil*, a subtle 'art of persuasion'), were little more than jottings from his commonplace books arranged into some sort of order.
They well illustrate the contemporary vogue for a
terse prose style, imitating Seneca (q.v.). In the second
edition (1612) the original essays were expanded,
especially with anecdotes and witty remarks, and
thirty new and rather less terse pieces were added.
The most informal (e.g. 'Of Masks and Triumphs', 'Of
Gardens') occur chiefly in the full edition of 1625.
Bacon's gift for the illuminating phrase and, notably,
metaphor merely reflect the precision and insight of
his mind and his immense knowledge of men. His
wisdom, though, had its limits: it is essentially practical. The *Essays* are written (like Elyot's *Boke of the
Governour*, or even *The Prince* of Machiavelli, qq.v.) as
advice for a monarch; their concern is constantly with
expediency and they reflect the preoccupation with
material advantage which may be traced also in his
scientific work.

His two great philosophical works are *The Advancement of Learning* (1605) and *Novum Organum* (1620). His
aim was to be the architect from whose plans men
might build a vast edifice of exact, scientific knowledge,
and for this purpose he laid down principles of inductive reasoning and scientific method, based upon observation, the study of nature, the accumulation of
instances and experimental verification. He held the
aim of knowledge to be not empty speculation but the
improvement of man's lot. In all this he marks a re-
action against Scholastic learning, with its verbal and
academic disputations; the Baconian method, as it is
called, has become the basis of modern scientific
achievement.

In his *Novum Organum* or 'New Instrument of Knowledge', Bacon describes what he calls 'the Idols of the
Mind', i.e. tendencies in the mind to false beliefs.
There are four such idols: (1) Idols of the Tribe, prej-
udices and wishful thinking inherent in human nature;
(2) Idols of the Den, tendencies in a person due to his
individual character, temperament, or background;
(3) Idols of the Market-place, false beliefs due to the
abuse of words or confused definitions of terms; (4)
Idols of the Theatre, blind adherence to some traditional system of thought or simply to authority in
general.

Legal works which appeared before his death include
De Sapientia Veterum, *The Maxims of Law*, *The Uses of
Law* and the *Instauratio*.

Maureen Ward-Gandy B Ed CDE BCFE

Professional Consultants

Part III Page 6

EVENING STANDARD" NEWS ARTICLE

Date July 1992

AUTHENTICITY OF DISPUTED MANUSCRIPT: Shakespeare or Bacon

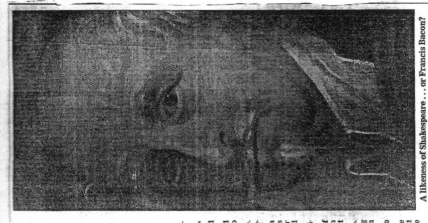

A likeness of Shakespeare ... or Francis Bacon?

Writing's on the wall for Shakespeare

by Heather Purchase

A HANDWRITING expert has added weight to claims that the Elizabethan author and philosopher Francis Bacon wrote the plays attributed to Shakespeare.

Maureen Ward-Gandy claims it is "highly probable" that Bacon was the author of a recently-discovered manuscript describing a scene which bears a striking similarity to one from Henry IV.

She compared a copy of the handwritten document, thought to date back to the 1590s when Henry IV was written and published, with the handwriting of 30 well-known scholars and statesmen of the Elizabethan era.

Mrs Ward-Gandy's strong belief that the handwriting is Bacon's has been hailed by Bacon supporters as a major breakthrough in proving the true authorship of the 38 plays, 150 sonnets and two long poems which bear William Shakespeare's name.

The debate over who wrote what, which has dogged literary critics for more than a century, resurfaced recently when the manuscript went on sale at Sotheby's.

Comprising a single sheet of 57 neatly-handwritten lines, the document was expected to fetch up to £12,000 but was unsold. It has since been returned to its secret owner.

Mrs Ward-Gandy, who outlined her findings in a 20-page report, is a forensic document examiner, a job which often involves studying handwriting for the police and Home Office to establish fraud.

She said: "The shapes of the letters and style of writing in the manuscript point to the writing being that of Bacon.

"It is very exciting and could settle the argument once and for all that the Shakespeare plays were in fact written by Bacon."

The scene in the manuscript describes a conversation in which an innkeeper tells two thieves of "a man that lodged in our house/ Last night that hath three hundred markes in gold".

Similar conversations in an almost identical setting are described in Henry IV.

Francis Carr, a historian and a director of the Shakespeare Authorship Information Centre in Brighton, believes the document was a reject script for Henry IV.

Mr Carr, who dedicated 30 years to proving authorship, believes Bacon was writing under the pseudonym of William Shakespeare.

"I think this is probably a breakthrough to the whole authorship mystery," he said.

"It could bring the whole subject into the open again. The information we have built up pointing to Bacon could blow the whole of Stratford sky high."

FSBT (Dip) MRMG (Dip) AHAF
(Registered with the British Law Society)

SIXTEENTH CENTURY STYLE OF
EMINENT PEOPLE FOR COMPARISON

Ann Boleyn: An able Ruler
and whose reign saw the
Great British Empire through the
best Great English navigators,

Elizabeth R

SIGNATURES & SCRIPTS OF SCHOLARS/Elizabethan Era	Description of the writer whose work is on Left	Comments observed from particular penmanship
	BURGHLEY, William Cecil. Lord 1520–98. The outstanding British statesman of the Tudor Age. Chief Secretary of State and for 40 years leading counsellor of **Elizabeth I**.	Long, narrow style with flourished adornment at end: Expressive style individually developed from copybook so likely to be a forceful and self-motivated person
	GRESHAM, Sir Thomas 1519–79. Tudor merchant, Lord Mayor of London. Founder of the Royal Exchange.	Inspired writing with many flourishes denoting a lover of splendour and one who likes to be impressive
	HAWKINS (or HAWKYNS), Sir John 1532–95. English sailor. **Drake's** cousin, he reconstructed the Elizabethan Navy.	Originality reigns in this legible and firm script: Clear thinker with a creative mind
	FROBISHER, Sir Martin c. 1535–94. English navigator and naval commander.	Natural, strong and disciplined writing should reflect similar tendencies in the man
	DARNLEY, Henry Stuart Stewart 1545–67. Second husband later murdered — of **Mary Queen of Scots**. A rare Scottish historical autograph. Variant signatures, one as King?	Precise, cautious with a liking for orderliness and highly self-aware

256

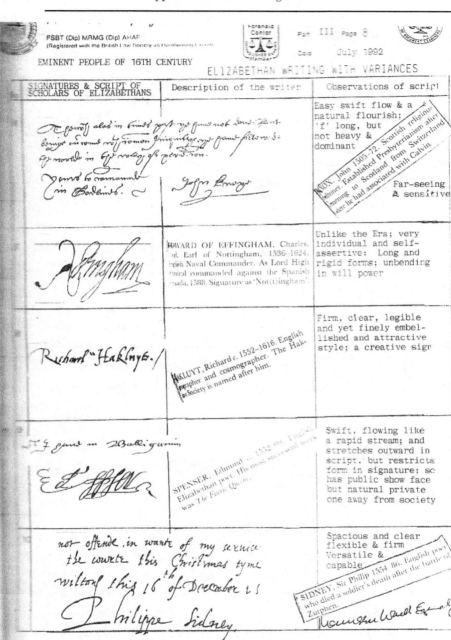

EMINENT PEOPLE OF 16TH CENTURY

ELIZABETHAN WRITING WITH VARIANCES

SIGNATURES & SCRIPT OF SCHOLARS OF ELIZABETHANS	Description of the writer	Observations of script
		Easy swift flow & a natural flourish; 'f' long, but not heavy & dominant
	KNOX, John 1505-72. Scottish religious reformer. Established Presbyterianism after returning to Scotland from Switzerland where he had associated with Calvin	Far-seeing & sensitive
	HOWARD OF EFFINGHAM, Charles. 2nd. Earl of Nottingham. 1536-1624. English Naval Commander. As Lord High Admiral commanded against the Spanish Armada, 1588. Signature as 'Not(t)ingham'.	Unlike the Era; very individual and self-assertive: Long and rigid forms; unbending in will power
	HAKLUYT, Richard c. 1552-1616. English geographer and cosmographer. The Hakluyt Society is named after him.	Firm, clear, legible and yet finely embellished and attractive style; a creative sign
	SPENSER, Edmund c. 1552-99. English Elizabethan poet. His most successful work was 'The Faerie Queen'.	Swift, flowing like a rapid stream; and stretches outward in script, but restricts form in signature; so has public show face but natural private one away from society
	SIDNEY, Sir Philip 1554-86. English poet who died a soldier's death after the battle of Zutphen.	Spacious and clear flexible & firm Versatile & capable

257

FSBT (Dip) MRMG (Dip) AHAF
(Registered with the British Law Society as Handwriting Expert)

EMINENT PEOPLE OF 16TH CENTURY

Center
Part *** Page 4
July 1992
Date

SIGNATURES & SCRIPT OF ELIZABETHAN SCHOLARS/	DESCRIPTION OF WRITER	Observations from the writing & signatures
	DRAKE, Sir Francis c. 1540-96. English Admiral and navigator. The greatest of the Elizabethan seamen, he was the first Englishman to circumnavigate the world. Variant signatures. Also part ALS about the defeat of the Spanish Armada. (Public Record Office, London.)	Very large, clear and flourishing: Confident and a flambuoyant manner Open and fearless looking script should be reflected in person
	LEICESTER, Robert Dudley, Earl of c. 1532-88. English courtier. For many years the favourite of Queen Elizabeth I.	Statuesque, slow and inner feeling of splendour is indicated in the extra twirls and elaboration
	HATTON, Sir Christopher 1540-91. 'The Dancing Chancellor'. A favourite courtier of Queen Elizabeth. Lord Chancellor 1587.	Rigidity with balance and personal style; firm and steady with a liking for being in the limelight, hence framed within the signature by own strokes
	GRENVILLE, Sir Richard c. 1541-91. Heroic British Admiral who with a single small ship, The Revenge, fought to the death against a fleet of 53 Spanish sail. Immortalised in Tennyson's poem 'The Revenge'.	Highly intense writing showing determination and endurance: Makes strong feelings work for him and not against
	RALEGH, RALEIGH in modern form. Sir Walter 1552-1618. English navigator, courtier and writer. Introduced potatoes and tobacco into England and tried to colonise Virginia. Two very different examples, both from the British Museum	Flexible form and easygoing rhythm; able to combine instincts with common sense is implied; quick to act in emergencies; able to pace himself – seen in clear spacing and bold, large signature

258

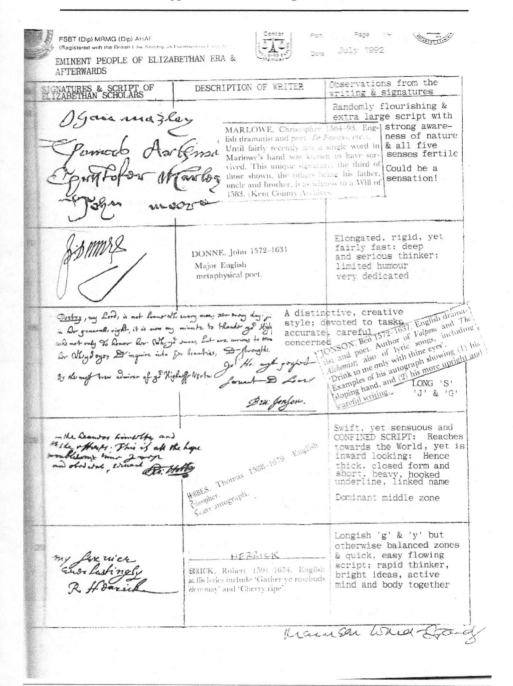

FSBT (Dip) MRMG (Dip) AHAF
(Registered with the British Law Society as Handwriting Experts)

Center

Part

Page

Date July 1992

EMINENT PEOPLE OF ELIZABETHAN ERA &
AFTERWARDS

SIGNATURES & SCRIPT OF ELIZABETHAN SCHOLARS	DESCRIPTION OF WRITER	Observations from the writing & signatures
	MARLOWE, Christopher 1564-93. English dramatist and poet. De Faustus, etc.). Until fairly recently no a single word in Marlowe's hand was known to have survived. This unique signature, the third of those shown, the others being his father, uncle and brother, is as witness to a Will of 1583. (Kent County Archives).	Randomly flourishing & extra large script with strong awareness of nature & all five senses fertile Could be a sensation!
	DONNE, John 1572-1631 Major English metaphysical poet.	Elongated, rigid, yet fairly fast; deep and serious thinker; limited humour very dedicated
	JONSON, Ben 1572-1637. English dramatist and poet. Author of Volpone and The Alchemist; also of lyric songs, including 'Drink to me only with thine eyes'. Examples of his autograph showing (1) his sloping hand, and (2) his more upright and careful writing.	A distinctive, creative style; devoted to tasks; accurate, careful, concerned LONG 'S' 'J' & 'G'
	HOBBES, Thomas 1588-1679. English philosopher. Scarce autograph.	Swift, yet sensuous and CONFINED SCRIPT: Reaches towards the World, yet is inward looking: Hence thick, closed form and short, heavy, hooked underline, linked name Dominant middle zone
	HERRICK, Robert 1591-1674. English poet. His lyrics include 'Gather ye rosebuds while ye may' and 'Cherry ripe'.	Longish 'g' & 'y' but otherwise balanced zones & quick, easy flowing script; rapid thinker, bright ideas, active mind and body together

FSBT (Dip) MRMG (Dip) AHAF
(Registered with the British Law Society as Handwriting Expert)

EMINENT PEOPLE OF ELIZABETHAN ERA &
BEYOND

Part III   Page 11

Case July 1992

SIGNATURES & SCRIPT OF ELIZABETHAN SCHOLARS	DESCRIPTION OF WRITER	Observations from writing
[handwritten signature sample — Sir Thomas More]	MORE, Sir Thomas. Saint Thomas More 1478-1535. English saint, statesman, scholar and writer. One of the most outstanding men of British history, the author of *Utopia* and Lord Chancellor. Beheaded as the result of refusing to accept the King, **Henry VIII**, as the head of the Church and to agree to a divorce from **Catherine of Aragon**.	Fast, legible, refined and sincere; clear to end letter
[handwritten script sample dated 25 Nov 1515] Elaborate & firm: Careful pedantic	WOLSEY, Thomas c. 1475-1530. English Cardinal and Lord Chancellor under **Henry VIII**. Signature as Cardinal and Archbishop of York 'Ebor'. latinised form). Also a Privy Council Warrant for the delivery of £2000 to the Merchants of the Staple at Calais. With this they are to buy two very different articles of merchandise. 'artillery habiliments of Warre' and wine for the King, (**Henry VIII**). Wolsey's signature 'Thomas Wulcy' is the last of the five Councillors who have signed. His rival Thomas Howard, Duke of Norfolk the victim of Flodden Field is the first and the others are Richard Foxe, Bishop of Winchester, Charles Somerset, Earl of Worcester and Sir Thomas Lovell. Receipted by the Merchants below. Dated 25 November 1515. Author's Collection.)
[handwritten signature samples] VARIOUS SCRIPTS OF WOMEN WHO MAY NOT HAVE WRITTEN FREQUENTLY YET EACH HAD A DIFFERENT & UNIQUE PERSONAL STYLE IN THE SAME ERA	CATHERINE OF ARAGON, 1485-1536. First wife of **Henry VIII**. Daughter of the Catholic rulers' **Ferdinand** and **Isabella** of Spain. *er also under* HENRY VIII.
	CATHERINE de MEDICI(S), 1519-89. Queen of **Henry II** of France and mother of **Francis II, Charles IX** (during whose minority she was Regent of France) and **Henry III**.
	CATHERINE (or KATHARINE) HOWARD, c. 1520-42. Fifth wife of **Henry VIII**. Beheaded on conviction for adultery. *er also under* HENRY VIII.
[handwritten signature: Katherina Regina]	CATHERINE PARR, 1512-48. Sixth wife of **Henry VIII**. *er also with* HENRY VIII.

Maureen Ward-Gandy B Ed A Gr CDE

FSBT (Dip) MRMG (Dip) AHAP
(Registered with the British Law Society as Handwriting Expert)

EMINENT PEOPLE OF ELIZABETHAN ERA & AFTER

Part III Page 12

Date July 1992

WRITING & SIGNATURE OF THE SCHOLAR/NOBLEMAN	DESCRIPTION/Observations
Marye the quene — *By the Quene*	MARY I. 1516–58. 'Bloody Mary' Tudor. Daughter of Henry VIII and **Catherine** of **Aragon**. Queen of England 1553–8. Document in English addressed to the Master of the Great Wardrobe, Sir Edward Waldegrave who has signed as receiving it (bottom right). Orders for the making of a uniform for the Royal Plumer. This includes a coat to be made of three yards of red with the Royal Cypher 'M.R.' embroidered on both the breast and back. Signed 'Marye the Quene', Westminster, 20 June 1557. (Author's Collection.)
	Rigid, bold & elaborate: very ornate and distinctive
Oliver Cromwell	CROMWELL, Oliver 1599–1658. Lord Protector of England. Cromwell's signature as 'Cromwell' is more scarce than as 'Oliver Protector'. For both signatures see with British Sovereigns pages 24 and 25.
	BOLD, EXTRA LARGE, ANGULAR & DOMINANT: FIERCE & FEARLESS
London Dec: y 10th 1707	Very rapid, flowing form with high intuition blending with logic and initiative signs: Creative mind, every alert perceptive and keenly aware missing nothing around him: always in haste
I desir as soon as this Comes to your hand you'll order the Striking the Third And all the Scaffolds about the Great Tower, with the Clearing of every place about the building that can be, both within and without. to have it to the best Advantage: for My Lord Duke comes down full of Expectation. I intend to be with you by Sunday Night, And my Ld Duke sets out on Monday: I am Yr faithfull humble Servt Vanbrugh	VANBRUGH, Sir John 1664–1726. English architect and dramatist. As a playwright a master of Restoration comedy. Designed Blenheim Palace for **Marlborough**. ALS concerning the building of Blenheim Palace, 1707. (The British Library.)
	Strong, humourous flourishes recur throughout the script: should be a versatile person with many different talents
	Maureen Ward-Gandy

FSBT (Dip) MRMG (Dip) AHAF
(Registered with the British Law Society as Handwriting Expert)

THE WIVES OF HENRY VIII in the pre ELIZABETHAN ERA

Forensic Center Member

Part **III** Page **13**

Date **July 1992**

30

(Collection)

YVIII, 1491-1547, King of England 7. Though cruel and despotic, Henry atron of the arts. His 'popular', if such can be used in his case, fame today rest in the fact that he had six wives. re (1) Catherine of Aragon signing as rina, the quene'; (2) Anne Boleyn as queen; (3) Jane Seymour, signed n; (4) Anne of Cleves, as 'Anna, the r of Cleves'; (5) Catherine Howard, ristian name only; (6) Catherine Katherina Regina, KP (Katherine

Parr)', and 7 in totally different handwriting 'Kateryn, the Quene Regente, KP'. The signatures of all the Queens of Henry VIII are rare, those of Jane Seymour, Anne of Cleves and Catherine Howard being excessively so. Above, an LS of Henry himself to the Duke of Florence sending a representative who was in fact intended to murder **Cardinal Pole**, 1545. (Author's Collection.)

Each signature of same Era differs in personal style or peculiarities

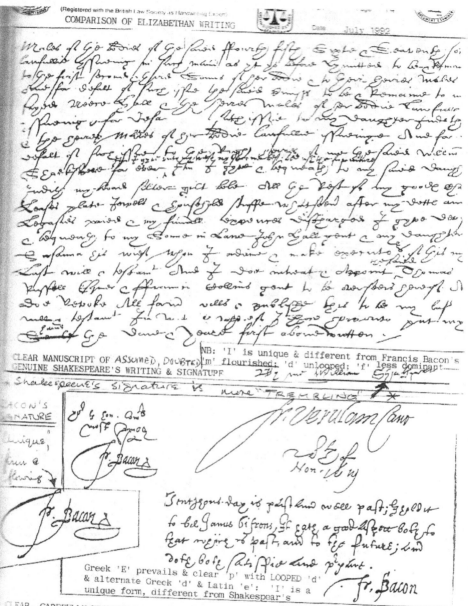

COMPARISON OF ELIZABETHAN WRITING   July 1992

NB: 'I' is unique & different from Francis Bacon's
CLEAR MANUSCRIPT OF ASSUMED, DOUBTED 'm' flourished; 'd' unlooped; 'f' less dominant
GENUINE SHAKESPEARE'S WRITING & SIGNATURE

Shakespeare's signature is more "TREMBLING"

BACON'S
SIGNATURE

Unique,
firm &
flowing

Greek 'E' prevails & clear 'p' with LOOPED 'd'
& alternate Greek 'd' & Latin 'e'; 'I' is a
unique form, different from Shakespear's

CLEAR, CAREFULLY WRITTEN FORMAL NOTE BY FRANCIS BACON WITH RIGHT SWING ON SWIFTLY MADE
FLOURISHING PARTS & MORE VERTICAL. CONSTRICTED STYLE IN THE MAIN TEXT NOTES

263

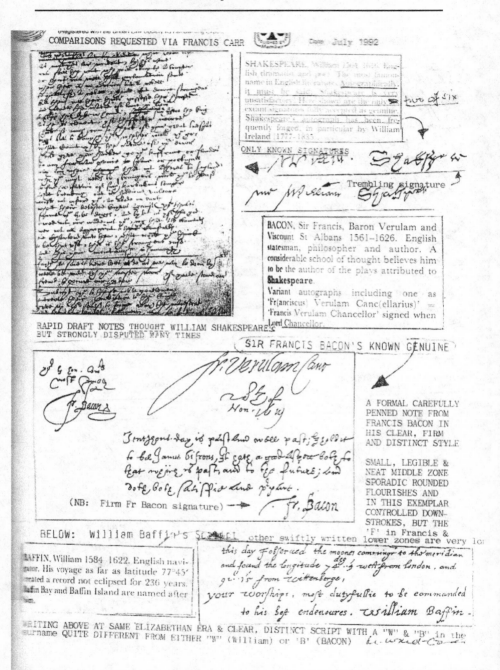

COMPARISONS REQUESTED VIA FRANCIS CARR   Date July 1992

SHAKESPEARE, William (1564-1616) English dramatist and poet. The most famous name in English literature. Paradoxically, it must be said, Shakespeare is very unsatisfactory. Here shown are the only extant signatures fully accepted as genuine Shakespeare's autograph has been frequently forged, in particular by William Ireland (1777-1835)

two of six

ONLY KNOWN SIGNATURES

Trembling signature

BACON, Sir Francis, Baron Verulam and Viscount St Albans 1561-1626. English statesman, philosopher and author. A considerable school of thought believes him to be the author of the plays attributed to **Shakespeare**.
Variant autographs including one as 'Fr(anciscus) Verulam Canc(ellarius)' and 'Francis Verulam Chancellor' signed when Lord Chancellor.

RAPID DRAFT NOTES THOUGHT WILLIAM SHAKESPEARE'S BUT STRONGLY DISPUTED MANY TIMES

SIR FRANCIS BACON'S KNOWN GENUINE

A FORMAL CAREFULLY PENNED NOTE FROM FRANCIS BACON IN HIS CLEAR, FIRM AND DISTINCT STYLE

SMALL, LEGIBLE & NEAT MIDDLE ZONE SPORADIC ROUNDED FLOURISHES AND IN THIS EXEMPLAR CONTROLLED DOWN-STROKES, BUT THE 'F' in Francis & lower zones are very lo

(NB: Firm Fr Bacon signature)

BELOW: William Baffin's SCRAWL other swiftly written

BAFFIN, William 1584-1622. English navigator. His voyage as far as latitude 77°45' created a record not eclipsed for 236 years. Baffin Bay and Baffin Island are named after him.

WRITING ABOVE AT SAME ELIZABETHAN ERA & CLEAR, DISTINCT SCRIPT WITH A "W" & "B" in the surname QUITE DIFFERENT FROM EITHER "W" (William) or 'B' (BACON)

Profession al Consultants

Registered with The British Law Society as
Forensic Handwriting / Document Expert

PEN CONTROL AFFECTING SCRIPT'S
RHYTHMIC FORCE & PACE FLUENCY

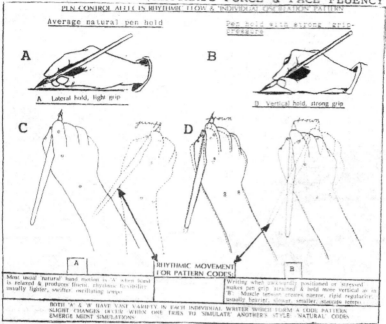

PEN CONTROL AFFECTS RHYTHMIC FLOW & INDIVIDUAL OSCILLATION PATTERN

Average natural pen hold

A

A   Lateral hold, light grip

Pen hold with strong grip pressure

B

B   Vertical hold, strong grip

C   **D**

RHYTHMIC MOVEMENT FOR PATTERN CODES:

Most usual 'natural' hand motion is 'A' when hand is relaxed & produces fluent, rhythmic flexibility usually lighter, swifter, oscillating tempo

Writing when awkwardly positioned or stressed makes pen grip strained & held more vertical as in 'B'. Muscle tension creates narrow, rigid regularity usually heavier, slower, smaller, staccato tempo

BOTH 'A' & 'B' HAVE VAST VARIETY IN EACH INDIVIDUAL WRITER WHICH FORM A CODE PATTERN
SLIGHT CHANGES OCCUR WHEN ONE TRIES TO 'SIMULATE' ANOTHER'S STYLE: 'NATURAL' CODES
EMERGE MIDST SIMULATIONS

The Script of Sir Francis Bacon looks as though he wrote with a Lateral light pen hold & his rhythmic, fluent flow has a strong, regular oscillation from vertical 90° - 53° from his known handwriting of which there are abundant examples as he was a known prolific writer of impressive style:

The only known to be genuine samples of William Shakespeare are shaky & very irregular and weak in pen control with an indeterminable oscillation ratio owing to the vague alignment

SLANT OSCILLATION RATIO FROM AXIS

BASIC SCRIPT VARATION AVERAGE FROM VERTICAL TO LATERAL SLANT

PRIMARILY LATERAL WRITING   PRIMARILY VERTICAL

EXPANDED WRITING

CONDENSED WRITING

SLANTS ILLUSTRATED FROM LATERAL (RIGHT) & VERTICAL AVERAGES IN
VARIATIONS OF CONDENSED & EXPANDED WIDTHS: (Individual codes exist)

NB   PEN FLOW & TEMPO ARE ALSO AFFECTED BY COMBINED HAND MANIPULATION OF PAPER
BENEATH PEN   LEFT HANDED USUALLY ADOPT MORE VERTICAL & RIGHT-HANDED MORE LATERAL
BUT THIS AGAIN VARIES

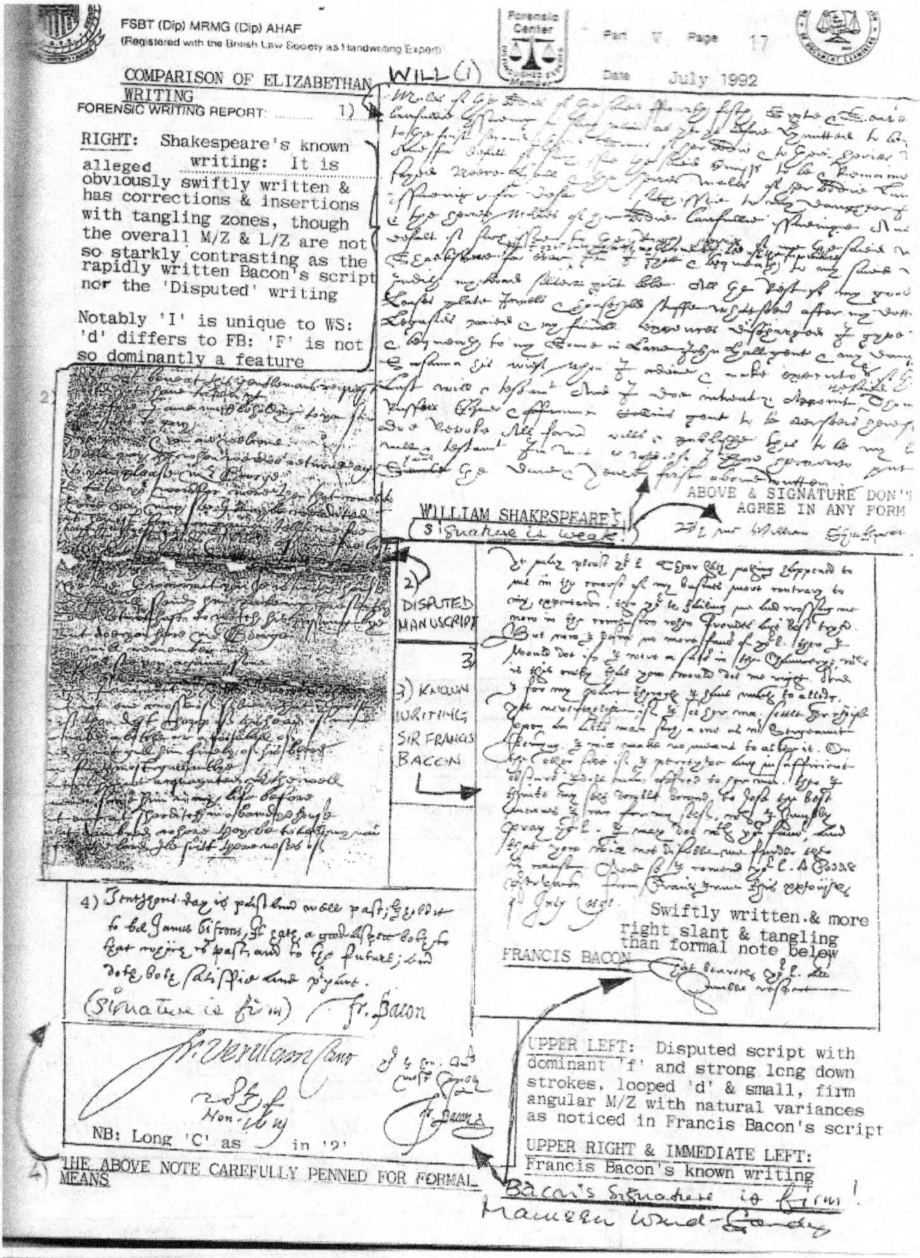

FSBT (Dip) MRMG (Dip) AHAF
(Registered with the British Law Society as Handwriting Expert)

Forensic Center

Part V Page 17

Date July 1992

COMPARISON OF ELIZABETHAN WRITING

FORENSIC WRITING REPORT:

WILL (1)

RIGHT: Shakespeare's known alleged writing: It is obviously swiftly written & has corrections & insertions with tangling zones, though the overall M/Z & L/Z are not so starkly contrasting as the rapidly written Bacon's script nor the 'Disputed' writing

Notably 'I' is unique to WS: 'd' differs to FB: 'F' is not so dominantly a feature

ABOVE & SIGNATURE DON'T AGREE IN ANY FORM

WILLIAM SHAKESPEARE: Signature is weak

2) DISPUTED MANUSCRIPT

3) KNOWN WRITING SIR FRANCIS BACON

Swiftly written & more right slant & tangling than formal note below

FRANCIS BACON

(Signature is firm) Fr. Bacon

NB: Long 'C' as in '2'

THE ABOVE NOTE CAREFULLY PENNED FOR FORMAL MEANS

UPPER LEFT: Disputed script with dominant 'f' and strong long down strokes, looped 'd' & small, firm angular M/Z with natural variances as noticed in Francis Bacon's script

UPPER RIGHT & IMMEDIATE LEFT: Francis Bacon's known writing

Bacon's Signature is firm!

Maureen Ward-Gandy

FSBT (Dip) MRMG (Dip) AHAF
(Registered with the British Law Society as Handwriting Expert)

COMPARISONS OF ELIZABETHAN Part V Page 18
WRITING

Fr. Bacon

No	First Script FB	Second Script FB	OBSERVATIONS	Manuscript DISPUTED & for MV comparison
1			Zonal difference parallel in all: small, neat M/Z Extra dominant L/Z esp 'f' form	
2			Links from Greek 'E' form from L/Z: 'I' unique in 1st & 2nd Row Flow, slant and rhythm constant	
3			'p' clear, firm Natural variance of some Italic 'f' forms: 'm' angular, rigid	
4			Rounded strong initial Capitals 'B' similar, L/Z flourish same	
5			'g' like '8' often, but varies; sometimes long curve & unclosed See 'd' RIGHT	
6			Remarkably same 'f' alternate & like a 'p': firm 'i' dots, midway 't' bar on right	
7			'd' mostly with loose: Greek 'e' mixed with Latin 'e', but larger	
8		Assorted end letter flourishes similar NB: 'd'		
9				NB: 'd'

FSBT (Dip) MRMG (Dip) AHAF
(Registered with the British Law Society as Handwriting Experts)

Part VI Page 19

Date 24th July 1992

<u>CONCLUSIVE EVIDENCE</u>

I   REVIEW OF EVIDENCE   AUTHENTICATION OF DISPUTED MANUSCRIPT

(a)   <u>Writing known genuinely by Francis Bacon</u> (SHAKESPEARE OR BACON?)

There were two exemplars; one sent to me by Mr Carr; the other from my personal collection: Mr Carr's exemplar was more swiftly written than mine: The former being more flowing, with some tangled long lower zone letters; the latter being more formally written with slower strokes, but were distinctly familiar in style and 'peculiarities' being:-

1   Set around central on the page with fairly regular spacing between letters, words and lines

2   DOMINANT feature being the long heavy downstroke at an angle about 85° to the right, especially on the letter 'f': This feature being more prominent on the writing from Mr Carr (more swiftly penned and less formal) than from my collection where the whole zone structure was carefully restricted for balance, but even then the 'f' stood out firmly

3   The rare p.p. 'I' appearing like an 'F' in Francis Bacon's exemplars was distinctly different to that appearing in the William Shakespeare exemplars, although the 'Disputed' note did not appear to have any 'I' letters (or I could not find them in the background shadow interference)

4   The Greek 'E' was predominant and had a similar form linking the lower to middle zones in all exemplars which is a style made by some writers of the Era under study now: Mixed with the Greek 'E' are sporadic Latin 'e' forms evident again in all exemplars, but more recurring in the Bacon exemplars where carefully penned and again in the 'disputed' exemplar

5   The dominant long, heavy 'f' has a natural variant Italic form of normal size which also occurs in the 'Disputed' exemplar

6   The letter 'g' is mostly written like an '8', but occasional 'g' with open curve, as made in the 'y' is noted; this recurs in the 'disputed' THE 'y' & 'g' in Shakespeare's writing tends to have a strong swing to the right in an open stroke rather than the commonly used curve to the left in Bacon's and the 'disputed' style lower zones (see July 'y' in Bacon's writing and the mid letter 'g' of the 'disputed' in word looking like 'cargo' (two lines above is a 'g' like an '8' in the disputed exemplar

7   The letter 'd' in the Copybook style of 1600's, has a looped or unlooped form: Shakespeare's known writing seems to have more unlooped 'd' forms; Bacon's and the 'disputed' exemplar are definitely predominant with use of the 'looped d' as highlighted and arrowed in the comparison tables I have created for visual quick viewing

(b)   <u>Writing known genuine by William Shakespeare</u>

The two exemplars are rapidly written in draft with corrections, and are not as centrally balanced on page nor even on the margins; the flow is flexible and oscillates a little more than Bacon's; the spacing is less regular and the middle zone less precise and angular; generally, though 'f' is long, it does not DOMINATE the appearance of the page as does Bacon's and the 'disputed' writing: The fact that Shakespeare's and the 'disputed' are both rapidly penned is significant that more similarities exist in the carefully penned of Bacon's most DISTINCTIVE & BEAUTIFUL STYLE: (Elizabethan with his own peculiarities).

(* Allegedly believed, now doubted)

Maureen Ward-Gandy B Ed A Gr CDE

FSBT (Dip) MRMG (Dip) AHAF
(Registered with the British Law Society as Handwriting Expert)

National
Forensic
Center

PRIVATE & CONFIDENTIAL

Part IV Page 20

Date 24th July 1992

CONCLUSIVE EVIDENCE

II PROFESSIONAL OPINION   DISPUTED MANUSCRIPT – BACON OR SHAKESPEARE?

Although the writing on the 'disputed' exemplar is obviously not as clear to examine as the other exemplars, it does reveal definitely the long, strong, heavy thrusts of pen from upper to lower zone on letter 'f' ('f' being the only letter in our alphabet having all 3 zones)

Natural variances always exist where a writer will use more than one style in the same letter, commonly the 'f', 'e'. 'g', 'd', 't' and 'y': In both the Bacon writing and the 'disputed' there are two forms made of the 'f' (the dominant and the smaller Italic); there are both a Greek and Latin style 'e' with lower to middle zone connections like an 'E' in all exemplars); the 'd' is mostly looped in the Bacon and 'disputed' with 'd' mostly angled in the Shakespeare exemplar

In both the Bacon & disputed there are 'g' letters formed like an '8' and also formed in a long open curve as in most of the 'y' letters; this occurs in the Bacon's known writing and the 'disputed'; but the lower zones tend to flow rightward at the end mostly in Shakespeare's

Taking into consideration that the writing under examination is from the Elizabethan Era; I took the advice of The Independent Journalist and made a study and comparison with writing of that Era, both the copybook style taught, and people involved with the Queen, or who did prolific writing within that Age; I found that - just as we have now in the 20th Century - there are copybook similarities, but also very special personal peculiarities or characteristics of style which are 'unique' to the writer and not able to be 'absolutely' compared as an 'Era Style' (not so many people were able to write in that Era also, so styles would be less likely to vary so vastly)

However, there were distinctly 'different' penmanships seen in the many eminent people's writing I studied, and few had much in common with the named strong similarities and peculiarities of Bacon and Shakespeare; they had some which can be attributed to stemming from the same Latin and Greek source - which still applies in Today's comparisons for forgery

When comparing writing for forgeries; it is helpful to be familiar with variances of style in individual letters as some can be written in more ways than others, and some letters recur in average writing more than others: Dominant features are imperative to find when having to study 'disguised' writing: This is where a 'peculiarity' of personally developed style can be the betrayer of a guilty party

Although I am unable to state DEFINITELY owing to not having ORIGINAL documents: My comparison and careful study of all writings in this matter, brings me to the conclusion that there is a stronger probability of the 'disputed' writing being by Francis Bacon than by William Shakespeare; and I conclude that likelyhood of 'COMMON AUTHORSHIP' between The known by Francis Bacon & the 'Disputed' script is of HIGH POBABILITY

Maureen Ward-Gandy

FORENSIC DOCUMENT &
HANDWRITING SPECIALISTS

Maureen Ward-Gandy B Ed CDE BCFE

FSBT FABFE NADE NFC RMGA

Professional Consultants

CURRICULUM VITAE

Maureen Ward-Gandy graduated in EDUCATION from The UNIVERSITY of LONDON, and from the USA *(1967)* she gained a Credit Diploma in Advanced SCIENTIFIC GRAPHOLOGY (Behavioural Profiling) at The ROCKY MOUNTAIN INSTITUTE OF GRAPHOLOGY: Later she achieved distinction in the ADVANCED FORENSIC DOCUMENT EXAMINATION of the NATIONAL ASSOCIATION OF DOCUMENT EXAMINERS: Further merits were attained through The AMERICAN BOARD OF FORENSIC EXAMINERS: Professional Membership of many relevant Societies of the UK & USA are held by her, and she was awarded a FIRST FELLOWSHIP of ABFE, and appointed as their UK Representative for countries outside the USA:

Mrs Ward-Gandy taught English, Art and Secretarial Skills in high schools and business colleges in the UK & USA from 1960 – 1980: While teaching in USA from 1964 – 1970 she studied, researched and applied Behavioural Profiling and Graphotherapy, enhancing her teaching with positive student benefits and better pupil/teacher rapport: By helping Denver's Forensic Squad Detectives solve forgery, arson and drug offences in Colorado; Mrs Ward-Gandy experienced her early forensic casework:

After returning to the UK in 1970, she successfully applied her skills in teaching, career guidance and counselling: Continuing her empirical study on the affects of health and other circumstances on handwriting, improved her authentication of questioned script: Research of foreign writing improved her liaison with overseas clients; particularly where forensic document disputes contained alien scripts: Demand for her help in Recruitment, Security Vetting and Forgery Detection grew rapidly in 1970's, motivating her resignation as a School Teacher to embark on a full-time Handwriting Consultancy, thus in 1981 she registered as a PRIVATE COMPANY and with the LAW SOCIETY:

Such vast, varied experience with historical research of handwriting and circumstancial affects upon it, have enabled Mrs Ward-Gandy to write articles and present academic papers Universally: Her widely published articles on writings of Christopher Columbus, Queen Victoria and other eminent characters have received high acclaim: Children still benefit from her help through Graphotherapy to overcome learning problems, and many international organizations use her skills for product promotion or charity fund-raising:

In addition to her lecturing internationally to different establishments; Mrs Ward-Gandy is a seasoned Radio Pundit, amazing listeners with penetrating character & health analyses of their handwriting; so often that BBC televised a broadcast on a QED Science Review: The News Media frequently seek her professional advice and publish her many activities:

With a desire to up-date and improve her forensic expertise; she participated in annual UK and USA's many Societies' Seminars, where pooling ideas expanded her knowledge; and forensic apparatus experiments led to adequate purchases: Recommendation extended her clientele Worldwide, bringing regular projects from Lawyers, Airlines, Local Governments, and Trading Standards Authorities: Over 2,000 cases have amassed since 1968:

Registered Business as required by
Section 29 of Companies Act 1981

INTERNATIONAL NETWORK

National
Forensic
Center

Registered with The British Law Society as
Forensic Handwriting / Document Expert

OF FORENSIC EXAMINERS

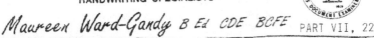

FORENSIC DOCUMENT & HANDWRITING SPECIALISTS

Maureen Ward-Gandy B Ed CDE BCFE PART VII, 22

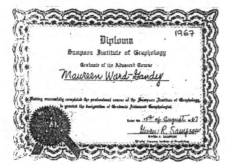

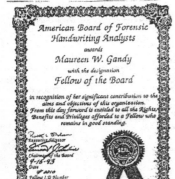

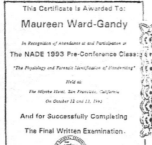

WILLIAM SHAKESPEARE OR SIR FRANCIS BACON?
AUTHENTICATION OF DISPUTED SCRIPT

PART VII, 23

Commendations

Commendations

NB: 'The Solicitors in following extracts wrote to The Law Society'

REED EMPLOYMENT (1983)
'We advertised 'Nationwide' for a GRAPHOLOGIST, and from over 60 responses to tests, we found MAUREEN WARD-GANDY was the only Candidate to score FULL MARKS on all Graphoanalyses tests.'
A E Reed, Chairman
(pp Shiela Grant PA)

TARRAN-JONES & CO. (Solicitors) (1972) — Crawley, Sussex
'Maureen Ward-Gandy is always pleasant, with work done efficiently and expeditiously.'
Jeremy Tarran-Jones, Director/ Solicitor

NORTH BRITISH MARITIME GROUP (1976 - 1982) — Hull, Yorks
'It's 6½ years since you accurately analysed 15 applicants. We disregarded a warning re one of the 3 chosen which proved later to be just as you had clearly defined: Such long-standing results are the highest commendation on the excellence of your skills.'
A B Wilbraham, Chairman

MECCA LEISURE (15th July 1980) — London, England
'This analysis was a test for this Company, and our inexperienced were very surprised: I, having used Maureen Ward-Gandy's services in a former Company, knew she would again be accurate.'
John Brown, Personnel Director

ELECTRONICS RENTALS GROUP Plc (4th Feb 1989) — Crawley, Sussex
'In analyses of staff and applicants, Mrs Ward-Gandy has always given detailed, accurate information of considerable value to us: Her work is of a high and most professional standard and I confidently recommend her.'
C Anne Bathgate, Personnel Director

THOMAS PINK (June 1988) — Dublin, London & New York
'Thank you, Maureen, for the superb & speedy job you did on analysing the applicants for the New York post. I am thrilled with the results as you identified some qualities I knew, but you unearthed new facts to their characters.'
James Mullen, Director

BRITANNIA ROW (6th October 1986) — London, England
'I gladly confirm that the Detective handling our Embezzlement Case commented that your Report was the best and most comprehensive of its type he'd ever seen.'
Norman Lawrence, Managing Director

D ANTHONY PROMOTIONS (4th May 1989) — Manchester, Lancs
'Thanks for standing in at the last minute on the Vodka Tour: Your Graphology Talks proved fascinating to all, and your Radio Broadcasts were astounding.'
David Warwick, Director

T I CLOUGH & CO (SOLICITORS) (14th Feb 1990) — Bradford, Yorks
'Maureen Ward-Gandy impressed us with a thorough report of conclusive evidence which undermined all credibility of the Applicant to clear our client beyond doubt, saving time and Court costs convincingly.'
Philip A Hirst, Solicitor / Manager

Continued

PRICE WATERHOUSE (16th May 1990) — London, England
'My experience with Graphology in recruitment had been disappointing, until Maureen Ward-Gandy's incisive, accurate & professional analysis impressed me to find it exceeds psychometric tests with depth, insight, accuracy & cost: She brings credit to her profession.'
Barrie A Whitaker, Consultant

ALPHA KOGYO KK (5th March 1990) — Yokohama, Japan
'Your analysis captured the essence of all personalities very well; Nakamura-san, I felt, was spot on! For Oigawa, your most perceptive remark, 'Power behind throne', was so accurate as he makes this Co. work!'
Giles Goldsbro, Director

WHITAKER & WOOD (SOLICITORS) (May, 1990) — Bradford, West Yorkshire
'We were pleased to note that Mrs Ward-Gandy's Forensic Report was extremely detailed; comprehensively covering all points to solve a complex authenticity case: An added bonus was her prompt efficiency throughout; thus we readily recommend her services to others seeking similar solutions.'
C Monagham LL.B

LEWIS & DICK (SOLICITORS) (July, 1990) — Surrey & Sussex Branches
'We called Maureen Ward-Gandy for an emergency authenticity opinion during a Drug Smuggling Trial in 1988: Her speed with an effective report helped towards successful conclusion.'
Paul Greenwood LL.B

WENDY DRAPER (SOLICITORS) (March, 1991) — Aldershot, Hampshire
'Since The Law Society gave me Mrs Ward-Gandy's name as an Expert in her field; she has undertaken work on behalf of this firm which has always been most satisfactory: One of her exceptional Court Reports brought about an out-of-court settlement: I would not hesitate to use her services again.'
Wendy M Draper, Director /Solicitor

BURSTOWS (SOLICITORS) (November, 1991) — Horsham, Sussex
'Neither Counsel nor ourselves had ever seen before a Report with such precision; we were very impressed; notwithstanding that Mrs Ward-Gandy found this case against our client: We have no hesitation in recommending her professional services to whomever needs a thorough Forensic Handwriting Expert.'
David Rodwell, Solicitor

WOKING HOMES (Railway Care Centre) (April, 1992) — Woking, Surrey
'We were glad we followed recommendation to use the expert services of Mrs Ward-Gandy as she convincingly solved an urgent, distressing case by revealing the author of disguised, anonymous letters: She adeptly demonstrates her testimonials.'
Mavis E. Champion, Director

WALKER WYLLIE (SOLICITORS) (July, 1992) — East Molesey, Surrey
'Mrs Ward-Gandy's comprehensive report impressed us as the most defined we had yet seen; and, despite being quite unfavourable for our client; we appreciated that she had concluded in a fair, professional manner: We recommend Mrs Ward-Gandy unreservedly to other firms requiring a good Forensic Writing Authenticator.'
John Farrar, Solicitor

BRIGHTON BOROUGH COUNCIL (Local Gov.) (March, 1993) — Brighton, Sussex
'Mrs Ward-Gandy supplied this Council with conclusive handwriting evidence which allowed us to recover monies from Parking Voucher Outlets: In similar circumstances, we would be pleased to use her competent services again.'
D Davey-Thomas, Parking Manager

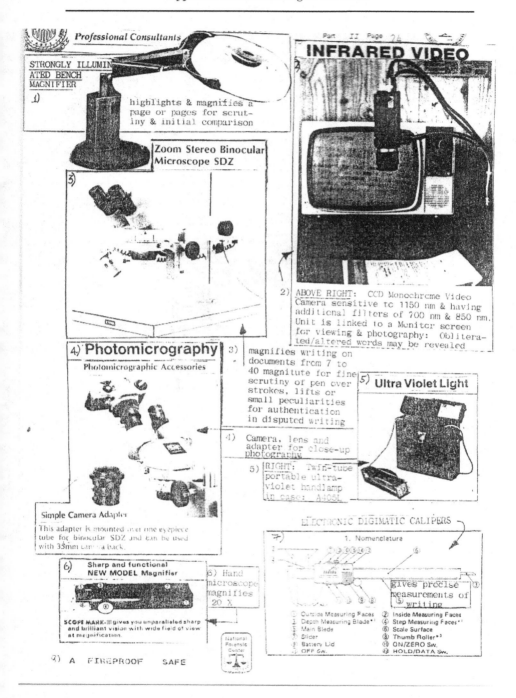

Professional Consultants

Part II Page 24

INFRARED VIDEO

STRONGLY ILLUMINATED BENCH MAGNIFIER

1)

highlights & magnifies a page or pages for scrutiny & initial comparison

Zoom Stereo Binocular Microscope SDZ

3)

2) ABOVE RIGHT: CCD Monochrome Video Camera sensitive to 1150 nm & having additional filters of 700 nm & 850 nm. Unit is linked to a Monitor screen for viewing & photography: Obliterated/altered words may be revealed

4) **Photomicrography**

Photomicrographic Accessories

3) magnifies writing on documents from 7 to 40 magnitude for fine scrutiny of pen over strokes, lifts or small peculiarities for authentication in disputed writing

4) Camera, lens and adapter for close-up photography

5) **Ultra Violet Light**

5) RIGHT: Twin-tube portable ultra-violet handlamp in case: A405L

Simple Camera Adapter

This adapter is mounted over one eyepiece tube for binocular SDZ and can be used with 35mm camera back.

ELECTRONIC DIGIMATIC CALIPERS

1. Nomenclatura

gives precise measurements of writing

6) **Sharp and functional NEW MODEL Magnifier**

6) Hand microscope magnifies 20 X

SCOPE MARK-III gives you unparalleled sharp and brilliant vision with wide field of view at magnification.

① Outside Measuring Faces   ② Inside Measuring Faces
③ Depth Measuring Blade*¹   ④ Step Measuring Faces*¹
⑤ Main Blade   ⑥ Scale Surface
⑦ Slider   ⑧ Thumb Roller*³
⑨ Battery Lid   ⑩ ON/ZERO Sw.
⑪ OFF Sw.   ⑫ HOLD/DATA Sw.

7) A FIREPROOF SAFE

THIS STUDY OF THE DISPUTED MANUSCRIPT & THE COMPARISON
WITH MANY WRITERS OF THE ERA, ALONG WITH SIR FRANCIS
BACON & THE LITTLE KNOWN BY WILLIAM SHAKESPEARE, WAS
REQUESTED AND EXECUTED AT SHORT NOTICE TO MEET A NEWS
DEADLINE WHEN AUTHOR WAS OVERCOMMITTED WITH COURT WORK

Professional
Consultants
in
FORENSIC DOCUMENT &
HANDWRITING SPECIALISM

(Registered with The British Law Society)

Maureen Ward-Gandy B Ed CDE BCFE

FSBT FRVFE NADE NFC MAGA

National
Forensic
Center

Also Written & had Published:

1. "Study of Queen Victoria's Handwriting throughout her Reign"

2. "The Lord Admiral, Christopher Columbus: His 4 Epic Voyages
   & Affects seen in his Writing"

3. "Graphology Enhances Education"
4. "Graphotherapy's Efficacy"
5. "The Hierarchy of British Rule & Law"
6. " The British Forensic Expert"

Selected Bibliography

Many sources were consulted and cited. To keep the size of the bibliography to a reasonable length, selection was arbitrary. In addition, some works neither consulted nor cited are included as suggestions for further reading.

1. Works of Francis Bacon
2. Language/Literature/Literary History and Criticism
3. Legal History/Law/Political science/Art history
4. Authorship Argued
5. Shakespeare, Law and Lawyers
6. Biography/History/Philosophy/Theology/Education/Science/Travel
7. Research Tools; Library Guides; Organizations
8. Information on *Processus* Books
9. Francis Bacon's Bi-literal (Bi-literary) Cipher; Acrostics

1. Works of Francis Bacon

Bacon, Francis. *Aphorismi de Jure gentium maiore, sive de fontibus Justiciae et Juris* ['Aphorisms on the greater Law of nations, or of the fountains of Justice and Law,' or, the *Aphorismi*]. Translated by Mark Neustadt. Appendix to Mark Neustadt, "The Making of the Instauration: Science, Politics and Law in the Career of Francis Bacon." Ph.D. dissertation, 1987, Johns Hopkins University, Microfilm, 1990.

Burgoyne, Frank L., ed. *Northumberland Manuscripts, Collotype and Facsimile Transcript of an Elizabethan Manuscript Preserved at Alnwick Castle, Northumberland.* London: Longman, 1904. Note: a modern font is used. Available at http://www.sirbacon.org/links/northumberland.html.   http://sirbacon.org/ResearchMaterial/nm-contents.htm.

Gregg, W. W., ed. *Gesta Grayorum*. London: Oxford University Press, 1914. First published in London, 1688. HathiTrust, https://catalog.hathitrust.org/Record/001017043.

The Oxford Francis Bacon Project. www.oxfordfFrancisbacon.com.

Tennison, Thomas. *Baconiana, or, Certain genuine remains of Sr. Francis Bacon Baron of Verulam and Viscount of St. Albans in arguments civil and moral, natural, medical, theological and bibliographical, now for the first time faithfully published.* London, 1679. Early English Books Online: Text Creation Partnership, http://tei.it.ox.ac.uk/tcp/Texts-HTML/free/A28/A28024.html,   also   http://name.umdl.umich.edu/A28024.0001.001.

Montagu, Basil, ed. *The Works of Francis Bacon, Lord Chancellor of England, a New Edition*. 16 volumes. London: William Pickering, 1825-37. HathiTrust. http://hdl.handle.net/2027/mdp.39015074712442?urlappend=%3Bseq=8.

_____. *The Works of Francis Bacon, Lord Chancellor of England, a New Edition: with a Life of the Author.* 3 volumes. Philadelphia: Carey & Hart, 1841-1853. Hathitrust, https://catalog.hathitrust.org/Record/006292551.

Spedding, James S., ed. *A Conference of Pleasure Composed for Some Festive Occasion About the Year 1592 by Francis Bacon, edited, from a manuscript belonging to the Earl of Northumberland, by James Spedding.* London, 1870. HathiTrust, http://hdl.handle.net/2027/mdp.39015053160555. Note: the font is difficult to read; see entries for "Burgoyne, Frank" and "Vickers, Brian," this subheading.

_____, Robert Leslie Ellis and Douglas Denon Heath, ed. *The Works of Francis Bacon, Baron of Verulam, Viscount St. Alban, and Lord High Chancellor of England.* 14 volumes. Longmans: London 1857-1874, 1887, 1889. Hathitrust. https://catalog.hathitrust.org/Record/006685889.

Vickers, Brian, ed. *Francis Bacon, a Critical Edition of the Major Works.* Oxford: Oxford University Press, 1996. Note: This edition benefits from several manuscripts not known to Spedding, including a better source for *Of Tribute, or Giving That Which is Due* (Spedding's *A Conference of Pleasure*). See pp. 515-516.

_____. *Francis Bacon, The History of the Reign of King Henry VII and Selected Works.* Cambridge: Cambridge University, Press, 1998.

The Works of Francis Bacon: The Wisdom of the Ancients and Other Essays. Roslyn, New York: Walter J. Black, 1932.

2. Language/Literature/Literary History and Criticism

Aristophanes, 'The Frogs.' In *Nine Greek Dramas by Aeschylus, Sophocles, Euripides and Aristophanes. The Harvard Classics*, vol. 8, edited   by Charles W. Eliot. Translated by E. D. A. Morshead et al. Released online April, 2005, first published

1909. The Gutenberg Project, ebook no. 7998. http://www.gutenberg.org/files/7998/7998-h/7998-h.htm.

Asquith, Clare. *Shadowplay, The Hidden Beliefs and Coded Politics of William Shakespeare.* New York: Public Affairs, 2006.

Baker, William and Brian Vickers. *The Merchant of Venice.* Shakespeare: The Critical Tradition, vol. 5. London: Thoemmes Continuum, 2005.

Barber, C. L. "The Saturnalian Pattern." In *Approaches to Shakespeare*, edited by Norman Rabkin. New York: McGraw-Hill, 1964.

Benston, Alice. "Portia, the Law, and the Tripartite Structure of 'The Merchant of Venice.'" In *The Merchant of Venice: Critical Essays*, edited by Thomas Wheeler. New York: Routledge, 2015. First published in *Shakespeare Quarterly* 30, no. 3 (Summer, 1979), pp. 367-385. JSTOR. http://www.jstor.org/stable/2869472.

Boyarin, Adrienne Williams. *Miracles of the Virgin in Medieval England: Law and Jewishness in Marian Legends.* Cambridge: D. S. Brewer, 2010.

Bryson, Michael and Arpi Movsesian. *Love and its Critics: From the Song of Songs to Shakespeare and Milton's Eden.* Cambridge: Open Book Publishing, 2017. https://www.openbookpublishers.com/htmlreader/978-1-78374-348-3/contents.xhtml.

Chambers, E. K. *The Medieval Stage,* vol. 2. London: Oxford University Press, 1925.

____. *William Shakespeare, A Study of Facts and Problems,* vol. 2. Oxford: Clarendon Press, 1930.

Clair, Jean, ed. *The Great Parade: Portrait of the Artist as Clown.* New Haven: Yale University Press, 2004.

Cohen, Adam Max. *Shakespeare and Technology: Dramatizing the Early Modern Technological Revolution.* New York: Palgrave Macmillan 2006; digital, 2008.

Collins, Hannah, "What Authors Need to Know About Commedia dell'Arte." Standout Books. August 16, 2017. https://www.standoutbooks.com/commedia-dellarte/.

"The Commedia dell'Arte homepage." Tim Shane. http://www.tim-shane.com/Commedia-Dottore.htm.

Conley, C. H. The First English Translators of the Classics. New Haven: Yale University Press, 1927. HathiTrust, https://hdl.handle.net/2027/mdp.39015005787463.

Cuffe, Henry. "The Earle of Essex his Bee, A Poem made on the Earle of Essex (being in disgrace with Queen Elizabeth): by mr. henry Cuffe his Secretary." Catalog of English Literary Manuscripts [CELM], EsR86, pp. 368-9 [Feilde MS, c. 1642]. 2005-2013. http://www.celm-ms.org.uk/repositories/pirie-robert-s-new-york.html.

Curran, John E., Jr. *Character and Individual Personality in English Renaissance Drama, Tragedy, History, Tragicomedy.* Newark: University of Delaware Press, 2014.

Davis, Gregson. "Coping with Erotic Adversity: *Carmen et Amor* (*Ecl.* 2 & 8)," chapter 6, *Parthenope: The Interplay of Ideas in Vergilian Bucolic*. Leiden: Brill, 2012.

DeGuileville, Guilliame de, *The Pylgremage of the Sowle*. Edited by Katherine Cust. Translated "prob. by Lydgate" in 1413. London, 1859. First published: London, William Caxton, 1483. HathiTrust. http://hdl.handle.net/2027/mdp.39015053 684802?urlappend=%3Bseq=14.

Douce, Francis. *Illustrations of Shakespeare, and of Ancient Manners with Dissertations on the Clowns and Fools of Shakespeare, on the Collection of Popular Tales entitled Gesta Romanorum, and on the English Morris Dance*, vol. 1. London, 1839.

Elze, Karl [Friedrich], ed. *Essays on Shakespeare*. Translated by L. Dora Schmitz. London, 1874. https://books.google.com/books/about/Essays_on_Shakespeare.html?id=_vlCFbCY_0AC.

Gesta Romanorum. Translated by Charles Swan, revised and corrected by Wynnard Hooper. London: George Bell & Sons, 1905. HathiTrust. http://hdl.handle.net/2027/hvd.32044010592095.

Giovanni, Ser. '*The Pecorone' of Ser Giovanni*. Translated by W. G. Waters. London, 1897. https://archive.org/stream/pecoroneofsergio00giovrich/pecoroneofsergio00giovrich_djvu.txt.

Haber, Judith. "*Si numquam fallit imago*: Virgil's revision of Theocritus," chapter 2, *Pastoral and the Poetics of Self-Contradiction: Theocritus to Marvel*. Cambridge: Cambridge University Press, 1994.

Hackett, Helen, *Shakespeare and Elizabeth, The Meeting of Two Myths*. Princeton: Princeton University Press, 2009.

Hardie, Philip. "The Eclogues," part 2, *Virgil*, Greece & Rome, vol. 28. Oxford: Oxford University Press, 1998.

Harrison, Frances Edward. "Some Notes on Language," *Millennium, a Latin Reader A.D. 374-1374*. Bristol, U.K.: Bristol Classical Press, 1991. First published, Oxford: Oxford University Press. 1968. https://books.google.com/books?id=5sC2pJYlzbsC&lpg=PP1&pg=PP1#v=onepage&q&f=false.

Helgerson, Richard. "Epilogue: The Folly of Maps and Modernity." In *Literature, Mapping and the Politics of Space in Early Modern Britain*, edited by Andrew Gordon and Bernhard Klein. Cambridge: Cambridge University Press, 2001.

Holderness, Graham, Bryan Loughrey, and Andrew Murphy. "What's the matter? Shakespeare and textual theory." In *Textual Practice* 9, no. 1 (1995), edited by Lindsey Smith. Taylor Francis Online June 30, 2008. pp. 93-119. https://www.tandfonline.com/doi/abs/10.1080/09502369508582213.

Huntington, John. *Ambition, Rank and Poetry in 1590's England*. Urbana: University of Illinois Press, 2001.

Iopolo, Grace. "Manuscripts Containing Texts by Shakespeare." In *The Cambridge Guide to the Worlds of Shakespeare*, edited by B. Smith. Cambridge: Cambridge University Press, 2016.

_____. "Some Recent Dramatic Manuscript Studies." In *Shakespeare Studies* 30, edited by Leeds Barroll. Cranbury NJ: Associated University Press, 2010.

Jenkins, Elizabeth. *Elizabeth the Great.* New York: Coward-McCann, 1959.

Joseph, Sister Miriam. *Shakespeare's Use of the Arts of Language.* New York: Hafner Publishing, 1966.

Kastan, David Scott, ed., *King Henry IV Part 1*, Arden Shakespeare, 3d series. London: Arden Shakespeare, 2002.

Kermode, Frank, ed. *Four Centuries of Shakespearian Criticism.* New York: Avon Books, 1965, p.b.

_____. *Shakespeare, Spenser, Donne: Renaissance Essays.* Oxford: Routledge, 2005. First published in 1971.

Kilpatrick, Ross S. "Two Horatian Proems, *Carmen* 1.26 and *Carmen* 1.32." In *Studies in Latin Poetry*, vol. 21, edited by Christopher M. Dawson and Thomas Cole. Cambridge: Cambridge University Press. 1969. pp. 213-241. https://books.google.ca/books?id=qLU8AAAAIAAJ.

Kitch, Aaron. "Shylock's Sacred Nation," *Shakespeare Quarterly* 59, no. 2. Summer 2008. pp. 131-155. https://www.bowdoin.edu/faculty/a/akitch/pdf/sacred_nation.pdf.

Kleefeld, John C. "From Brouhahas to Brehon Laws: Poetic Impulse in the Law," *Law and Humanities* 4. 2010. pp. 21-61. SSRN: http://ssrn.com/abstract=1937496.

Knight, W. Nicholas. "Equity, 'The Merchant of Venice,' and William Lambarde," *Shakespeare Survey* 27. Edited by Kenneth Muir. Cambridge: Cambridge University Press, 1974.

_____. Shakespeare's Hidden Life, Shakespeare at the Law 1585-1595. New York: Mason & Lipscomb, 1973.

Mallock, W. H. (William Hurrell), ed. and trans., *Lucretius.* Philadelphia, 1881.

Manly, John Matthews. "Familia Goliae," *Modern Philology* 5 (Oct., 1907). pp. 201-209. JSTOR. http://www.jstor.org/stable/pdf/432490.pdf.

Mapes (Map), Walter. *A Canticle of Wine, or, The Drinking Song of Walter de Mapes, Scholar and Satirist, Archdeacon of Oxford in the Reign of Coeur de Lion and of John.* Metrical paraphrase by Robert W. Arnot, with decorations by Blanche McManus. New York, 1898. HathiTrust. https://hdl.handle.net/2027/hvd.32044088986450.

_____. *The Latin Poems Commonly Attributed to Walter Mapes.* Edited by Thomas Wright. London, 1841. HathiTrust. https://hdl.handle.net/2027/uva.x000460059; Internet archive. https://archive.org/details/latinpoemscommo16mapw.

_____. *De nugis curialium distinctions quinque* [*Of Trifles*]. "Edited from the unique manuscript in the Bodleian Library at Oxford by Thomas Wright." London, 1850. HathiTrust. https://hdl.handle.net/2027/uva.x000195915; Internet archive. https://archive.org/details/gualterimapesde00mapgoog.

McQuain, Jeffrey and Stanley Malless. *Coined by Shakespeare, Words & Meanings First Penned by the Bard.* Springfield MS: Merriam-Webster, 1998.

Melchiori, George, ed. "Textual Analysis," *The Second Part of Henry IV*. Cambridge: Cambridge University Press, 1989.

Meres, Frances. *Palladis tamia, Wits treasury being the second part of Wits commonwealth. By Francis Meres Maister of Artes of both universities.* London, 1598. Early English Books Online: Text Creation Partnership. http://name.umdl.umich.edu/A68463.0001.001.

Morris, Richard, ed. *Cursor mundi (cursur o the world), Northumbrian poem of the XIVth Century in four versions.* Early English Text Society, original series 99, part 6. London, 1874, 1893. https://books.google.com/books?id=AAEVAAAAQAAJ. 1892 ed., scanned by the University of Toronto. http://scans.library.utoronto.ca/pdf/2/1/cursormundicupt600morruoft/cursormundicupt600morruoft_bw.pdf.

Peltonen, Markku. *Cambridge Companion to Bacon, The.* Cambridge: Cambridge University Press, 1996.

Plautus, Titus Maccius. *Amphitryo, Asinaria, Aulularia, Bacchides,...Captivi.* Edited and translated by Paul Nixon. Cambridge: Harvard University Press, 1916. Gutenberg Project. Released online Aug., 2005. http://www.gutenberg.org/files/16564/16564-h/16564-h.htm.

_____. *The Captivi and the Mostellaria [Haunted House] of Plautus, Literally Translated with Notes.* Translated by Henry Thomas Riley. Philadelphia, 189[?]. HathiTrust, https://hdl.handle.net/2027/ucl.c052820141.

Poole, Kristen. "God's Game of Hide-and-Seek: Bacon and Allegory." In *The Palgrave Handbook of Early Modern Literature and Science*, edited by Howard Marchitello and Evelyn Tribble. London: Palgrave Macmillan UK, 2017. pp. 115-138.

Ransom, John Crowe. "On Shakespeare's Language." *Sewanee Review* 55, no. 2 (1947). pp. 181-198, 1947. JSTOR. http://www.jstor.org/stable/27537724?seq=1#page_scan_tab_contents.

Rawley, William, ed. *Manes Verulamiani [Shades of Verulam], 32 Elegies Written on the Death of Francis Bacon.* Translated into English verse by Willard Parker. *American Baconiana* 5 (November, 1927). First published in London, 1626. "Electronically typed and edited by Juan Schoch for editorial purposes only." http://sir-bacon.org/Parker/Parker_ManesVerulamiani.pdf.

Rea, John D. "Shylock and the Processus Belial," *Philological Quarterly* 8 (1929). pp. 311-313. http://search.proquest.com/openview/ab2a34efac8128f15105dd5f789515af/1?pq-origsite=gscholar.

Restivo, Giuseppa. "Shylock and Equity in Shakespeare's *The Merchant of Venice*." Revised from the version in *The Concept of Equity, an Interdisciplinary Assessment*, edited by Daniela Carpi. Heidelberg: Universitaets Verlag, 2007. pp. 24-42. http://www.openstarts.units.it/dspace/bitstream/10077/3827/1/Tigor_3_restivo.pdf.

Reynolds, William. *The Merchant of Venice: (The Players Text of 1600, with the Heminges and Condell Text of 1623):[...].* The Bankside Shakespeare. Edited by Appleton Morgan. New York: Shakespeare Society of America, 1888. HathiTrust, https://babel.hathitrust.org/cgi/pt?id=mdp.39015082503056;view=1 up;seq=11.

Schuler, Robert M. "Francis Bacon and Scientific Poetry," *Transactions of the American Philosophical Society* 82, no. 2 (1992). pp. 1-65. JSTOR. http://www.jstor.org/stable/3231921.

Seneca, Lucius Annius. '*Ad Neronem Caesarem, de Clementia* [*To the Emperor Nero, On Mercy*],' *Seneca*, vol. 1, *Moral Essays*. Translated by John W. Basore. Loeb Classical Library (LCL) 214. Cambridge: Harvard University Press, 1928. pp. 356-357. https://www.loebclassics.com/view/seneca_younger-de_clementia/1928/pb_LCL214.357.xml?rskey=AEdHSL&result=5.

"Shakespeare, Henry IV, Part 1," The Schoyen Collection, https://www.schoyencollection.com/literature-collection/modern-literature-collection/shakespeare-henry-fourth-4-ms-1627.

Shell, Marc. "The Wether and the Ewe," *Money, Language and Thought: Literary and Philosophical Economies from the Medieval to the Modern Era*. Berkeley: University of California Press, 1982.

Stewart, Alan, *Shakespeare's Letters*. Oxford: Oxford University Press, 2008.

Syme, Holger Schott. *Theatre and Testimony in Shakespeare's England: A Culture of Mediation*. Cambridge: Cambridge University Press, 2012.

Tacitus, Cornelius. *Tacitus*, vol. 1, *Agricola, Germania, Dialogue on Oratory*. Translated by M. Hutton and W. Peterson; revised by R. M. Ogilvie, E. H. Warmington, and M. Winterbottom. Loeb Classical Library 35, Cambridge: Harvard University Press, 1914. pp. 22-23. https://www.loebclassics.com/view/tacitus-agricola/1914/pb_LCL035.23.xml.

Taylor, Sir Henry. *Henry Taylor's Correspondence*. Edited by Edward Dowden. London, 1888.

Thorns, William J. "Shakespeare in Germany." *Three Notelets on Shakespeare*. London, 1865. HathiTrust. http://hdl.handle.net/2027/uc2.ark:/13960/t9s17x33c?urlappend=%3Bseq=13.

Traina, A. "*Si Numquam Fallit Imago*: Reflections on the Eclogues and Epicureanism." In *General Articles and the Eclogues, Virgil*, edited by Philip Hardie. London: Routledge, 1999.

Traver, Hope. "The Four Daughters of God, a Mirror of Changing Doctrine." *Publication of the Modern Language Association* [*PMLA*] 40, no. 1 (March, 1925). pp. 44-92. JSTOR. http://www.jstor.org/stable/457268.

_____. *The Four Daughters of God, a Study of the Versions of this Allegory, with Special Reference to those in Latin, French, and English*. Bryn Mawr College Monographs, vol. 6. Bryn Mawr, 1907. Internet Archive. https://ia902704.us.archive.org/13/items/fourdaughtersgo02travgoog/fourdaughtersgo02travgoog.pdf; HathiTrust. https://hdl.handle.net/2027/hvd.32044021642061.

_____. "I Will Try Confusions with Him." *The Shakespeare Association Bulletin* 13, no. 2 (April, 1938). pp. 108-120, JSTOR, http://www.jstor.org/stable/23675765.

Usher, Roland B. "Francis Bacon's Knowledge of Law French." *Modern Language Notes* 24 (1919). pp. 28-32.

Vickers, Brian. "Bacon's Use of Theatrical Imagery." In *Francis Bacon's Legacy of Texts*, edited by W. A. Sessions. New York: AMS Press, 1990. pp. 171-213.

_____, ed. *Essential Articles for the Study of Francis Bacon.* Hamden CT: Archon Books, 1968.

Watson, George. "Shakespeare and the Norman Conquest: English in the Elizabethan Theatre." *VQR* 66, no. 4 (Autumn, 1990; online, Dec. 12, 2003). http://www.vqronline.org/essay/shakespeare-and-norman-conquest-english-elizabethan-theatre.

Wells, Stanley and Gary Taylor, with John Jowett and William Montgomery. *William Shakespeare: A Textual Companion.* New York: W. W. Norton. 1997.

Weston, Jessie. *From Ritual to Romance.* Mineola NY: Dover, 1997. First published by Cambridge: Cambridge University Press, 1920.

Wheeler, Thomas. *The Merchant of Venice: Critical Essays.* New York: Routledge, 2015.

Woodhuysen, H. R. *Sir Philip Sidney and the Circulation of Manuscripts, 1558-1640.* Oxford: Clarendon Press, 1996. https://books.google.ca/books?isbn=0191591025.

3. Legal History/Law/Political Science/Art History

Note: Items followed by the notation "(REB)" were provided by Professor Robert E. Beck, School of Law, Southern Illinois University, "Selected Materials on Anglo-American Legal History: The Development of a Legal System, 4th revised ed. Not for general publication. August, 1978" for the legal history course he taught, and which I took, in 1985.

Ames, J. B. *Selection of Cases in Equity Jurisdiction*, vol. 1. Cambridge: Harvard Law Review Publishing Association, 1901-1904. HathiTrust. http://catalog.hathitrust.org/Record/100627172.

Andrews, Mark Edwin. *Law v. Equity in The Merchant of Venice, a Legalization of Act IV, Scene I with Foreword, Judicial Precedents, and Notes.* Boulder: University of Colorado Press, 1965.

Andrus, R. Blaine. "Daniel, 'Public Defender,' and the Art of Cross-Examination," *Lawyer: A Brief 5,000-year History.* Chicago: American Bar Association, 2009.

Ascheri, Mario. *The Laws of Late Medieval Italy: Foundations for a European Legal System (1000-1500).* Leiden: Brill, 2013.

Baildron, William Pailey, editor for the Selden Society 1896. *Select Cases in Chancery (A.D. 1364-1471).* London, 1896. HathiTrust. http://babel.hathitrust.org/cgi/pt?id=njp.32101073364646;view=1up;seq=9. (REB).

Baker, J. H. *An Introduction to English Legal History*, 3d ed. London: Butterworths, 1990; 4th ed., 2002.

_____. "Law and Legal Institutions." In *William Shakespeare: His World, His Work, His Influence*, vol. 1, edited by John F. Andrews. New York: Charles Scribner's Sons, 1985.

Bathurst, T. F. (Hon.), Chief Justice of New South Wales. "The History of Equity" (speech). October 27, 2015. http://www.supremecourt.justice.nsw.gov.au/Pages/sco2_publications/SCO2_judicialspeeches/sco2_speeches_chiefjustice.aspx.

Bellomo, Manlio. *The Common Legal Past of Europe 1000 to 1800*, vol. 4. Translated with permission of the author by Lydia G. Cochrane. Washington D.C.: Catholic University of America Press, 1995. First published as *L'Europa del Diritto commune*. Rome: Il Cigno Galileo Galilei, 1988, 1989.

Brasington, Bruce. *Order in the Court*. Leiden: Brill, 2016.

Coquillette, Daniel R. *The Civilian Writers of Doctors' Commons, London: Three Centuries of Juristic Innovation in Comparative, Commercial, and International Law*. Berlin: Duncker & Humblot, 1988.

_____. *Francis Bacon*. Stanford: Stanford University Press, 1992.

_____. "Legal Ideology and Incorporation I: The English Civilian Writers, 1523-1607." *Boston University Law Review* 61 (1981). pp. 10-89. http://works.bepress.com/daniel_coquillette/; http://lawdigitalcommons.bc.edu/do/search/?q=coquillette&start=0&context=1184401.

_____. "Legal Ideology and Incorporation IV: The Nature of Civilian Influence on Modern Anglo-American Commercial Law." *Boston University Law Review* 67 (Nov., 1987). pp. 877-970. http://works.bepress.com/daniel_coquillette/.

_____. "Past the Pillars of Hercules: Francis Bacon and the Science of Rule-Making." *University of Michigan Journal of Law Reform* 46, no. 2 (2012). pp. 549-592. http://lawdigitalcommons.bc.edu/cgi/viewcontent.cgi?article=1495&context=lsfp; https://works.bepress.com/daniel_coquillette/.

_____. " 'The Purer Fountains': Bacon and Legal Education." Boston College Law School, Legal Studies Research Paper Series, no. 52 (Jan. 27, 2005). SSRN: http://ssrn.com/abstract=655261; http://works.bepress.coquillette. Also in *Francis Bacon and the Refiguring of Early Modern Thought: Essays to Commemmorate "The Advancement of Learning,"* (1605-2005), edited by Julie Solomon and Catherine Gilmetti Martin. (2005) New York: Routledge, 2016.

Crowe, Michael Bertram. *The Changing Profile of the Natural Law*. The Hague: Martinus Nijhoff, 1977.

Coulson, Doug. "The Devil's Advocate and Legal Oratory in the *Processus Sathanae*." *Rhetorica: A Journal of the History of Rhetoric* 33, no. 4 (March 9, 2016). SSRN: http://ssrn.com/abstract=2745281.

Dauchy, Serge and Georges Martyn, Anthony Musson, Heikki Pihlajamäki, Alain Wijffels, *The Formation and Transmission of Western Legal Culture: 150 Books that Made the Law in the Age of Printing*. Cham, Switzerland: Springer International, 2016; e-book, 2016.

Dawson, J.P. "Coke and Ellesmere Disinterred: The Attack on the Chancery in 1616." 36 *Ill. L. Rev.* 127 (1941). (REB).

Donahue, Charles, Jr., "Aggadic Stories About Medieval Western Jurists?" *Diné Israel*, vol. 24 (2007). https://cardozo.yu.edu/sites/default/files/Charles%20 Donahue%2C%20Jr.%2C%20Aggadic%20Stories%20About%20Medieval%20Western%20Jurists.pdf, pp. 209 to 215, 209.

_____. "Bassianus, that is to say, Bazianus? Bazianus and Johannes Bassianus on Marriage," *Rivista international di diritto commune* 14 (2003), pp. 41-82. http:// www.law.harvard.edu/faculty/cdonahue/writings/RIDC14_41_82.pdf.

_____. "The Case of the Man who Fell into the Tiber: the Roman Law of Marriage at the Time of the Glossators," *The American Journal of Legal History* 22, no. 1 (Jan. 1978), pp. 1-53.

_____, ed. *Tractatus Universi Iuris* (Venice 1584-86 Authors,). July, 2014. The Ames Foundation 1999-2018. http://amesfoundation.law.harvard.edu/digital/ TUI1584/TUI1584Metadata_Authors.html.

_____, and Kenneth Pennington. Bio-Bibliographical Guide to Medieval and Early Modern Jurists. August, 2016. The Ames Foundation 1999-2018. http://ames-foundation.law.harvard.edu/BioBibCanonists/HomePage_biobib2.php.

de Zulueta, Francis and Peter Steen. *The Teaching of Roman Law in England around 1200.* London: Selden Society, 1990.

Fortier, Mark. *The Culture of Equity in Early Modern England.* New York: Routledge, 2016.

Fowler, Russell. "A History of Chancery and its Equity, from Medieval England to Today's Tennessee." *Tennessee Bar Journal* (January 25, 2012). Reprinted by permission from Capital Area Bar Association, May 2012. http://caba.ms/articles/ features/history-chancery-equity.html.

Goodrich, Peter. *Law in the Courts of Love, Literature, and Other Minor Jurisprudences.* London: Routledge, 1996; Taylor & Francis e-Library, 2003.

_____. *Oedipus Lex: Psychoanalysis, History, Law.* Berkeley: University of California Press, 1995.

_____. Satirical Legal Studies: From the Legists to the *Lizard*," *Michigan Law Review* 103, no. 3 (2004). pp. 397-517.

_____, and Valerie Hayaert, eds. *Genealogies of Legal Vision.* New York: Routledge, 2015.

Gordley, James. *The Jurists: A Critical History.* Oxford: Oxford University Press, 2013.

Gratian, *Decretum.* The Medieval Canon Law Virtual Library. September 24, 2009. http://web.colby.edu/canonlaw/2009/09/24/decretum-decretists/.

Gray's Inn. 2018. "Benchers." https://www.graysinn.org.uk/history/past-members/ benchers; "Treasurers." https://www.graysinn.org.uk/history/past-members/ treasurers (1608 to 1617). https://www.graysinn.org.uk/sites/default/files/ documents/history/Treasurers%20websitre%202016%20updl.pdf.

Helmholz, Richard H. "Assumpsit and Fidei Laesio," *Law Quarterly Review* 91 (1975). pp. 406–432.

_____. "Canonical Remedies in Medieval Marriage Law: The Contributions of Legal Practice Founding," *University of St. Thomas Law Journal* 1 (2003). pp. 647-655. Chicago Unbound. http://chicagounbound.uchicago.edu/cgi/viewcontent.cgi?article=2479&context=journal_articles.

_____. *Roman Canon Law in Reformation England.* Cambridge: Cambridge University Press, 1990. http://catdir.loc.gov/catdir/samples/cam034/89035785.pdf.

_____. "Usury and the Medieval Church Courts," *Speculum* 61 (1986). pp. 364–380. http://chicagounbound.uchicago.edu/cgi/viewcontent.cgi?article=11246&context=journal_articles.

Holdsworth, William S. *A History of English Law,* 3d ed., vol. 1. Boston: Little, Brown, 1922. HathiTrust. http://hdl.handle.net/2027/njp.32101075729283?urlappend=%3Bseq=9. (REB).

Ibbetson, David. *Law and Equity: Approaches in Roman Law and Common Law.* Edited by E. Koops and W. J. Zwalve. Leiden: Martinus Nijhoff, 2014.

James, Sarah N. "Elizabethan painting: the portrait," in chapter 8, *Art in England: The Saxons to the Tudors 600-1600.* Oxford: Oxbow Books, 2016. pp. 307-311.

Kantorowicz, Ernst. *The King's Two Bodies: A Study in Medieval Political Theology.* Princeton: Princeton University Press, 2016. First printed in 1957.

Kantorowicz, Hermann. "The Poetical Sermon of a Medieval Jurist: Placentinus and his 'Sermo de Legibus,'" *Journal of the Warburg and Courtauld Institute* 2 (1938). pp. 22-41. JSTOR. www.jstor.org/stable/750022.

_____, William Warwick Buckland and Peter Weimar, eds. *Studies in the Glossators of the Roman Law: Newly Discovered Writings of the Twelfth Century.* Cambridge: Cambridge University Press, 1938.

Kirshner, Julius. "A Critical Appreciation of Lauro Martinez' 'Lawyers and Statecraft in Renaissance Florence.'" In *The Politics of Law in Late Medieval and Renaissance Italy, Essays in Honor of Lauro Martinez,* edited by Lawrin Armstrong and Julius Kirshner. Toronto: University of Toronto Press, 2011.

Kocher, Paul H. "Francis Bacon on the Science of Jurisprudence," *Journal of the History of Ideas* 18, no. 1 (Jan., 1957). pp. 3-26. JSTOR. http://www.jstor.org/stable/pdf/2707577.

Kuttner, Stephan. "A Forgotten Definition of Justice." In *Melanges Gerard Fransen* 2, edited by A. M. Stickler and S. Kuttner. Rome: *Studia Gratiana* 20. Rome, 1976. Reprinted in *The History of Ideas and Doctrines of Canon Law in the Middle Ages* 5, edited by S. Kuttner (London 1980, 1992). pp. 75-109.

Lauer, Rena, "Jewish Law and Litigation in the Secular Courts of the Late Medieval Mediterranean," *Critical Analysis of Law* 3, no. 1 (2016). pp. 114-132.

Main, Thomas O. "Traditional Equity and Contemporary Procedure," *Scholarly Works.* Paper 740 (2003). http://scholars.law.unlv.edu/facpub/740.

Maitland, F. W. *Equity, also the Forms of Action at Common Law, two courses of lectures.* Edited by A.H. Chaytor and W. J. Whittaker. Cambridge: University Press, 1909. Internet Archive, https://archive.org/details/equityalsoformso00mait.

_____, ed. *Select Passages from the Works of Bracton and Azo.* Publications of the Selden Society 8. London, 1894.

Mastroberti, Franceso. "The Liber Belial," *Historia et ius*, paper 12 (Jan., 2012). www. historiaetius.com.   http://www.historiaetius.eu/uploads/5/9/4/8/5948821/ mastroberti.pdf.

McGlynn, Margaret. *The Royal Prerogative and the Learning of the Inns of* Court. Cambridge: Cambridge University Press, 2003, 2004; first online 2009. www.cambridge.org/core_title/gb/201690.

Moglen, Eben. "English Legal History and its Materials, Political Refugees' Property." Aug. 23, 2014. http://moglen.law.columbia.edu/twiki/bin/view/ EngLegalHist/RefugeeProperty.

Murray, David. *Lawyers' Merriments.* Glasgow: James Maclehose and Sons, 1912. HathiTrust.   http://hdl.handle.net/2027/hvd.32044010322881?urlappend=%3Bs eq=17.

Padovani, Andrea, "The Metaphysical Thought of Late Medieval Jurisprudence." In *A Treatise of Legal Philosophy and General Jurisprudence*, vol. 7, edited by Andrea Padovani and Peter Stein. Dordrecht: Springer Netherlands, 2007. pp. 31-78.

Pennington, Kenneth. *The Biography of Gratian, The Father of Canon Law. Vill. L. Rev.* 59 (2014). pp. 679-706. http://digitalcommons.law.villanova.edu/cgi/viewcontent.cgi?article=3226&context=vlr;   http://scholarship.law.edu/cgi/viewcontent.cgi?article=1839&context=scholar.

_____. "Gratian and the Jews," *Bull. Medieval Canon L.* 31 (2014). pp. 111-124. http:// scholarship.law.edu/scholar.

_____. "Lex Naturalis and Ius Naturale." In *Crossing Boundaries at Medieval Universities*, edited by Spencer E. Young (Leiden: Brill, 2010), online, 2011. Pp. 227-254. Chapter DOI: 10.1163/ej.9789004192157.i-352.39.

_____."Medieval and Early Modern Jurists: A Bio-Bibliographical Listing." http:// legalhistorysources.com/; http://legalhistorysources.com/biobibl.htm; with Charles Donahue. August, 2016. The Ames Foundation 1999-2018. http:// amesfoundation.law.harvard.edu/BioBibCanonists/HomePage_biobib2.php.

_____. "Politics in Western Jurisprudence." In *A Treatise of Legal Philosophy and General Jurisprudence*, vol. 7, edited by A. Padovani and P. G. Stein. Dordrecht: Springer International, 2007. First published online, March 13, 2015. pp. 157-211.

_____. *Roman and Secular Law in the Middle Ages.* In *Medieval Latin: an Introduction and Biographical Guide* , edited by F. A. C. Mantello and A. G. Rigg. Washington D.C.: Catholic University Press of America, 1996. pp. 254-266. http://legalhistorysources.com/Law508/histlaw.htm.

Pettus, Isabella M. "The Legal Education of Women," *The Albany Law Journal* 61 (Jan.-June 1900). pp. 325-331. HathiTrust. https://hdl.handle.net/2027/osu.32437010639850.

Price, Polly J. "Natural Law and Birthright Citizenship in Calvin's Case (1608)," *Yale Journal of Law & the Humanities* 9, no. 1 (2013). http://digitalcommons.law.yale.edu/cgi/viewcontent.cgi?article=1170&context=yjlh.

Rechtshistorie. A Gateway to Legal History. http://www.rechtshistorie.nl/en/home; http://www.rechtshistorie.nl/en/medieval-law.

Reid, Jr., Charles. "Conjugal Debt." In *Women and Gender in Medieval Europe, an Encyclopedia*, edited by Margaret Schaus. New York: Routledge, 2006.

_____."Thirteenth Century Canon Law and Rights: The Word *Ius* and its Range of Subjective Meanings," *Studia Canonica* 30 (1996). pp. 295-342.

Resnik, Judith and Dennis Curtis. *Representing Justice*. New Haven: Yale University Press, 2011.

Roscoe, Thomas and Henry Roscoe. *Westminster Hall: Or Professional Relics and Anecdotes of the Bar, Bench and Woolsack.* London, 1825.

Ross, Richard J. "The Memorial Culture of Early Modern English Lawyers: Memory as Keyword, Shelter, and Identity, 1560-1640." *Yale Journal of Law & the Humanities* 10, no. 2 (May 8, 2013). pp. 229-326. http://digitalcommons.law.yale.edu/yjlh/vol10/iss2/1.

Rossi, Guido. *Insurance in Elizabethan England: The London Code.* Cambridge: Cambridge University Press, 2016.

St. Germain, Christopher. *The Doctor and Student, or, Dialogues between a Doctor of Divinity and a Student of the Laws of England [...]*. Revised and corrected by William Muchall. Cincinnati, 1886. First published in Latin, London, 1518. HathiTrust. http://hdl.handle.net/2027/uc2.ark:/13960/t1jh3nw58?urlappend=%3Bseq=28; http://lonang.com/library/reference/stgermain-doctor-and-student/.

Schrage, Eltjo. "'*Descendit ad Inferos:* And Belial Sues Jesus Christ for Trespass,"chapter 29. In *Critical Studies in Comparative Law, Ancient Law, and Legal History, Essays in Honor of Alan Watson*, edited by John Cairns and Olivia Robinson. Portland, OR: Hart Publishing, 2001.

[Seldeni, Ioannis]. *Ad Fletam Dissertatione.* Translated with introduction and notes by David Ogg. Cambridge: Cambridge University Press, 1925.

Selden, John. *A brief discourse touching the office of Lord Chancellor of England written by the learned John Selden of the Inner Temple, Esq., and dedicated by him to Sir Francis Bacon[...]; transcribed from a true copy thereof, found amongst the collections of[...] St. Lo. Kniveton[...]; together with a true catalogue of lord chancellors and keepers of the great seal of England, from the Norman conquest untill* [sic]*this present year, 1671*, by William Dugdale, Esquire[...]. London, 1671. Early English Books Online: Text Creation Partnership. http://name.umdl.umich.edu/A59075.0001.001.

_____, *The Dissertation of John Selden Annexed to Fleta.* Translated with notes by [Robert Kelham, the] editor of Britton. 1771. First published in 1647. HathiTrust, https://hdl.handle.net/2027/nyp.33433008667663.

_____, Adam Littleton, and Robert White. *The reverse or back-face of the English Janus to-wit, all that is met with in story concerning the common and statute-law of English Britanny, from the first memoirs of the two nations, to the decease of King Henry II, set down and tackt together succinctly by way of narrative: designed, devoted and dedicated to the most illustrious the Earl of Salisbury.* London, 1682. Early English Books Online: Text Creation Partnership. http://quod.lib.umich.edu/e/eebo/A59093.0001.001/1:8.1?rgn=div2;view=fulltext.

Shakespeare and the Law, Inner Temple Library. Exhibit. April 2014. http://www.innertemplelibrary.org.uk/displays/shakespeare.pdf.

Shapiro, Barbara. *A Culture of Fact.* Ithaca: Cornell University Press, 2003. http://www.cornellpress.cornell.edu/book/?GCOI=80140100453790.

_____. "Sir Francis Bacon and the Mid-17th Century Movement for Law Reform," *American Journal of Legal History* 24, no. 4 (Oct. 1, 1980). pp. 331-362. JSTOR. http://www.jstor.org/stable/844906.

Shoemaker, Karl. "The Devil at Law in the Middle Ages," *Revue de l'histoire des religions* 4 (2011). pp. 567-586. http://rhr.revues.org/7826.

Simpson, A. W. Brian. "The Early Constitution of Gray's Inn," in *Legal Theory and Legal History: Essays on the Common Law.* London: The Hambledon Press, 1987.

_____. The Place of Slade's Case in the History of Contract," *Law Quarterly Rev.* 76 (1958). pp. 381-396 (REB).

Smith, David Chan. *Sir Edward Coke and The Reform of the Laws: Religion, Politics, and Jurisprudence, 1578-1616.* Cambridge: Cambridge University Press, 2014.

Sokol, B. J. and Mary Sokol. "Shakespeare and the English Equity Jurisdiction, 'The Merchant of Venice' and The Two Texts of 'King Lear.'" *The Review of English Studies* 50, no. 200. Oxford: Oxford University Press (Nov., 1999). pp. 417-439. JSTOR, www.jstor.org/stable/517390.

Steinberg, Justin. *Dante and the Limits of the Law.* Chicago: University of Chicago Press, 2013.

Stephen of Tournai. *Die summa über das Decretum Gratiani.* Edited by Johann Friedrich von Schulte. Aalen: Scientia, 1965. First published in Giesen, 1891. http://works.bepress.com/david_freidenreich/12.

Stone, John. "John Cowell's *Interpreter*: Legal Tradition and Lexicographical Innovation," *Sederi* 10 (1999). pp. 121-129. www.sederi.org/wp-content/uploads/2016/12/10_12Stone.pdf.

Stretton, Tim. "Contract, Debt Litigation, and Shakespeare's 'The Merchant of Venice.'" *Adelaide Law Review* 31, no. 2 (2010). pp. 111-125. https://search.informit.com.au/documentSummary;dn=201100559;res=IELAPA.

Swindler, W.F. *Magna Carta, Legend and Legacy.* Indianapolis: Bobbs-Merrill, 1965 (REB).

Taliadoros, Jason. ch. 6, "Law and Theology in Gilbert of Foliot's (c. 1105/10 – 1187/88) Correspondence." In *Haskins Society Studies in Medieval History*, vol. 16, edited by Stephen Morillo and Diane Korngiebel. Woodbridge UK: The Boydell Press, 2006.

Taylor, Scott L. "*Vox populi e voce professionis: Processus juris joco-serius. Esoteric Humor and the Incommensurability of Laughter,*" chapter 17. In *Laughter in the Middle Ages and Early Modern Times: epistemology of a fundamental human behavior, its meaning and consequences*, edited by Albrecht Classen. Berlin: Walter de Gruyter, 2010.

Thorne, Samuel E. and J. H. Baker, eds. *Readings and Moots at the Inns of Court*, vol. 2. London: Selden Society, 1990.

Van de Wiel, Constant. *History of Canon Law*. Louvain: Peeters Press, 1991.

Vervaarts, Otto. Rechtsgeschiedenis. Legal History with a Dutch View. Blog.https://rechtsgeschiedenis.wordpress.com/2012/04/21/a-mosaic-of-digitizedmedieval-legal-manuscripts/.

Vinci, Stefano. "Liber Belial, a vademecum for roman-canonical procedure in Europe." *Forum historiae iuris* (Feb., 2015). http://www.forhistiur.de/es/2015-01-vinci/.

_____. "La diffusione del processo romano-canonico in Europa: Il Liber Belial tra fonti giuridiche canonistiche e romanistiche" ["A Diffusion of the Roman-Canonical Procedure in Europe: 'Liber Belial' between Canon Law and Roman Law Sources, in Italian"], Max Planck Institute for European Legal History Research Paper Series No. 2012-03 (Sept. 9, 2012). SSRN: http://ssrn.com/abstract=2139529 or http://dx.doi.org/10.2139/ssrn.2139529.

Wheeler, Harvey. "Francis Bacon's *Case of the Post-Nati:* (1608), Foundations of Anglo-American Constitutionalism; An Application of Critical Constitutional Theory". Paper delivered at the University of London Symposium, September 1999. http://www.sirbacon.org/wheelerpostnati.html; http://www.constitution.org/hwheeler/hwheeler.htm.

_____. "Francis Bacon's 'Verulamium': the Common Law Template of the Modern in English Science and Culture." *Angelaki* 4, no. 1 (1999). pp. 7-26. www.constitution.org/wheeler/bacona.doc; http://www.sirbacon.org/wheelerv.html.

Wiener, Frederick Bernays. "Did Bracton Write Bracton?" *American Bar Association Journal* 64, no. 1 (1978). pp. 72-75. JSTOR. http://www.jstor.org/stable/20745182.

Williman, Daniel. "Legal Terminology, an Historical Introduction to the Technical Language of Law." http://www.corsanoandwilliman.org/latin/work/legalterminology.htm.

Winroth, Anders. "Where Gratian Slept: The Life and Death of the Father of Canon Law." 7/04/13. pp. 105-106. https://classesv2.yale.edu/access/content/user/haw6/Law/KA03_Winroth_Gratian_K2-1.pdf.

_____, and Michael Widener. "The Pope's Other Jobs: Judge and Lawgiver." *Italian Statutes*, book 6. Exhibit. 2015. http://digitalcommons.law.yale.edu/itsta/6.

Witt, Ronald G. *The Two Latin Cultures and the Foundation of Renaissance Humanism in Medieval Italy*. Cambridge: Cambridge University Press, 2012.

4. Authorship Argued

Alexander, Mark. *Shakespeare Authorship Sourcebook*. 2018. http://www.sourcetext.com/sourcebook.

Bacon Is Shakespeare. Blog. http://baconisshakespeare.blogspot.com/. "Bacon versus Shakespeare, A Judicial Decision . . . ." http://www.sirbacon.org/links/nytimes.html.

Bacon Was Shakespeare-Authorship Evidence. Blog. http://bacon-shakespeare-evidence.blogspot.ca/search?q=Merchant+of+Venice; "Was Shakespeare a Lawyer?" June 5, 2011 et al. In twenty-four parts. Posted by "Unfold Yourself." http://bacon-shakespeare-evidence.blogspot.com/2011/06/shakespeare-lawyer-1-introduction-1.html.

Baconiana, journal of the Francis Bacon Society. London, 1886–present. http://francisbaconsociety.co.uk/the-society/baconiana/. See also HathiTrust. https://catalog.hathitrust.org/Record/000676348.

"Baptismal Registration of Francis Bacon from St. Martin-in-the-Fields." http://www.sirbacon.org/baptismalregistration.htm.

Bassano, Peter. "Shakespeare." http://peterbassano.com/shakespeare.

Biddulf, L. "Lord Bacon and the Theatre," *Baconiana*, no. 108 (July, 1943). http://www.sirbacon.org/links/lord_bacon_&_the_theatre.htm.

"Binder's Waste Discovery of a Manuscript Similar to Shakespeare," Sotheby's July 21, 1992 (*Henry IV*). http://www.sirbacon.org/graphics/sothebys.jpg.

Bormann, Edwin. *Francis Bacon's Cryptic Rhymes* and the Truth They Reveal. London: Siegle, Hill, 1906. HathiTrust, http://hdl.handle.net/2027/ucl.$b681854. For an excerpt, "Did Mr. James Spedding Really Know Everything about Francis Bacon?" (appendix to chapter one. pp. 217-226), see http://www.sirbacon.org/boranonspedding.htm.

_____. *The Shakespeare Secret*. Translated from the German by Harry Brett. London, 1895. HathiTrust, http://hdl.handle.net/2027/ucl.b4500360.

Bridgewater, Howard. *Evidence Connecting Sir Francis Bacon with 'Shakespeare.'* London: George Lapworth, 1943. http://sirbacon.org/ResearchMaterial/evidence.htm.

Brown, Basil. *Supposed Caricature of the Droeshout Portrait of Shakespeare, with Fac-Simile of the Rare Print Taken from the very scarce Tract of an Elizabethan Poet.* New York: 150 copies printed for private circulation, 1911. HathiTrust, http://hdl.handle.net/2027/loc.ark:/13960/t1rf6ng94?urlappend=%3Bseq=14.

Carr, Francis. "Bacon's Royal Parentage." http://www.sirbacon.org/parentage.htm.

_____. "The Writer's Finger Prints." http://www.sirbacon.org/links/carrlegalquixote.html.

Clarke, Barry R. *A Linguistic Analysis of Francis Bacon's Contribution to Three Shakespeare Plays*. A Ph.D. Thesis, Brunel University, 2013. http://barryispuzzled.com/PhDThesis.pdf.

_____. *The Shakespeare Puzzle, a Non-Esoteric Baconian Theory*. Online, 14 Feb. 2007. http://barryispuzzled.com/shakpuzz.pdf. http://citeseerx.ist.psu.edu/viewdoc/download?doi=10.1.1.116.944&rep=rep1&type=pdf.

Cooper, D. W. and Gerald, Lawrence. "A Bond for all the Ages: Sir Francis Bacon and John Dee: The Original 007." http://www.sirbacon.org/links/dblohseven.html.

Dawkins, Peter. Francis Bacon Research Trust: *Bacon-Shakespeare Timeline*: http://fbrt.org.uk/pages/essays/Bacon-Shakespeare_Timeline.pdf; "The Name 'William Shakespeare,'" http://fbrt.org.uk/pages/essays/The_Name_William_Shakespeare.pdf; "Baconian Philosophy," http://www.fbrt.org.uk/pages/hermes_philosophy.html; "The Bacon Brothers and France," http://fbrt.org.uk/pages/essays/Bacon_Brothers_and_France.pdf.

Des Moineaux, Edwin J. *Manuscript Said to be Handwriting of William Shakespeare Identified as Penmanship of Another Person. Mystery of "Sir Thomas More Document" Unraveled. An Entirely New Phase of the Bacon-Shakespeare Controversy*. Los Angeles: printed for the author, 1924. http://www.sirbacon.org/stmcover.htm, http://www.sirbacon.org/stmcontents.htm.

Dixon, Theron Soligman Eugene. *Francis Bacon and his Shakespeare*. Chicago, 1895. Internet Archive. https://archive.org/details/cu31924013153402.

Dodd, Alfred. *Francis Bacon's Personal Life Story*, vol. 1: London: Rider, 1949. Vol. 2: London, Century Hutchinson, 1986. See http://www.sirbacon.org/links/dodd.html. For "Francis Bacon and his Nemesis Edward Coke," an excerpt of the chapter, "The Last of the Tudors," see http://www.sirbacon.org/cokeandbacon.htm.

_____. "The Sublime Prince of the Royal Secret," *The Marriage of Elizabeth Tudor*. London: Rider, 1940. For excerpts, see http://www.sirbacon.org/links/marriageofet.htm and http://www.sirbacon.org/doddsublimeprince.htm.

Dupuy, Jr., Paul. An Authorship Analysis, Francis Bacon as Shakespeare. http://fly.hiwaay.net/-paul/.

Durning-Lawrence, Sir Edward. *The Shakespeare Myth*. London: Gay & Hancock, 1912. HathiTrust. http://hdl.handle.net/2027/mdp.39015030034436. Pages 27-30, "Francis Bacon and the English Language," are excerpted at http://www.sirbacon.org/links/BaconEnglishLanguage.htm.

Freeman, Arthur. "The 'Tapster Manuscript': An Analogue of Shakespeare's *Henry the Fourth Part One*." In *English Manuscript Studies, 1100-1700*, vol. 6 (1997), edited by Peter Beal and Jeremy Griffiths.

Gentry, R. J. W. "Francis Bacon and the Stage" (from *Baconiana*). http://www.sirbacon.org/links/bacon&_the_stage.htm.

Gililov, Ilya. *The Shakespeare Game: The Mystery of the Great Phoenix.* New York: Algora Publishing, 2003.

"H. S." "Hayward's 'Henry IV,' *Baconiana*, IV, third series, no. 13 (Jan., 1906). pp. 5-14.

James, George. *Francis Bacon: The Author of Shakespeare.* London, 1893.

Johnson, Edward D. "A chapter from "Francis Bacon's Promus" in *The Shaksper Illusion* . 1947. 3rd ed.: London: Mitre Press, 1965. http://www.sirbacon.org/links/notebook.html.

Leith, Alicia Amy. "Bacon on the Stage." *Baconiana* (1909). http://www.sirbacon.org/leithbaconstage.htm.

Lochithea. *Baconian Reference Book,' Commentarius Solutus.'* New York: iUniverse, 2009. Online, https://www.fbrt.org.uk/pages/essays/baconian_reference_book_archive.pdf; https://archive.org/stream/BaconianReferenceBook/baconian_reference_book_archive_djvu.txt.

_____. *Sir Francis Bacon's Journals: The Rarest of Princes.* New York: iUniverse, 2007. http://www.sirbacon.org/FBs_Journals/FBs_Journals.pdf.

Loerzel, Robert. "Judge: Bacon Wrote Shakespeare Plays." 2003. http://www.alchemyofbones.com/stories/shakespeare.htm.

Miles, Simon. "The Francis Bacon Society Lectures with Simon Miles. 'Francis Bacon and the *Merchant of Venice.*' March 2015, pub. on Aug. 27, 2015. https://www.youtube.com/watch?v=KcQCljc1Mv8.

_____. SAT [Shakespeare Authorship Trust] Conference 2017-5–Simon Miles–Francis Bacon and the Mystery of the Phoenix and Turtle. Published online, January 11, 2018. Youtube. https://www.youtube.com/watch?v=HjxlobZKzZI.

The Morning Oregonian 46, no. 17,368 (July 22, 1916). p. 1. http://oregonnews.uoregon.edu/lccn/sn83025138/1916-07-22/ed-1/seq-1.pdf.

Niederkorn, William S. "To Be or not To Be Shakespeare." *New York Times*, Learning Network, Student Connections. August 21, 2004. http://www.nytimes.com/learning/students/pop/20040823snapmonday.html.

"The Northumberland Manuscript, Bacon and Shakespeare Manuscripts in one Portfolio!" http://www.sirbacon.org/links/northumberland.html.

Pott, Mrs. Henry [Constance]. *Did Bacon Write Shakespeare?" Thirty-two Reasons for Believing that He Did.* Parts I and II: London, [1884 to 189-?]. Parts III to V: London, 1900.

_____. "*Francis Bacon and Shakespeare, the promus of formularies and elegancies, being private notes, ca. 1594, being hitherto unpublished . . . illustrated and elucidated by passages from Shakespeare.*" Edited with preface by E. A. Abbott. London, 1883. For similar works, see the Online Books Page for Mrs. Henry Pott, http://onlinebooks.library.upenn.edu/webbin/book/lookupname?key=Pott%2C%20Henry%2C%20Mrs%2E%2C%201833%2D1915.

Price, Diana. *Shakespeare's Unorthodox Biography, New Evidence of an Authorship Problem.* Westport CT: Greenwood Press, 2001.

Purchase, Heather. "Writing's on the Wall for Shakespeare," *London Evening Standard* (July 30, 1992). http://www.sirbacon.org/links/handwriting1.html.

Saunders, Walter. "The Identification of 'Labeo' and 'Mutius' as Francis Bacon in Hall and Marston's Satires." 2011. http://sirbacon.org/wsaundersHallandMarston.htm.

_____. "The Northumberland Manuscript and a Remarkable Discovery by Simon Miles." 2007. http://www.sirbacon.org/nmsaunders.htm.

Stewart, Alan. "The Case for Bacon," chapter 2. In *Shakespeare Beyond Doubt: Evidence, Argument, Controversy,* edited by Paul Edmonson and Stanley Wells. New York: Cambridge University Press, 2013.

Stronach, George. Letter to editor. "Shakespeare, Bacon, and Dr. Murray," The Academy and Literature 64 (April 25, 1903). pp. 421–423. https://books.google.com/books?id=xvXQ3PTqthYC.

Ward-Gandy, Maureen. "Elizabethan Era Writing Comparison for Identification of 'Common Authorship,'" Shakespeare vs. Bacon 1992, Originally Examined 24 July, 1992. Reviewed for Mr. Lawrence Gerald 2 July 1994. Published with permission of Maureen Ward-Gandy and Lawrence Gerald.

5. *Shakespeare, Law, and Lawyers*

a. "Shakespeare Had Great Legal Knowledge."

Briggs, Arthur E. "Did Shaxper Write Shakespeare?" *American Bar Association Journal* (April, 1960). pp. 410-412. JSTOR. http://www.jsor.org/stable/25721149.

Carr, Francis. "The Writer's Finger Prints, Francis Carr Explores the Legal Link between Quixote and Shakespeare," *New Law Journal* (Jan. 31, 1997). http://www.sirbacon.org/links/carrlegalquixote.html.

Castle, Edward J. *Shakespeare, Bacon, Jonson, and Greene: A Study.* London, 1897. https://books.google.com/books?id=vDQ_AAAAYAAJ.

Cockburn, N. B. *The Bacon Shakespeare Question, The Baconian Theory Made Sane.* Guildford and Kings Lynn UK: printed for the author, 1998. http://www.sirbacon.org/cockburn.htm (outline); http://www.sirbacon.org/anonymous.htm (excerpt from ch. 4). Review by Mather Walker http://www.sirbacon.org/mcockburnreview.htm.

Greenwood, G. G. *The Shakespeare Problem Restated.* London: John Lane, 1908. HathiTrust. http://hdl.handle.net/2027/njp.32101067185445?urlappend=%3Bseq=11.

_____. *Shakespeare's Law.* London: C. Palmer, 1920. HathiTrust. https://catalog.hathitrust.org/Record/001019050.

_____. *Shakespeare's Law and Latin: How I Was 'Exposed' by Mr. J. M. Robertson.* London: Watts, 1916. HathiTrust. https://catalog.hathitrust.org/Record/001366923 (refutation of J. M. Robertson, *The Baconian Heresy: a Confutation.* London:

Herbert Jenkins, 1913. For more by Greenwood, see the Online Books Page for G. G. Greenwood, http://onlinebooks.library.upenn.edu/web-bin/book/lookupname?key=Greenwood%2C%20G%2E%20G%2E%20%28Granville%20George%29%2C%20Sir%2C%201850%2D1928.

Holmes, (The Hon.) Nathaniel. *The Authorship of Shakespeare, with an appendix of additional matters including the recently discovered Northumberland MSS, a supplement of additional proofs that Francis Bacon was the real author, and a full index. In two volumes.* London, 1866. HathiTrust. https://hdl.handle.net/2027/hvd.hw2cb8; http://www.sirbacon.org/holmes.htm.

Pares, Commander Martin. "Francis Bacon and the Knights of the Helmet," *American Bar Association Journal* (April, 1960). pp. 402–409. JSTOR. http://www.jstor.org/stable/25721148; https://books.google.ca/books?id=IHARbvm-CwwC.

_____. "Parallelisms and the Promus." *Baconiana* (August, 1963). http://www.sirbacon.org/mp.html.

Reed, Edwin. *Bacon vs. Shakspere, Brief for Plaintiff,* 7th ed. Boston, 1897. HathiTrust. http://hdl.handle.net/2027/hvd.hw20tk.

_____. *Coincidences, Bacon and Shakespeare.* Boston: Coburn Publishing, 1906. HathiTrust. http://hdl.handle.net/2027/cool.ark:/13960/t56d6d75z. For more by Reed, see the Online Books Page. http://onlinebooks.library.upenn.edu/webbin/book/lookupname?key=Reed%2C%20Edwin%2C%201835%2D1908.

Roe, J. E. [John Elisha]. *Sir Francis Bacon's Own Story.* Rochester NY: DuBois Press, 1918. HathiTrust. http://hdl.handle.net/2027/njp.32101068587755.

Rushton, William Lowes. *Shakespeare a Lawyer.* London, 1858. HathiTrust. https://hdl.handle.net/2027/hvd.32044009633488. For more by Rushton, see the Online Books Page. http://onlinebooks.library.upenn.edu/webbin/book/lookupname?key=Rushton%2c%20William%20Lowes&c=x.

b. "Shakespeare Did Not Have Great Legal Knowledge."

Barton, Sir Dunbar Plunkett. *Links Between Shakespeare and the Law.* London: Faber & Gwyer, 1929. HathiTrust, https://hdl.handle.net/2027/ucl.b3293657 .

Beeching, D. H. C. *William Shakespeare, player, playmaker, and poet: a reply to Mr. George Greenwood, M.P.,* 2d ed. London: Smith, Elder, 1909. HathiTrust. https://catalog.hathitrust.org/Record/009392575.

Brune, C. M. *Shakespeare's Use of Legal Terms.* London: Straker, 1914.

Davis, (Hon.) Cushman K. *The Law in Shakespeare,* 2d ed. St. Paul, 1884. HathiTrust. http://hdl.handle.net/2027/loc.ark:/13960/t07w6z849?urlappend=%3Bseq=7.

c. Literature and Law

Conter, David. "Eagleton, Judge Posner, and Shylock v. Antonio," in "Notes," *McGill Law Journal* 35 (1990). pp. 905-920. http://lawjournal.mcgill.ca/userfiles/other/2931026-Conter.pdf.

Fields, Bertram. *The Players, The Mysterious Identity of William Shakespeare.* New York: HarperCollins, 2005.

Friedler, Edith Z. "Essay: Shakespeare's Contribution to the Teaching of Comparative Law— Some Reflections on The Merchant of Venice," *La. L. Rev.* 60, no. 4 (Summer, 2000). pp. 1087-1102. LSU Law Digital Commons. https://digitalcommons.law.lsu.edu/lalrev/vol60/iss4/6/.

Keeton, George W. *Shakespeare and his Legal Problems.* London: A. & C. Black, 1930.

_____. *Shakespeare's Legal and Political Background.* London: Pittman 1967.Kornstein, Daniel. *Kill All the Lawyers, Shakespeare's Legal Appeal.* Princeton: Princeton University Press, 1994.

Normand, Lord [Wilfred; W. G.]. "Portia's Judgment," *University of Edinburgh Journal* (1939–40), pp. 43–45.

Raffield, Paul. *The Art of Law in Shakespeare.* Oxford: Hart Publishing, 2017.

_____, and Gary Watt, eds. *Shakespeare and the Law.* Oxford: Hart Publishing, 2008.

Phelps, Charles E. *Falstaff and Equity, an Interpretation.* Boston: Houghton Mifflin, 1901. Internet Archive. https://archive.org/details/falstaffequityin00phel.

Phillips, O. Hood. *Shakespeare and the Lawyers.* New York: Routledge, 2013. First published, 1972.

Shakespeare Cross-Examination: a compilation of articles first appearing in the American Bar Association Journal. Chicago: Cuneo Press, 1961.

Sinsheimer, Hermann. *Shylock.* New York: Benjamin Blom, 1963. First published in 1947.

Yoshino, Kenji. *A Thousand Times More Fair: What Shakespeare's Plays Teach Us about Justice.* New York: Ecco, 2011.

Warren, Christopher N. *Literature and the Law of Nations, 1580-1680.* Oxford: Oxford University Press, 2015.

Wilson, Luke. "Drama and Marine Insurance in Shakespeare's London." In *The Law in Shakespeare*, edited by Constance Jordan and Karen Cunningham. Houndsmills UK: Palgrave Macmillan, 2007.

Zurcher, Andrew. "Consideration, Contract and The End of The Comedy of Errors," chapter 2 in *Shakespeare and the Law*, edited by Paul Raffield and Gary Watt. Oxford: Hart Publishing, 2008.

_____, ed. *Shakespeare and Law.* London: Arden Shakespeare, 2010.

6. Biography/History/Philosophy/Theology/Education/Science/ Travel

Armstrong, Chris. "The darker side of the chief King James Bible translator." Grateful to the Dead, a church historian's playground. Dec. 30, 2010. https://gratefultothedead.wordpress.com/2010/12/30/the-darker-side- of-the-chief-king-james-bible-translator-lancelot-andrewes/.

Armstrong, Lawrin David, *Usury and Public Debt in Early Renaissance Florence: Lorenzo Ridolfi on the Monte Commune.* Toronto: Pontifical Institute of Medieval Studies, 2003.

Barrow, Henry and John Greenwood. *A collection of certain letters and conferences lately passed betwixt certaine preachers and two prisoners in the Fleet.* [Dordrecht?: S.n.], 1590. Early English Books Online: Text Creation Partnership, http://name. umdl.umich.edu/A05036.0001.001;

_____. *A collection of certain sclandalous [sic] articles given out by the bishops against such faithful Christians [...].* [Dordrecht? S. n.], 1590. Early English Books Online: Text Creation Partnership, http://name.umdl.umich.edu/A05037.0001.001.

Bowen, Catherine Drinker. *The Lion and the Throne, The Life and Times of Sir Edward Coke (1552-1634).* Boston: Little, Brown, 1956.

Brown, Brendan F. "St. Thomas More, Lawyer," *Fordham L Rev.* 4, no. 3, (Nov., 1935) pp. 375-390. http://ir.lawnet.fordham.edu/flr/vol4/iss3/1.

Brown, Campbell and Steven Wiggins. *St. Andrews and Fife Walks.* Edinburgh: Black and White Publishing, 1992.

Campbell, John Lord. *Lives of the Chief Justices,* vol. 1 (4 volumes). London, 1849. https://archive.org/stream/liveschiefjusti06campgoog/liveschiefjusti06camp-goog_djvu.txt; vol. 2. https://archive.org/stream/livesofchiefju02camp/livesof-chiefju02camp_djvu.txt.

_____. *Lives of the Lord Chancellors and Keepers of the Great Seal of England[...],* vol. 1, 2d ed. Edited by John A. Mallory. Toronto, 1876. HathiTrust, https://catalog.ha-thitrust.org/Record/100266555.

The Church of England. "History." https://www.churchofengland.org/about-us/history.aspx.

Collections of Epitaphs and Monumental Inscriptions: Chiefly in Scotland. Glasgow, 1834.

"Coram Rege Rolls initial detail Elizabeth I," National Archives, UK, http://www. nationalarchives.gov.uk/education/resources/the-english-reformation-c1527-1590/coram-rege-rolls-initial-detail-elizabeth-i/.

Cullhed, Anders. *The Shadow of Creusa, Negotiating Fictionality in Late Antique Latin Literature.* Berlin: Walter De Gruyter, 2015, e-pub. 2015, www.jouve.com.

Ditchfield, P. H. *Books Fatal to Their Authors.* New York, 1895. HathiTrust, http://hdl. handle.net/2027/uc2.ark:/13960/t84j0jh8z.

Dixon, William Hepworth. *Personal History of Lord Bacon.* 2 vols. "From unpublished papers." Leipzig, 1861. HathiTrust. http://hdl.handle.net/2027/uc2.ark:/13960/t8v982b7k?urlappend=%3Bseq=7.

Dox, Donnalee. *The Idea of the Theatre in Latin Christian Thought: Augustine to the Fourteenth Century.* Ann Arbor: University of Michigan Press, 2004.

Duby, Georges. *The Knight, the Lady, and the Priest, the Making of Modern Marriage in Medieval France.* Translated by Barbara Bray. New York: Pantheon Books, 1983.

Duff, E. Gordon. *The English Provincial Printers, Stationers and Bookbinders to 1557.* The Sandars Lectures 1911. Cambridge: Cambridge University Press, 1912.

Ellison, Katherine, "Early Modern Cryptology as Fashionable Reading," *Journal of the Northern Renaissance*, no. 6 (2014), digital only. http://www.northernrenaissance.org/114400072777760780000-wayes-early-modern-cryptography-as-fashionable-reading/.

Erasmus, Desiderius. *The Praise of Folly,* with a life of the author and illustrations by Hendrik Willem van Loon. Translated by John Wilson (1627-1696). New York: Walter J. Black, 1942. First published, Paris, 1511.

"Fool's Cap World Map." Royal Museums Greenwich Collection. http://collections.rmg.co.uk/collections/objects/206385.html.

Forshaw, Cliff. "'Cease to bawle, thou wasp-stung Satyrist": Writers, Printers and the Bishops' Ban of 1599.' Brunel University. *Renaissance Renegotiations. EnterText* 3, no. 1 (May 22, 2003; online, June 12, 2004), pp. 101-131. https://www.brunel.ac.uk/__data/assets/pdf_file/0005/111020/Cliff-Forshaw,-Cease-Cease-to-bawle,-thou-wasp-stung-Satyrist-Writers,-Printers-and-the-Bishops-Ban-of-1599.pdf.

Goldring, Elizabeth. *John Nichols's 'The Progresses and Public Processions of Queen Elizabeth I,' a New Edition of the Early Modern Sources,* vol. 1 (1579-1595). Oxford: Oxford University Press, 2014.

Guzzetti, Linda. "Women in Court in Early Fourteenth-Century Venice," chapter 4. In *Across the Religious Divides, Women, Property and Law in the Wider Mediterranean (ca. 1300-1800),* edited by Jutta Gisela Sperling and Shona Kelly Wray. New York: Routledge, 2010; Taylor & Francis e-library, 2009.

Hall, Grace. "Felix and the Spider." *The Baldwin Project.* 2000– 2018. http://www.mainlesson.com/display.php?author=hallg&book=saints&story=felix.

Haskins, Charles Homer. *The Renaissance of the Twelfth Century.* Cambridge: Harvard University Press, 1982. First published, 1927.

Haugaard, William P. "Elizabeth Tudor's Book of Devotions: A Neglected Clue to the Queen's Life and Character." *The Sixteenth Century Journal* 12, no. 2 (Summer, 1981). pp. 79-106. JSTOR, http://www.jstor.org/stable/2539502.

Havry, Ofir. *John Selden and the Western Political Tradition.* Cambridge: Cambridge University Press, 2017.

Hekala, Tamsin. "Who's a Relative? Kinship Terminology in the Middle Ages," *The ORB: On-line Reference Book for Medieval Studies.* ARLIMA [*Les Archives de literature du Moyen Age*]. 1996. pp. 1-8. https://www.arlima.net/the-orb/essays/text03.html.

The History of Parliament. First published as *The History of Parliament: the House of Commons 1604-1629.* Edited by Andrew Thrush and John P. Ferris. Cambridge:

Cambridge University Press, 2010. 1964-2017. www.Historyofparliamenton-line.org.

Hoftijzer, P. G. "British books abroad: the Continent." In *The Cambridge History of the Book in Britain*, 1557-1695, vol. 4, edited by John Barnard and D. F. MacKenzie. Cambridge: Cambridge University Press, 2002.

Holmes, Arthur F. Wheaton College. "The History of Philosophy, Lecture 29, Francis Bacon," in the series, *The History of Philosophy*. Youtube. Published online April 21, 2015. https://www.youtube.com/watch?v=gARxnOJDI-w&index=29&list=PLjpbX0XZ76T2suXhHqGkINqzAhE4dknQB.

Hook, Walter F., "Theobald," *Lives of the Archbishops of Canterbury*, vol. 2, *Anglo-Norman Period*. London, 1862.

Hughes, R. E. "Francis Bacon, the Renaissance State, and St. Augustine: a Chapter in the History of Education." *History of Education Journal* 9, no. 2 (Winter, 1958). pp. 32-36. JSTOR, http://www.jstor.org/stable/3692579.

Hughson, David. *London, Being an Accurate History and Description of the British Metropolis*, vol. 2. London, 1805.

Huizinga, Johann. *Homo Ludens, a Study of the Play-Element in Culture*. London: Routledge, 1949. http://art.yale.edu/file_columns/0000/1474/homo_ludens_johan_huizinga_routledge_1949_.pdf.

Hyde, John Kenneth. *Padua in the Age of Dante*. New York: Barnes & Noble, 1966.

Jacobs, Frank. "#480. The Fool's Cap Map of the World." The Big Think. 2007–2018. http://bigthink.com/strange-maps/480-the-fools-cap-map-of-the-world.

Jacobs, Rita D. "Fare of the Country; English Trifle; Serious Dessert." Travel Section, *The New York Times* (March 27, 1988). http://www.nytimes.com/1988/03/27/travel/fare-of-the-country-english-trifle-serious-dessert.html?pagewanted=all.

Johnston, Douglas M. *The Historical Foundations of World Order: the Tower and the Arena*. The Hague: Martinus Nijhoff, 2008.

Kelsy, Harry. *Sir John Hawkins: Queen Elizabeth's Slave Trader*. New Haven: Yale University Press, 2003.

Klein, Jürgen. "Francis Bacon," *The Stanford Encyclopedia of Philosophy. Edited by N. Zalta* (Summer, 2015). http://plato.stanford.edu/archives/sum2015/entries/francis-bacon/.

Kunow, Amelie Deventer von. *Francis Bacon, Last of the Tudors*. Translated by Willard Parker. New York: printed for the Francis Bacon Society of America, 1924. Electronically typed and edited by Juan Schoch at http://www.sirbacon.org/vonkunow.html.

Langman, Peter. "I Give Thee Leave to Publish: New Atlantis and Francis Bacon's Republic of Knowledge." In *Centres and Cycles of Accumulation in and Around the Netherlands during the Early Modern Period*, edited by Lissa Roberts. Zurich: Lit Verlag, 2011. pp. 53-73. http://www.academia.edu/946407/Centres_and_cycles_of_accumulation_in_and_around_the Netherlands.

Leonard, A. B. *Marine Insurance: Origins and Institutions, 1300-1850.* Houndsmills UK: Palgrave-Macmillan, 2016.

"Lot 53, Elizabeth I, Queen of England. Cicero, Marcus Tullius. Orationem volume primum 1543. Bound for Queen Elizabeth. Live auction April 9, 2015: *sold.*" Swann Auction Galleries. Copyright by Invaluable (1986-2018). http://www.invaluable.com/auction-lot/elizabeth-i,-queen-of-england.-cicero,-marcus-tu-53-c-5da482eb94.

"Magna Carta and the Rule of Law from the Knights Templar," Order of the Temple of Solomon. 2016. http://www.knightstemplarorder.org/templar-magna-carta/.

Martin, Patrick. *Elizabethan Espionage, Plotters and Spies in The Struggle Between Catholicism and the Crown.* Jefferson NC: McFarland, 2016.

Matthews, Nieves. *The History of a Character Assassination.* New Haven: Yale University Press, 1996.

Matthews, Steven. *Theology and Science in the Thought of Francis Bacon.* Aldershot: Ashgate, 2008.

Mays, Andrea. *The Millionaire and the Bard: Henry Folger's Obsessive Hunt for Shakespeare's First Folio.* New York: Simon & Schuster, 2015.

Miceli, Augusto P. "Forum Juridicum: Bartolus of Sassoferrato." *Louisiana Law Review* 37, no. 5 (Summer, 1977). pp. 1027-1036. LSU Law Digital Commons. https://digitalcommons.law.lsu.edu/lalrev/vol37/iss5/3/.

Minkov, Svetozar Y. *Francis Bacon's Inquiry Touching Human Nature: Virtue, Philosophy and the Relief of Man's Estate.* Lanham MD: Lexington Books, 2010.

Parker, J. H. *The Library of Anglo-Catholic Theology: Ninety-six Sermons by the Right Reverent and Father in God Launcelot Andrewes[...],* vol. 2. Oxford, 1874. https://books.google.com/books/about/The_Library_of_Anglo_Catholic_Theology_N.html?id=BzDxoQEACAAJ.

Parry, Graham. *The Trophies of Time.* New York: Oxford University Press, 1995.

"Portia Catonis, Life of Portia." http://portiacatonis.weebly.com/.

Riga, Frank G. "Rethinking Shylock's Tragedy: [Director Michael] Radford's critique of anti-semitism in 'The Merchant of Venice.'" Mythopoetic Society (2010). The Free Library by Farlex, 2018. http://www.thefreelibrary.com/Rethinking+Shylock%27s+tragedy%3a+Radford%27s+critique+of+anti-semitism+in...-a0227196961. Roe, Richard Paul. *The Shakespeare Guide to Italy, Retracing the Bard's Unknown Travels.* New York: HarperCollins, 2011.

Ronald, Susan. *Heretic Queen: Queen Elizabeth I and the Wars of Religion.* New York: St. Martin's Press, 2012.

Ross, Janet. *Florentine Palaces and their Stories.* London: J. M. Dent, 1905.

Saveli, Rodolfo. "The Censoring of Law Books." Translated by Adrian Belton. In *Church, Censorship, and Culture in Early Modern Italy.* Edited by Gigliola Fragnito. Cambridge: Cambridge University Press, 2001.

Schaff, Philip, ed. *Nicene and Post-Nicene Fathers, First Series,* vols. 1 and 2. Buffalo, 1887. Revised and edited for New Advent by Kevin Knight. http://www.newadvent.org/fathers/1102055.htm.

Schoch, Juan. "The Private Manuscript Library of Francis Bacon." http://www.sirbacon.org/Tottel.htm.

Sennis, Antonio. *Cathars in Question.* Rochester NY: York Medieval Press, 2016.

Shuger, Deborah. *Censorship and Cultural Sensibility: The Regulation of Language in Tudor-Stuart England.* Philadelphia: University of Pennsylvania Press, 2006.

Spedding, James. *Evenings with a Reviewer: Or, Macaulay and Bacon.* 2 vols. Boston, 1881–82. HathiTrust. https://hdl.handle.net/2027/wu.89095710323. vol. 2, HathiTrust, https://hdl.handle.net/2027/wu.89095710414.

Stephen, Leslie and/or Sidney Lee, ed(s). *Dictionary of National Biography.* London, 1885-1900; 1901 Supplement.

Strong, Roy. *The Cult of Elizabethan Portraiture and Pageantry.* London: Thames & Hudson, 1977.

Tallan, Cheryl and Emily Taitz. "Learned Women in Traditional Jewish Society," *Jewish Women: A Comprehensive Historical Encyclopedia,* vol. 1. Jewish Women's Archive. March, 2009. https://jwa.org/enccyclopedia/article/learned-women-in-traditional-jewish-society.

Temkin, Owsei. *The Double Face of Janus and Other Essays in the History of Medicine.* Baltimore: Johns Hopkins University Press, 1977.

Thuerck, Robert. "The Fool's Cap Map — Solving a 450 Year Old Mystery." Sustainable Diversity. July 16, 2013. www.sustainablediversity.com/?p=208.

Tosi, Laura and Shaul Bassi. *Visions of Venice in Shakespeare.* Farnham UK: Ashgate, 2011.

Warren, Jonathan. "Lancelot Andrews, the Star of Preachers." Anglican History, Anglican Pastor. June 30, 2014. http://anglicanpastor.com/lancelot-andrewes-the-star-of-preachers/.

White, Michael. *The Pope and the Heretic, The True Story of Giordano Bruno, the Man who Dared to Defy the Roman Inquisition.* New York: HarperCollins, 2002.

Wintrol, Kate. The Intrinsic Value of the Liberal Arts: Cicero's Example." *Journal of the National Collegiate Honors Council* 15, no. 1, paper 131 (Spring/Summer 2014). pp. 129-134.

Withers, Hartley. "The Rise of Insurance." *The Cornhill Magazine* 22, new ed. (Jan.-June 1907). Edited by George Smith and William Makepeace Thackeray. pp. 661-677.

7. Research Tools; Library Guides; Organizations

Abarim Publications. Free Online Encyclopedia of Biblical Names. 2002-2017. http://www.abarim-publications.com/Meaning/index.html.

"Belshazzar." Bible Study Tools. public domain. copyright 2018 by Salem Media Group. http://www.biblestudytools.com/dictionary/belshazzar/.

"The Bibliographies." www.sirbacon.org/biblio.html.

Catalog of English Renaissance Literature [CERL] Thesaurus. https://thesaurus.cerl.org/.

Dawkins, Peter. Francis Bacon Research Trust, Gateways to Wisdom. 2018. http://www.fbrt.org.uk/.

English 2220: Introduction to Shakespeare: Find Websites. Columbus State Library. http://library.cscc.edu/shakespeare/websites.

English Legal History. Duke Law. Duke University. https://law.duke.edu/lib/researchguides/englishlegal/.

Fehrenbach, Robert J. and E. S. Leedham-Green. *Private Libraries in Renaissance England: a collection and catalogue of Tudor and early Stuart book-lists.* Binghamton, New York Medieval & Renaissance Texts and Studies, 1992. https://archive.org/stream/privatelibraries01fehr/fehrenbach_djvu.txtO2IabQ.

Francis Bacon Society. http://www.francisbaconsociety.co.uk/. Jastrow, Jr., Morris and Ira Maurice Price, Marcus Jastrow, and H. M. Speaker. Full text of the *Jewish Encyclopedia.* 2002-2011. First published in 1906. http://jewishencyclopedia.com/articles/2846-belshazzar.

Mabillard, Amanda. '*The Merchant of Venice Q & A.*' Shakespeare Online. Aug. 20, 2000. http://www.shakespeare-online.com/faq/merchantfaq.html.

_____. "Words Shakespeare Invented." http://www.shakespeare-online.com/biography/wordsinvented.html.

Medieval Genealogy.org. "Some publications of the Selden Society available online." http://www.medievalgenealogy.org.uk/links/selden.shtml.

Open Source Shakespeare, an Experiment in Literary Technology. Search engine. 1864 Globe edition to the complete works of Shakespeare online. Program code and database, copyright 2003-2018 by George Mason University. All works are in the public domain. https://www.opensourceshakespeare.org/.

Shakespeare Authorship Research Centre, Concordia University. http://www.cu-portland.edu/academics/colleges/college-arts-sciences/shakespeare-authorship-research-centre-sarc.

Shakespeare Authorship Studies, Brunel University, London. 2018. https://studylink.com/institutions/brunel-university/courses/cid-si-8273.

Shakespeare Oxford Fellowship. https://shakespeareoxfordfellowship.org/.

Shakespeare Studies: Authorship Studies, Library and Information Services, The University of Winnipeg. http://libguides.uwinnipeg.ca/c.php?g=124979&p=817288.

Shakespeare Studies: Shakespeare and Law, New York University Libraries. http://guides.nyu.edu/c.php?g=276645&p=1848006.

Shakespearean Authorship Trust. http://shakespeareanauthorshiptrust.org.uk/.

Wall, Bill. "The Etymology of Chess." March 24, 2015. http://www.chessmaniac. com/the-etymology-of-chess/.

"Word of the month: Anglo-Norman chess terminology (and how to find it)." Anglo-Norman Words. Oct. 23, 2014. http://anglonormandictionary.blogspot. com/2014/10/word-of-month-anglo-norman-chess.html.

8. Information on Processus Books

Ancharano, Jacopo. *Consolatio peccatorum, seu Processus Luciferi contra Jesum Christum.* Yale University Library. http://brbl-dl.library.yale.edu/vufind/Record/3443008. [145?]. "Frequently referred to as the *Processus Belial* or *Luciferi.*"

Ayrer, Jakob, Leonard Burck, and Jacopo Theramo [Jacopo Ancharano, Palladini]. *Historischer processor iuris : in welchem sich Lucifer uber Jesum, darum das er ihm die, hellen zerstoret, eingenommen, die, gefangene darauss erlost[...].* Leonard Burck: Franckfurt am Main, between 1604-1625. "A free translation and adaptation of Theramo's work." HathiTrust. http://hdl.handle.net/2027/ucl.31175035211260?urlappend=%3Bseq=246.

"Bartolus de Saxoferrato (1313-1357)." *CERL Thesaurus.* https://thesaurus.cerl.org/record/cnp00397421.

Heubach, Dittmar, *Der Belial. kolorierte Federzeichnungen aus einer Handschrift des XV. Jahrhunderts, herausgegeben von Dittmar Heubach, mit 17 Tafeln in Lichtdruck.* Strassburg: J. H. E. Heitz, 1927. Note: "With reproduction of 33 miniatures in ms. 66 of the Landesbibliothek at Weisbaden, containing Palladini's *Consolatio peccatorum, seu Processus Luciferi contra Jesum Christum,* frequently referred to under the title *Belial.*" HathiTrust. http://hdl.handle.net/2027/mdp.39015015853511?urlappend=%3Bseq=9. Note: limited search.

Mosaico, Modello *Processo di Satana,* 2009, CIRSFID, University of Bologna, http://mosaico.cirsfid.unibo.it/templates/index.php?table=SATANA&action=show mokup.

Processus Sathanae contra genus humanum. Rome: Steffanum Plannk, 1486. "Erroneously attributed to Bartolus Saxoferrato." Special Collections, University of Glasgow Library. http://eleanor.lib.gla.ac.uk/record=b2665638.

Theramo, Jacobus de. Fragment in Czech. Vienna: Johann [Schilling] Solidi of Vienna, 1478. Royal Collection Trust. http://www.royalcollection.org.uk/collection/1071393/consolatio-peccatorum-seu-processus-belial.

9. Francis Bacon's Bi-literal (Bi-literary) Cipher; Acrostics

Booth, William Stone. *Subtle Shining Secrets Writ in the Margents of Books.* Boston: Walter H. Baker, 1925.

Friedman, William F. and Elizebeth S. Friedman. *The Shakespearean Ciphers Examined.* Cambridge: Cambridge University Press, 1958. Reprinted in 2011.

Gallup, Elizabeth Wells. *The Tragedy of Anne Boleyn, a Drama in Cipher Found in the Works of Sir Francis Bacon, from original editions in the British Museum 1579 to 1590. Deciphered by Elizabeth Wells Gallup from the Novum Organum of Sir Francis Bacon by means of the Bilateral Cipher, described in his Advancement of Learning.* Geneva IL: Riverside Laboratories, 1916. HathiTrust. https://hdl.handle.net/2027/hvd.hnlczc.

_____. "The Bi-Literal Cypher of Sir Francis Bacon, a New Light on a Few Old Books." *The Pall-Mall Magazine* 26. Edited by George R. Halkett (1902). pp. 392-401. http://copac.jisc.ac.uk/id/29622417?style=html.

_____. *Bi-Literal Cipher of Sir Francis Bacon; Replies to Criticism.* Detroit, 1902. HathiTrust. https://catalog.hathitrust.org/Record/007025589 (limited search). For more by Gallup, see the Online Books Page. http://onlinebooks.library. upenn.edu/webbin/book/lookupname?key=Gallup%2C%20Elizabeth%20 Wells%2C%201846%2D.

Groenewegen, Carla. "Dr. Orville Owen's Cipher Wheel, Past, Present, and Future," *Baconiana,* the online journal of the Francis Bacon Society 1, no. 6, June, 2017, http://francisbaconsociety.co.uk/the-society/baconiana/baconiana-issue-1/#orville-owens-cipher-wheel. Note: Dr. Owen wrote five books on a cipher in Shakespeare.

Leary, Penn. *A Reply to 'The Code that Failed' by Terry Ross.* July 20, 1996 http://shakespeareauthorship.com/bacpl2.html.

_____. *The Second Cryptographic Shakespeare.* Omaha: Westchester House Publishing, 1990, online copyright 1990, revised from *The Cryptographic Shakespeare* 1987. https://www.baconscipher.com/.

Patton, Kenneth R. "www.SirBacon.org Presents: *Setting the Record Straight: an Expose of Stratfordian Anti-Baconian Tactics. Book One: The Vindication of William Stone Booth, a Detailed Critical Analysis of Chapter IX: The String Cipher of William Stone Booth in Elizabeth [sic] S. and William F. Friedman's The Shakespearean Ciphers Examined.*" All rights reserved worldwide, copyright Sept. 2000, published online only. http://www.sirbacon.org/pattonstrs.htm.

Printed in the United States
By Bookmasters